RUXTON *of the Rockies*

AMERICAN EXPLORATION AND TRAVEL

RUXTON OF THE ROCKIES

Collected by CLYDE *and* MAE REED PORTER

Edited by LEROY R. HAFEN

293426

NORMAN

UNIVERSITY OF OKLAHOMA PRESS

The Chapters

The Illustrations

Foreword

Few men have crowded so much adventure and
achievement into so few years as did George Frederick Ruxton. As
if forewarned that but twenty-seven short years had been allotted
him, he set about to cram them full of travel and observations in many
lands.

With all the enthusiasm he expended upon novel scenes, strange
peoples, and primitive life in Spain, Africa, Canada, Mexico, and the
American West, he was not so absorbed in their enjoyment as to lose
his perspective. He had the foresight to keep notes and diaries of his
unique experiences, and the wisdom to distill his observations into
articles and books.

George Ruxton was a precocious youth. Expelled from the Royal
Military Academy of Sandhurst at fifteen, he was soon a full-fledged
soldier in war-torn Spain. At seventeen he was wearing the Cross of
San Fernando with the title of knight; at nineteen he was a lieutenant
in Ireland; at twenty he was serving the military, contacting Indians,
and hunting the forest of Upper Canada. At twenty-three he was
experiencing life in the desert of Morocco, at twenty-four exploring
South Africa, at twenty-five adventuring in Mexico and the Rocky
Mountains, and at twenty-six writing scholarly articles on ethnology
and graphic accounts of his adventures. Then, just as he turned
twenty-seven, while on the way to his beloved Rockies and beyond,
he died in St. Louis.

In a period when literary persons were romanticizing life and
creating fantastic stories of unreal characters, Ruxton ate and slept
with his heroes and recorded them as human beings.

He was first among writers to portray the wild life of the Far
West as it was. He realized that the Mountain Man of the American
West was a natural as literary material, more intriguing in the flesh

than as fancifully portrayed by literary lights of the day. So he described the buckskin-clad hunters and fur men, portrayed their fascinating life, and expressed their thoughts in their own colorful jargon.

As a youth he had been transported to the backwoods of America by J. Fenimore Cooper and had stalked the deer and the enemy beside Uncas, Hawkeye, and other of the novelist's romantic heroes. But when Ruxton came to write of similar men and adventures, his portrayal was in a new and truer pattern. With such a presentation he was to become an important figure in American literature.

Ruxton was a born traveler and explorer. In the spring of 1848, he thus expressed his yearning for adventure and discovery: "My movements are uncertain, for I am trying to get up a yacht voyage to Borneo and the Indian Archipelago; have volunteered to Government to explore Central Africa; and the Aborigines Protection Society wish me to go out to Canada to organize the Indian tribes; whilst for my own part and inclination, I wish to go to all parts of the world at once."

His great affection for the Far West gleams in his book published in 1847: "Although liable to an accusation of barbarism, I must confess that the very happiest moments of my life have been spent in the wilderness of the Far West; and I never recall but with pleasure the remembrance of my solitary camp in the Bayou Salado, with no friend near me more faithful than my rifle, and no companions more sociable than my good horse and mules, or the attendant coyote which nightly serenaded us."

It was his love of the western wilds of America and his effective portrayal of life there that gave him, even in his own day, the appropriate sobriquet "Ruxton of the Rockies."

We have chosen to give his story almost entirely in his own words. Chapters one through sixteen are Ruxton's own reporting. Only minor changes involving the mechanics of style have been made for the sake of uniformity. Necessary connecting links and condensations are enclosed in brackets.

The extent and nature of explanatory notes to be inserted in a work of this sort constitute a problem. Many pages could be filled with scholarly comments upon the flora and fauna mentioned by Ruxton, and upon the peoples and tribes and cities he visited. One might exhibit erudition with elaborate annotations, but for most readers these would only burden the narrative. On the other hand, a complete absence of notes would probably be equally unwise. The identification of certain men and places seems advisable. Since the book is planned for a wide popular audience rather than a limited scholarly one, we have thought best to forego extensive annotations and reserve our explanations primarily for matters relating to Ruxton's Rocky Mountain adventures, which are the core of the present volume.

New biographical data and the writings now made available for the first time will be enthusiastically welcomed by those who have already known and enjoyed Ruxton's two books of travel and adventure. For those who have not heretofore known Ruxton, a new, intriguing character and author now challenges the attention. Anyone who relishes hunting and wilderness life, enjoys travel in strange lands, or is fascinated by the frontier life of the American West will find in this young Englishman a most remarkable adventurer, explorer, and writer.

LeRoy R. Hafen

Denver, Colorado
April 24, 1950

Introduction

To the readers of Western Americana one of the most delightful of the early-day itinerary narratives was left by one George Augustus Frederick Ruxton, who as a result of his all but solitary wanderings in our West and in Mexico produced two books that for over a hundred years have been considered indispensable treasures in libraries devoted to tales of rambles into the Indian country. His *Adventures in Mexico and the Rocky Mountains* and his *Life in the Far West*, full of the lingo of the Mountain Men of the period, are as fascinating to the reader of today as they were in the late eighteen forties, when they first appeared in print.

While his books have been reproduced a number of times since then, his likeness had never been found and only the briefest outline of his life's story had ever been published. This challenge fired my husband, Clyde Porter, and me with the desire to hunt the necessary materials in the hope that an illustrated reissue of some of his works with a more detailed story of his life, might serve as a memorial to the young Englishman on the one hundredth anniversary of his death.

In an effort to pry into Ruxton's life story, several years ago Mr. Porter made inquiry of several libraries, historical societies, and military records offices in this country and in England, hoping to find his picture and something of his story. For a time their answers contained only meager information about the man, and there was no word of his portrait. Discouraged and wondering where to turn next, in May, 1947, Mr. Porter received a letter from the librarian of the town of Tonbridge, England, stating that he had located the school records of young Ruxton, but, the boy having left the school at the age of thirteen, there was very little information of value and nothing whatever to indicate performance of later years.

Since I had in prospect a plan for spending the summer of 1947

in Europe, the Ruxton quest was transferred to me, and a trip to Tonbridge for a visit with the librarian became one of my objectives.

I deferred my trip to Tonbridge until twenty-four hours before
boarding the *Queen Elizabeth* for the voyage home, and on a sunny
day in late September took train for the hour's ride to that city with
only the vaguest hope that anything in the way of information would
materialize. But when, on leaving the train, I saw the town library
across from the station, I took its easy accessibility for a good omen,
and so it proved to be.

The librarian, remembering his correspondence, produced the
school records, which revealed that our George Ruxton was one of
six brothers who had left elementary school records, and that the
eldest brother, John Henry Hay Ruxton, had been living in Brenchley
in 1893. The librarian suggested that a trip to Brenchley and a call
upon the vicar—since vicars know their flocks—might be a good idea.
And with that slim clue and instructions about the bus changes, I set
out for Tunbridge Wells, and there took another bus for the twelve-
mile ride to Brenchley.

It proved to be a residence crossroad instead of a conventional
town with stores and mercantile establishments, and as I stood in front
of its very old church, rapt in admiration of the old neighboring
houses, along came a small boy. On my inquiry as to where the vicar
might be found, he told me to climb to the top of the hill ahead of me
—then to turn left, and at the end of the street I would see a large
white house with a "Vicarage" sign upon the gate. After a ten-minute walk I found the sign, and although I did not then know it, as I
opened the gate I was stepping into the boyhood yard of George
Ruxton.

A housekeeper answered my knock, and soon the kindly vicar,
who proved to be Sir Henry Fitzmaurice, was hearing my story. Although he had been in residence but four years, he knew that the
Ruxton family home of Broad Oak had been torn down to make way
for the vicarage, but he could recall no member of the Ruxton family
in his church. Suddenly his face lighted and he said, "I believe an
elderly Mr. Turner, who lives in the next village, Castle Hill, is the
son of a woman born a Ruxton." With that he went to the telephone,
but the butler who answered refused to call his master, explaining that
at that hour Mr. Turner always listened to the London news over his
radio and then had his lunch and that if we wished to talk with him
we might call at two-thirty. The vicar then said, "Will you tell Mr.
Turner there is a woman here from America asking information about

a George Ruxton of one hundred years ago?" At that, Mr. Turner came to the telephone; and when to my question about the possibility of his owning a likeness of the young man, he replied, "I have a miniature—come over," you may imagine my delight.

The housekeeper accompanied me through the verdant bit of forest that lay back of the house, but it was soon left behind, and we came out upon a lovely country lane atop a high hill. Beautiful Kent lay spread out below, and since it was hop-picking time, there were color and action in the fields and the air was filled with the strange perfume from the hop ovens running for the drying process. After a ten-minute stretch we met the vicar's vegetable boy. The housekeeper took his sack of cabbages, sending him back with me, and in another twenty minutes he delivered me at the Turner gate.

I went through the rose garden, and at the door of his four-hundred-year-old Elizabethan home stood the eighty-year-old Mr. Turner, a tiny man with snowy beard and a mass of curls atop his handsome head. We passed into the beautifully furnished library and soon turned to a group of objects Mr. Turner had placed upon the table. He opened a leather case, and I saw the ivory miniatured face of young Ruxton, regular featured and goateed, and he was wearing a plaid waistcoat of dark green and black. Then from a smaller case came two medals—received in 1839 from Queen Isabella II of Spain for the boy's participation, between the ages of fifteen and seventeen, in a campaign being waged to keep the nine-year-old girl's regency alive against the claims of her pretender uncle, Don Carlos. There was besides the medals, a paper-covered notebook filled with penciled descriptions of soldiering in Spain and in Canada, and containing a drawing of Ruxton in a Canadian wood. A second volume, bound in leather, proved to be a memorial scrapbook compiled by his mother. It held the installments of *Life in the Far West* that had been appearing in *Blackwood's Magazine* at the time of the author's death, followed by the publishers' four-page memorial tribute to the young writer; an article from the *Nautical Magazine and Naval Chronicle* of January, 1846, describing Ruxton's disastrous four months' trip to Africa; a copy of his pamphlet on the Oregon Question; and obituary notices from various newspapers. The final pages of this book held copies, made in ink by Ruxton's mother, of some of his unpublished manuscripts, describing his hunting experiences in Canada and the expedition to Spain, along with reminiscences of his unhappy school days. Pasted into the book, there were some pencil drawings signed by George Ruxton, and loosely within the cover were a number of letters from Mr. Blackwood and others, written to Hay Ruxton and to Mrs. Ruxton, expressing regret at George's passing.

The richness of this find was breath-taking, and after I had explained our plans for a memorial volume, great was my delight when Mr. Turner asked, "Would you like to take these things to America?"

As he found a piece of wrapping paper and a cord, I expressed my gratitude and assured him that we were accustomed to the handling of valuable historical materials and would be doubly careful with his. After a walk through the rose garden and a good-bye, I set off down the lane in the direction of Brenchley.

Later, at home, as we began studying the material, it seemed a pity that we could not know what Ruxton's home had looked like; so off went a letter to Mr. Turner. His reply was discouraging, but several months later two photographs of handsome Broad Oak arrived, along with heartening news that he had communicated with another grandnephew of Ruxton's, Major C. M. Roberts, and found that he had a number of letters and some of the personal effects of our man. In time those came to us in Kansas City, where by right of purchase they and the four items supplied by Mr. Turner will remain.

Ruxton's last letters to his mother and his brother William, a long letter to the *London Times* pleading for a commission sending him into the Arctic to search for the lost party of Sir John Franklin, and three letters from a younger brother, Augustus Alexander, recounting to the family details of the illness, death, and burial of Ruxton were included in the Roberts packet.

Two tan leather pocket notebooks bore further record—one filled with passports and with notes from which Ruxton was to fashion his *Adventures in Mexico;* the other, a *Punch Pocket Book Almanac* of 1845, holding notes on his African expedition. Among the passports was the travel card which he refers to in his Mexican adventures as being full of magic in affecting his treatment by Mexican officials.

There were numerous rather crude drawings in the packet: plans for a trophy case to hold his mounted heads and horns and sketches of his tomahawk and butcher knife, his guns and powder horn, and an Indian coupstick. A drawing of his Canadian camp showed the little tomtit mentioned in his manuscript perched upon the roof. Glimpses of his Indian guides and one sketch in color of his hunting party among the natives of a giraffe-infested African veldt completed his sketches.

Major Roberts' possessions included a large photograph of Broad Oak made before the trees had grown up about it. A handsome closed carriage drawn by four white horses and manned by three liveried coachmen stood before the door. A number of photographs of brothers and relatives having little importance to our narrative, completed the collection.

It has been a tedious but not too difficult undertaking to trace the detailed chronological order of Ruxton's adventures, and considering his life span of only twenty-seven years, their variety is amazing. Study of the Turner-Roberts materials showed some important information missing, and it took much letter-writing and the help of a professional research assistant in London to fill the gaps. As we went along with this investigation, we had the benefit of coming upon the writings of people who had at one time or another searched for information on Ruxton's life story. We gratefully acknowledge the help and inspiration we derived from their labors. In the British publication *Good Words* for August, 1893, J. Munro, under the title, "Ruxton of the Rocky Mountains," set out the results of an investigation made while some of the people who knew Ruxton were still alive. It is a most interesting and informative article, and we quote from it frequently. We were sorry to find that any additional information, other than the notes Mr. Horace Kephart included when he republished Ruxton's works between 1916 and 1937, perished when Mrs. Kephart's home burned after his death. We enjoyed Mr. Bruce Sutherland's article, "George Ruxton in North America," published in the *Southern Review*. He plainly not only put in a great deal of study on Ruxton's works but made himself familiar with much of Ruxton's route of travel in the Rocky Mountains. Mr. Frederic E. Voelker of St. Louis, after many years of research and study, has written a masterly article on Ruxton's life, published as "Ruxton of the Rocky Mountains" in the January, 1949, *Bulletin* of the Missouri Historical Society.

Our thanks to Mr. Marcus S. Crouch, branch librarian at Tonbridge, who first started us on the right path. Without the help of Sir Henry Fitzmaurice and his housekeeper and the vegetable boy we would have missed Mr. F. H. Turner, grandnephew of Ruxton, who lent us the medals, miniature, notebooks, and papers that make up the bulk of the new material we are able to present. Mr. Turner brought us in touch with Major C. M. Roberts, another grandnephew, who provided the last two letters from Ruxton to his mother and the rest of the new manuscript material. Miss Margaret Franklin's untiring search through the Central Records Office and the Royal Geographical Society's files in London has helped to establish the chronological order of Ruxton's life. Mr. G. Lanctot, deputy minister of the Public Archives of Canada, rendered invaluable aid, as did Mrs. Brenda R. Gieseker, librarian of the Missouri Historical Society at St. Louis. Mr. G. D. Blackwood and Mr. H. Carson of Blackwood's London offices sent information about Blackwood's letter files of a hundred years ago and the publishing of their book *Life in the Far West*. Mr. Henry R. Wagner contributed information about a rare illustrated copy of *Life in the Far West*, purchased in England years ago; and Mr. Leslie E. Bliss, of the Huntington Library, sent further information concerning it.

Major Earl, adjutant of Sandhurst, and Major A. J. Morris, historian of the Irish Fusiliers (successor to Ruxton's old Eighty-ninth Foot Regiment), provided information about Ruxton's school experience and regimental connections. From Mr. David P. Botsford came data on the old post at Amherstburg. Catherine Phelan, of the Wyoming State Library, speculated with us about the actual existence of the trapper La Bonté. We want to thank Arthur Hoskins of St. Louis, who many years ago introduced us to Ruxton by giving us our first copy of *Adventures in Mexico and the Rocky Mountains*. Mr. Wright Howes of Chicago and Mr. Fred Rosenstock of Denver, dealers in rare books on American history, helped gather our collection of Ruxton editions, and Mr. LeRoy Hafen, Mr. Herbert Brayer, and Mr. Fred Rosenstock, through their affiliation with the Denver Westerners, have been instrumental in bringing the book to publication, for which we shall forever be indebted to them.

Thomas Hornsby Ferril's poem "Ruxton Creek" sums up in its few lines the gist of our story, and we appreciate permission for its use.

MAE REED PORTER

Kansas City, Missouri
April 25, 1950

Ruxton Creek

By Thomas Hornsby Ferril

Alone thru dusk he sat—
Safe in Bayou Salade above the Platte,
Safe from the rumbling dust to Santa Fé,
Cool in the woven spruce that curtained day,
*   While good Panchito browsed along the sage*
Beyond the picket fire; it was an age
For picket fires.
*   Broiled beaver tail was good,*
Better than dripping hump-ribs—cedar wood
Was sweet in flapping, snapping, crackling bright—
Alone, the boy, Bayou Salade and Night.

And much was in the fire; green Sandhurst, cricket—
(What would Panchito think of Sandhurst cricket,
Or Euclid, Covent Garden, polka dancers?)
Panchito would not mind Diego's lancers,
*   For there was fine, hot galloping in Spain,*
Good fun, those civil wars, to come again.
And more was in the fire. How might he seek
A trail thru Africa to Mozambique,
Or track from Liverpool to Borneo,
*   Or down thru Canada to Mexico?*

An idle hand crept thru his hunting vest,
*   Where Isabella's cross had touched his breast,*
And Drake and Cook and Raleigh stood around
Till he was sound asleep upon the ground,
And stars swept up in royal gallopade,
And night was purple in Bayou Salade.

xvii

Shout, little stream, burst into racing flame,
For in you burns the spirit of a name.
Sweep till the seven seas have felt your foam,
Thunder on every shore. The world is home.

NOTE: This poem was written by Mr. Ferril, an outstanding
Colorado poet, when he was twenty-five—the same age that Ruxton
was when he hunted on the creek that now bears his name. The writing was induced by the receipt of a dispatch from Manitou that Ruxton Creek was booming. This stream enters Fountain Creek in the
center of the business district of the resort town of Manitou, Colorado. Much of Ruxton's spirit and career are embodied in this poem,
which was first published in the *Denver Times* of June 18, 1921.

RUXTON *of the Rockies*

CHAPTER I

Youth and Background

M Y MEMORY carries me back to the fourth year of my age.[1] Even then I was a vagabond in all my propensities, for there was not a dark closet or interdicted staircase or corner under taboo of nursemaid that I had not explored ready to battle with the bogle who, the nursery legends affirmed, inhabited it and devoured the naughty children who were rash enough to enter his retreat. I rejoiced in the distinctive and honourable soubriquet of "the pickle" of the family, which enviable title I bore away from the attempts of five brothers, amongst whom my position with regard to seniority was central, having two older and three younger than myself.

Until my eighth year or ninth I continued at home, my wayward disposition increasing with my years, and with little prospect of being checked, for at that critical period I lost my father, and, left to the control of a too indulgent mother, I did not pay due deference to those whose years and experience made them fitted to advise and instruct me. My schoolboy days it is hardly necessary to describe. They were such as might be expected from my truant and wayward disposition. Everything like restraint, and consequently all application to studies, was irksome to me, and but that I had fortunately a tolerable share of ability, a quick and ready talent, and a clear intellect which enabled me to seize at once upon ideas and adapt them to practical purposes, I should have entered the world totally uneducated. My life at school was therefore spent in a succession of scrapes and

[1] Mr. J. Munro, who obtained his Ruxton family history from Captain John Ruxton (George's brother), gives the date of George F. Ruxton's birth as July 24, 1821. (See Munro's "Ruxton of the Rocky Mountains," published in *Good Words* (London), August, 1893, p. 547). This tallies with the records at the Sandhurst military academy, given below, and with Ruxton's statement of his age upon entering that school. His parents were married July 28, 1817, and he was the third son born to them.

3

schoolboy atrocities which it is not worth while to inflict upon the reader. At thirteen I was sent to a military college, where I learnt to drink and smoke, to say nothing of the art of wiring hares and rabbits, and other accomplishments too numerous to mention.

On my first entering the college, I had determined to give myself a fair chance, and if moderate application was sufficient to ensure my passing through the usual course of study, I made up my mind to work away cheerfully and to do my best to perform what was expected of me. Three days' experience of the drudgery of mind imposed by the wretched system pursued at this school sufficiently proved that four years of my life would be passed in a state of confinement, both of mind and body, which would be insupportable. I therefore threw aside my books, took to wires and cricket bats; foremost in every row going on, I spent the greater part of my time in the black hole and at the end of two years was invited to make myself scarce, which I did with infinite satisfaction, cordially detesting the system which expects boys to be men and men boys.

I was now a strong, active boy of fifteen, with a mind filled to overflow with a love of adventure and excitement, which at that early age, even, was necessary to me. Everything quiet and commonplace I detested, and my spirit chafed within me to see the world and participate in scenes of novelty and danger. My friends held *in terrorem* over me the necessity of my return to school, being very properly averse to my entering the world at so early an age. To this, however, I put a very determined veto, and they knew my character too well to attempt to enforce anything so repugnant to me. This disobedience to those whose natural duty it was to control my actions, I do not for an instant palliate. Pride and determined self-will had been my stumbling blocks; but my disposition was such that ordinary measures would have had no effect, and violent ones been attended with most injurious consequences, and not the slightest good effect.

[This revealing but all too brief account, written by George F. Ruxton, can be supplemented by family records, school and academy reports, and the recollections of a brother and a fellow cadet.

Fighting spirit and adventure flowed naturally in the blood of George Ruxton. On his father's side he came of the Ruxtons of County Louth, which half encircles Dundalk Bay and faces the stormy Irish Sea, about midway between Belfast and Dublin. From ancestral estates on the banks of the Dee, Ruxtons for generations had gone to the Irish parliament, representing the borough of Ardee.[2]

George's grandfather, Henry T. B. Ruxton, had two sons and six daughters. The eldest son, John Ruxton, became an army surgeon.[3] On July 28, 1817, Surgeon Ruxton, then of the Twenty-fourth Dragoons, married Anna Maria, youngest daughter of Colonel Patrick Hay, of the great East India Company. This couple became the parents of George Frederick Ruxton.

Red blood of Scotland came to George through his mother. His grandfather Hay, a scion of the Scottish Hays of Alderstone, was related to the noble houses of Errol and Tweeddale. Anna Hay Ruxton's granduncle was historic John Hay, secretary to Bonnie Prince Charlie in the romantic uprising of '45.

Both the Ruxton and Hay families boasted long lines of soldiers and adventurers. Stories of these heroes must have been powerful determinants in the career of George Ruxton.

To John and Anna Ruxton six sons were born, three of whom were to choose military careers.[4] George, the third in the brood and hero of our story, was born July 24, 1821, at Eynsham Hall, England, an estate his father had leased from Lord Macclesfield. The fine mansion was set in a handsome park overlooking the wooded banks of the Isis—the upper reaches of the famous Thames that flows through London. Eynsham Hall was in Oxfordshire, not far from the ancient walled city of Oxford, seat of England's oldest university.

While George was an infant, his father bought Broad Oak, in Kent, southeast of London, and moved his family there. This estate lay near the village of Brenchley, about three miles south of Paddock Wood. Broad Oak was set on a secluded upland summit. "In the sleepy hamlet below there are cottages hundreds of years old, with timbers in the walls and peaked gables, and funny little porches overgrown with honeysuckle."[5] In this charming countryside George Ruxton spent his impressionable early years.

George began his education at the school in Tonbridge, where the brief reports are still preserved. The training received there must

[2] See Burke's *Landed Gentry*.

[3] John Ruxton joined the 61st Foot (South Gloucestershire) in 1798, was with the 6th Dragoons in 1806, with the 24th Dragoons from 1806 to 1812, and was placed on half pay July 25, 1818. See the *Naval and Military Gazette*.

[4] The sons were: Captain John Henry Hay Ruxton, Rev. William James Mylne Ruxton, Lieutenant George Augustus Frederick Ruxton, Charles Dashwood Ruxton, Rev. Frederick Wardell Ruxton, and Augustus Ruxton.

[5] J. Munro, "Ruxton of the Rocky Mountains," *Good Words*, August, 1893, p. 547.

5

have been of that sound and thorough kind characteristic of English schools, for George had little formal education beyond this, and yet his writings reveal a trained mind and well-stored head. The Sandhurst records show that he entered the Royal Military Academy on July 14, 1835.[6]

One of George's comrades at the military academy became General Robert Beaufoy Hawley, C.B. The General thus remembered George Ruxton:

"He was a fine boy, his head well set on his shoulders and such a straight, grand neck and carriage—a beaming expression—his figure strong and good; but what he used to complain of in joking in his later days was that his legs were too short! But he had strong hips, and square useful shoulders. Mind, he was neither big nor bulky; he may have reached five feet ten inches at his full growth." Hawley recalled that George was a lonely boy. "His delight as a cadet was to wander on the heather between the Royal Military College and Bagshot, then as wild as a Devonshire moor."[7]

The freedom of the moor was a foretaste of later wanderings in many lands. The happiness of these excursions fed the boy's wanderlust and brought dreams of long journeys to far places. With J. Fenimore Cooper's Leatherstocking heroes he penetrated the leafy wilderness of America, to match skill and wits with savages and wild game. Perhaps of more immediate influence was a retired sergeant whom he found keeping bees on the moor near Sandhurst. This former officer of the Third Light Dragoons had volunteered for service with DeLacy Evans in the Carlist War and had great stories to tell of romantic adventures.

George's eldest brother, John, reported that a venturesome spirit and disregard for rules got the young cadet into trouble at the military academy. On one occasion, while being helped through a window, George was impaled on a hook by the wrist. Thereupon his assisting comrades fled, leaving him in agony and in certainty of being caught in his misdeed. He was expelled from the academy. According to his own statement, quoted above, he had been in the school two years.

---

[6] The record at Royal Military Academy, Sandhurst shows: George A. F. Ruxton, Cadet No. 47. Admitted on July 14, 1835. Age on admission, 13 years, 11 months. Height, 5 feet, 4½ inches. Father (deceased) Surgeon 24th Light Dragoons. Left R. M. A. 31st December, 1835. Returned to friends.

Ruxton may have returned again to the school, as he says he spent two years there.

[7] Munro, *loc. cit.*, 547.

6

Freed now from the restraints of Sandhurst, George determined to be upon his adventuring. The story continues in his own words.]

About this time commenced the civil war which for so many years devastated unhappy Spain. In the wild and sanguinary partisan warfare which characterised the commencement of that bloody struggle between the adherents of the Pretender and the legitimate Queen, I took the greatest interest and delight and determined at all hazards to proceed to the theatre of war and join one of the belligerent parties. Spite of the obstacles thrown in my way by reluctant friends, I carried my point and made preparations for carrying out my cherished object.

7

CHAPTER 2

Adventures in Spain, 1837-39

I SHALL NEVER FORGET the delight with which I stepped on the deck of the steamer which was to convey myself and my traps to Havre, whence I intended proceeding by way of Paris and Bordeaux to Spain. My heart bounded within me as I saw the everyday smoke and mists of London clear away before me, and visions of coming excitement danced before my eyes as I paced the deck of the vessel, for the first time entirely my own master. Although I had determined to proceed through France as quickly as possible, yet Paris, Bordeaux, and Bayonne had such charms for me that it required some two months, and the strong hint of a fast-consuming purse, to withdraw me from their allurements.

One fine cold morning in December, at break of day I looked out of my window in Bayonne and saw waiting beneath, a horse and two mules, attended by a Basque, which were to carry me and my kit to San Sebastián. A crisp frost covered the ground, and a cold but bracing air, sweeping from the snow-clad Pyrenees, made me don my sheepskin jacket as we emerged from the town into the open country. The few miles between Bayonne and Behobie were soon trotted over and the lofty mountains, stretching away from the sea to the southward, were before us, their snow-clad summits appearing to hang in mid air, as the mists of morning hanging round the bases disclosed only their ragged peaks, standing out of the background of clear blue sky.

Passing through the village of Behobie, the Bidassoa, boundary of France and Spain, appeared before us, crossed by a wooden bridge, at each extremity of which was a guard of French and Spanish soldiers. The French sentinel was clean and soldierlike while at the other end of the bridge paced slouchingly the ragged-looking ruffian in the pay of Spain. Having exhibited to this worthy my passport, we passed the bridge, and with a cry of delight I threw my cap in the air and hurrahed for Spain—Spain, land of love and war, of romance and robbery, of murder and miracles, of curiosities and contrarieties, of *cuchillos* and castanets. *¡Viva España!* Bless your sunny skies and sunnier eyes. Bless your *chiquitas* who are so *guapitas*, and your wine which is so *bueno*. Last as you once were first, may you remain as you are and have been, *país de romance*, land of the Cid. May the whistle of the snorting locomotive never desecrate your plains and valleys, and dispel the vapoury clouds of soft romance which still hang over them. Long may the rueful Knight and faithful Sancho wander through the burnt-up plains of thirsty La Mancha without recourse to the Villain Ticket of a third-class up; and Heaven forbid that he of Santillana should ever exchange his *macho* and *alforjas*, or the *galera* of the Astorgan Carrier, for the speedier transport in the luxurious conveyance of the "Great North of Spain" with branch to Salamanca and Oviedo.

"*¡Jesús, qué demonio!*" exclaimed an old Basque woman who was sitting by the side of the road, as at the conclusion of an excited demi-volt, which I executed in honor of my first entry into Spain, my cap flew into her face. "*Por Dios, caballero, una limosnita en el nombre de la santíssima Virgen, a la pobre vieja que más que cien años tiene de una vida desgraciada*"—a little sixpence, my lord, in the name of the most holy Virgin, for a poor old body more than a hundred years old, a hundred years of miserable life—and truly her appearance confirmed the assertion of extraordinary age. Sitting in a cowering attitude on a large stone with her long chin resting on her knees and her bony hands clasping a wrinkled and leathern countenance, she mumbled out her whining prayers for alms. Throwing a piece of money into her lap, which she clutched with idiotic rapacity, we passed on the road to Fuentarabia.

Along the heights which overhung the left of the road, numerous picquets of Cristino troops formed a chain of communication from San Sebastián to the French frontier. It was, however, no uncommon thing for small guerrilla parties of the Factions to pass this line and waylay travellers whom they thought worth an attack, to rid them of their baggage. The knowledge of this caused my guide to quicken the pace of his *macho*, on which he sat perched upon a pile of packs, and to bring to conclusion the Basque song which he was roaring out at the top of his voice. When we approached lonely parts of the road I observed him examine the priming of the *trabuco* which hung at his saddle and look cautiously around.

9

We halted at Irún in order to submit the baggage to the examination of the *aduanero*, or custom house official. This matter was easily arranged by the judicious application of a *peso fuerte* which at once closed the eyes of the conscientious worthy to the sight of a sufficiency of English contraband goods to stock the best shop of the Calle Alcalá of Madrid. At Irún too we entered a *posada* and discussed the merits of a puchero, my first initiation into the mysteries of the Spanish cuisine. With this, and a draught of potent *zacoli*, the inward man refreshed, we proceeded on to San Sebastián.

A heavy snow storm pelted upon us as we descended into the valley of Urumea, and as we forded that river a column of infantry debouched from the broken hills on our left, amongst the files of which several stretchers were borne along on men's shoulders, containing wounded men. They had been engaged with a part of the enemy whilst relieving picquets and were now returning to San Sebastián with their wounded. The faces of the soldiers begrimed with powder, and their round red *boynas* covered with snow which hung in half-frozen masses from their long hair and moustaches, gave them a fierce and warlike appearance, with the appropriate adjunct of the wounded on the stretchers with bandaged heads and bloodstained countenances. They were chorusing as they marched, the well-known Basque song eulogizing the celebrated corps to which they belonged, the Chapelgorris, and their popular leader Gaspar Jáuregui.

> *Don Gaspar de Jáuregui comandante ya*
> *A Tolosa con escacha cortejeria a*
> *Ay, ay, ay, mutila Chapelgorri, a, a,*
> *Ay, ay, ay, mutila Chapelgorri, a, a.*

It was dark when we entered the town; and, slipping and scrambling through the dirty narrow streets, we made for the Posada Ysabel, a hostelry much frequented in those stirring days. Here I quickly ensconced myself by the huge fire in the kitchen round which was a goodly company of *arrieros*, soldiers, and *paisanos*, the smoke from whose *pipas* filled the room with a thick cloud. A man with his face buried in the collar of his *zamarra* made room for me on the bench on which he was sitting, and, turning to me as he offered me a cigar from his *petaca*, I remarked his extraordinary expression of face. He was evidently a Jew, with the strongly marked and prominent features peculiar to the Hebrew race, and a swarthy complexion; but his eyes, small and deeply set, were of an iron grey colour and wore a most peculiar expression of cunning and evident determination. His eye-

GEORGE AUGUSTUS FREDERICK RUXTON
from a miniature painted on ivory

HALIF
a pencil drawing in Ruxton's Spanish passport

brows were marked in the figure of a reaping hook and gave expression to a forehead of great breadth, furrowed over with deep wrinkles. But the most unpleasant feature in his face was a sneering grin playing about the corners of his mouth, and rendered an otherwise handsome countenance almost repulsive. In stature he appeared to be above the ordinary height and in figure was robust and well proportioned. I am thus minute in describing this man as he takes rather a prominent position, and I met with him so often and under such strange circumstances and in different quarters of the globe, that at length I looked upon him as a sort of "familiar" and never felt surprise in meeting him wherever I might be.

The kitchen of the inn presented a picture worthy of a painter. It was a large room, with a clay floor indented with numerous holes full of water from the snow which the guests had brought in on their clothes and shoes. In the large open chimney was a roaring fire round which many ollas were gently simmering. On benches inside the chimney and before the blaze were grouped in every picturesque attitude and costume, soldiers, muleteers, peasants of Navarre and Aragón, with many cavalry officers, hale fellows, amongst them. All were armed with the fragrant weed, and *botas* well filled with strong Navarre wine and potent *zacoli*[1] were passing quickly amongst them. Two or three *criadas*, sturdy Basque wenches, were tending the pucheros, giving opportunities to little gallantries from the guests, through whom they had to make way to reach their charges. Every now and then a trooper would enter bringing his saddle and accoutrements on his head, which he would hang on the wall and join the party round the fire.

The conversation turned altogether on the struggle, then at its height, between Carlist and Cristino. The man in the *zamarra* I remarked appeared the only one who dared or cared to utter any opinions concerning the justice of the question. He, however, flung about his ideas in anything but a flattering way to either party. This man, be it [recalled?], was no Spaniard, although he spoke the language perfectly.

"*Pues señores*," he remarked, taking his *papelito* from his mouth and at the same time vomiting forth a dense volume of smoke from his mouth and nostrils, "*a mí, me parece* that all this fighting will lead to no ultimate good to this poor country. *Viva Ysabel Segunda* and we lose our rights, our ancient *fueros*, our nationality, and our Church.

[1] Ruxton's original, the greater part of which is missing, is followed from this point through the next eight paragraphs.

New men will spring up with new ideas and no *Españolismo.* Spain will not then be *España Antigua* but a new country—*como Francia—como Ynglaterra. Pues señores, lo que falta es éste*—what we require is this—*por los Castellanos, España*—Spain for the Spaniards—*y Españoles sobre todo*—and Spaniards before the world. *Pues señores,* on the other side, if we cry *Viva Carlos Quinto,* Spain will not then be for Spaniards—no—for priests and friars and monks; then comes the inquisition, slavery to the church. *Entonces adiós. Ni rey ni reyna*—neither king nor queen for this country but a republic, as in Spanish America—this is what we want. *Pero, vaya*—what use is it to speak? *Por este país no hay otra cosa que desgracia*—*vaya, vaya*—nothing but misfortune for this poor country."

These bold maxims, rattled out in pure Castilian and with a volubility and gesticulation surprising, were received in silence, no one daring to acquiesce or dissent from any of the opinions, until an old weatherbeaten officer whose *galones* on the sleeve of his coat proclaimed him a *comandante,* and who was drying his clothes saturated with snow water, by the fire, turning suddenly round and casting a fierce look at the speaker of all this heresy, who, however, continued unconcerned puffing huge clouds of cigar smoke from his mouth, exclaimed:

"*¡Carajo!* Who's this we have speaking thus? *Factioso—me parece sin duda traidor. ¡Carajo!* Who are Spaniards that they are to have no king or queen?"

"*Halto, amigo mío,*" broke in the first speaker. "*A mí es lo mismo*—It's the same to me. No Spaniard I. *Gracias a Dios, de otra tierra vengo yo*—From other lands I come, my soldier, perhaps better, perhaps worse, *¿quién sabe?* But this I say, if Carlos Quinto or La Chiquillita herself heard me, *Ni rey ni reyna.*"

"*¡Caramba!*" bellowed the old officer. You no Spaniard? *¡Mentira!* Who but a Spaniard can speak Spanish? *¡Indigno que eres, falso, puñetero!*

"*Anda, anda—mala lengua tiene el viejo.* But what matters? *Patrona, vino y aguardiente. Vamos beben una brindacita:*

"*Que se j—— rey y reyna*
Viva vino y hora buena."

All this in so offhand a way in such a matter of fact tone that even the choleric old *comandante* could not help smiling, and soon all the party were enjoying the treat of the strange being in the *zamarra.*

I sat enjoying the scene, occasionally smoking and plying the *bota* as it made its rounds, when my friend in the *zamarra*, turning to me, asked me in purest English, "Well, sir, what do you think of Spain and Spaniards? You are, I see, going to join the Queen. Hard service— all hard knocks and no pay. Youngsters never listen to reason, so no use giving it. Perhaps we shall meet again, and if my poor services will be of use never fear to apply to ———.

"*Señores*," turning to the others, "a very good night to all."

The next morning I was up by times and before breakfast saun-tered round the walls which still bore evident marks of the good prac-tise of Wellington's artillery during the siege. The breach was still in ruins as were many houses in the neighbourhood.

On entering the plaza, I found two battalions parading prepara-tory to a sortie against advanced work of the Carlist lines, which they had thrown up and occupied the preceding day. It was a novel sight to me to watch the minute inspection of the men, the careful scrutiny of the arms and ammunition, loading with ball cartridge, and telling off the files to carry the stretchers for the wounded, which leaned, bloodstained from former use, against the colonnade of the square. This, thought I, looks like earnest.

At length came a roll of drum and a few words of command and the little column filed, with music playing and colours flying, across the plaza and out of the gate. Mechanically I followed in the rear, for-getting my breakfast, and regardless of the danger I was incurring by exposing myself where I could be of no use.[2]

After a few days spent in San Sebastián, I determined upon com-mencing my journey into Navarre to join, if possible, the French Legion, which I understood was to be met with either in that province or in lower Aragón.

Here I concluded the purchase of a horse and mule, paying of course for my whistle. I also secured the services of an Aragonese as a servant, one Manuel Orteiza, as big a rascal as his country ever pro-duced, but an excellent *criado*, and honest, I do believe, to me, al-though at war with the rest of the world. My intention had been to have gone round by Santander and Bilbao and so by the Ebro and Logroño into Aragón or Navarre.

A foul wind, which had lasted many days, and promised to con-tinue foul as many more, however, prevented the *chasse-marée* from putting to sea. I therefore lost patience and started off one morning

2 From his mother's copy of an original.

at daylight by Pasajes and Irún to Bayonne. From thence, skirting the Pyrenees, I passed Toulouse [Tolosa?], Pau, and Oloron, from which last place I provided myself with a guide [Miguel] and extra mule, in order to cross the somewhat hazardous mountain pass of Urdos into Spain. An unusually severe winter and great quantities of snow rendered the passage exceedingly difficult, and I was strongly urged to wait for more favourable weather. This, however, with my usual obstinacy, only determined me the more strongly to proceed. And one evening I found myself and caravan halting at the miserable inn in Urdos, which is the last civilised halting place before entering the pass of the mountains. Here we heard alarming accounts of the difficulties we were to enter upon in the morning. The paths, bad enough at all times, were now completely blocked and hidden by snow. The least deviation from them would perhaps hurry us down a precipice. The wolves were down from the mountains in great numbers, and many tales of devoured travellers and other horrors were poured into our ears. Manuel scratched his head, opened his mouth ejaculating, "*¡Jesús María, Jesús María!*" While my Oloron guide, albeit an old smuggler, and used to the mountain passes all his life, shrugged his shoulders, and it required an extra dollar or two to induce him to undertake the journey.

A *bota* of brandy was added to our stock and other creature comforts provided, and leaving directions to Manuel to call me an hour before daylight, I turned in.

Next morning when I rose I found the guide and Manuel preparing the chocolate and frying some ham and eggs. The people of the house were snoring in their different beds in the kitchen, from one of which the daughter of the house, too lazy to rise, was pointing out the locale of the different articles required. Into her hands as she lay half asleep, I was requested to pay the *cuenta*, and with mumbled prayers for our safety from the old landlord and landlady in one corner, we sallied out.

It was a piercingly cold morning, the sky clear and bright with countless stars. The lofty Pyrenees frowned over head, their snowy sides reflecting the brightness of the sky, while the snow-clad ground appeared studded with scintillating jewels. Borne by the wind we could plainly hear the howling of the wolves, as they returned to the mountains from the predatory visits to the sheepfolds in the valley, whilst the deeptongued bay of the noble Pyrenean watch dogs resounded from all sides, taken up as by a chain of sentinels and giving notice that they were awake and alert on their posts. A cold, biting wind poured down the gullies of the mountains, causing us to pull up over our ears the collars of our *zamarras*, and scattering the ashes from our cigars in our rear like the sparks of a furnace. We proceeded slowly and with great difficulty, as a recent fall of snow had obliterated the tracks in the road. Several times a large wolf bounded across, causing our beasts to start and tremble violently, as they instinctively recognised their natural enemy. As morning dawned, a striking and beautiful scene presented itself as the first streaks of daylight appeared behind us in the east, dimming at once the brightness of the stars. The lofty masses of mountain gradually lost their distinctness. First the bright reflection of the snow faded away leaving a dim shadowy form looming through the gloomy twilight. Soon, however, as the light increased, the outline became clearer and more defined, but leaving the mass itself still cloudy and indistinct. The outline of the ridges, the peaks and valleys became more and more exposed, until suddenly, the upper limb of the bright orb of day, appearing upon the horizon of the plains, tinged the edges of the mountains with a golden hue and at once brought into sight the colossal figure of the mountains themselves, now clearly drawn against the clear blue sky. Now the summits of the lofty peaks became distinct, and the ragged outline of the chain, those nearest to us fringed with snow-weighted pines. The sun, bursting out at length in all its power and majesty, threw its glittering beams upon the walls of snow which, throwing back the reflection, dazzled the eyes until they were unable longer to look upon the glorious picture. High up above the highest peaks floated a canopy of golden clouds, changing into gorgeous tints as the sun rose higher and higher in the heavens.

Often as I have seen the sun rise in many different parts of the world, I never have been so struck with the natural beauty of such a scene, as on this morning. I well remember the feeling of gratitude, nay of devotion, to nature for providing so gorgeous a spectacle to her children which took possession of me. My whole heart felt an ecstasy I have seldom since experienced, and struck with the unusual feeling I remembered asking myself, "Surely this after all is devotion?" And so it was, and is. And the heart and not the lips is a universal prayer.

With the world for our cathedral and nature for an altar, what meretricious aid do we require to stir up in our hearts sensations of awe or of devotion? In the valleys and the mountains, in the seas, the lakes, and rivers, God speaks through his high priest, Nature, the word of power and truth. What seek we more to prove his omnipo-

15

tence and glory; for us his loved children doth he not provide spec-
tacles of awful grandeur, scenes of soft and pleasing beauty, compared to which the cunningly devised allurements wrought by the
children of men are as fire sparks in lustre to the stars of heaven?
Doubt, if your soul allows you, his power and truth.

Go abroad then, unbeliever, and cast your eyes around you: look
to yonder mountain piled in stupendous blocks up to the clouds of
heaven. Behold its gorgeous canopy of painted vapours through which
the sun imparts its hues of endless splendour and variety. See its dazzling mantle of purest white clothed by the snows of winter with a
spotless garment, symbol of the glory and perfection of its maker.
What human hands, think you, could effect this? What human mind
conceive it?

Look over head. Doth not the burning orb of day, which warns
your eyes of their arrogance and pride yet remind you too of your
littleness? From morn to night, it wends its impartial way distributing
to every portion of the globe its share of warmth and life and happiness. See this and doubt not, for to doubt is to die here and hereafter.

As the day advanced, we proceeded somewhat more briskly, interrupted and delayed though now and then by one of the *machos*
tumbling into a snow drift, from which it required an hour or so of
pulling and shouting and numerous volleys of Basque and Spanish
oaths, startling and horrible enough in their sentiments to split one
up the back, *como se dicen en América*. One scene will suffice. We
were proceeding in Indian file, along a narrow track of barely three
feet width. On one side rose abruptly the rocky side of the mountain
against which the well laden baggage frequently rubbed and jostled;
on the other some thousand feet of perpendicular descent, at the bottom of which rushed headlong amongst falling masses of snow, and
icicles of huge dimensions, though hardly "bergs," a roaring torrent,
its bed choked with rocks, over which we could occasionally discern
a string of loping wolves following on our flank. In most places between the track and the precipice there was a ledge of snow some
four or five feet broad; beyond this, *facilis descensus Averni*. In round-
ing a corner, the leading *macho* would strike his well-secured load
against an abutting angle of the rock. In an instant, slipping, by the
force, off his legs, down he would thud on the ledge of snow with his
head over the side, enjoying the view of the "gentle descent" below.

Here, perfectly aware of the insecurity of his position and taking
in at one glance of his brown expressive eye, the critical juncture, for
in his struggle to rise with his back encumbered, the chances were

less than even he would topple over—all these considerations being at once grasped in his sagacious mind, Mulo at once determined on "letting well alone," when "in the kettle, jump not into the fire," &c. So without so much as a move of his tail, there he remained, nor *carajos*, nor curses, nor *puñetas*, nor *puños*, were sufficient to induce him to move a muscle of his frame. "*Aquí estoy*," he argued, "*más me gusta quedar*"—Here I am, and I'd rather remain. "*Más valen palos que lobos*"—cuffs [clubs] before wolves. And there he *would* remain, until —what any but a Spaniard would have done at first—the load was removed from his back. Then commenced a conversation between our *mayoral* and the *macho* on the ground. In deprecating tones, half crying, half sarcastically, such as a Spaniard alone can command when talking to his mule, he would expose the cutting conduct and insulting obstinacy of the prostrate beast, his coadjutors the while standing by, manufacturing their cigars and occasionally dovetailing in an epithet of objurgation.

"*Ahora, indigno ¿quieres levantarte? ¡ar-r-hé! Ingrato, maldita sea la madre que te parió ¡ar-h-r-hé! ¿Porqué me das estas malas palabras? Tu cochino, ar-r-r-hé, macho, maldita sea la hora que te ví. Ar-h-r-hé, faccioso, pronta sea su muerte digo yo, ar-r-hé, cobarde. Que te olvide Dios, bruto, ¡ar-r-he!*"

At length the last package is removed. Mulo measures his distance, gives a flop and a flounder, kicking a storm of snow upon us, and is once more on his legs.

About noon the dull and leaden clouds gathering to a head above us suddenly discharge their freight, in the shape of a storm of snow such as I have never witnessed, although I have passed a winter in the woods of Canada. Thick as falling leaves, and equal in size to leaves of books, down pelted the flakes. In a few minutes, the track was filled and the sagacity of our mules alone could discover the line of path. It was impossible to see before one the length of an arm, and we could only advance at a snail's pace. At length we were brought to a halt, the leading mule refusing to advance a step. With pricked up ears and staring eyes, his neck bent to the snow, and trembling violently, he stood stock still.

The application of the *mayoral's* lasso and his language of coaxing, promises, and threats were equally unavailing, until at length Miguel, thinking there might be some obstruction which we could not see, crept past and advanced a few paces into the track.

17

In a few seconds I saw him bound like a hot pea, into sight, from the wall of falling snow, which at the distance of a few yards hid everything from our sight. With a face as white as the snow itself peeping from the collar of his *zamarra*, he began to creep back stealthily, as one would retreat when in momentary expectation of a double thong application to his rear. When he had placed the mule between himself and the danger, whatever it was, he gasped out in faltering accents the following disjointed explanation.

"*¡Jesús María, Jesús María! Viene la hora última, perdóneme, santa Virgen. Ya ha venido el demonio, alante él qui quiere verlo—* The devil has already come for us; let him who wishes go forward and see him—*grande y negro, grande y negro, y con zamarra como Cristiano ¡ay de mí, ay de mí!—*big and black, big and black, and dressed in a *zamarra* like a Christian. Lackaday! Lackaday, that I should see this! *Por Dios, caballero, habla con él—*For God's sake, sir, speak to him! *Somos Cristianos todos—*We are all Christians tell him."

The ridiculous fright of Miguel was so exquisitely absurd that I thought I should have rolled off my mule with laughter. He was beating the snow with his feet in short jerks, turning round and round, bemoaning his hard fate, and uttering a sentence every now and then of an Ave María, or Pater Noster.

His companions were speechless with fright or frozen into dumbness by the unexpected announcement of the arrival of the old gentleman.

As, however, I saw that something must have caused the sudden fright of the mule as well as Miguel, I dismounted from my mule and, wading through the snow, crept under the belly of the leading mule, for I was unable to pass, and advanced a few yards before him.

The track here was gradually ascending, and here and there a mass of rock almost filled up the narrow path. One of these was about six yards in advance of the leading mule, and indeed rising some three feet from the ground appeared a sufficiently serious obstacle to oppose our progress. But on this was seated an object which at first sight seemed indeed enough to account for Mulo's trepidation and Miguel's fright. The side of this hump of rock facing us, being to leeward and at the same time abrupt, was uncovered with snow, looking something like a chair. On this was seated, dressed, it seemed at the first blush, in a *zamarra* and with collar well up over the ears, powdered with snow and with head bent down over his chest, the old gentleman himself, for I saw at once that the little of his face which was exposed from the collar of his coat, was not human. I could see, too, his shaggy eyebrows laden with snow flakes and encircled with icicles, beneath which peered a pair of small but twinkling eyes.

I *was* taken aback. That's the truth.

However, seeing that Sir Diablo was disposed to be civil and retained his cool seat quietly, only grumbling audibly at the wretched weather, so unlike what he had been accustomed to further south, I regained my presence of mind, and thinking that such an opportunity might not be presented again even in a long life, I advanced a pace nearer and determined to have a good look, cost what it might.

Demonio evidently considered himself affronted by my propinquity, for he raised his head and mumbled in a low indistinct tone and in a language I was ignorant of, a few words, perhaps of displeasure. I feared, too, he was going to punish my aggression, for rising from his sitting posture, he lifted his hand; but just as I expected to see his Satanic Majesty rise upon his hoofs and unfold his unmistakable posterior appendage, what should I behold but a fat and shaggy bear stand grinning on me.

Here's a chance, flashed across my mind. My pistols were in my valise, and loaded. I crept back. *"Por Dios silencia,"* I exclaimed to Miguel, as I fumbled for my pistols. Of course every strap was frozen and obstinately fastened.

But at length, I reached them. Creeping past the mule again, during which I heard a muttered *"¡Cuidado, por Dios; cuidado! No es del mundo"*—For God's sake, take care. He's not of this world. I, when within sight of the place, was just in time to see Bruin dodge off the rock and shuffle along the path. Bang! bang! I cracked at him, which elicited a sharp growl, but only made him quicken his pace, and, scrambling down the face of the precipice, I saw him cross the torrent below and disappear among the pines on its bank.

It required some time to restore Miguel and his comrades, and when I had prevailed upon him again to proceed, we found we were completely hemmed in by the snow, and after surmounting the block where the bear had perched himself, we were quite unable to make out the track any further. Miguel, however, declared that we were within a short distance of a hut, which was the residence of a family of those unfortunate outcasts known in the Pyrenees as *Cagots.* Nor was he wrong, for in a few minutes we heard a shout, and answering it by a lusty halloa, we soon had the satisfaction of seeing a man wading through the snow, staff in hand, along the track we wished to proceed.

Through Miguel I understood—for the *Cagot's* tongue was perfectly unintelligible to me—that the hut was within two hundred yards of us, and that we should be obliged to put up there for the night, it being perfectly impossible either to advance or retreat.

Led by our guide, we turned an angle of the rock and came upon a small level plateau, where under the shelving rock, which seemed to threaten momentary destruction, we dismounted at the door of the *Cagot* hut.

Such a hut! I have lived in the wigwam of the Indian and the windbreak of the Bosjesman of South Africa. Compared to the miserable abode of these poor creatures, outcasts from the laws and all society, yet existing in the bounds of a civilised country, they were as splendid palaces.

Formed of the rough logs of the pine, laid one upon the other, their inequalities and interstices admitting everywhere the chilly blasts of this inhospitable region, without windows, low roofed, if roof it can be called, and about thirty feet square, this hut formed the residence of a family of thirteen individuals.

Its floor, of damp and miry clay, with here and there holes filled with water, was taken up by hogs and goats and naked children, snuggling for warmth in the breasts of beasts almost as much entitled to humanity as themselves. In the large chimney, a pile of green and wet pinewood sent forth huge volumes of stifling smoke filling the chamber and almost concealing from view its motley inmates. Almost scorching themselves in the fire, over which they were holding their skinny hands, crouched three or four old men and women, the latter naked save by a sacking mat which barely covered, in the shape of a loose frock, their attenuated and filthy frames. From the neck of every individual, save the younger children, the hideous goitre depended in disgusting flakes. There seemed, however, no lack of provision, for a newly killed bear hung from a beam near the fire, and the children were picking off pieces of the fat and stealthily conveying them to their mouths, whilst two enormous, gaunt, lank-sided hogs roamed at will among the children and a sow with young about her was lying on her side before the fire, one child feeding her while another was drawing from her teats that sustenance denied by its sickly, emaciated mother.

The filth everywhere apparent beggars description, and on entering I looked in vain for a nook or corner where I might ensconce myself apart from the poor disgusting objects which surrounded me. This, however, was impossible, so making the best of it, I shook my *zamarra,* pulled the cover over my ears and my cap well over my head, and drew near the fire, where I had leisure to remark this extraordinary colony.

Poor and degraded as they were, yet the simple natural kindness and hospitality of these poor creatures would shame the well fed indifference of the civilised inhabitants of the world. Seeing me young and a stranger, I was immediately marked out as the object of their attention. Whilst one woman beat the snow from my sheepskin jacket, another scraped the frozen masses from my boots and trousers, dried my cap and shawl by the fire, and stirred up the blaze, inviting me to draw near and enjoy it.

A gourd of *aguardiente* was produced from which, their whole store of the precious liquid, I was forced to drink, a rasher was quickly cut from the bear, and broiling on the coals for our supper, and the women of the house, prepared and spread their best goat and sheep skins in the corner by themselves for my bed at night. Two of our mules found shelter in a shed, near at hand, one was brought into the hut, where it shared a corner with an old ass and her colt, and the goats and hogs were forcibly ejected to make more room for the advent of strangers. The old goitred crones who were huddling by the fire vacated their seats when the muleteers, having cared for their beasts, entered, and enveloping themselves in skins, huddled like witches in a corner, mumbling discordantly to themselves.

Night drew on apace. Dry logs were piled in profusion on the fire, soon kindling up into a cheerful blaze. Huge rashers of bear's meat smoked upon the embers, to which we paid out duties as they in turn became "cooked." Our *botas* of wine and brandy went their rounds, gladdening the hearts of our hospitable entertainers. After it was dark, three men entered bearing the carcase of a large bear which they had killed, probably our old acquaintance. These people were all extremely diminutive in stature, and in form loose and ungainly. To a man they all bore the brand of the horrible goitre.

I had resolved on passing the night by the fire, notwithstanding the preparations which had been made for my repose.

Drawing my cloak round me, I thrust myself, cigar in mouth, in a corner of the chimney and, puffing away complacently, enjoyed the scene around me.

Enlivened by the unwonted stimulus of wine and spirits, the *Cagots* soon forgot their miseries and wretched condition in the pleasures of the moment.

21

They sang and danced, apparently apostrophizing the muleteers for their unlooked for munificence in bestowing upon them the unconsumed fragments of their *puros*. Producing a cracked instrument, the like of which was never conceived by votary of Orpheus, one of them strummed a strange discord to which the men sang and the women danced.

Their wan and squalid figures, "lit into life" by the mad excitement, moving here and there through the smoky atmosphere, and occasionally drawing near the fire, where their disgusting peculiarities became hideously apparent, appeared to me who sat in the clearer light of the blaze as a chorus of imps seen through the mists of a conjurer's mirror. I sat and puffed and enjoyed the scene, saw the excitement become "fast and furious," the muleteers joining in an Aragonese-*Cagotjota*, gradually lost my powers of vision, and, leaning back, spite of the uproar was soon fast asleep.

When I awoke, the fire was almost burned down, not a sound was heard but the deep breathing of the muleteers, who lay around the fire enveloped in their *mantos*. In one part of the hut the whole family of *Cagots* were huddled in a pile of skins indiscriminately seeking warmth from each other. A huge mastiff and myself shared the chimney, nor was I displeased at having him for a bedfellow in preference to anything human I saw around me.

The next morning before daylight I was out seeking the relief of the cold fresh air from the smoke-filled atmosphere of the hut.

The snow was still falling thickly; the little plateau on which we were, was literally enclosed with walls of snow. Ingress or egress was alike impracticable. The morning dawned without a prospect of relief. The leaden, murky air seemed laden with snow, the fall of which in steady flakes was uninterrupted by a breath of wind. Everywhere around, and in startling propinquity, resounded the howling of wolves, driven to the enclosure by extremity of hunger. When Miguel made his appearance, accompanied by one of our hosts, they at once pronounced our departure impossible for that day. We therefore made up our minds to pass it with our present entertainers.

One of the men was dispatched to the nearest hut for a supply of black bread, without which we found the tough bear's meat was anything but palatable. Our mules suffered the most, for there was nothing for them but very little of the coarsest hay and the little corn we carried with us.

All that day I remained out in the air, for the filthiness within, which was in some measure hidden by the night, now appeared with all its morning horrors. My party, too, in no way more fastidious than their countrymen, shared with me my disgust, and together we breakfasted outside the hut, and at night I betook myself to the stable, where in the manger, wrapped in my cloak, I enjoyed a tolerable night.

During the night I was awakened by a terrible din amongst my four-footed bedfellows, caused by the onslaught of a gang of wolves on the pigs and poultry. The mules were the first to give the alarm, and the first howl also brought to the rescue the large mastiff, who quickly seized and secured one, until one of the *Cagots* came up and dispatched it. It was a large grey wolf but in the last stage of starvation. Its bones literally appeared through the skin.[3]

[So ends this fragment of the story. We wish we could read the rest of this experience and learn how Ruxton reached the army and how he became a soldier of the Queen.]

About two miles from Tafalla and between that town and Olite, once the residence of the kings of Navarre, but now a small *ciudadilla* famous alone for its olives and wine, and situated in a beautiful and fertile plain watered by the little river ———, lies a tract of marshy land running to the foot of the mountains and within sight of the little mountain village of San Martín, celebrated, during the late war which so cruelly devastated this fine province, as being the abode of a most ferocious *alcalde*, who was well known to be heart and soul in the Carlist interest, although the vicinity of the neighbouring garrison of Tafalla restrained him from openly espousing the cause of the Pretender.

During a rather protracted stay in this fine province, Tafalla was my headquarters, and I made several excursions to the Olite marsh to enjoy the sport the abundance of snipe and wild fowl afforded. My companion in these expeditions was always a stump-tailed Spanish pointer, who, if his qualifications in the qualities of his breed were not surprising, yet had the advantage of being too slow and lazy to prove a mar-sport, and would occasionally even come to a point if by chance a snipe or quail was rash enough to run against him.

One cold snowy morning in December, my *patrón* roused me up, as I had directed him, before daylight, in order that I might make an early start to my shooting grounds.

"*Vamos, don Jorge,*" he cried, thrusting a small cup of chocolate into my hands. "*Vamos, levanta. Son las seis ya*—It's past six and all

[3] From MS in Ruxton's handwriting.

23

the snipes are waiting to be killed. *Pero toma usted cuidado de este alcalde maldito*—But take care of this cursed *alcalde*. Two golden ounces he gives for the ears of *un Ynglés, y más por la cabeza*—and more for his head. And the *paisanos* of San Martín *mala gente son. Cuidado don Jorge*—Take care of the wicked people of San Martín."

With this advice to beware of the dangerous vicinity of San Martín, my worthy *patrón*, or landlord, after seeing me finish the little cup of exquisite chocolate, such as only a Spaniard can concoct, went off to his *campo*, or farm. And I, donning my shooting jacket &c. and taking my gun, whistled to lazy old Tigre, who was lying in a corner of the room snuggled up on my *zamarra*. I sallied into the kitchen, where *patrona*, assisted by several sturdy girls, was preparing a puchero for the noonday meal. I was immediately pulled into a corner by the good woman, who repeated earnestly the advice given by her husband as to the danger of my shooting in the neighbourhood, where it was well known people from the village of San Martín were continually in wait to pick up stragglers. Indeed, I had been, I knew, marked for some time, but nothing could prevent my enjoying my favourite sport.

Better than all the advice, my kind hostess stuffed my pockets with a savoury *salchichón*, a bunch of hot peppers, and a twist of bread, and adding a flask of *aguardiente* to the commissariat, off I started.

See a figure clocking me through gateway.[4]

When I entered the marsh, which in many places was up to my waist in water, the snow was falling in heavy flakes, but the snipe were plentiful and laid like stones. Following a ditch, I popped away, bagging several couple, and occasionally knocking over a mallard as he rose quacking at my feet, when, feeling somewhat peckish, I adjourned to a dry spot and produced the sausage. As I sat munching away, old Tigre suddenly raised his head and gave a short bark; and looking up I saw the same figure I had observed on leaving the town, stealthily picking his way over the marsh in the direction of the mountain. I thought nothing of it at the time and, having finished my tiffin, I again turned to at the long-bills.

Some excellent sport had led me on beyond my usual hour of returning when just before sunset a lot of teal swept whistling over my head and lit on the snow in a field outside the marsh. To get a shot at them I had to take a circuitous route by keeping round the foot of the mountain and proceeding under cover of a wall. As I was

---

[4] Fragment roughly interlined in penciled MS.

creeping stealthily along, a stone suddenly rolled down to my feet, and looking up, to my no small dismay I saw three figures behind the upper wall of the field in which I was walking, most deliberately pointing three villainous looking *escopetas* at my head. To dodge behind a small rock and quickly slip a ball into each of my barrels was the work of an instant, and as I rammed a wad over each, I thought it prudent to parley with my friends, who were shouting at me loudly to throw down my gun and surrender.

"*Date, Cristino, date, a los soldados del Rey. Abajo el escopeta y toma quartel*"—Surrender, Cristino, to the king's soldiers. Down with your gun and receive quarter.

Finding, however, that I paid but little attention to their recommendations, they commenced a perfect shower of abuse, banging Billingsgate hollow, occasionally raising their heads above the wall and taking a crack at the rock behind which I was safely ensconced, with loud cries of "*Alza, Ynglés, al frente alante, vamos hablar un pocito* [*poquito*]—Come out of your hole and talk to us. *Estamos amigos.*"

The approaching darkness favoured me, and I knew if I could only draw their fire on me at once, I might then make a bolt over the wall and trust to my legs, for of course to attempt to attack them in their strong position would be certain death. Taking a couple of wild ducks from my bag, I tied them to my gun barrel, fixing my cap on the top. Raising this suddenly, and feinting from one end of the rock to the other, it had the desired effect of drawing a simultaneous volley from the Carlists or robbers, whichever they were, probably both. And, jumping over the wall, I was safe from their fire in an instant. One fellow being exposed, I took a snap shot at him, but one of my caps snapped, and as soon as I had fired they sprung over their wall and, spreading in guerrilla, rushed down to the one I had just cleared, loading their guns as they came. I was determined to hold my place now. And as I was again loaded and had put a fresh cap on the other muzzle, I waited 'til two of them came jumping at the very spot behind which I was placed. Covering the breast of the foremost, I awaited his approach until he was within two yards of the muzzle of my gun. To do the fellow justice, he charged manfully although he saw my barrels peering over the wall and staring him in the face. Waving his *boyna*, he was shouting to his comrades, "*Alante, alante, ahora tenemos*—Come on, come on, now we have him." His sheepskin jacket was almost brushing the muzzle of my gun, and he was in the act of raising his own piece to fire, when I pulled the trigger. Be-

25

fore I knew that the gun had missed fire, I had turned the other barrel on one of the others who was now scrambling over the wall. But the dull sound of the hammer striking the cap without its exploding alone struck upon my ear, and then I was aware of my first barrel having also snapped. My first antagonist was now on the top of the wall with one leg over it, and in another instant would have shot me when I gave a point with the barrels of my gun right into his face, for I had not time to administer a good round blow with the butt, and he stumbled and fell over to the ground, his piece going off harmlessly in the fall. At the same instant I bolted down the hillside into the marsh as quick as lightning, followed by two shots from the others, and jumping into a pool five or six feet in depth, I swam to the other side and getting some reeds between me and my pursuers, splashed and spluttered through the marsh as fast as my legs would carry me.[5]

When the belligerent parties were on the point of entering into an arrangement which ended by the memorable Convenio of Vergara, the Navarrese seeming determined to resist the proposed accommodation, the Cristino government resolved to treat them with the greatest severity in order to compel them to submission by the dread of remaining alone exposed to all the horrors of a civil war carried to extermination. Orders were forwarded to General León to act towards those populations who were known to be fervent adherents of the pretendant with the utmost rigour.

Obliged to conform himself strictly with his duty, although his heart was grieved at the idea of the sufferings he was thus compelled to inflict upon his unhappy countrymen, General León prepared to accomplish his painful task. He issued proclamations to the inhabitants of the villages in the Carlist lines, who generally used to abandon their dwellings on the approach of the troops of the Queen, threatening to burn their habitations should they thus persist in abandoning them.

The Division of Navarre having received orders to occupy Allo and Dicastillo and the General finding that despite his warnings the greatest part of the people had fled carrying away all they had been able to remove, he consequently ordered the immediate execution of his threats.

Allo and Dicastillo, which might be considered as two of the advanced posts of the Carlists' lines, were therefore devoted to the flames. In consequence of some order of the General not having been communicated in proper time, the artillery and munition waggons had

[5] From Ruxton's original in pencil.

remained in the square and the fire was already raging on every side. The General, informed of the danger to which the neglect of his orders had thus exposed the safety of the whole army, instantly hastened to the spot, followed by his staff, in hopes that his presence would prove efficacious for the better accomplishment of the measures which the imminence of the peril rendered more difficult.

The crash of the walls and the crackling of the flames frightening the mules, they refused to advance through the narrow streets, and every moment rendered the situation more dangerous, for if unfortunately a single spark had entered one of the munition boxes the whole material of the division would unquestionably have been lost. Amidst the scene of confusion which necessarily ensued, General León remained in the midst of the peril calmly giving his orders and surveying their execution. He retired the last when secure that no one remained exposed to danger.

On reaching the outside of the village, his attention was attracted by a small group who were following with looks of despair the progress of the fire. A woman was sitting upon the ground whilst a female child of about twelve years of age, hiding her face in her mother's lap, was weeping aloud. Heavy tears that were silently trickling down the careworn cheeks of the poor woman told eloquently the tale of anguish and despair that was working in her breast. A young man whose uniform was that of one of the free corps raised in Navarre for the service of the Queen was standing by her side. One arm was leaning upon his gun whilst his other hand pressed that of the woman who was sitting at his feet. The paleness of his features, the dark flashing of his eyes, and his under lip which he bit convulsively easily told the violence of the inner emotions which he was struggling to repress. On seeing his general approach, he turned his head aside, unwilling no doubt to see his grief witnessed by stranger's eyes. León, however, drew near to the unfortunate mourners and enquired into the subject of their distress. In a few words the young soldier related the melancholy circumstances. A small house situated at the extremity of the village and to which he pointed was the only property of his widowed mother.

The dwelling was already enveloped in flames and therefore could no more be spared. The former inmates now remained without hope or shelter, exposed to all the pangs of misery and want. Two mattresses, a broken chest, of which the contents had been plundered, and a few utensils of their household furniture were the only remains of their little property. However afflicting, their situation, too frequently witnessed during the horrors of a civil war, attracted but little notice, and few showed pity for misfortunes they could not relieve.

The feelings of the noble León were highly excited at the sight of the distress of this poor family. The idea of the many wrongs and sufferings under which were labouring his countrymen and of which his military duty had obliged him to be the instrument struck forcibly upon his mind. "Unhappy Spain!" exclaimed he, "and must the hands of thy own sons thus wound thee to the heart?" Then spurring his horse, he rode away full speed as if desirous by the violence of corporeal exertion to master his emotions, lest the tears that were filling his eyes should betray his feelings.

The same day he ordered the sum of ten ounces of gold to be delivered to the unfortunate family to supply their first wants, promising at the same time to take the young soldier under his protection and to advance him in his career.[6]

[It is unfortunate that Ruxton's descriptions of all the battles he took part in have not survived. It would be interesting to read his account of the action of Villatuerta; the affair of the Ega; the taking of the fortified height of Belascoain, for which he was made a knight of the first class of the Order of San Fernando; the four-day action of Arroniz; and the two actions in the Val de Berrueza.

One wonders if the wild spirit of the young boy did not feel he had had enough fighting and adventure in a foreign land; if in the dirt and grime and privation he did not look with longing toward the home and the school he had left so early. One last story from Spain follows.]

The Division of General Diego León, viceroy of Navarre, having lain for some months in a state of monotonous inactivity at Tafalla (the only break in our lazy life being an occasional march from Pamplona to the Solano, and vice versa) hailed with delight, on the morning of the second of December, 1838, the *toca de la trompeta*, sounding the well known *orden general*, or general orders.

As a rumour had been some time afloat that our General had determined to make an inroad into the Carlist lines for the purpose of obtaining provisions, of which his troops were much in need, their hopes were raised by the expectation of something to do, no part of the Division more anxiously wishing it than the gallant little squadron

[6] From a manuscript in a flowing hand, obviously not Ruxton's, but possibly his mother's.

of Reyna Ysabel Lancers, who, fire-eaters all, hailed the prospect of a fight with all the ardour of boys for a game of cricket. The *adjutantes* of corps having received the orders from the chief of the Estado Mayor, all doubts as to meeting the Factions were removed.

The Division was to be under arms by twelve o'clock and at that hour were already formed on the Solano road. About this time a *confidente*, or spy, reported to the General that the enemy were in some force in the valley of the Solano.

During the night of the second, the troops occupied the villages of Carcar and Andosilla, and a number of mules and cars were collected for the carriage of provisions. Before daybreak on the morning of the third, "Armada de Tropa" was beating through the streets, and the Division was formed on the road to Los Arcos, then occupied by the Carlists.

The road from Carcar to Los Arcos lies over a plain, several miles in extent, broken here and there by ridges of hills, affording no verdure but wild thyme and heath. After passing Sesma, a village situated on an abrupt hill, the plain becomes more level, but on the right of the road, or rather track, to Los Arcos is a range of hills, with groves of dwarf oak and an occasional olive tree.

The troops had passed these hills, with the exception of the rear guard, which had been detained in bringing up a broken gun carriage, and which consisted of a half troop of the English Lancers, and half a company of the Saragoza regiment. The first appearance of the Factions was on one of these hills, where a squadron of lancers shewed themselves, and trotting down, charged the rear guard, the infantry of which retreated on the main body, covered by the Lancers, who were repeatedly charged but succeeded in keeping them off the company of infantry. The officer in command of the Lancers had a narrow escape, for when at last compelled to go "files about," being in the rear of his retreating men, he was attacked by a Carlist officer and three troopers and received three lance wounds, only escaping by the speed of his mare.

On getting up with the main body, the rear guard was soon informed of the state of affairs. To the right, in an open space between the olive groves, were formed up eight squadrons of Carlist cavalry, with their skirmishers thrown out, whilst General León was busily engaged forming his straggling division in order of battle, sending four squadrons of his cavalry, including one squadron of lancers of the Royal Guard, and the grenadiers of the same corps to attack the Factions, who, now becoming more emboldened by their evident superiority of cavalry, had advanced their skirmishers and commenced firing on our advancing squadrons.

As yet no infantry had appeared, but shortly several dark columns were seen moving on the distant hills, in rear of the cavalry, and it became evident that Maroto with his whole division was advancing, instead of, as we were led to believe, the smaller one of Elio, which consisted of but ten battalions and some four hundred cavalry.

The Cristino horse had by this time approached to within two hundred yards of the enemy, who quietly awaited their attack. Now was seen in perfection the usual ridiculous preface to a Spanish cavalry combat. The adverse squadrons commenced holloaing and complimenting each other in a strain in every way worthy of Billingsgate. *Cobardes, Puñeteros, Muerte a la puta,* and *Mueren los Facciosos* were among the most frequent compliments. Now a trooper would ride from the ranks and, bringing down his lance to the charge, shout out, "*Adelante, vamos, mujer,*" inviting one of the "women," as he was pleased to term his adversaries, to come out to fight him.

At length being sufficiently worked up, the two parties neared each other till within twenty yards, when the *comandante* of the Lancers of the Guard, riding out from his men for the purpose of leading the charge, and in the act of waving his sword to them, was shot dead, the charge of a *trabuco* or blunderbuss completely blowing away his right breast and shoulder. The lancers and grenadiers now charged in earnest, but after a few minutes were seen galloping out of the melee in disorder. The remaining squadrons then charged, and a beautiful sight presented itself; from the force of the last charge, the Factions were in some measure scattered, and the combat became more animated from its being carried on in detached fights.

Here might be seen a giant grenadier defending himself from two or three Carlists, wheeling round him on their active little horses, prodding with their lances, shouting *¡Viva Carlos Quinto! ¡Muerte a la Reyna!*; here, amongst the trees, a Carlist skirmisher coolly pinking off with his carbine any unlucky Cristino who came within range; or another might be seen stripping a fallen trooper; cries of "*¡Quartel, quartel, por Dios!*" from some wounded wretch, the words most probably thrust down his throat by a lance blade, all the quarter he had a right to expect; or here, another thrown from his horse, curling up his body to receive the *coup de grâce* of some butchering lance.

At length might be seen grenadiers riding bleeding and minus their bearskins out of the melee, pursued by Factions; and troops of yellow-jacketed heavies flying from the fight, the Carlists shouting in triumph. Our four squadrons, though they fought well, when once in the thick of it were evidently overmatched and had to contend with more than double their own number.

León, seeing this, and fearing that a panic might seize his troops and render them unmanageable, immediately sent off an aid de camp to the English Squadron, who by a mistake of a staff officer had been left in the rear, with the order, "*Al frente los Yngleses.*"

"Front form squadron," shouted the *comandante*, as they moved by files in their place of column. The little squadron wheeled rapidly into line, trot-canter, the General and his staff vivaing and waving their hats as they galloped past. "Charge!" and with a most infernal shout, comprising the war cries of every nation in Europe, the squadron, not numbering more than one hundred horses, was in the midst of more than eight hundred Carlists, flushed with victory and presenting an ugly appearance to the little troop which now charged them.

The officer commanding the squadron, an immensely powerful young Irishman, was the first amongst them as he charged, in front of his men, in line with his other officers. Bringing the butt of his lance to the front, he used it as a round parry, and soon cleared a lane, followed closely by his orderly trumpeter, who sabred those whom his major knocked off their horses. The other officers showing a good example, cut and stab was the order of the day, and after showing fight for some time, the Factions fairly turned tail and ran for it, leaving three hundred on the field. No quarter was given or expected, and a scene of butchery commenced which defies description, and which our men could not be restrained in.

As our men were being re-formed, a Carlist who had been stripped and left for dead suddenly jumped up, at a distance of about two hundred yards, and immediately ran towards the Carlist squadrons, which were also re-forming for the purpose of again charging. The sergeant-major of the English Squadron, an ex-sergeant of the Blues, perceiving him, immediately pursued, and came up to the fugitive, who, poor wretch, immediately threw himself on the ground and, curling himself up like a ball, demanded, "*¡Quartel, por la Virgen, quartel!*"

He raised his lance, saying, "*Recorde usted el quartel a Andoain,*" alluding to the massacre of the legion at that place; he drove it through the body of the unfortunate Faccioso till the lance flag was dyed in his blood. This same sergeant-major was seen to cut down eight of the enemy during the action, and was promoted on the field, by the General, to the rank of officer.

31

After the bodies had been stripped (the invariable custom on both sides) and the squadron got together and formed, the General with his staff rode up to thank us, as he was pleased to say, for saving his Division. There might be some truth in his remark, for the columns of Maroto were seen rapidly advancing, about twenty-five thousand strong, and we were instantly obliged to retreat, the cavalry covering the column, but the Carlist horse had evidently had enough and did not molest us.

The rain now coming down in torrents, we halted at Mendavia, where we found, on calling the roll, that we had lost but one man killed and but few wounded.

Next day we returned to Carcar, and to our former monotonous life, which continued till spring and the breaking up of the winter called us again to the field. We were shortly after reviewed by Espartero, the commander-in-chief, who complimented the Squadron on its gallant conduct at Sesma, for which we were well repaid by a gazette-ful of promotions and decorations, granted by the Queen.[7]

[7] From original Ruxton MS.

CHAPTER 3

Military Service in Ireland and Canada, 1840-43

[$\mathcal{A}$ T THE CLOSE of his fighting career in Spain, Ruxton returned home to England, a military veteran at the age of seventeen. At the Battle of the Bridge of Belascoain, April 29 to May 1, 1839, he had so distinguished himself that the commander, Don Diego León, selected him for special honor. Following the fight, when the army was paraded, Don Diego rode with Ruxton down the ranks and called on all to note and imitate the young Englishman. For his gallantry in the battle, he was awarded the Cross of the First Class of the National Military Order of San Fernando, which carried with it the title of knight. The Queen Mother, then Regent, had promised him a large ring engraved with the English lion astride the broken bridge of Belascoain.[1] Ruxton had learned the Spanish language and much about the Spanish people and their customs, all of which would subsequently serve him well during travels in Mexico and New Mexico.

[1] Munro, *loc. cit.*, 547–48, quoting General Robert B. Hawley, Ruxton's schoolmate, and Captain John H. H. Ruxton, eldest brother of George F. Ruxton.

Subsequently, on December 28, 1841, Queen Victoria gave Ruxton, in the following order, permission to wear the Spanish cross:

"The Queen has been pleased to grant unto Ensign George Frederick Augustus Ruxton, of the 89th Regiment, late a Cornet of Lancers in the British Auxiliary Legion, Her Majesty's royal licence and permission, that he may accept and wear the cross, of the first class, of the National Military Order of San Fernando, conferred upon him by the Queen of Spain, in testimony of Her Catholic Majesty's royal approbation of his services in the actions of the 29th and 30th of April, and the 1st of May, 1839, at the bridge of Belascoain; provided, nevertheless, that this Her Majesty's licence and permission doth not authorize the assumption of any style, appellation, rank, precedence, or privilege appertaining unto a Knight Bachelor of these realms;

"And also to command, that this Her Majesty's concession and especial mark of Her royal favour be registered, together with the relative documents, in Her College of Arms."

Hardly had he arrived home before he found himself gazetted to a lieutenancy in the Ceylon Rifles, August 2, 1839. Then, without joining the Rifles, he was transferred on September 20 to the Eighty-ninth Foot, a regiment later to be known as the Second Battalion Royal Irish Fusiliers. The service corps of the regiment was in the West Indies; so on November 15, 1839, Ruxton joined the home depot at Forton Barracks, Gosport. This was in Hampshire, southwest of London. Here he remained through July, 1840.[2]

We have found no Ruxton writings recounting his experiences at Gosport or in Ireland after his removal there. But we know he took every opportunity to indulge his love for hunting and dogs. A fellow officer in both Hampshire and Ireland was Ensign Robert Hawley, Ruxton's schoolmate of Sandhurst days. From him we get a glimpse of Ruxton during this period. Hawley says:

"We became fast friends, our pursuit of shooting and fishing giving us a mutual topic for talk. Even in that over-inhabited country we managed to get, perhaps a snipe, an 'awl,' or some winged creature. Ruxton at Forton R. M. S., though quarters were small, and not even a back yard, had at times half a dozen dogs of parts; and I recollect, too, a monkey in his room which clawed at the prints on the white-washed walls cut out of the 'Book of Beauty.' Soon we were ordered to Fermoy (Ireland). There we used to fish the Funcheon. How he used to laugh when by some half poacher's trick he killed what his Irish attendant declared to be the biggest fish that was 'iver' killed in the Funcheon. Next we were quartered at Clonmel. There he and I strolled along the Suir, day by day, to knock down a moorhen; and when no one was on the look-out we left the river and beat any bit of wood and the mountain-side opposite Clonmel. One day we were very proud, he having killed a hare and I a woodcock."[3]

[2] The record at the Royal Military Academy, Sandhurst, has an entry against George Ruxton's name which reads: "Commissioned Ceylon Rifle Corps, Lieut., August 2nd, 1839." But his name does not appear on the lists of that regiment.

The *Army List* of 1840 shows: "Ruxton, G.A.F., Second Lieut., 2nd August, 1839, Ensign, 20th September, 1839. Rank in Regiment, Ensign; rank in Army, Lieutenant."

In the files of the Central Records Office, London, are the following: W. O. 17/924, *Monthly Returns*, 89th Foot, 1839, 1 December, H. Q. Forton Barracks, Gosport, officers who have joined the Regiment during the preceding month, Ensign G. A. F. Ruxton, 15 November 1839; W. O. 17/934, *Monthly Returns*, 89th Foot, 1840, 1 January–1 August, H. Q. Forton, Barracks, Gosport, list of officers includes Ensign G. A. F. Ruxton.

[3] Quoted by Munro, *loc. cit.*, 548.

34

From this period in Ireland, apparently, come Ruxton's earliest extant literary and artistic efforts. These, found in his notebooks, are the verses below and the signed sketch reproduced on the following page:

AN IRISH SUB'S LAMENT

Oh! There's nought in the world like the life of a Sub
With no care but for how he's to pay for his grub,
Which the Guards in its love for his comfort have strove
To compel him to swallow in style.

Ochone! Wirrasthru!!

Two and sixpence no less I must pay for my mess
Oh! Whether I ate it or no.
At home I could ate without silver or plate;
A joint would content me, or roast, or biled mate.
But because I'm an Ensign, then fane must I dine
On ill cooked made dishes and stews.

Ochone! Wirrasthru!!

I wish I'd my prog in my own native bog
In county Roscommon or Meath.
Och! The first of the month and the mess bill's to pay—
Eight pounds ten, out of five and three pennies a day;
The wine will be ten, and my washing again
Three months in arrear I declare.

Ochone! Wirrasthru!!

In Ireland I think 'twould be whisky I'd drink,
To drink no more sherry I'll swear.
Oh what do we suffer, who live on our pay
Toiling hard in our rank till our heads become grey.
On promotion we look as an ever sealed book,
In fine misery we live and we die.

Ochone! Wirrasthru!!

Why feast I so rare when my back it is bare?

Ochone! Why are mess bills so high?

35

The Irish Sub. paying his monthly Mess bill

The military records in London show that on August 4, 1840, Ensign Ruxton was transferred to Fermoy, Ireland. On September 15, 1840, he was transferred to Clonmel, where he remained until March, 1841. After a brief leave of absence, March 25 to April 10, Ruxton prepared to join his overseas regiment, which had been transferred from the West Indies to Canada.[4]

Of his journey across the Atlantic and to Upper Canada we have no record, but he joined his service company on July 8, 1841, at Amherstburg.[5] This post was on the Detroit River, in the heart of country made famous by campaigns of the War of 1812. More recently had occurred the Canadian uprising of 1837, but it had been amicably settled and British military service here was now largely routine. Consequently Ruxton was able to devote much of his time to his loved hunting excursions. Fortunately, well-penned accounts of some of these experiences are preserved in Ruxton's notebooks, from which the following extract is quoted.]

During the autumn and winter of last year [1841–42] it was my lot to be quartered in an out of the way post in Upper Canada. Amongst the several sportsmen of the regiment to which I belonged, just arrived in the country, not a little rivalry existed as to who should attain the reputation of a hunter by killing the first deer or wild turkey. The gun had ever been my delight and my *ardor venandi* had been worked up to the highest pitch by reading the adventures of Natty Bumppo and his friends the Mohegans in the admirable romances of Cooper. I had always longed to pull a trigger in the woods of America, and now the opportunity had arrived. Many wagers were laid by our confident sportsmen as to flooring the first deer or turkey. I had sternly resolved that I should be the man. On our arrival I had formed an acquaintance with an old Indian hunter and had hunted with him once (unsuccessfully) in the summer. However, I had found out the way in which the Indians followed their game, and treasured the knowledge carefully in my mind. It was the month of October that one of the officers had been asked to join a hunting party under the direction of one of the most reputed hunters of the Chippewas, and there was little doubt that something or another would be slaughtered. I was agonized at the idea of being beaten, and resolved to hunt the same day by myself. I had previously been some eight or ten miles

4 Central Records Office, W. O., 17/934, *Monthly Returns*, 1840, and W. O. 17/944, *Monthly Returns*, 1841.
    5 Central Records Office, W. O. 17/544, *Monthly Returns*, 1841.

back in the forest and on one occasion had wounded a buck, so that I had some little knowledge of the bush.

Before daybreak on the day in question, I was equipped and off for my hunting ground. For hours I had toiled without coming on the track of game, when in the hollow occasioned by a tree being torn up with its roots, and filled with water, I descried a turkey track and soon after the tracks of a flock. For several miles I followed it up, sometimes losing it for a mile together, then discovering it on the log of a rotten tree where the brood had been scratching and dusting themselves. I forgot to mention that I was accompanied by a dog of the Romney Marsh breed who had been very useful in running up the track.

The sun was beginning to get low, and being a long way from home, I was on the point of giving up in despair, when I noticed the dog hunting more keenly, and presently he struck off, with his nose down, at a gallop. He had left me some ten minutes when I heard a loud clucking noise and the flapping as of fifty pheasants on the wing. I immediately cocked both barrels, one of which was loaded with buckshot and the other with ball. Scarcely had I done so when with a tremendous flapping I saw to my inexpressible delight a large turkey flying right upon me. On seeing me, however, he turned off to the right, flying high over the tops of the trees. I gave it up for lost, when I again caught sight of the bird and quick as lightning brought my gun to bear on it and fired. Down crashed the fine fellow through the branches, and had hardly reached the ground when Dash and I had thrown ourselves on him, so fearful was I lest he might be only wounded and escape. He, however, was shot dead, three buckshot having pierced his body, and proved to be an old gobbler with a splendid black plumage. Dash started off again and, knowing there were more of them near, I hastened to reload. Slinging the dead bird on my shoulder, I followed in the direction the dog had taken. In this way I had proceeded for about an hour when I caught sight of the whole flock running before the dog. On seeing me, they took wing and I marked one settle on the topmost branch of a tall hickory tree. The thickness of the branches prevented my seeing the bird except at some distance, nearly a hundred yards, so that I resolved upon trying him with a ball and killed him.

No sport pleased me like the cock shooting in Upper Canada. Fancy the dawning of a superb day in July; the magnificent Erie smooth as a looking glass lighted up by the first gleam of the sun as he shows over the forest that bounds the eastern shore, the mist slowly rising from the water and gradually uncovering the objects on its bosom—perhaps a schooner bound to the Western Lake lying lazily with its sails flapping against the mast or slowly drifting with the current, or a canoe darting along paddled by a dusky Indian seeking his fishing grounds thus early in some of the numerous islands which lie, picturesquely beautiful in their varieties of foliage and situation, along both shores. As the mist gradually disperses, ducks of all varieties may be seen enjoying themselves in the morning sun—the wary and stately loon leaving a long wake in the glassy water as, startled by some object, he swims swiftly towards the islands, amongst the reeds of which he finds a sure harbour. Not unfrequently I have seen a deer stretching across the head of the lake, leaving behind him a wake like a steamboat. Nothing is more exciting than a chase in a canoe after a strong buck.

On such a morning as this I would turn out an hour before daybreak and, rousing Dash from his deerskin, would sally down to the wharf where I kept my skiff. Stowing away a ration and a small bottle of brandy-pounce in the locker, and perhaps a lump of ice, gun, shot belts, powder, and game bag, almost filling the little craft, I would then stretch across to some of the islands which lie in the Detroit River —some eleven miles wide, by the way. Choosing a sheltered nook in which to run the boat, I would commence operations. These islands are generally surrounded by a narrow belt of flags under which the soil is soft and spongy. Here the cock feed in the mornings and evenings. Dash, some fifteen or twenty yards in advance, would soon flush one, which would make off into the cover unless a snap shot— and a quick one it required, too—stopped him. I would lie in the middle of the island until noon, where I could shoot with comfort, the sun not being able to penetrate the thick foliage.

After having beaten round the island and shot or driven every cock into cover, I would make for the boat, take a pull at the brandy, light a cigar, and away to another island. My fun was often diversified by a crack at a wood duck or a flock of pigeons. Sometimes an otter would dart out from the reeds, and many a muskrat has old Dash brought me in his mouth, and often a tortoise. About noon I would again make the boat and prepare for lunch, ice a bottle of porter or cider, take a snack of pemmican, a shaugh of a pipe, and snooze in the shade for a couple of hours. If I was on the shady side of the island, a plunge into the lake and I was fresh as a lion for the afternoon's work, which was the cream of the thing, as it always and everywhere is.

About sundown another bath and home with a boatload of cock—say sixteen or twenty brace—a brace or two of bittern, two or three duck, a snipe or two, with pigeons and a black squirrel or so, killed for the express gratification of Dash, who had a particular fancy for the black long-tails.

In the evening the water would be alive with mosquito hawks, the whippoorwill, in shape and size resembling the ferm owl or night jar of the British Islands. The cry from which they take their name and which is as plainly, "Whip poor Will," as a child could speak, is only heard when the birds are single, and not when in numbers. The Indians frequently eat them, as indeed they do owls and hawks, but I don't envy them their taste.

I once, whilst still hunting in the woods came across an Indian boy some twelve years of age, with a rifle on his shoulder and some dozen large hawks and whippoorwills he had shot with ball, and which he was carrying to his camp for dinner. I came upon the little fellow suddenly, for I had hid behind a tree to surprise him, and in an instant his rifle was thrown forward to the ready, and his hand on his knife. But I was an old friend and made him happy with a little good powder and some percussion caps.

This boy was the son of a Chippewa with whom I frequently hunted. On one occasion whilst sitting over the fire with Peshwego, for so he was called, I asked why he did not allow his son to hunt. He answered that he could not spare him ammunition, but on my promising to supply him with powder and caps he consented that he should go out on his first hunt on the morrow. Consequently, when he and I turned out the next morning, we found that the boy was already off with his rifle.

That day we were most unsuccessful, not getting a shot or coming up to deer on account of the stillness of the day, but we found, on returning to camp, that the boy had returned some hours before with a turkey and a fine young doe which he had killed. Subsequently he often accompanied me in my hunts, and I never had a better hunting companion, for no labour was too much for him, no day too long. His father, who was a Chippewa, was a perfect specimen of an Indian hunter—his instinct was almost animal. However, Peshwego was addicted to firewater, and sometimes when knocking up his wigwam at daylight I have found him and other Indians in the midst of a carouse, the effects of which were very evident during the day by his unsteady hand and frequent misses, to say nothing of the frequent and copious draughts of water he took whenever that element presented itself. However, he was a good hunter, was Fred Fisher, that being his English name, and a most amusing fellow at night when sitting over the campfire smoking, for he had been his life long in the woods and knew the furry inhabitants thereof as well as he knew his own people, and many a yarn of b'ar hunts &c. has he spun for me.

I remember my most successful day's duck shooting was on a Sunday in April of 1842. It was as ugly a day as I ever had the misfortune to be out in. The wind blew great guns and the rain was not backward in its desire to saturate my old velveteen. I was sitting very miserable over the stove in my quarters dozing over the locks of my double, which for want of anything better to do I was cleaning up for the opening of the spring campaign, when a half-breed who was frequently coxswain of my canoe on my ducking expeditions knocked at my outer door and on entering informed me of the arrival of large flocks of ducks in a marsh on the lake shore some five miles off. In spite of the weather, I immediately donned my foul-weather toggery, clapped my heavy double into its waterproof case, and calling Dash, who was evidently aware of my intentions and was capering eager for the fray, I followed Domene to his canoe, which he had left lying at the wharf. After a two-hour paddle against a heavy stream and wind, we made the edge of the marsh, which was alive with ducks flying about very wildly, as they usually do in stormy weather.

Finding that they were too wild to come at in the marsh, I paddled to the shore, determined to drag myself along the mud to some of the numerous pools surrounded with rushes, which extended along the muddy banks for miles in length and some seven or eight hundred yards in width, and on which the ducks were alighting in immense numbers and every variety. Flocks of wild geese were also turning into the marsh, their long line of march extending as far as the eye could reach. Most of the pools were surrounded by an edging of flags, but the greater part of the marsh was without cover of any kind, the summer growth of reeds and flags not having as yet made its appearance, and the only thing to cover one's approach was a few heaps of cat reeds at some distance from each other.

On one of these pools, which was even more scantily edged than the others, I saw a large team alight and determined to have a crack at them. Putting my ammunition in my breast pockets and turning up the skirts of my jacket, I drew myself along the mud followed by Dash, who was up to this style of work and quiet as a mouse. After a long and not very enviable drag, I got within some thirty yards of my birds and raised my head to reconnoitre. In a space of not more than thirty yards square some five hundred ducks—teal, widgeon, pintails, ruddy ducks, canvasbacks, and numerous other kinds—some with their doups stuck up diving for weed, some fighting, and others now and then rising and settling again. I remained in this bog for some minutes, waiting for a good opportuntiy to get a shot at a knot of grey ducks. When at length I let drive my right barrel into the midst of them, the others immediately rose with a tremendous quacking and as soon received my other barrel into the thick of them. I saw clouds of feathers and birds dropping from the mass as they flew off, but not waiting to bag them, I loaded as fast as I could and got another double shot as they wheeled over my head, knocking over nine by both shots.

Dash and I then commenced the work of collecting the slain, nor did we desist till thirteen fine fellows were lying at my feet, making twenty-two by the four shots, six of which were the large grey duck or mallard, the rest teal, widgeon, and pintails. By this time I was wet through and through and my clothes freezing to me, but I determined to have a blaze at some of the geese, which were still coming in in long lines. Charging both barrels with buckshot, I waded into a pool in the middle of which was a clump of flags, under cover of which I waited with Dash till the geese came over me.

Whilst I was thus waiting, Dash made a bolt into the water and came out with a tortoise in his mouth, numbers of which are found in the marshes.

After remaining up to my middle in water for some time, I at last saw twenty or thirty geese flying slowly towards me headed by a huge old gander, who alighted in the pool some seventy yards from me, but a movement of mine scared him and he rose again, the others turning off to my left, out of shot. However, I drove at the gander and knocked the feathers out of him the first shot, but instantly [firing?] the second barrel at him, was more successful, turning him over, and he fell plump into the water. Dash immediately started off to bring him but found he had enough to do as the old fellow shewed fight with wings and beak. However, Dash got him by the neck and brought him up to me, where a *coup de grâce* with the butt of the gun settled him.

I had several other shots, bagging nine or ten teal and widgeon and one more goose, when my powder became so wet that I found it useless remaining. Collecting the slain, I dragged them to the canoe, which was nearly filled with them. On counting the birds, I found I had bagged thirty-three ducks and two geese, not a bad three hours' work. But tell it not in Gath—this was on a Sunday, so the better day the better deed. Paddling home through the marsh, I came upon an Indian in a canoe laying up for ducks, concealed in the rushes of the marsh with an old flint gun such as is served by government as presents to the Indians and the cost price of which is nine shillings six. He had killed twenty-nine ducks and three geese, and with every prospect of killing twice that number before nightfall. This day's work nearly cost me dearly, as Dash took cold from staying so long in the cold water and was within an inch of dying. No sum of money could have induced me to part with this dog, who was invaluable in every species of shooting, from wild turkey to quail.

[Ruxton remained in Upper Canada until August 1, 1842, when he obtained a leave of absence for five months to attend to "private affairs."[6] He returned to Britain and spent the winter there. Apparently his original leave was extended, for it was late in May, 1843, before he began his return to Canada. He was at Cork, Ireland, on May 20, ready for embarkation.[7] His brief notes supply some data on the voyage.]

May 23rd, 6½ A.M. On board tug steamer. Baggage and troops to cove. Embarked *Marquis Bute* 10½ A.M. Wind E. S. E. light and as usual rain. All confusion—making the berths comfortable. Discover loss of keys. Short the portmanteau. Nothing to hand. Dash miserable. Skipper surly. No sheets forthcoming. Sew up two old shirts. Case of pictures in imminent danger. First dinner—symptoms of a famine. Grease and dirt in abundance. Turned in at 12 P.M. to an atmosphere of ———.

24th–25th. Lay at cove. No prospect of sailing. 25th. At 2 A.M. weighed and stood out of harbour. Wind from the southeast, light, with rain.

26th. Rain—head wind. No progress. Got a kennel built for Dash, who had been lying under the lorry boat smothered by coils of rope.

27th. Almost a calm. Shark near the ship. Unpacking of guns and rifles. Blazing at gulls and boobies. Black steward. Dignity hurt.

28th–31st. Fine breezes from the southwest and south by west. Every chance of a good run. Taken aback night of 29th.

[6] Central Records Office, W.O. 17/1546, *Monthly Returns*, 1842, and W.O. 17/1547, *Monthly Returns*, 1843.
[7] *Naval and Military Gazette*, May 20, 1843, p. 306, column 3: "89th Foot., Lieut. Ruxton has arrived at Cork for Embarkation for Canada."

July 4th. Heavy squall—taken aback. 6th. Lost M.T.G. mast in a squall. Snapped at the chesstrees.

[A fuller description of experiences on the boat and some observations made while ascending the St. Lawrence are supplied by Ruxton.]

One morning when I turned out to breakfast I found the mess-cabin table covered with guns, rifles, &c., with which some of the sporting people were preparing to have a shot at the whales which were surrounding the ship. As I had a reputation of being a bit of a rifle shot, a D–6 W. R. [Westley Richards] was put into my hands with which I blazed away for some time at long distances. As I sat on the taffrail with the rifle in my hands, I saw the water about twenty yards right astern appear suddenly of a dull yellow colour in a space of about ten feet square. Guessing that a whale was about to make its appearance, I cocked both barrels, nor was I deceived, for slowly and by degrees up he came to the surface, first shewing his head, into which an ounce ball from my rifle whisked instantly, and as soon as the shoulder was exposed—bang went the other with a sounding thud as it told, and which was plainly heard. Neither seemed to have inconvenienced the monster, though a streak of blood was left in his wake as he slowly made off, snorting and blowing the water many feet into the air. Hundreds were at this time sporting in the water, and all taking the same track, apparently into the Gulf of St. Lawrence. I made a good shot at a seal which rose in our wake some three hundred and fifty yards astern. Poising the long sight, I managed to send a ball into him, but he immediately dived and we lost sight of him.

After passing the Manicouagan shore, the seals again made their appearance, and again the rifles were called into requisition, but they never came within fair range. A few white porpoises also shewed about the ship. On the seventh of July we passed the mouth of the Saguenay, a fine river about a hundred and twenty miles from Quebec and rising some two hundred miles to the N. N. E. This river opens a fine field for the sportsman, unfrequented hunting grounds abounding with deer, bears, and moose, and streams full of salmon. Now and then a more than usually enterprising party from the Quebec garrison sets out on a fishing excursion some little distance up and is well repaid by the number of fish killed. A steamer sometimes with a pleasure party on board, in summer, explores the river, some eighty or ninety up, with a band of music on board, and great shindy, much to the astonishment of the solitary Indian trapping on its banks. I have long projected a hunting trip *this-a-way* and *Deo volente* intend to carry it into effect the very first opportunity, and this summer, if the powers that be are propitious. My idea is to ship self, Dash, and skiff into any vessel bound down river and turn adrift when near the mouth, and then paddle and sail up. A bucket of salt pork and a hundred of biscuits, an anker of brandy, cooking apparatus—such as gridiron, frying pan, and kettle—lashins of tobacco, rifle and smooth bore and fishing rod, galore of powder and shot, and a pair or two of blankets, buffalo skin, &c.—and hey for a couple of months of liberty.

A companion is desirable if a hard worker can be procured and heart and soul in the business, but your milk-and-water sportsmen who, when game is scarce or work harder than usual, put on a long face and hint that they do not see the fun of the thing and evidently wish to put about—that style of bird, I say, had better remain in his wigwam. I once knew a party of officers who, having obtained a two or three months' leave of absence, set off to have some hunting in a wildish sort of country. One or two were inclined to do the business properly, but one of the least red-hot of the number—old, seventy-one, sergeant—mutinied the third day because there was no Harvey sauce to his catfish or jelly to their venison. This worthy started off townwards in search of what he deemed the absolute necessaries and returned with a hamper of sauces and pickles, hams, tongues, porter, beer, wine, &c. Loading some half-dozen canoes with this freight, [he] returned to the camp where he had left the others, but to his disgust they had changed their ground and he had the satisfaction of eating and paying for all the trash himself.

The country north of this river, that is, beyond its source, which is properly the Lake St. Johns, is totally uninhabited. A few Iroquois and Algonquins camp on its upper waters for the summer's hunt, and there is a trading post of the Fur Company some ninety miles from its mouth. The current runs seven knots out of its mouth, and no anchorage is found for some miles up, the banks being precipitous. At the mouth, it is said, two hundred and fifty fathoms of line cannot find bottom. The almost monopoly of this country north of the St. Lawrence and east of Quebec by the hunters and Indians in pay of the Company prevents these hunting grounds being sought by white hunters, collision with the above worthies some hundreds of miles from civilization partaking rather too much of a "to walk with the weak" system to please the more peaceably inclined amateur hunter. The Indians are extremely jealous of their country being encroached

45

upon, and there might be some little danger in attempting an excursion of the kind, at least to any considerable distance, without the escort of an Indian or hunter of the Company.

People at home are much mistaken in thinking that the North American Indian is now rarely if ever met with in anything like his original character. In some parts, particularly in the Huron district of Upper Canada, where they are now located in considerable numbers, they still retain all the characteristics of their race, not having even as yet imbibed *all* the vices of their white supplanters in their land. There they maintain their old customs and live as primitively as in the days when the Leatherstocking and the Mohegan chief followed the Mingo Trail in the woods of the Susquehanna. Living wholly by the chase, their wants are few and easily supplied. Pemmican and bear's meat, fresh and dried, furnish their food the year round, and unless the destructive "firewater" is introduced by casual white visitors, nothing like discord breaks the harmony of their camps. But when spirits are to be obtained, every other consideration is drowned in their passion for it—to which all the debasement of the red men, owing to the cruel policy of their European conquerors, is to be attributed.

I have hunted and lived among Indians of almost every nation, and when in their primitive state have always found them strictly honest, kindhearted, and hospitable. In the neighbourhood of the large towns, which is the locale from which most travellers draw their sample of Indian manners and customs, it cannot be denied that they are seen in a very unfavorable light. But when it is considered that these are men debased by imitating the vices of their white neighbours, of inferior blood, and not depending on their own resources for subsistence (most of them live by begging), it would be unfair to condemn the many for the sake of the few.

Some are found endued with even extraordinary qualities—for instance, Tecumseh and other chiefs, who exhibited in the last war wonderful appreciation of the arts, and from whom our generals derived great assistance, both bodily and mentally.

Whilst on the subject of Tecumseh, let me add a trait in the Indian character which redounds as much to their good feeling as their generosity. It is well known that the gallant Brock, when killed on the heights of Queenston, was accompanied by a body of Indian warriors who had been attached to his division during the war. When some time afterwards it was proposed by the inhabitants of Upper Canada to erect a monument to his memory on the scene of his death, the Indians in a body, through their different superintendents, handed in their subscriptions with many expressions of their deep regard and affection for their White Chief; and lately—though that generation had almost passed away and the memory of the love for the general might be supposed to have been lost—when this monument was destroyed by a band of cowardly ruffians, the Indians were the first in the field, coming forward with their mites to contribute to the rebuilding of the column. Councils were called by their chiefs at which speeches were made on the subject and were forwarded to the governor general by the superintendents, reflecting the highest honour on these red children of the forest, not only on account of their sympathy for the deed but for the elegance and beauty of their language. Some time after this, it was proposed to erect a monument to the memory of Tecumseh, and I blush to say that after many fruitless attempts to raise subscriptions, the project fell to the ground.

An officer of the government, superintending the interests of the Indians in the Huron and Manitoulin areas, assured me that though he had some thousands constantly under his eye, crime was almost unknown amongst them, and he never had the slightest difficulty in arranging their differences, which happily were few and far between.

These superintendents are appointed by government with a liberal salary, for the sole purpose of attending to the interests and supervising the affairs of the Indians in their respective districts. They are generally men well acquainted with their habits, customs, and language, and in many cases themselves of Indian blood. To these the Indians look as a channel through which their wrongs and grievances are made known to and redressed by government. They likewise see to the fair and equal distribution of the presents annually supplied by the Queen and which I hope may be forever continued, although it has more than once been proposed to discontinue them on the score of economy; however, when it is considered that is the compensation for the whole of their country, it is to be hoped that such a design could never be for an instant seriously considered. Policy, indeed, would never allow the affections of the Indians to be alienated from British interest.

It has been sufficiently proved that no war can be successfully carried on in the Canadas without their assistance. The nature of the country and the enemies we have to contend with render it necessary always to employ them. It would be vain for regular troops to attempt to move through the woods in this country without the protection of Indians on their flanks and rear.

47

No scenery can be more perfect than that of the river St. Lawrence, which may justly be deemed the first river in the world. The alternation of hill and dale, bold headlands and capes, with distant mountains clad with pine forests, either tinged by a setting sun or grey with mist, the broad, clear waters of the magnificent stream covered with vessels, the distant settlements and partially cleared lands—all combine a picture unrivalled in beauty in any part of the world. On land the scenery is equally attractive—the picturesque villages all white and clean as driven snow, the tin-spired churches shining and dazzling the eye in the sun, luxuriant fields and gardens, and the happy, healthy faces of the habitants add tenfold to the scene and make us wonder that so much of the land is still unoccupied and that the tide of emigration has not yet set in in this direction.

Few people can appreciate the joy and excitement of being on terra firma like those who, after a long sea voyage, set their foot on land for the first time. After a couple of months at sea, with a full allowance of gales and constant foul winds, great was our satisfaction in at length arriving in the river, with land on both sides, wild and uncultivated at first, but gradually presenting a pleasanter view as it became partially cleared, with white, shining houses on its banks and the cultivated land with its patches of green offering a pleasing contrast to the dark, sombre hue of the forest.

Many and speculative were the opinions, as to the capabilities, in a sporting sense, of the different ridges of forest and wild country, of many of our old-country sportsmen. One would exclaim, "By Jove, what splendid cock covers!" his eye wandering over miles and miles of larch forests. Another would ejaculate a wish to draw them with a pack of fox hounds, whilst one simple gentleman from Sussex remarked that they must be full of pheasants. I, having been before in the country, and having the credit of being a bit of sportsman, was constantly appealed to. When a chance of landing appeared, out came the gun and rifles of all kinds and denominations, Westley Richards in a majority; though the most useless of all arms in Canada, namely three-ounce ball rifles, were in greater plenty than anything—and all red-hot with the idea of landing and notions of bear and deer killing.

The wind being dead against us and it being therefore impossible to get up the river except by tides, on making Kamouraska we let go the anchor, and the skipper with two officers, and myself as interpreter, went ashore to procure fresh provisions, of which we were much in want. Of course in an expedition of this kind all were for being of the party. So to prevent all discussion, lots were drawn by the twenty-four on board. And I, procured as interpreter, with another fortunate put off for the shore, which lay some four miles from the ship. On pulling to the land, we passed a small rocky island, at the extreme point of which lay the body of a sailor in a natural grave, the body lying between two rocks with a large stone and some branches on the top. The poor fellow had been wrecked and perished of cold before reaching the shore.

Kamouraska is a small village twenty leagues from Quebec, to which there is a tolerable road, though little used. It is, with the exception of two families, exclusively inhabited by French Canadians, who live in the most primitive yet perfectly happy state, having all the comforts and some of the luxuries of Canadian life. There are two inns in the village, one kept by an Irishman of the name of Wood, whose success in life may be taken as a sample of that of every successful adventurer from the old country. Fifteen years before, he had migrated from Ireland with some £20 of property. Being wrecked in the river near this place and losing everything he possessed, he determined to remain at Kamouraska until he had by work accumulated sufficient to take him to Quebec. However, day after day, week after week, month after month, he still knocked on without getting farther, till at last, by dint of industry, he found he had amassed sufficient to set up a small store, which he gradually increased, and, still prospering, now owns several capital houses in the village, including the two large inns, is married to a French Canadian, educates his daughter at a convent at Quebec, and is in every sense of the word well to do in this world. The village is very pleasantly situated on the banks of the river and consists of some fifty houses and a large, and as usual in Catholic countries, handsome church, capable of containing twelve or fourteen hundred people.

On gaining the beach, the whole population turned out to see us. Mr. Wood immediately laid claim to us as countrymen and took us off to his hostelry where we were soon pitching into soft tack (the nautical term for fresh bread), fresh butter, and—oh, mention it not in Gath—onions, which we ate and ate and ate till we became so many onion beds, washing down the same with copious draughts of excellent Quebec beer. After our regale, and seeing to the wants of the boat's crew, we started off to see the town. Everything presented a pleasing view of the happy and contented state of the Canadians. Houses well built, clean as silver, and healthy faces peering out of the windows—all betokened comfort; nothing like poverty or misery of any description. The bell of the church was tolling for evening mass,

49

and the inhabitants were all thronging towards it. I never saw prettier girls or stouter men, and all dressed extremely well, the women even with great taste, as French women always do. The best houses belonged to the priest and the seigneur of the district. The land appeared to be well cultivated. Though wheat is not abundant, the soil not being adapted to its growth, fruits and vegetables in abundance. We found no difficulty in procuring fresh provisions. Customers being scarce, they were but too glad to supply us.

We soon bargained for *un veau gras*, a couple of porkers, potatoes, bread, butter, salad, onions, beer, &c., for which, to give an idea of the prices of provisions in this part of Canada, we paid not quite £2, including the calf, 10 s., pigs 3 s. 6 d. each. We also procured a dish of strawberries for the ladies on board. After having consumed a prodigious quantity of soft tack, &c., we saw all the lions of the place, over which, by the way, we were ciceroned by the mate of a vessel which had been wrecked on the reef off the town, and who had been hanging on during the winter in charge of the hull, which he expected to get off and up to Quebec for repair by the middle of the month. He gave us a good account of the hospitality and sociability of the people of Kamouraska. Great gaiety was constantly going on during winter, when dancing and sleighing were the order of the day.

There is no game in the vicinity, with the exception of a few geese and ducks which appear in spring and fall. A short time before we visited the place, two huge animals, or as the native informed me, *deux animaux grands comme ça*, pointing to a large cow, appeared near the town, with hoofs and large horns—he knew no name for them, but I concluded they were elk or moose—and swam across to the opposite shore. Deer are unknown, and but few Indians ever make their appearance, and then on their way to their fishing grounds towards Gaspé. However, I saw a brace of decent-looking pointers, so perhaps there may be a few quail in the swamps.

[The narrative ends abruptly. The official record states that Ruxton reached his station at Montreal on July 12, 1843.

Lieutenant Ruxton grew dissatisfied with the army; the life apparently was too dull for his active spirit. His discontent reached such a point that on September 10, 1843, he requested permission to retire by the sale of his commission. The permission was granted on October 6. Companions persuaded him to endeavor to recall his request, but action upon it had already been taken, and was not revoked.[8]

[8] Public Archives of Canada, Ottawa, File No. 30518: "Lieutenant Ruxton

General Hawley throws light upon the matter, offers an appraisal of Ruxton, and marks the loss sustained by the army in the retirement of Lieutenant Ruxton:

"When in garrison at Montreal he made up his mind to sell out, and wished me to do the same. I was, however, too matter-of-fact to throw up what I had been brought up in—tempting as the companionship would have been. We persuaded him to withdraw his 'papers' as they were called—he agreed—but the 'authorities' refused the request, and as fine a fellow as ever breathed was lost to the English army. Mind," says this distinguished soldier and Crimean veteran, "I have met many, and my appointments have been many, too—still, but one (who served as a sub. in the 60th Rifles, now the head of the staff of the army) was his equal."[9]]

requested permission to retire from the army by the sale of his commission under date of September 10, 1843; C. 1005, p. 109. Permission to retire was granted October 6th, 1843; C. 1005, p. 115. Later correspondence shows that Lieut. Ruxton made application to withdraw his resignation, but action having already been taken regarding his retirement, the request was not granted."

[9] Quoted by Munro, *loc. cit.*, 548.

CHAPTER 4

A Winter Hunt with Chippewas
in Upper Canada, 1843-44

[OUT OF THE ARMY, foot-loose, and free to follow his natural bent, Ruxton was not long in choosing his course or selecting the ground. He would make a winter hunt with his Indian friend Peshwego in the forest of southeast Ontario. The story of this experience he supplies in gratifying detail.]

It was a cold rainy day in October of last year [1843] that I put myself and traps, a brace of setters, and three gun cases on board the little steamer plying between Chippewa and Buffalo.

After having myself portered my luggage on board—for with the usual civility ever of Canada, I was left to my own care—and tying the dogs behind the little miserable hurricane house, called, par excellence, "the ladies' cabin," I looked about me to endeavour to discover some familiar face, but nothing met my eye but the long-haired greasy countenances of rowdy Canadians and Yankee loafers. These gentry were lolling about the deck, chewing and spitting, and swearing in a most disgusting manner. So quitting the deck, I essayed to enter the cabin, but here a collection of the most cutthroat looking villains, squirting showers of tobacco juice, soon compelled me to make myself scarce, and I had recourse to the companionship of my dogs, by far the less brutish of the two.

On nearing the mouth of the Niagara River, we found the wind blowing so hard directly in, that it was impossible to make any headway, and a heavy sea on the lake deterred us from reaching Buffalo, so the boat was steered into Little Rock, a miserable place consisting of some dozen houses and one tavern. Into this all the passengers rushed, leaving me to follow, as best I could, with dogs and baggage. On entering the tavern, which was filled with loafers, a rather respectable looking man came up to me and, saying that he was the custom-house officer, asked if I had anything excisable in my trunks. On my offering him the keys, he very civilly said it was quite unnecessary, as he presumed I was on a sporting expedition and he had orders to give as little trouble as possible. What a lesson, by the way, our custom-house people at home might learn from the American authorities, from whom I have always met with the most obliging civility and attention.

I found that there was a railroad to Buffalo, the cars being drawn by horses, but the only two were then both on the road, from whence they would arrive in an hour or two, so there was nothing for it but to wait in the tavern until their arrival. The bar was filled with a strange medley of Yankees and Canadians and Irish, Scotch, and English immigrants who were on their way up the country. The natives were holding a very animated discussion of Canadian affairs and seemed to anticipate another disturbance, for with many oaths and blasphemies too horrible to mention, they were bragging of what they had done in the last rebellion, or "patriots' war," as they called it, and what they would do in the next, heaping imprecations on Britishers, whom they intended to "chaw up right off."

The car returning and again being ready to start, I gladly left these gentlemen to their gin and sugar and in an hour reached Buffalo, where I was soon snugly ensconced in the excellent American Hotel, and my dogs under the care of the Irish porter. After remaining here for one day, as there was a gale blowing on the lake which prevented the steamer's putting to sea, I embarked on board one of the splendid Western boats bound for Chicago.

The gale having abated, we steamed out of the harbour with some nine or ten others, which had been detained by the weather and soon shot out into old Erie, which was alive with steamers and schooners. This being the last trip, there must have been at least five hundred passengers on board and an immense freight for the Upper Lakes. Indeed, I heard the captain say that this one passage would cover the expenses of the boat, both the building and fitting, and leave a hand-some balance besides.

On ascending the promenade deck, which was crammed and had the appearance of a crowded street, I was soon detected as a foreigner and consequently became a sort of lion. One citizen with a very broad-brimmed chimney-pot hat soon accosted me with,

"Well, stranger, I guess you're off to the West, a-hunting. Con-siderable clever dogs them of yourn. You call them greyhounds, I b'lieve, in your parts. Well now, what may they cost? Well now, that's a heavy total."

53

I had a pair of cloth boots on, with cork soles, which gave rise to the following remarks from a gent from Ohio, who, after gazing at me from head to foot, deliberately stooped down and felt the cloth and buttons and soles of the boots.

"Well, those be handsome shoes now, and considerable neat. I suppose you think we han't got nothing like those in these parts. Well we make pretty handsome boots in Detroit, we do. I guess you're from the Canadas, you are. Well now, how do they git on there now? I onderstand the French have a strong party agin the Queen. You Britishers will never keep the Canadas, anyhow you fix it. They was meant for the States and the States will have it, that's what they will."

The bell for dinner stopped the discussion, and my friend bolted like the wind down the stairs, closely followed by the crowd, cramming and jamming each other on the steps and making frightful attemps on the door of the saloon, where the dinner was laid. They did not immediately take their places, for it is etiquette on the Lake boats to wait for the captain and lady passengers before the word is given to fall to. However, they hug the backs of the seats, looking daggers at the viands on the table, until the skipper passes through to the ladies' cabin, from whence he soon emerges with a *lady* under each arm, followed by the others, and moving to the head table, arranges them on his right and left.

All this time it is most amusing to watch the countenances of the *gents* who surround the tables. They all appear as if about to be led to execution, their eyes fixed dismally on the dishes, which are evidently undergoing a refrigerating process, whilst they remove the quid of tobacco from their cheeks and either stow it away in their pockets or deposit it under the table. At length the captain seats himself—and then such a rush it is impossible to describe. Each gentleman and lady seizes every dish within reach and piles the contents on his or her plate, which is soon a chaotic heap of beef, pork, fowl, cabbage, applesauce, pumpkin, corncob, sausage, pudding, pie, &c., at which they drive pell mell, shovelling in immense slabs with their knives, performing feats of conjuring in the way of swallowing blades of knives &c. that would eclipse the "Wizard of the North."

However, as this is a match against time, everyone seeming to lay himself a wager that he can eat sufficient for three persons in five minutes, it of course is soon over, when, the wreck being cleared, the negro servants and forward cabin passengers rush in and perform a second edition.

As soon as the dinner was cleared away, I saw two citizens emerge from their staterooms, with each a pack of small cards in his hand, which he began dealing over and along the table. My curiosity being excited, I took one up and read, "Mr. Milo Ruggles can be consulted in Stateroom No. 95 on diseases of the stomach and organs of digestion." On the other was, "Elam Peck, Surgeon and Dentist, No. 5 Stateroom, will extract and clean teeth during the passage to Chicago between the hours of nine and four." Catch a Yankee allowing an opportunity to slip of making a dollar!

Preferring the deck to the close, heated staterooms, as the night was fine, I rolled myself in a grego and slept on deck, watching the huge snorting chimney as it coughed out flames of fire into the dark night, and enjoying a cigar the while. My two dogs I had smuggled aft, though against orders, and made a pillow of one whilst the other lay at my feet and kept them warm.

In six and thirty hours, we entered the Detroit River, or rather straits, which separates Lakes Erie and St. Clair, and were soon lying alongside the wharf at the city of that name. Here, after a stay of two or three days, enjoying the hospitality of the American officers, I recrossed to the Canadian side and, leaving my baggage in the little village of Malden, prepared for my campaign with my red friends.

Two years before, I had been the hunting companion of a Chippewa called Peshwego, who, on my leaving the country, had said that I was the last paleface who would ever hunt with him and that he would never be able to get powder and lead after my departure. This man, who was a great hunter, I determined to take as a guide to the Indian country, with which he was well acquainted and understood the different languages.

Him I first set about finding. So the day after my arrival, I took my dog and gun and set off to the Indian village where he lived. I had approached near the camp and was passing a wigwam outside of which was a fire, round which three or four Indians were sitting smoking, when in the one who was sitting with his back to me I thought I recognized my old friend, Peshwego. So stealing quietly up, I put my hand on his shoulder. When he turned round, he appeared scarcely to believe his eyes, although he betrayed not the slightest emotion. At length, after satisfying himself that it was indeed the Saganach [Englishman], he held out his hand and began laughing immoderately, though without giving utterance to the slightest sound.

On telling the other Indians who I was, some of whom indeed recollected me, the pipe was immediately handed to me, and soon after a tin bowl of soup made of whitefish and corn was set before me. Peshwego then related to me what he and his tribe had been doing, what successful hunts they had had, and how they had been expecting that the war hatchet was to be dug up between the British and Americans.

One old Indian was the most ridiculous looking figure I ever beheld. His face was as flat as a pancake, with a piece of putty stuck on for a nose, and most fantastically painted. His head and scalp lock were ornamented with about twenty skins of the blue jay, which hung around his face. A blue calico shirt, very short, with a red sash round the waist, no leggings—that is, limbs à l' écossais—and a pair of moccasins completed his equipment. This worthy, who boasted of the name of "Devil's Son," set up for a bit of a medicine man, although he was not recognized as that functionary by his tribe. He affirmed that although his name was "Devil's Son" yet the moon was his father, who told him everything that was going to happen.

The moon had paid his son a visit the night before and had explained to him that the hatchet was dug up and they were to put on the war paint, for scalps were soon to be taken. This they were discussing when I made my appearance.

"Devil's Son," who was an old ally of mine, was overjoyed to see me and persisted in constantly shaking hands with me every minute, which incensed Peshwego so much that at last he administered a rap on the head, which had the effect of quieting him for a short time. Peshwego was delighted with the idea of going off to hunt with me.

November 4. A northeaster was blowing a gale on the lake when we put off for Michigan. I found Peshwego and Alec had provided a large dugout, in which we laid our guns and provisions and, hoisting a blanket, with Alec steering with the paddle at the stern, we soon shot out from the low shores of the Canada side. When in the middle of the river, which is here about eight miles wide, we had enough to do to keep her head on, as the wind had shifted and was blowing a hurricane in our faces, with a heavy swell, over which the canoe, being heavily laden, was with difficulty propelled by our four paddles. However, thanks to the skill of our Palinurus, the canoe danced at length into the smooth waters of Miami River, up which we glided, disturbing myriads of wild fowl from the reeds which line the river. I made one or two successful shots with my rifle at the large grey ducks and secured enough for supper. After following the course of the river for some five miles, we made our canoe fast and, hiding the paddles, proceeded a mile or two more along the banks until we found a suitable spot for camping for the night.

We were soon engaged cutting wood and building a fire, whilst Peshwego rigged up the tent cloths and made all snug. The pot was soon boiling away over the fire, with a huge piece of pork and maize in it, and the ducks split in two and broiling on the embers. This, by the way, I can recommend as one of the best methods of dressing birds in the woods, as they retain their juiciness and are exceedingly palatable. After having had the usual smoke, we rolled up in our blankets and slept till the blue jay's chattering on the tree over the tent warned us that day was breaking.

Our tents were soon struck, blankets rolled, and before the sun had peeped over the trees, we were on our way to the hunting grounds. As soon as the light broke through the trees, the woods seemed alive with the noisy greetings of their numerous inhabitants. As we walked silently on in Indian file, a black squirrel would start from a log where it had been enjoying a breakfast of nuts and, chuck-chucking at our approach, dart up the body of a tree, where, out of reach, it would face us, chattering and beating the bark with its tail. Joe, an Indian boy who accompanied us, soon had his belt strung with them, tumbling them down with his pea rifle, seldom failing to bore their heads with his bullet.

A deer would now and then, too, jump across the track, though so quickly as to prevent our getting our rifles to bear upon him. Tracks of all kinds of game became frequent. The broad handlike track of the bear often gladdened our eyes. Magua, however, was never seen *in propria persona*, though he left plenty of evidence to shew that he had been taking a nocturnal ramble in our neighbourhood.

After two or three hours through the woods, we arrived at the creek where we purposed camping, and as we were to remain several days, great care was taken in the choice of a good site. Having found a spot to our liking, the underbrush was cleared away and a huge fire kindled, over which a pot containing six or seven squirrels was soon simmering for our breakfast, whilst poles were cut for our tent and logs chopped for a supply of firewood.

The Indian method of pitching a tent camp—though few are rich enough to possess tent cloths, and content themselves with a bark substitute—is this. In the first place, the fire is some six feet long. About three feet from the fire, and from its center, a pole of hickory sapling is driven into the ground. A similar one is driven in about eight feet from the first, the two forming a right angle to the fire, both being

57

chosen with a fork at the top, across which another pole is laid. Over this the cloth is drawn and secured by pegs to the ground, the cloth being of sufficient length to draw in at the end farthest from the fire. This kind of tent will hold about three, wood fashion, and is a tolerable protection from wind and rain.

When the camp was finished and the squirrels accounted for, we took our rifles and sallied forth to hunt, Peshwego and I together, in order that he might show me the ground, for otherwise Indians are averse to hunting in company. Indeed, it is almost impossible to hunt successfully unless by oneself, as the most perfect quietness is required to get up to deer, and which is difficult when two persons are together, as the deer is alarmed by the cracking of a twig or the shaking of a branch when passing under it.

This was the first day of a new double rifle I had brought out with me, and I longed for an opportunity of displaying its merits to Peshwego, who had looked with contempt on its light handsome barrels—perfect popguns compared to the heavy metal of the American rifles. He would not at first believe that it was rifled and said it was "a good gun for ducks, but that thing can't kill deers—too light."

We soon came on a fresh track, on which we trotted merrily, till the state of the track indicated that the deer was close, and we crept silently along. However, with all our caution, the deer saw or heard us before we caught a glimpse of him, and throwing up his white tail, away jumped a fine buck at a tremendous pace. Six deer we found with the same results, when the sun beginning to dip warned us to beat a retreat towards camp. Giving up, therefore, all hopes of hunting for that day, we lighted our pipes and moved homewards. We had proceeded some little distance when a buck started up close to us, and running some little distance, stopped and gazed at us. Peshwego immediately dropped down and motioned me to fire, but wishing him to try my rifle, and the uncertain light rendering it doubtful to me where I should hit the deer, I whispered the Indian to take my gun and try his luck. Peshwego, with a look of contempt as he took it, cocked the right barrel and, taking a steady sight, pulled the trigger. To my astonishment, the buck started off seemingly unhurt, and Peshwego, throwing down the gun, exclaimed, "I knew these light guns were of no use. They can't kill deers."

However, having great confidence in his eye, as well as in my Westley Richards, I ran up to the spot where the deer was standing when shot at, and discovered a spot of blood, which at once started me on the track; and calling to Peshwego that the deer was hit, I ran for about a hundred yards when, looking ahead, I saw something lying on the ground, which I concluded was the deer. The Indian by this time came up, and I said to him, "You have something in your eye today to miss such an easy shot."

"Oh, no! I told you your gun would never kill a deer—shoot fifty times, never kill one."

Then I walked up and kicked over the body of the buck, which had been shot through the heart, the ball passing completely through the body, notwithstanding which he had run a hundred yards before he fell. I have seen, several times, deer shot through the heart and yet run at the top of their speed many yards, when they would invariably drop dead. The hunters assert that a deer breathes slowly and will always have sufficient strength to run whilst the inhalation lasts which it was taking when the wound was received.

Peshwego looked at the rifle with greater respect after this, and shots he saw me make with it caused him to swear by the Saganach's rifle.

We soon had the carcase rigged with traces of hickory bark and, not being far from home, dragged it along the snow to the camp, where a collop was soon broiling on the embers for supper.

[Ruxton does not tell us how long he stayed on the American side in this hunt and does not recount the return to Canada, but it was not long until they were off again.]

I had long meditated a hunt in that section of country lying immediately on the banks and to the back of Lake St. Clair, a place which the Indian Peshwego had assured me abounded in game, as he had hunted and trapped there the preceding winter and with great success. He had built himself a small shanty eight miles back from the lake on a beech ridge, where the deer were to be found as plentiful as squirrels. Hitherto I had been prevented from going by the want of snow and hard frosts, which precluded all thoughts of hunting. One morning, however, on opening my eyes, I was delighted to perceive that snow had fallen plentifully during the night and was still coming down in a way which promised to last. The first thing after breakfast I sallied off with my gun and dogs to the Indian camp, knocking over a brace of quail on my road.

I found Peshwego engaged in cleaning up his rifle and making preparations for a hunting expedition. He said he was just coming to fetch me and that our best plan would be to start first thing in the morning for our hunting grounds. After desiring his boy to come with the horse in the afternoon for the prog, I returned home to complete my preparations for the start. My hunting shirt, moccasins, &c. were overhauled, bullets run, powder dried, tobacco bag filled, and a couple of leather shirts stowed away in my knapsack; pork, Indian corn, biscuit, and peas stowed in sacks, and my blankets rolled up, ready for Joe. Everything being prepared, I stowed away my civilised toggery, donned my blanket coat, leggings, and moccasins, and about an hour before sundown (Joe having duly made his appearance and packed the kit on the pony) I accompanied him to the camp, where I intended to sleep that night.

I found Peshwego busy preparing supper, and a pot of corn and some dried venison was already simmering on the fire. The wigwam was full of Chippewas who were camped near waiting for the distribution of the government presents, which, though already December, had not as yet been issued to the unfortunate Indians, who, by the shameful neglect of the authorities, had been away from their homes and hunting grounds since the summer and were literally starving. Many and bitter were the complaints of these poor despised creatures of the want of faith and broken promises of the government, who had wrung from them their lands and hunting grounds for the paltry consideration of receiving a present of a blanket or so once a year, and even this irregular and uncertain.

I was rather amazed at finding that my host had a supply of whisky in the wigwam, which was produced after supper, and I feared a regular drinking bout was to come off, in which case I knew it would be very doubtful whether my red friends would be in fit state for the march of tomorrow. However, the carouse was carried on with great moderation amidst many tales of hunting and scalping, of many tales by "flood and field." It was near midnight before the lodge was cleared of the red carousers, who all shook me by the hand on departing, wishing me a successful hunt. My host then laid a couple of deerskins by the fire for me, on which I lay rolled up in my blanket and slept comfortably until morning.

It was still dark when Peshwego shook me by the shoulder, and, rubbing my eyes, I saw that the pot was already off the fire and the pemmican ready for our meal. Soon after, four dusky forms moved quietly into the lodge and, squatting down by the fire without saying a word, were soon deep in the mysteries of the caldron. These, as they brought their rifles and blankets and were otherwise equipped for a move, I concluded were to be my companions, who, with Peshwego and his son, completed the party. Joe appeared with the horse, a regular Indian mustang, strong and hardy as a bear. Blankets and kettles, provisions, &c. were piled on his back, and Joe perched on the top. Strapping my pack on my shoulders and taking up my rifle, we sallied out, Peshwego leading, myself and the other Indians following in Indian file, and Joe bringing up the rear.

It was a cold, clear morning, the grey of dawn just peeping over the eastern trees and lighting us over the creek, or small river, on the banks of which lay the encampment. The village was still as death, not a stir among the gloomy bark wigwams, from the tops of which, however, the white smoke was slowly curling into the clear, cold air, shewing that the attentive squaws were at work by times preparing the morning meal of venison and corn for their still snoring and lazy lords. Soon a gaunt-looking dog would push aside the deerskin, which serves as the only door to the wigwams, and eye enquiringly the party as it wound among the lodges, giving me a snarl as it recognised the pale face of the Saganach. Presently the sounds of an ax, and a squaw might be seen chopping a load of firewood. And before we had passed the village, many a dusky face peered from the huts looking for signs of a good hunting day, which the thick carpet of snow and the rising wind sighing and singing over the treetops already promised.

With an occasional greeting of "How, how," we passed the village and filed into the creek, over which was a convenient sheet of ice. Whilst crossing, Peshwego called our attention to the track of a wildcat which had just passed, and, halting, he called out to the nearest lodge, from which issued an active boy of about twelve or thirteen. The track being pointed out to him, he returned to the lodge, reappearing with a rifle, and on looking back, we saw him trotting merrily up the track of the animal.

Our way lay for many miles through the forest, not a track to guide us. But the wonderful sagacity of the Indian treats such a difficulty with contempt, and never once during our march of sixty or seventy miles did Peshwego for an instant waver in his choice of a line. Our course lay about northeast, and I found on frequently consulting my compass that we were proceeding in as straight a line as it could be run by a surveyor. We saw plenty of deer tracks, and towards evening came across a colony of black squirrels, against which we waged a successful war for ten minutes, bagging sufficient for a meal. With scarcely an intermission, we continued our march till sundown, when Peshwego came to a halt and, laying down his rifle and pack, said, "Maybe we better camp here. Plenty water," pointing to the hole caused by the tree being blown down from its roots, which was filled with water.

We soon began preparing the camp, some cutting wood, others making the fire, and we found plenty of occupation for half an hour. Joe unpacked the horse and, tying the forelegs with a bond of hickory bark, set him at liberty to roam as far as his well-tied limbs would permit, first taking the precaution of tying a bell round the beast's neck that his whereabouts might be ascertained in the morning.

Round the blazing fire we chatted and smoked our kinnikinek while the squirrel bubbled merrily in the pot amid a handful or two of sweet corn. And here let me for an instant digress to pay tribute to thee, O Black Squirrel, than whose delicate and juicy flesh no gourmet ever dreamed of anything more appetizing. How often after a week of tough stringy buck venison, unseasoned by salt and unassisted by bread, after a world of damage done to ivories by its sinewy meat or vain and fruitless mastication of a bit of tough old bear, how often have I gloated on your fair proportions, as, divested quickly of your suit of mourning by the skilful hands of Peshwego, your plump carcase plunged into the hissing corn, where you would sing and dance for twenty minutes, when head, legs, and all, piece by piece, you would disappear down my relishing throat, whilst Joe would cunningly pick your little *caput* of those delicious brains, revelling in the delicate feast. Tender as a chicken, rich as a ground hog, delicate as a porcupine—meat, you embody the idea of an Indian delicacy.

However, there is an end to all things, even to a squirrel feast, and we were soon snoring under our blankets.

On awakening next morning, and shaking off the snow which had fallen during the night and completely covered up my blanket, I cast my eye round the little mounds of snow, looking like grave hills in a churchyard, under which my red friends were sleeping as quietly and as luxuriously as many under the weight of sheets, blankets, and coverlid, and posted bed.

The fire required a little coaxing before it would burn, being almost extinguished by the snow, and the huge logs with which it had been piled the last thing at night, being burnt through, had fallen off. Soon, however, its crackling blaze melted the snow hanging on my blanket, and I roused the Indians to prepare breakfast, which this morning consisted of pork and biscuit. Joe was dispatched to find the horse whilst we packed up everything, leaving them for Joe to bring on. And again we were en route.

Our [burme?] still lay through the gloomy forest, nothing relieving the monotony of the scene. Not a bird or living creature was to be seen, and on we marched, till evening again threw her shadows on the trees and we drew near the spot where Peshwego purposed to camp. We were now moving on the banks of a small creek, which wound and wriggled like a snake through the woods, frozen over except here or there, where deer had broken the ice in crossing. We had just taken to the bed of the creek, where the walking on the ice was easier than on the banks, when suddenly the sharp report of a rifle saluted our ears, and almost immediately two deer, a noble buck and a doe, bounded over the creek, the buck dripping blood plentifully as he ran. However, his wound seemed slight, for he went off at a tremendous pace. We stood gazing at the deer as they flew over the creek, when an Indian suddenly darted down the bank on the track of the deer and, without a look upon us, quickly followed up the bank and into the woods, where we shortly heard another shot, which was doubtless the *coup de grâce* to the wounded buck.

Moving a little farther along the creek, we were looking out for a good spot to build our camp, when, turning a bend of the creek, we came suddenly upon an Indian hunting camp, where a squaw was engaged in dressing a deerskin whilst two or three children were playing round the fire. The woman informed us that she had been there with her husband three or four days, who had been hunting, and who was the man we had seen just before. We resolved to camp in his neighbourhood for the sake of company and soon erected a sort of shed of bark near the Indian's, great quantities of which were lying about, and from the remains of poles, old fires, &c., we concluded it was a favourite spot for hunting camps. The neighbour's hut was a very primitive affair, the order of which was this. Two upright poles some six feet high, and forked at the top, were driven into the ground, across the forks of which was laid another. Against this, long pieces of bark were laid slanting to the ground, leaving some six feet by five inside, where the family was stowed. The fire was made opposite and close to the open front, and the crevices back of the hut were stuffed with moss and leaves. As a mansion of this kind takes but little time and trouble in the erection, we set about and completed one for ourselves and were solaced with the prospect of an unusually comfortable night.

By the time that darkness had set in, the Indian whom we had seen in the woods came into camp sleighing along a fine buck, the one he had wounded before he met us. He immediately skinned and presented us with a large hind quarter, which we thankfully received and prepared for supper. This over, Peshwego and I adjourned to hold a talk and smoke with our kind neighbour, and found him and his family discussing the heart, kidneys, &c. of the fresh-killed deer. A present of tobacco made him quite communicative, and he gave us such accounts of the number of deer about that we resolved to remain a day to hunt. As we were going to leave, he asked me for a few good caps. His own, he said, were *pis qui*, not worth anything, and a score of large fuzees soon made him superlatively happy, and we left him cleaning up his rifle for the morrow.

Daylight the next morning saw us equipped and starting for our hunt. Following Peshwego some distance along the creek, we separated, taking each an opposite direction. I had scarcely crossed the creek and turned into the woods when I came upon a fresh track, or rather tracks, of a large buck and two young does. They had seemingly crossed the ice but a few minutes before me, so I trotted warily on, keeping a sharp lookout ahead. And now I try the snow and find that they *must* be close at hand. Gingerly I tread over the crisp snow, taking a cast round the track that I might come upon the flank of the deer. And now so cautious I fear to lean my weight on my foot, lest a treacherous twig should snap and alarm the game, quietly yet at a good pace, on I move, my heart thumping against my ribs. Again I make the track. The deer have left their file march and have spread to feed. I see where those noses have probed the snow for the hidden grass. By certain signs I know them to be close. I halt and try to pierce the gloom of the forest. Presently, straining my eyes, I descry a moving figure some two hundred yards. On I crawl on my knees, dragging myself to the cover of a fallen oak, when I cautiously raise my head and look over. Hurrush! There they are—a buck and two does, sure enough, quietly cropping the herbage, and turning up the snow as they move slowly past. Now one of the does turns round and approaches where I am concealed. Confound her! I wanted the buck. Suddenly she throws up her tail and gives a bound. I am in an agony lest she is off—but no, she means play, and the other two are following her. The doe, a small one, passes the log within fifty yards, but I am all intent on the neat horns of the two-year-old buck. He and his companion are trotting past, when I give the "ye-k, ye-k," and he stops. Now, good rifle, do your work, but wait till I can draw a fine bead on his shoulder. Now then! Bang! ping—down drops the buck. And bang goes my other barrel at the doe, who flies, bound, bound, bound, away unhurt.

And now for a hickory sapling. Here I have one—bark soon stripped and fashioned into a serviceable rope. My knife through the gristle of the nose and above the hoof of the forelegs, through which the bark is passed, and round my shoulders, and in this fashion I sleigh the venison to the camp; and leaving it in charge of the squaw, off I start again for another shot.

I soon came upon the track of a deer, but after following it some distance, I found the track of one of the Indians on it, so I was obliged to give it up.

As I was sitting on a log, having just lit my pipe, I saw Peshwego coming towards me dragging a deer. He was passing within a few feet of me without seeing me when a "How! how!" made him turn his head and indulge in his usual quiet laugh.

"You see no tracks?" he asked. "You must have no eyes. Great many tracks and plenty deer." When I told him that I had already killed one and deposited in the camp, "Maybe you'll come and help me cut down a raccoon tree?" he asked. "I find one, about six raccoons in it."

On my agreeing to assist him in the expedition against the 'coons, we hastened to the camp and took our axes.

Peshwego's 'coon tree was about three miles off and was a large tree of a species called, in that country, buttonwood. The tracks of the 'coons were easily to be seen, though they appeared to be old. However, we set to work, and the woods soon resounded with the noise from our axes. After an hour or more of hard work, the tree began to nod, and, "Look out," cried the Indian as it cracked through the tops of the surrounding trees and with a noise like thunder crashed to the ground. We found the 'coons, after searching all the hollow limbs, snugly ensconced in the middle of the trunk, from whence the fat little fellows were speedily withdrawn and knocked on the head, slung with hickory bark, and fastened on our backs en route to camp.

By this time the sun was going rapidly down, and on our return we found the other Indians dropping in, and three more 'coons and a porcupine were added to our larder. Though they had not succeeded in killing a deer, Joe, the boy, had wounded a buck, and had come upon the track of a large bear in a swamp he thought could not be far off, as the tracks were quite fresh. This, Peshwego and I resolved to follow up in the morning, sending the other Indians on to build the shanty, or rather to repair the old one which Peshwego had left the preceding winter.

That night we feasted on two of the raccoons, and I was initiated into the mysteries of a most piquant dish. First be it known that the trail [entrail] of the 'coon is esteemed beyond everything else. The Indians take this out of the animal, together with the heart, kidney, liver, &c., which they do not wash. They then take a long hickory stick as thick and as long as a ramrod, pointed at the end, with which they skewer the giblets, one on the other. Round this they bind the trail, which, however nasty it may sound, is perfectly clean, and cover the [giblets] with two or three layers of it, looking like white macaroni. They then lay the stick before the bright fire and toast it slowly, and when nicely browned, serve up hot, as Mrs. Glass says. This, I can answer for, is the best dish I ever ate and, cooked by a Chippewa, equals anything—[word illegible] ever attempted. This night we found it so palatable that every 'coon was robbed of its treasures, and the feast continued till the small hours.

Early next morning, Joe led us to the spot where he had seen the bear track. To make sure of finding it, he had blazed the trees on his return to camp, so that he now led us in a direct line to the spot. We found, as he had said, a track of a bear of the largest size, which we followed to a large swamp, which was strewed with fallen trees, and where Magua had evidently been searching for a soft log to lay up in. He had evidently been fastidious in his choice, as he had climbed and explored every decayed and *holy* tree in the swamp without finding one to his liking. His tracks then left the swamp, and we followed on it until we came to where he had camped two nights before. On we trotted at a killing pace, and so till nightfall, but no sign of our approaching Bruin, and were fain to return to camp, quite tired out and disgusted with the fastidiousness of Magua.

Nothing is more uncertain in "woodwork" than tracking a bear. Sometimes, on discovering his fresh track, we come up in twenty minutes to the tree where he has made up his mind to take up winter quarters; sometimes follow him for days, and still he gives no evidence of tiring or seeking to lay up. Again, he always shows when least expected, but go out bear hunting, and of course not a sign of him. However, he is sometimes so incautious as to allow a bead to be drawn on him—and then *adiós!* His fair broadside anywhere within a hundred and fifty yards is scarcely missable, and his skin and rich meat amply repay the persevering hunter.

The next morning we were astir betimes, and before daylight were already on our way. About noon we came upon a back settlement, where a number of emigrants were located. The country here might be taken as a fair sample of the [remotest?] settlements in Upper Canada. A line for a road had been run from a town on the shore of Huron called Goderich to Chatham, which as yet was merely cleared of the trees, leaving space sufficiently wide for waggons to pass, though of these there were none within a hundred miles. On this road lots of lands were granted free to anyone choosing to take out the patent, the only condition being that it was required of the settler to clear a certain portion, embracing the whole front of his lot which abutted on the road. These lots were of one hundred acres each and ran back from the road, the front being about two acres. It was also necessary for the holder to build a log house and a barn and bona fide to live on the lot five years. If these conditions were broken, the lot was taken away and given to another.

Along this road, which was some one hundred fifty miles long, here and there clearings might be seen in every stage of improvement. Here the partially cleared fields, dotted with blackened stumps, of one of the first settlers, who had perhaps got some ten or twelve acres under some kind of cultivation and then desisted from further attempts at improving in disgust, his seeds being washed out of the ground by the floods of spring, at which season the whole face of the country in this district is under water. Here again, the lot of a recent settler with some two acres of felled trees lying in all the confusion of scattered limbs and faggot wood, with tall, half-burnt trunks standing like blackened ghosts amidst the wreck. The quaint little shanty of rough logs plastered with mud, looking gloomily into the road, is not the least curious part of the scene. For the most part, the road is run in a perfectly straight line, and as the country is perfectly flat, you see ahead for a long distance, the road appearing like a large slice cut out of the forest, the trees of immense size forming a wall of timber on each side. The trees in the line of road have, for the most part, been burned, and the long blacked logs are left standing amidst the underbrush which has grown up. The settlers are, for the most part, Irish and Scotch and with few exceptions are a rough, discontented set of people. Some few have cattle and sheep, but lose a great number of the latter by the wolves, great numbers of which are in the woods.

We followed this road for about fifteen miles, and a more dismal looking country it is hard to imagine. Night coming on, we were compelled to camp, and soon commenced cutting down an abundance of firewood as the night set in excessively cold and the wind howled and moaned through the woods. Peshwego evidently feared the cold, for we had but one blanket each, the rest being on the horse. However, we cooked part of a leg of venison which we had with us and made a huge fire which, large as it was, was not able to keep us warm, for sitting almost in it, our backs were quite numbed, and the pot of water, though standing quite close to it, was frozen in five minutes. To add to this, the snow was coming down fast, and we promised ourselves a night of unusual severity.

We made out to sit out half the night smoking and chatting, but at last the cold made us drowsy, and we both fell asleep. How long I had been asleep I know not, but I was suddenly roused by a most infernal howl close to my ear, and jumping up, saw by the light of the fire a large wolf making off into the darkness, whilst the howling of twenty others resounded on all sides. Peshwego seized his rifle and told me to keep a lookout as they were uncertain in hard weather. Though, generally speaking, cowardly brutes, they have been often known to attack men when pressed by hunger, as I had an opportunity of witnessing shortly after. They continued treating us to a concert of much horrible howling until morning, when we saw a string of six loping past the fire, and as soon did two balls from my rifle and one from the Indian's ping after them, making them stick their tails between their legs and make themselves scarce in no time. After breakfasting on some of the venison we had cooked the night before, we set off on our last day's march.

This day we turned off the road and kept the course of a creek which ran in a northerly direction. This we followed the whole day, seeing occasionally a deer bound across, until about an hour before sundown, when we came upon numerous tracks, which Peshwego said were the tracks of the remainder of our party, which had gone on before, and that we were close to the camp.

Presently the sound of an ax was heard, and soon, turning a bend of the creek, we came upon the little shanty, and our Indian friends engaged in making it habitable. The stages which Peshwego had erected the winter before were still standing, and the skulls and legs of deer and bears shewed that he had been busy with his rifle. The shanty itself was a unique affair ten feet long by six, made with a sloping roof, and about five feet high, much resembling—with the difference that it was built of rough logs and thatched with bark— the pigsties met with in the country. It was entered by a hole about three feet square in one of the gable ends, and inside, the floor was laid with bark on each side the fire, which ran the entire length of the hut. The whole top of the roof was left open to allow the escape of the smoke, as were also the interstices of the logs, the lower ones alone being filled up with moss. One side of the fire Peshwego immediately appropriated for himself and me, leaving our friends to pack themselves as best they could on the other.

A roaring fire was burning, and after depositing my pack and blanket in a corner, I turned out to assist in stowing away the meat we had brought with us. This was soon effected by hanging it out of reach of wolves on the stages, after cutting off some choice bits to smoke dry for future use. On taking an inventory of the larder, I found we had one whole carcase of a deer and part of another, with four raccoons and a porcupine, so that with the pork and biscuit I had brought we ran no chance of starving for some time to come. Two of the 'coons and some pork were cooked for supper, after we had discussed which, pipes were lit and we were all as jolly as could be.

Next morning at break of day we all sallied out to hunt, each taking a different direction. For myself, I came upon fresh tracks almost immediately and followed four deer the whole day, but as there was no wind, I was unable to get a shot till near sundown, when I knocked over a young doe. In this way we passed a week more, slaughtering the deer most successfully, and already the stages round our wigwam groaned under their loads of venison. At the end of the week, however, the frost began to show symptoms of breaking up, and thaws commenced in the middle of the day. One morning Peshwego and I had been to examine some of our traps, and were crossing what is termed in that country a "windfall," which is where a hurricane has blown down a long line of trees, leaving a straight open space in the woods extending often a mile or two and having the appearance of a clearing. We were crossing over the fallen logs when suddenly Peshwego, who was leading, came to a dead halt and pointing down muttered, "Magua," and there, sure enough, I descried the track of a large bear, and apparently fresh. "Maybe, we'll have that fellow," said the Indian. "I don't think he's a great way off." We both judged him to be laid up in the windfall under some log. However, on following the track, it took directly away from it; and turning and twisting and examining every log and hollow tree, up several of which we could see he had climbed, the bear had evidently been in a hurry to find some suitable place to lay up. We still followed up the track, going round and round to every point on the compass, till at length it doubled back and entered the windfall, where we had first discovered it.

Peshwego now declared he had no doubt but that the bear was here, and freshed up his priming and looked to his flint. All eager, we moved cautiously on, and as the snow had disappeared from some of the logs which the bear had passed over, we spread out that we might not lose the track. On reaching within five hundred yards of the end of the windfall, we found he had crossed and recrossed the track several times, so that it was difficult to follow, and we examined every hollow trunk and peered under every log, thinking to descry his brown coat. At last as I was looking ahead, I saw the trunk of a tree which had been blown down some fifteen feet from the ground, and perfectly hollow, with a small hole about the size of a plate three feet from bottom. This, I at once felt certain, held the animal, and calling to Peshwego, "*Ye-tsis Magua*"—Here's the bear—off I ran towards it. Sure enough, the track ran up directly to the tree, which it did not leave again; therefore I knew the bear to be at home. I saw plainly where he had climbed up the trunk, stripping off great pieces of bark with his claws in his ascent.

I put my ear to the lower hole and to my delight heard him plainly snore. Peshwego coming up, we held a council of war and determined to attack him from the top, where sufficient light would be thrown down to enable us to shoot him. We collected some of the larger limbs which lay scattered about in plenty, and raised a sort of ladder, placing other pieces across the top, thus forming a stage on which to stand. On climbing up and looking into the hollow trunk, we plainly descried Bruin lying curled up amongst the tan dust in the bottom, his head being well exposed, and though it was certainly taking a dirty advantage of a sleeping enemy, we both at the same instant drove two balls through his skull, and without a groan or growl or even unrolling himself, Magua slept with his fathers.

How to get him out was the next thing. To pull him up from the top was no easy matter, as we had no ropes, but by enlarging the hole at the bottom we might easily get at him. We soon had the hole of sufficient dimensions to allow Peshwego to enter, when he fastened a rope of hickory bark round the bear's neck, and we pulled him out bodily. He proved to be a seven-year-old bear of unusually large size and had a beautiful fur. We dragged our prize to camp, much to the delight of the Indians, who prize bear's meat above that of every other animal. We soon had his coat off and his carcase most artistically cut up, myself operating on his hams, which I wanted to be shipshape to take to the settlements.

After this, we lay idle for several days, the frost completely stopping our hunting, so much so, that as we had sent home great quantities of venison and the whole of the bear's meat, we soon ran short of provisions and were compelled to be very sparing of what was left.

Another week passed, and still the frost continued without a flake of snow being on the ground, the cold being at the same time intense. At length we arrived at the end of our stock of venison. The last leg was cooked and finished at a sitting, though our party was reduced to four, the others having been sent on with the game. The morning after our last meal, when I awoke and unrolled from my blanket, my eyes sought the bubbling pot, which had always heretofore been filled at daybreak and boiling away with our breakfast in it. Instead of this, however, there was the hooked stick dangling over the blaze and scorching in the smoke, but no pot hanging from it, and the Indians sitting up round the fire looking exceedingly solemn and breakfasting off their pipes. Feeling very peckish, I turned out and rummaged the biscuit bags, thinking that one might have been, by a remote chance, left undiscovered at the bottom, but not a crumb was there.

Determining not to be done out of breakfast, I seized my rifle and went out to look for a squirrel, but returned at the end of an hour's unsuccessful hunt. The cold had driven them all into their holes, and not even a chipmunk was to be seen. So I followed the Indian's example and took to my pipe. About noon a wind sprang up and, though with but little chance of success, we determined to try to kill a deer. Sundown, however, saw us return, one after the other, with the same tales of disappointment. Though plenty of deer were seen, it was impossible to get near them. The leaves and twigs snapping and cracking in the intense frost caused us to make as much noise as a cow going through the woods. With appetites sadly increased by the hunt, we sat disconsolate round the fire, and again were compelled to dine, as we had breakfasted, on our tobacco and kinnikinek.

The next day we were lucky enough to catch a couple of squirrels in one of the mink traps, and one of the boys found a couple of ears of maize under a heap of deerskins, which we quickly made into soup and discussed with infinite relish after our fast of thirty-six hours. Two squirrels between four did not, however, provide a very lavish dinner, and only served to make us more savagely hungry.

Towards evening I caught Peshwego looking daggers at an unfortunate dog, which had kept its flesh wonderfully on a diet of deer's legs and an occasional munch at one of the freshest skins, and

71

was soon undeceived as to his intentions by seeing him suddenly, and without saying a word, seize the slut by the leg and whip out his knife. In another instant it would have been into the dog's throat, when I interfered and with great difficulty saved its life.

The next morning set in cloudy and the air seemed full of snow, the cold not being so intense; and thinking the squirrels might be out, we all took our rifles, intending to remain out the whole day in hopes of killing sufficient for a good meal. One of the boys accompanied me with the dog whose life I had interceded for, and we hunted about the beech ridges for four or five hours without seeing a living creature. At last we heard the joyful sound of the slut's bark and, running to the spot whence it proceeded, found she had treed a couple of squirrels, which were half way up the tree, lying almost concealed in the fork of a branch. However, the quick eye of the Indian boy discovered them, and they were soon tumbling to the ground with a couple of holes drilled through their heads. Just as the boy had tucked them under his belt, the dog started off after something she had caught a glimpse of, and we heard her again giving tongue. This time we saw five squirrels jumping along the topmost branches and springing from tree to tree. At length they reached a tree where they seemed disposed to give us a chance, and after a good many shots we killed four of them.

Having now done my share, I returned to camp, killing another on the way. The Indians soon came in, one after the other, bringing twelve more, which together with my seven were soon divested of their jackets, popped into the boiling water, and in half an hour were safely stowed under our belts at the rate of four apiece, which with the soup made us a very tolerable meal, and which, it may be imagined, we stood much in need of.

Spite of our prognostications of a fall of snow, three more long hungry days saw us continuing our banyan, two squirrels being the only food we tasted during that time, and we were becoming gaunt as wolves. One day on returning from a fruitless hunt, we found that one of our party, a Chippewa named Kis-Kis, or the Young Pine, had deserted. He had doubtless anticipated famine, packed up his blanket, and started home. Peshwego began to look serious upon it and recommended that we should hold a council and have a talk of what was to be done. So after gravely lighting a pipe, first taking a whiff himself and then passing it round to myself and the two other Indians, he commenced an harangue in nearly these words.

He didn't know what he'd done, but he'd gone and done something very bad. The Great Spirit was angry and kept the snow away and drove off the deer and bears. He had hunted for twenty-five winters and had never seen so little snow. A Saganach chief (meaning myself) had come a long way to hunt with him, and on leaving the village the medicine men had promised a good hunt—but there was no snow, no deer, no bears, and no raccoons, and they were obliged to make new holes in their belts every day. Their bellies were very empty. The Great Spirit had hidden the snow and driven the deer over to the hunting grounds of the Pottawatomies. They had better pack the blankets and make tracks for Moon River, where there were plenty of fat elk; or if the Saganach wished to get back to his people, twelve suns would take them to the Great Lake, and they might take catfish on the creeks by the way. For himself, he thought the medicine man was wrong, and that they ought not to have started. When he got back to his village he would tell the chiefs that the medicine man was a snake with two tongues, that they might take away his medicine bag. He had spoken. What had the Saganach to say?

I waived my right of addressing the very respectable meeting in favour of my two other red friends, who both in their turns agreed with Peshwego that the Great Spirit was angry and had withheld the snow from us for something that we had done, and also that the medicine man was clearly wrong in promising a good hunt. They thought the best thing we could do was to return as speedily as possible to their village and wait till the Great Spirit was propitious, but still they would go to Moon River if the Saganach wished. As the vote for the return to the village was unanimous, we prepared for our departure early on the following morning, first caching our skins.

Daybreak saw our gaunt party issue from our little shanty, the scene of many a feast and many a fast, and as I looked behind and saw the blue smoke ascending in thin wreaths from its open roof, I almost regretted leaving the little kennel. A little tomtit was perched on the doorsill chirping and pecking at the skull of a deer which protruded from between the logs. This little fellow had been our guest for a long time, paying us a visit as soon as the deerskin was withdrawn from the door in the morning, and entering boldly would attack the dried venison that hung from the roof poles. Regularly as the sun rose we heard his twit-twit-twit, and though we were fasting, he always found something to peck at.

On we went, silent and surly, each no doubt with his mind full of corn soup, pemmican, and pork. Scarcely a word was spoken,

Peshwego only remarking on starting that we had forty miles to go that day. And stepping out, we soon left our little camp far behind. Glad was I when the sun, already sinking beneath the lofty forest trees, warned us to take up our camping ground for the night.

Fire kindled and sufficient fuel being cut to burn during the night, no sooner had I cast my weary body along a prostrate log than I fell asleep; our long march, in the weak and half-starved state in which we were, had completely worn me out, and before closing my eyes I saw the Indians were already enveloped in their blankets and, forgetting hunger, were snoring away their cares.

The stars were shining brightly in the clear, cold sky, and the moon, then near its full, was just rising above the trees when, numbed and stiff with cold, I awoke. The fire had nearly burned out, and as I crept close to throw on an additional log and rake up the embers, I looked on the dark slumbering forms of the Indians, rolled to the eyes in their single blanket, and their naked feet almost among the embers of the fire. The boy, who was a fine, handsome little fellow of thirteen, was mumbling in his sleep, dreaming, most probably, of the good things in his mother's wigwam.

Just then I heard the twigs snapping a little distance from the fire, and presently, as the log blazed up for a moment, I saw a loping wolf skulk past, giving a most dismal howl as he disappeared in the darkness. Hunger prevented me from sleeping, so I filled my pipe and, wrapping my blanket round me, crept close to the fire and smoked. Presently the Indians, one by one, awoke and sat up, each drawing out his pipe and puffing away.

Towards the break of day the sky became overcast with thick clouds, and snow commenced falling in small, thin flakes. Peshwego looked up and, after taking a long inspection of the clouds, predicted a fall of snow. We thought it advisable, if there was a sufficient fall, to remain and hunt for one day, that we might have some provision for our homeward march.

Whilst plodding along, following one after the other in Indian fashion, the report of a rifle, just before us, caused us to come to a sudden halt. We presently heard the snapping of twigs and noise of some animal bounding over the brittle twigs, and soon three deer leaped across our path, a fine buck leading at a tremendous pace. To cock my rifle and let drive at him was the work of an instant, but I had the mortification of seeing the hairs fly from his back by the ball as the deer bounded off unhurt.

Hunting in the Canadian woods—a sketch from
Ruxton's notebook

Ruxton's sketch of his Canadian camp—the little tomtit
perched atop the roof of the shanty

An Indian soon after emerged from the shadows of the trees, and approaching, we at once knew him to be a Pottawatomie, by his paint, and particularly by a peculiar kind of turban which is much worn by this people.

He told us that many of his people were out in the woods, but from the unpropitious state of the weather had been as unfortunate as ourselves in killing game, that many of them were nearly perishing from want of food, and that he himself had been two days without food other than a few frozen acorns.

He had shot at the deer which passed us, but they were running, he imagined, before wolves, and too rapidly to give him a chance of hitting one. However, he told us that he had seen some raccoon tracks not far off and we might succeed in finding and killing one of these animals. The anticipation of a roasted 'coon soon put us on the track, and following our Pottawatomie guide a short distance through the woods, he pointed to a log, along the top of which there was still a little snow and where the luckless raccoon had imprinted his not to be mistaken track. However, the ground was so intensely frozen that on leaving the log no trace of our game was perceptible even to an Indian eye, and, dispersing, we sought a long time in vain, in different directions, for any evidence of the fugitive. At length a shout from one of the Indian boys proclaimed his success, and following the sound to a lofty hickory, we found the boy carefully examining the bark of the tree, where, sure enough, we perceived the marks left by the animal's nails whilst climbing up the trunk.

A brace of axes were soon thundering into the body of the tree; and presently a warning shake of its lofty head cautioned us to stand clear of its fall, when at first with a graceful bow it inclined towards the surrounding trees. Quickly losing its centre of gravity, down it crashed to the ground, stripping limbs and bark from the others in its descent, bringing with it a perfect wreck of branches. As soon as it was down, we rushed to the fallen trunk, from which, as soon as it touched the ground, bolted a fine fat raccoon. Before we could stop him, he had sprung on a hickory tree, up the trunk of which he was scudding with the activity of a cat, when a ball from my rifle, drilling his skull, brought him dead to the ground.

"Ti-ya," grunted an Indian standing by the prostrate log as out bolted another, almost upsetting him in its course. A tomahawk of another [Indian] whirled in the air as the animal gained a tree, and, swift as an arrow, cleaving the head, transfixed it to the trunk. An expressive "howgh" from all present showed their admiration of this snap shot. In a short time another fine fat fellow was drawn from a hole in the tree and quickly dispatched, and before five minutes were over, one was already divested of his jacket and broiling over a fire, which one of the party had promptly kindled. It required neither bread nor salt to flavour this meal, which after a fast of thirty-six hours was opportune enough, and to which it may be imagined we did ample justice, as the well-picked bones testified after our repast. Presenting one raccoon to our friend who had so timely informed us of the game, and carrying the other with us, we proceeded on our journey.

The Pottawatomies as they now exist are the remains of what was once one of the most powerful nations on the Lakes; but long and bloody series of wars with the Chippewas and Hurons, and other causes, have now reduced them to a par with other nations once their inferiors in numbers and power, and having lost their hunting grounds, they wander from one place to another, wherever game may happen to be abundant, but leaving behind them a bad name for treachery and other crimes, perhaps not unmerited.

They have the credit of being the most determined horse and hog stealers, and amongst the Chippewas, Pottawatomie is only another word for thief. However, little credit can be attached to the character of an Indian given by one of a different tribe, for an hereditary enmity, or rather jealousy, is characteristic of these peoples, whose different tribes have been natural-born enemies from time immemorial. Knowing this, I did not listen with much attention to the following remarks of Peshwego, who, after proceeding some way in silence, commenced an abrupt harangue to me on the Pottawatomie character.

"Maybe," he began, "you like these peoples. Well they fine tall mens and great hunters. They almost good as Chippewas, and long time ago they great warriors."

"Howgh!" exclaimed an old Indian, who understood the subject.

"Well they got plenty horses," continued Peshwego, "plenty guns—maybe they got five thousand. Well *they* don't hunt none, they just steal, steal all the time. They bad peoples. Maybe they just come and tomahawk us tonight."

"Howgh!" assented the old Indian.

"Well," again broke out Peshwego, "they bad peoples. They just scalp everybody they find in the woods, just like minks. I never want to see Pottawatomie in the woods—Bad peoples."

An exclamation of surprise from one of the party interrupted this charitably drawn character—caused by the fall of several heavy flakes of snow, which, by the appearance of the sky, appeared to be the forerunner of a good fall.

The Indians halted, and I could see by their looks and exclamations that they considered this a proof of the Great Spirit being angry with them, having sent a hard frost while they were hunting, and now on their return a heavy snow, when they did not require it. Peshwego had before declared to me his belief that the Great Spirit was angry with us and had punished us by driving away the deer and snow.

"Well, we've just gone and done something very bad. Great Spirit, he's very cross, and made the deer very wild, and melted all the snow. We'll kill no deers here in twelve moons. I don't know what we've done—maybe drunk too much whisky."

He said, too, that he had not consulted the medicine man before starting, and could have no luck in consequence.

The snow now came down in a heavy fall, and the ground was quickly covered. We reached our intended halting-place about sunset, devoured the other raccoon, and rolled up in our blankets before the fire. As the snow would render the hunting excellent, I was anxious to return to our camp, but the Indians were determined to wait until the Great Spirit was propitious; so finding they were not to be induced, the next morning before daylight I shouldered my traps and returned alone to the shanty. I was within sight of it when I came upon the tracks of three deer, which had passed only a few minutes before, and though the daylight was fast waning, I followed them until the track led me to a ridge of beech saplings, where I discovered the deer browsing. I quickly levelled my rifle at the nearest and killed it, brought it to camp, skinned and cooked a collop for supper, after which, much fatigued, I slept soundly until morning. On leaving the hut the next morning, I found that several wolves had been round the deer, which was lying on a gallows, and had carried off the head and neck.

The next day I had a long hunt. The deer were wild, and though in great numbers, were difficult to approach within shot, so that after following some for many hours, I found myself far from camp, and evening already closing in. Looking at my compass, I struck through the woods in the direction of the shanty, but night was fast coming on, and the woods being as dark as pitch, I had great difficulty in keeping a straight course. The wind was moaning in fitful gusts through the tops of the trees, through which not a ray of light penetrated to enable me to consult my compass, save by removing the glass and feeling the direction of the needle with my fingers. Heavy flakes of snow were falling, which ever as I emerged into a more open part of the woods, drifted into my face, adding to my discomfort. I was never out in a darker or more dismal night. Occasionally I heard the deep, baying howl of a wolf on the track of a deer, or the dismal hoot of an owl close to my ear, than the shriek of which bird, nothing living is more unearthly. Stumbling over logs, running against trees, falling into root holes full of snow, on I floundered, but I hit upon an expedient by which I was enabled to steer by the compass, which was simply by lighting my pipe, which I had only to hold near the compass to afford sufficient light for the purpose.

I had been many hours on my march, when at a moment that I was thinking of lying down for the night on the first log which presented itself, I perceived a small speck of light, apparently in the branches just beside me, and which seemed to be moving in the darkness. I at once set it down as a wolf, the eyes of which, it is known, shine in the dark like a cat's. Therefore, cocking my rifle and throwing it forward into my arm in readiness, I approached cautiously the spot where I fancied the wolf might be standing watching me.

However, as I drew near, the beast did not seem to change its position, the speck of light appearing in the same place; but as I approached I thought it grew larger. At length, somewhat doubting, I quickened my steps towards it, when I saw more of the same light, and presently many sparks flew into the air. I was now convinced that the light proceeded from my shanty, through the crevices of which the flickering light came; but as I most certainly had extinguished the fire before leaving in the morning, I was unable to account for it, except by supposing that some Indians had rekindled it.

Approaching the shanty as noiselessly as I could, I soon perceived that a roaring fire was blazing within; and, creeping up, I looked through a chink in the wall and beheld a sight which did not altogether delight me.

Spreading his hands over the fire, sat an Indian, in the well-known dress of the Pottawatomie. So motionless was his posture that for some moments I fancied it was a sleeping figure. He sat opposite to where I was looking, so I had a good opportunity of inspecting him. He was a tall, powerful-looking savage with his naturally swarthy face rendered more striking by lines of red paint which crossed transversely his whole countenance. A picturesque sort of turban of red cloth, in which was stuck a single feather, covered his head, while a shirt of deerskin, but a sorry covering from the cold of winter, confined at his waist with a belt in which was the usual hunting knife, and leggings of the same, with moccasins completed his costume. No sooner had I caught a full glimpse of his countenance than I was aware that my approach had been heard by him. His whole face gave at once the idea of the most intense watchfulness, though to one unaccustomed to the study of the immovable features of the redskin, his whole appearance might have indicated the perfect repose of security.

The head was a little inclined to one side, and slightly raised, as a dog may be seen to do when listening attentively, the mouth partly open, and the muscles of the body, though in apparent repose, were rigid as stone. Nor did it escape me that the rifle stock was at his side within grasp, and the knife loosed in the sheath. Though I confess that I might have been better pleased with other guest than a Pottawatomie, particularly after my friend Peshwego's description, yet I made up my mind to enter, without any appearance of distrust. So throwing aside the deerskin which served as door, I entered at once, with the usual Indian salutation of "Howgh, howgh" and proceeded to disencumber myself of my rifle and pouch, during which the Indian relapsed into a perfectly indifferent posture.

When I had taken off my wet leggings and moccasins, I sat down opposite to my dusky guest and had more leisure to observe him. His cheeks, I observed, were fallen in and his whole face painfully attenuated; his long body, too, appeared gaunt and half famished, which indeed I found was literally the case. He had actually been three days without food, for although he had seen many deer, his rifle was out of order, so that he could not get it off. Having seen my tracks in the snow, he had followed them to the shanty; but though venison was hanging from the roof and he was famished for food, he had waited till my arrival, which he said he was certain of, because I had left my blanket behind me, before he satisfied his hunger—not the custom of the woods.

I soon had a pot on the fire with some choice pieces of venison, which the poor fellow watched like a famished wolf. He had neither pipe nor tobacco, and whilst the meat was boiling, I gave him a pipe, which he greedily devoured. The hot venison broth soon restored him, and after having done ample justice to the tender meat, he lit his pipe and we chatted, as well as my imperfect knowledge of the language allowed me, till late. He told me that many of his people were hunting in the woods, but the weather had been so unfavourable that they had been very unsuccessful, and many were almost starving. He himself had been out for weeks, but had killed nothing but a few squirrels &c. and had subsisted entirely on what few nuts and acorns he could find in the woods.

He remained my guest for a few days, and I frequently hunted in his company. He was one of the best rifle shots I ever met with, and with my rifle performed many wonderful feats in fine bead drawing. He was also a good hunter, particularly after turkeys, which he never failed to come up to, if once on the track.

A turkey hunt, which we made in company, was very successful. One night he returned to the camp with a fine gobbler and told me that a flock of thirty were roosting on a beech ridge within a mile of our shanty.

Accordingly, some hours before daylight we were on the ridge, waiting quietly until the morning broke, when the turkeys would leave their roost. The Indian had seen them take wing for the trees the night before, when he had killed one, and not far, he thought, from the spot where we then were.

In the interim we lit our pipes, sitting quietly on a log amongst a thick clump of beeches. Just as day was breaking, a rustling in the branches of a tree over my head roused me, followed by a loud, clear call from the same tree. It was instantly answered by another, at a little distance, and taken up by the rest, until the woods seemed to resound with the noises on all sides.

The Indian, at the first alarm, had pulled me behind the log, where, with rifles cocked, we awaited our opportunity. It was just light enough to enable us to look along our barrels, when a commotion in the same tree from whence the first call had proceeded warned us to prepare. Now, as the light first disclosed the top of the tree to us, we saw a large, dark body descending from branch to branch, occasionally uttering a loud cluck. When it came to the first branches, I could plainly see the figure of a large turkey, and was on the point of firing at it, when the Indian restrained me. I soon found the wisdom of this proceeding, for as soon as the bird hopped to the ground, a few loud repeated calls brought the remainder of the flock, one after the other, running swiftly over the snow.

Two or three had joined the old gobbler, when the Indian motioned that now was our time; so levelling at the father of the flock, I laid him sprawling and fluttering on the snow, where another victim was also soon fluttering, shot by the Indian. The reports of the pieces did not appear to alarm the others, for my companion, putting his fingers in his mouth, soon brought them trooping up by his imitation of the call. And as soon as we had again charged our rifles, at least twenty were within thirty yards of us. This time firing at two which were in a line, my ball, passing through the body of the first, broke a wing of the other, which instantly set off at a round pace, followed by the others, not, however, before the Indian had turned over a second. Loading as quickly as possible, and leaving the four dead birds hanging on a tree, we soon followed on the tracks of the game, which left us far behind, although the long swinging trot led by my companion brought us up to the wounded bird, which was lying panting and bleeding on the snow, where it had sunk exhausted from loss of blood.

In the evening, towards sundown, we again came upon the flock, this time feeding in apparent security, but two quickly succumbed to our rifles, thus making a bag of seven of these magnificent birds. When we had collected the slain, we found we had enough to do to carry them all, but staggering as well as we could under our load, we reached the camp after sunset and feasted on part of one of the birds— and delicious eating it proved.

Two or three days after, I had a close view of the remainder of the flock, which had fallen a victim to their stupidity in an Indian trap or pen. I had followed several tracks for some time when I suddenly heard a tremendous uproar a short distance ahead of me. Hastening on, I came upon a turkey pen, which some Indians had formed and which had entrapped eleven fine full-grown birds. These silly fowls are taken in the following manner. In a part of the woods, where turkeys are known to resort, the Indian or white hunter forms his pen. It is merely a square enclosure of rough logs about six feet square and four feet in height, the top covered with smaller logs, with an interval of six or eight inches between each. At the sides the lower bar is wanting, leaving a space clear from the ground of eighteen inches or two feet. A train of Indian corn is then laid from different parts of the woods, leading to the pen, which is also strewed with corn. The turkeys coming upon the train follow it, picking it up, until they reach the trap, when, entering, they quickly devour the remainder. When all is consumed, they attempt to find an exit, but all their endeavours are exerted to get out at the top, through which they thrust their long necks, but without attempting to escape by the way they entered. Thus a whole flock is often captured in a day.

My Pottawatomie friend rejoiced in the euphonious patronymic of To-ti-ka-sa-mame, signifying "the man who holds his face to the thunder," and was the son of a chief. He had even distinguished him-

self during the Canadian Rebellion, having on one occasion brought
in prisoners four sympathisers whom he had taken crossing the Saint
Clair River in a canoe, with dispatches to one of the so-called patriot
leaders. For this deed he had received a rifle, which he greatly prized
on this account, but which was now a most dilapidated affair, the lock
being tied on by a thong of buckskin, and the stock broken in many
places.

Four hunters of his nation joined us one evening, having come
upon our camp during their hunting. I spared them some powder and
lead, which they were quite out of, and they departed in great spirits,
taking my friend with them.

During my solitary sojourn in the woods, I had a daily visitor in
the person of a little tomtit which every morning, on the first appearance of dawn, awakened me with its lively twit-twit. Whilst
venison or other meat was hanging outside the shanty, it fared sumptuously enough, and I constantly, on turning out in the morning,
saw it perched on a leg of venison or the carcase of a raccoon. When,
however, the meat was brought into the wigwam to dry in the smoke,
the little fellow became bolder, and on my return from hunting, I
invariably found it pecking away at something or another inside.

It gradually grew tamer, and at last, when I raised the deerskin in
the morning, would at once hop into the shanty and sit by my side
whilst I was eating my breakfast, and willingly take pieces of meat
out of my hand. The shrill twit-twit invariably served as a reveille to
me in the morning, and if by chance I awoke earlier than usual, I always waited for my little friend, knowing that until he made his appearance, it was still dark.

On the return of the Indians, it still flew in and out, although
there was scarcely an inch of standing room to spare, and would sit
on my legs, which were stretched before the fire, waiting patiently
for its share of the meal. When one morning after many weeks' sojourn in this wild and solitary spot, I turned out of the shanty for the
last time, my poor little companion was perched on the skull of a
bear which was lying before the door, waiting for the signal to enter.
And when the deerskin was removed from the door and he hopped
in as usual, he appeared to know that I was about to desert him, and,
perching on the sill, uttered a long, mournful twittering. I felt quite
sorry to leave the old camp and the sociable little tit, but threw a
large piece of meat into the shanty which would last him till the snow
disappeared, and bid both farewell.

[Ruxton, on his return to the settlements, encountered an American frontiersman clad in a fringed buckskin hunting shirt belted at the waist and] reaching nearly to the knee, with trousers of deerskin and mocassins. A few locks of straggling, grizzled hair escaped from a small skull cap of raccoon skin shading a face well tanned by many years of exposure to sun and snow. Seeing us approach, he addressed one of the Indians who happened to be foremost, but not being understood, he turned to one of his sons with,

"Injuns, by C——. Gone deer now Bill," I say. "What brings these d——d critturs yere I wonder? And a white amongst 'em! I declare! Wall, stranger, where away now? After the deer in these parts now, I calculate. Wall now that's a smart piece you carry anyways. Smooth bar'l—no, grooved, by C——, and two bar'ls. Wall now that beats all! Look here, Bill—look, Barnaby—at this hyar piece. Wall it beats. A costly piece of timber that (admiring the stock) as I've seen. Wall, stranger, you conceed that ar's a piece now, I am bound, but yar's your true rifle," taking up his own, a heavy Kentucky piece carrying fifty to the pound (mine was a double twenty-five gauge), "and can shoot smart, too, I tell you. If you've a mind to chance a bead, why I'm your man. Ninety yards, a dollar mark—but your piece won't throw that-a-way—make it fifty."

"One hundred fifty," said I. "My piece won't throw under a hundred. One hundred fifty yards and a dollar a shot."

"Wall now, that beats. Your gun go a hundred and fifty yards! Ha-ha-ha! Chalk it off, boy. Size of a plate at that distance and give us my gun."

The Yankee carefully loaded his rifle and, taking a long aim on a rest, fired. As I anticipated, leveling as he did point-blank, the ball struck a bush two feet under the white spot, but in good line.

"Whar it strike, boy?" he cried.

"A whole way down, Father."

"Well that beats! Who'd think it? But a hundred and fifty yards is a long chalk, that's a fact, and your piece won't do as well as that, stranger, I'm a-thinking."

My essay, however, was far more successful, for from my shoulder, I threw my ball almost in the center of the mark, making a chip fly high in the air.

"Darn me, Father. Stranger's struck it, if he hasn't, right in the soft cut, by Sambo! Well that beats!"

Without replying, the Yankee, throwing his rifle onto his arm, stalked up to the tree, which stood one hundred fifty yards distant, to satisfy himself of the truth of his son's report. Without speaking, he returned and took the rifle out of my hand, examined it minutely, raised it to his shoulder several times, and returning it said,

"A right smart piece, stranger, that's a fact! You draw a tight bead, you do! Come, let's liquor."

Leading the way into his house and producing a large jar of Monongahela, we pledged each other in a bumper of the cratur and, finding ourselves comfortable, agreed to take up our quarters with him that night in order that we might have a 'coon hunt in company the next day.

The interior of our entertainer's shanty was a fair sample of the houses of new settlements. Built of rough logs [phrase illegible], it boasted of none of the comparative elegance of a house in an old settlement. One small square window, filled with green-looking glass, afforded light enough for the short time it was tenanted during the day, for to a hunter indoors is unbearable, and at night a blazing fire brilliantly illuminated it. A rough table, two or three stools of primitive fashion, and a long, wide settee, covered with blankets and buffalo robes (the common bed), completed the furniture. Three rifles leaned against one corner, with their corresponding pouches and horns. A pile of skins in another testified that the weapons were not for mere show. Dried venison and hams of bear's meat dangled from the roof, where too were many heads of fine Indian corn.

Three half-bred hounds lay before the fire and shared the hearth with a couple of raccoons lying snuggled up into a ball and almost in the blaze.

Books there were none. A pair of shelves which had evidently once borne a more honourable load now supported sundry paraphernalia of the chase.

[One last fragment tells of Ruxton's]

Arrival in the Settlements after a Long Hunt

At noon we made the lake shore, and breaking through a narrow strip of brambly thicket, which lay between the woods and the clearing, we entered an open field, where some men were working rooting up stumps.

"Hallo, Injuns!" cried one of them, as he saw my party climb the snake fence. "You mighty handy, I guess, a-comin' into my lot. Who asked you to shew your d——d red skins here-away? I guess now you'd a sight better make tracks out of this now. None of your tricks won't do here now. That's a fact."

Notwithstanding this inhospitable reception, I made up to the speaker, who eyed me as if he wondered what on earth I was; and certainly my *tout ensemble* was anything but orthodox. My blanket, hunting pack, deerskin leggings, and moccasins had the marks of hard service, whilst my cap, adorned with a buck's tail and pulled over my eyes, effectually concealed my face, whether white or red.

However, when I approached and, throwing down my heavy packs, sat down on them, throwing my rifle over my knees, he had a better glimpse of my countenance, not the more Christianlike for being adorned with a several months' beard.

"How now!" he exclaimed, "why h——l, who's this d——d half-Injun, half-bull cat? Why, stranger, you're a white man, I do guess! What deviltry *are* you up to now with these red devils?"

"Morning, boss," I said. "Maybe you want some venison, and if you do, we've a buck you may pick the titbits out of, and if you want venison, we want bread and salt—so let's trade."

"Well now, if you've not come a-stealing hogs and horses now, with your red Injuns. I see now you're a Britisher. We'll try and trade a bit if you've any peltries. What do you say venison's worth now?"

"I do not know. We're just in from the woods and have only a buck we killed this morning, but give us a bag of potatoes, a gallon of meal, and a pound or two of salt pork and you shall have the deer."

"Well now, you're clever, you are! Where on airth do you think money's made here in Sampson? A bag of potatoes—why there's not a bag grown in this township. And as for meal and pork, we've to feed on what we get, we have—that's a fact. But if you're thirsty for corn doings, why my missis will let you have a score or two Johnnies (meal cakes) for the meat, I'm thinking."

I myself saw a boy as he entered the clearing carrying a large basket of potatoes from the heap to the house, so I knew my friend was saying what was not the fact; but pretending to be indifferent about it, I replied, "Well then, since you have not got the things, we'll clear out. And good day to you." And shouldering my pack, off I went.

"Now, stranger, I'd a rather have that buck because my old mother likes a bit of venison, and maybe we *have* a few 'tatres in the shanty, but there's no pork, I know, that's a fact."

"Oh, never mind, we'll try at the next lot."

"Well now, you're rustsome now, I think. Step in and talk to missis and she'll fix it, now, in no time."

Entering the log house, we found missis in the act of washing half a bushel of potatoes, whilst a daughter was preparing a mess of mush (Indian corn meal) for dinner. The rafters were plentifully garnished, too, with hams of pork, notwithstanding my friend's assertion as to the scarcity of these articles in the new township of Sampson. I was introduced with,

"Here, missis, here's a hunter with some venison now, and if you've any pork and 'tatres to trade, fix it with him somehow, for he's too hard on me, now that's a fact."

The good woman, a hustling, good-looking housewife, good-naturedly told me to draw near the fire, and having asked what we required for the venison,

"Well now," she said, "that's not much, anyhow, and we could afford to give you that for nothing, only Silas is so fond of raising a good trade, he's hardly Christian. But where are them poor Injuns I saw with you? They'd be glad of a warm and a drop of whisky now, I'll swear. Call 'em in, stranger, and Mercy will get you all some mush in no time. Silas," she continued, calling to a pocket edition of the father, "cut off a side of the hog hanging in the off house and fill these poor people a bag of meal, quick now. How many potatoes can you carry with you? Come in now, poor critturs, come in"—to my six Indians who were crowding into the room. "You'll be for a drop of whisky now, I wager," at the same time fitting out seven tin pannikins with good Ohio whisky and handing them to us. Our kind hostess quickly spread before us a large kettle of boiled Indian corn in which was immersed a huge lump of pork which had been boiled in the soup, and Silas and the other men coming in, who were all his sons, we sat down together and made the most luxurious meal we had tasted for many months.

After thanking our kind, hospitable friends—for Silas, to do him justice, except in the matter of "raising a bargain," was a good fellow—and, in addition to the buck, presenting our hostess with a couple of dressed skins, we sallied out and resumed our march through the settlement of Sampson.

CHAPTER 5

Two Trips to Africa, 1844-45

UXTON RETURNED from Canada in the spring of
1844. Of his homeward trip and his doings in Britain we have no
record. But it was soon apparent that he was not content to remain
inactive. Presently he had decided to travel in Africa. What induced
him to undertake the journey is not known.

At any rate, late in June, 1844, he secured a passport to journey
through France and Spain. He seems to have crossed the frontier into
Spain at Behobie, July 8, and it is likely that he visited some of his
old friends and familiar places in Spain, as he did not check into the
British legation at Gibraltar until July 31, when his passport was
stamped for a visit to Madrid. He visited Barcelona and Málaga before he had his passport stamped on August 27 as "about to proceed
to Cádiz," from which place he travelled to Tangier, in Morocco.
When the French fleet bombarded that city, he moved on to Tetuán,
which he left under escort at 3:00 A.M., September 12, "with hopes of
visiting the Rif," but his notes remaining to us show that the country
was too full of unrest for him to get very far.[1]

One of his first acquaintances assured him that, "Christians and
caliphs were made to pave the way to the believer's paradise." And
when he had travelled only thirty-seven miles from Tetuán, he notes
that, "A Jew swears I am a Frenchman and nearly causes me to lose
my ears." He says again, "Beware of the —— dog of a Cadi, who
nothing short of a bag full of dollars will satisfy." Whether or not
this cadi took all his cash is not clear, but he did spend the night in
the market place with only dates and camel's milk for supper. At
2:00 A.M. on the nineteenth, he started for the interior with a caravan of sixteen camels belonging to a man named Halif, who seems
to have greatly irritated Ruxton.

[1] Data from Ruxton's notes and papers.

Why these notes end abruptly, with Ruxton in a dry, hot camp, he does not explain. He did, however, make a little sketch of the object of his dislike, which is reproduced herewith, together with two pages of his notebook. Since the French and the Moroccans made peace on September 18, he probably did but little more travelling in North Africa and went back to England as soon as possible, for it was only a little over two months after the last entry was made in his notes on North Africa that he was on his way to South Africa.

His object was geographical discovery, as revealed by the president of the Royal Geographical Society, who soon after Ruxton's departure spoke thus in his anniversary address (1845):

"To my great surprise I recently conversed with an ardent and accomplished youth, Lieutenant Ruxton, late of the 89th Regiment, who has formed the daring project of traversing Africa in the parallel of the southern tropic, and has actually started for this purpose. Preparing himself by previous excursions on foot in North Africa and Algeria, he sailed from Liverpool early in December last in the *Royalist* for Ichabo, now so well known for its guano.

"From this spot he was to repair to Walwich Bay at the mouth of Kuissis River, where we have already mercantile establishments. The intrepid traveller had received from the agents of these establishments such favourable accounts of the natives towards the interior, as also of the nature of the climate, that he has the most sanguine hopes of being able to penetrate to the central region, if not of travelling it to the Portuguese colonies of Mozambique. If this be accomplished (and there are traditions of its having been done in former times by the Portuguese), then indeed, will Lieutenant Ruxton have acquired a permanent name for himself among British travellers, by making us acquainted with the nature of the axis of the great continent, of which we possess the Southern extremity."[2]

In December, 1844, Ruxton prepared to sail from Britain. His South African notebook is a little tan leather-bound pocket-book, printed by Punch, for the year 1845.[3] On the inside cover he wrote his list of ammunition, which included 125 lbs. of bar lead, 25 lbs. of tin, 50 lbs. of powder, 10,000 caps, 12 muskets, 12 dozen flints, 500 musket balls, 1 single rifle, 1 double rifle, 1 double shotgun, 1 elephant gun, two pistols, and bullet moulds. His other supplies are not listed.

The daily notes of events during the voyage are a little monoto-

[2] Quoted by Dr. Richard King in his obituary notice of Lieutenant Ruxton which was published in the Ethnological Society *Journal* of 1848.

[3] In the Ruxton collection.

nous, as the voyage must have been, lasting as it did for more than three months. We extract some of the more interesting entries.]

11. [December, 1844]. Heard of barque *Royalist.* Saw Capt. Lownis. Took passage for 25 and got kit ready.

12. Baggage on board—all but powder. Busy with last preparations.

13. Gave steward £1 to lay in soap and necessaries for cabin. Did not make his appearance. Moved out of dock. Decks crowded. Pilot refuses to take her out to sea.

14. Cleared out with fair breeze S.E.—freshened when out of river. At night took in M.T.G. Wind fresh from east and good run down channel during night.

15. Wind shifted a point to westward. Still fresh. During night blew strong. . . .

19. Fair wind from E.N.E. Going 5½. Passed a small sloop, *Earl Spencer,* fruit trader from Azores. Continues fair. Breezes and occasional showers. Warm weather. Wind E.S.E. . . .

28. Terrible gales—at times a hurricane with violent squalls—heavy thunder and lightning. Under a close-reefed topsail. . . .

Jany. 1st [1845]. Wind directly aft, but light. Rolling violently. Light airs during day, and vessel quieter. Great relief from the violent motions of the last 80 hours. Weather mild and soft—like entering a new world. Unsuccessful search for my sextant and chronometer—fear they are left behind. . . Light airs from N.E. Course S.W. Weather mild and genial trades.

2. Sighted Palmas, Canary Isles, before sunrise. Although we were running down with a spanking breeze, going from 6 to 10 knots, we did not get to land a team till 12 M. At 2 abreast of town. Looking out for Peak of Teneriffe. Everything set and going well. 10 knots. Trades. . . .

5. Stiff breeze from the N.N.E. Going 9 knots during the 24 hours. Saw several flying fish, and porpoises. Made 230 miles in the last 24 hours. Weather cool—sky cloudy and watery looking. Strong current to S.S.W. Trades strong.

6. Strong breeze from same quarter. Flying fish flew on board—ate him for supper. . . .

8. Breeze moderated—almost a calm at night. Sudden change of weather. Mercury at 85. North Star fast disappearing. Night hot and sultry with thunder and lightning. Red appearance of heavens. New moon. . . .

12. Calms and heavy rain. All hands washing. Caught a shark and 2 dolphins. *Duke of Brontë* in company. Cloudy towards night.

13. Calm and heavy squalls of rain. Barque on starboard quarter. Occasional baffling airs and heavy rain all day—filled up two casks. ...

16. At noon—36 miles from the equator. Thermometer in cabin 100° degrees. Fell calm in evening. Heavy squall of rain. Dutch barque in company. Dirty-looking weather—strong breeze at night from S.E.

17. Light breeze from S.E. Spoke the barque *J. Walker* from Liverpool to Ichabo. She, carrying more canvas, went ahead and at midnight was 4 miles ahead. . . .

22. Strong breeze from S.E. Less than 200 miles coast of Brazil. Breeze lighter. *J. Walker* coming up fast—passes us at 6 P.M.—4 miles ahead to W. at midnight. . . .

25. At noon the sun perfectly vertical—no shadow cast on deck. Latitude 28° 22′ south. Light breeze during day. Night clear. First time for a fortnight again observed comet 45° south of Pegasus.

26. Light airs and calms. In the afternoon a large brig in company. Very hot. Comet plain at night. 4 A.M. heavy squall. Light airs from S.S.E.

27. Calm weather and very hot. Nothing new. Heavy dews at night.

28. Pleasant breeze from the N.N.E. Exchange numbers with barque *Oriental*, from London to Calcutta, 48 days out.

29. Fine breeze from E.N.E. at sunset. Spoke a man-of-war brig standing to northward—did not hear her name—carrying topgallant and royals.

30. Fine breeze from E.N.E. Brig in sight standing to southward.

31. At 3 A.M. heavy squall of rain, which continued for 2 or 3 hours, soaking everything in cabin. Spoke a South Sea whaler bound to America. . . .

February 5. At 6 A.M., 4 sharks astern—harpooned one and shot another through the head. The one brought on board measured 10 feet. Calm during 24 hours.

6. Calms during day. At sunset black squally weather. Light breeze from S. by E. Clouds pass off without wind or rain.

7. Light breezes from E.S.E. Capt. of American whaler *Poka-nunket* came on board—14 months out, bound to Bahia. Nell pupped— 7 pups. . . .

10. Calms and hot weather. Run balls for guns. Saw Cuerpo Santo floating on water.

11. Calms and dull weather. At sunset light breeze from W.S.W. Run balls for guns. 29° 23.'

12. Calms and light airs from westward. At noon spoke barque *Eagle* (Kerr) of Liverpool—said she was bound to Java, but saw in papers that she cleared for Ichabo—steering like ourselves E.S.E. Saw brilliant meteor at night.

13. In morning calms and light breezes. Numerous waterspouts on the horizon to leeward. . . .

21. Tack ship every watch. Strong breeze from S.E. Pass Greenwich meridian. Blows from the same quarter all day and night with little more E. or W.

22. Breeze from E.S.E. Tacking to eastward. Two Cape pigeons about the vessel. . . .

28. Tacking to eastward, with wind at E.S.E. and hauling continually to N. and S. Spoke brig *Mercury*, 75 days from Liverpool, becalmed three weeks. At night light breeze from S.W.½S. Brig going ahead fast. Pleasant breeze during night.

March 1. Light breeze from E.S.E. and variable. Caught a dolphin. Weather pleasant.

2. Dead calm. Caught a shark 11 feet long. At sunset breeze from southward. Midnight hauled on larboard tack, with breeze strong from E. by S. . . .

4. Strong breeze from S.E., with nasty sea, and cold, unpleasant weather. In the afternoon large barque in sight on starboard tack, standing to S. and W. Backed main yard and spoke the *John Walker*, our old friend, whom we spoke nearly 2 months ago—86 days out—had had calms and easterly winds—intends to stretch to southard. At night strong breeze from S.E. . . .

13. Strong breeze from S. with short sea. Many albatrosses and birds about the ship—water very muddy. 2 P.M. pass through large patches of water as red as boiled coffee. Sharks astern. Blows a stiff gale from S. by W. with heavy sea. Take in topgallant sails and reef topsails over courses. 'Bout ship at 8 P.M.

16. Moderate weather. Breeze strong from S.S.W. At 10 A.M. land on larboard and lee bow. Tack towards anchorage during afternoon. At night stand out to sea.

17. At 9 A.M. drop anchor off N. end of Ichabo Island. Visit the fleet. Bad news.

[Ruxton related his experiences and gave his observations upon South Africa in an article published in the *Nautical Magazine* for

January, 1846. The account is longer than can be utilized here, but we present the major part, omitting only unimportant sections.]

17th [March, 1845]. Anchor off the north end of the island, and find twenty-two vessels lying at anchor. The island cut down nearly to the water's edge, and all the guano removed. On landing, which owing to the surf is always difficult, I found the whole surface of the island covered with skins and carcases of seals and penguins, in every stage of decay. At the southwest point, are the graves of thirty or forty seamen and labourers, killed whilst working in the pits, by the fall of guano. The skins and bodies of the seals and penguins had been originally the surface covering of the valuable deposit underneath; and had to be removed in order to reach the guano, to which they served, not only as a protective covering from the damp and spray of the sea, but also, in course of time decomposing themselves, formed new layers of this extraordinary substance. There was still a depth of many feet, in many places, of an inferior guano but too much impregnated with moisture and sand to be worth removal, though at the same time very valuable as a manure.

The island is of primary formation, exhibiting no traces of a volcanic origin; granite white and red, resting on quartz, compose the rocks. Lumps of ammoniacal salt exist in the guano in a comparatively pure state. Notwithstanding that the island had been occupied for nearly two years, during which time, thousands upon thousands of penguins had been wantonly destroyed, on the cessation of work, these birds again flocked to their old haunt, where they had again commenced laying their eggs. The rocks round the island are literally covered with penguins, cormorants, and albatrosses. The former, wedged together in a dense phalanx, have no more dread of man than ducks in a poultry yard, although they have met with such persecution on the island; and any number might be taken by the hand without any difficulty.

The sailors eat the livers and hearts, which are exceedingly palatable, but the flesh of the body is rank and oily. Hearing that *H. M. S. Thunderbolt* was on the coast and supposed to be lying in the Bay of Angra Pequeña, I determined to proceed overland to that place, distant from Ichabo by land about fifty miles, as I expected to find letters from the Admiralty with instructions to the officers in command to assist me in reaching Walwich Bay. For two or three days after my arrival on the coast, the sea was too high to allow a boat to land on the main. On the eighteenth, however, I succeeded in landing through a very dangerous surf, at a bay two and one-half miles south of the island, accompanied by a volunteer from the ship I arrived in. As I was led to believe that we should find vessels at Angra Pequeña, I only carried sufficient water and provisions for two days for myself, desiring my companion to carry a sufficiency for his own use. By some mistake, he neglected to provide himself with any, and the few biscuits I carried were completely spoiled in landing through the surf. Unfortunately I was not aware of our want of provisions until we halted for the night, when it would have been useless to return, as a gale of wind was blowing, which would have prevented our getting off to the ship for a further supply. On landing I kept a course S.S.E. by compass, passing through a valley deep with soft and yielding sand, into which sinking at every step to our ankles, and being laden with heavy packs and ammunition, we found our progress very laborious, particularly as it was the first time I had been on land for upwards of three months.

About four miles south of the island, we passed a valley which had been swept by a tornado. Although the surrounding hills were many feet deep in sand, the surface of this valley had been completely swept, as by a broom, and was as hard as a beaten road, with small triangular points or ridges sticking out of the sand sufficiently hard to wound the feet. These all pointed to the northwest or mouth of the valley, so that the tornado which had caused this appearance, must have blown with great violence from the southeast, and probably caused the phenomenon common on this coast of the sand pillar. The sand was piled up fifty or sixty feet in height at the mouth of the valley, which appears to me to have once been the bed of a water course or river. The rocks are all of primary formation, with the rare exception here and there of blocks of limestone further inland. . . .

As night was approaching, I struck off to the sea shore, along which we proceeded with no little toil. The coast is strewed with fragments of wrecks. Boats, spars, casks, &c. are met with at every step. A large longboat was cast high and dry on some rocks, and near it were many barrels, bamboos, cocoa nuts, &c., from which I inferred she must have belonged to an Indiaman. . . .

Along a distance of thirty or forty miles on this inhospitable coast, I saw parts of wrecks of at least six different vessels. . . .

About ten o'clock at night we halted and set about building up a fire, which a biting wind and intense dew rendered necessary. This we were able to effect with very little difficulty, abundance of firewood being at hand. . . .

Here I found, on examining our stock of provisions, that we had but three eatable biscuits and two quarts of water, in which my companion had already made a hole.

The moon was yet high when we resumed our march, leaving the log still burning. The sand on the shore was so soft that we sank to our ankles at every step; I therefore struck in amongst the sand hills, hoping to find a harder track. As we were floundering through the sand, I perceived a peculiar smell issuing from a dark patch of brush a little distance before me. Approaching the spot, I found it proceeded from a native hut, or rather den of brush and sand bushes, piled round a framework of rib bones of whales, with which, by the bye, the coast is plentifully strewed. Bones of this fish were also stuck up in the sand, and the ruins of two or three more huts were visible. From the abominable odour which hung around the place, and which exactly resembled the stench proceeding from the den of a wild beast, or the nest of an eagle or vulture, I concluded it had recently been inhabited by natives. Inside the hut were some broken ostrich eggs, and several large, flat, and exceedingly heavy stones, which from the weight I imagined to be ironstone.

On leaving this primitive retreat, we again floundered over the sand hills, which were continual stumbling blocks in our way; for the darkness prevented our perceiving the inequalities of the ground, and we were constantly tumbling over them and into holes. At length, finding it impossible to proceed, I lay down under the lee of a sand hill, and slept till daylight. An intense dew was falling, and in the morning my clothes were saturated with the damp, and my gun and pistols a mass of rust; our limbs, too, were stiff with the laborious walking and with lying on the damp sand.

We persevered, however, and leaving the sand hills, again steered for and reached the sea shore as the sun was rising; and we continued our course to the southward, passing, as the day before, many wrecks lying on the beach, and the same monotonous line of sandy plains and hills on our left. Fourteen miles from Ichabo, we entered a bay where the sand hills rose perpendicularly from the water's edge; and it being high-water at the time, we were obliged to walk up to our knees in the water. This bay must be frequently impassable when the tides are high; at any time there is considerable danger of being washed back by the sea. Passing the long circuitous shore, we found some rocks at the southern extremity, on which were some limpets. We found them tolerable eating, but I was seized shortly after with pains in my chest, which I afterwards found out was occasioned by eating these fish—some species of them being poisonous.

Leaving Sandhill Bay, on crossing a point, we entered another of equal extent. Here lay several fragments of the wreck of a vessel, which had, apparently, but recently been broken up. India baskets and some Japan bowls lay in profusion on the sands; and amongst other things, I picked up a bottle of Harvey's sauce, which still contained the greater portion of its original contents, and which, strange enough, were as fresh and well-flavoured as the day it was made. There was no mark or name on any of these fragments; but at a little distance, a broken oar had the name "Heart of Oak," stamped upon it.

At sunset of the twentieth we were in sight of Angra Pequeña, and, to my great disappointment, but one vessel was to be seen, and she was in the act of getting under way. A dense mist almost hid the coast from my view, and might also have concealed any vessel lying off the land. The vessel in sight was so distant that all attempts to attract her attention would have been futile. We had at least fifty miles before us over the sand, to reach our vessel, which was to sail on the fifth day after our departure; so that no time was to be lost in our return. Our food and water were also exhausted, which rendered our situation anything but pleasant. A biscuit each had been our only food, with the exception of the few limpets, for three days; and we already felt exhausted with fatigue and hunger. We, therefore, with a very bad grace, turned our backs upon the bay.

On the maps, a river is laid down as running into Angra Pequeña, called Fish River. No such river exists. From the Gariep, or Orange, River to Walwich Bay, no river runs into the sea, although in some maps of Africa I have seen three or four laid down. Imagining that water was to be procured here in the river, was the cause of my not providing myself with a larger supply; and the consequence was that we nearly perished. Angra Pequeña was first discovered more than 360 years ago, by Bartholemew Diaz, on his first voyage of discovery. Whilst lying here, he erected on a rock, which abuts from the southwest point of the bay, a marble cross—both as a memento of his so far prosperous voyage, and also as a testimony to his primary discovery, and as a symbol of his having taken possession of the country in the name of his king. Here it remained upwards of 300 years undisturbed, an honourable memorial of the skill and enterprise of the old Portuguese. For three centuries it had braved the elements, when, a few years ago, it was destroyed by some modern Vandals, and now lies, broken and unheeded, buried in the sand. Of the many ships of war which have put into this bay, not one has ever thought of raising the old cross to its former position. To the view, the whole line of coast presents but one cheerless, inhospitable aspect. Sand hills rising from the water's edge, until in the distance they are lost in more elevated hills as miserably sterile as themselves. Not a patch of verdure relieves the eye, but everywhere shining, glassy sand glares in the sun, broken on the ridges of the hills by abrupt masses of rock, which shut out a view, many miles beyond, of a desert equally wretched. A few half-starved jackalls are occasionally seen prowling near the shores, where—worthy denizens of such a waste—some wretched bushmen resort, seeking a subsistence on any offal cast on shore by the sea. Wherever water is to be procured, two or three families reside, living on beetles, the carcases of seals, which they devour in the last stages of putrefaction, and the few shellfish they may find on the rocks.

Quitting Angra Pequeña about sunset, we proceeded northward for a few miles, and slept under the lee of a sand hill, in a plain abounding with myrrh plants. Scooping a hole in the sand, I slept until sunrise, when I was so weak and exhausted I could scarcely rise. My companion was in a still worse plight, and it was with great difficulty I could induce him to rouse himself.

The sun was exceedingly powerful, and we were tormented by excessive thirst. A plunge every now and then into the sea, regardless of the sharks which were swarming within the surf, refreshed me for the time, but only increased the thirst. Every few yards we would fall from sheer weakness, when in an instant I would be fast asleep, and it was with great difficulty I could resist the drowsiness which was stealing over me. The long Sandhill Bay took us five hours to pass; and having to ascend a range of high sand hills, we abandoned our packs, blankets, ammunition, and—what I regretted more—some beautiful skins of the fur seal which I had shot.

We experienced a temporary relief from this, but in a short time were in as hopeless a state as before. Choked with thirst, and stumbling at every step, at length simultaneously we threw ourselves down; and I was just giving way to the drowsy stupor which was coming over me, when, looking down the beach, I perceived the figures of several natives, seated round a fire. Knowing that water could not be far distant, I imbibed fresh strength from the anticipation of a draught, and was soon amongst them. The party consisted of six women and as many children, all perfectly naked. On seeing us approach, they all dashed up the sandbank, squatting like crows on the top. On my making signs, however, one of them came down, and, to my great joy, with two ostrich eggshells of water, which refreshed us wonderfully, and enabled us to accompany them to their village, which was about half a mile from the shore. The village consisted of six or seven huts, formed of bushes raised against rib bones of whales. The only tenants of these were a few old men and women, who were crouching, enveloped in greasy sheepskins, over a fire. On our arrival, a boy, who seemed to anticipate our wants, ran to the well, and brought several ostrich eggshells of water, which, although very brackish, I esteemed the sweetest draught that ever passed my mouth. I found the well to be a hole dug in the sand, about four feet deep, from which about a gallon of water could be procured at a time. Experience afterwards taught me that water is to be procured at almost any spot on this coast, and often in the driest-looking and sandiest parts. We rested in the village for several hours; but the only food they could give us was a dozen of roasted limpets.

A present of tobacco amply repaid their hospitality; and when we left them in the evening, old and young were sitting in a circle, and enjoying a regular smoke over the fire. These natives were the wandering Bushmen of the coast.

We arrived opposite our ship late at night, and made a large fire to notify our arrival. It was with great difficulty that we were got through the surf the next day, almost famished with hunger. I remained some days at the island before I could get an opportunity of proceeding down the coast. . . .

Many vessels have arrived on the coast, seeking an island said to lie a few miles north of Ichabo, and of which a chart had been published. It was reported to be covered with guano, and to be situated in a bay affording good shelter and safe anchorage. More than 300 vessels had arrived, with instructions to take cargo from this island, which was called Gallovidia. No such island exists. I made an unsuccessful search for Gallovidia Island, pulling along shore in a boat to the latitude assigned to it, and closely examined every bay between Ichabo and Hottentot Bay. I also walked overland to the spot laid down in the chart as the locality of this newly-discovered island.

On the thirtieth of March I proceeded down the coast in a vessel in which I had taken a passage for that purpose, running along shore during the day, and closely examining the line of coast.

On approaching Mercury Island, the coast presents a rather bolder appearance; masses of granite rising abruptly from the shore, and of considerable height.

Mercury Island, as well as Ichabo, is of primitive formation. It is merely a mass of rock, lofty and precipitous, in the hollows and interstices of which were the deposits of guano, which have now been entirely removed. The bay is small, and affords little or no shelter from the prevailing winds. A heavy, rolling swell sets in with the strong southerly winds, and breaks with great force on the beach, where boat-landing is very dangerous. It is, however, of easy access, either from the north or south; and in case of a gale, vessels can easily get to sea. The rocks on the north and south ends of the bay rise abruptly and to a great height from the water's edge, and between them is a lower range of sand hills, through which the points of quartz rocks shew themselves. From this a curious ridge ascends to the high land, which exactly resembles the backbone of a fish. No vegetation is to be seen, beyond the stunted sand plant common to the whole coast.

On arriving at Walwich Bay, from whence I had intended proceeding into the country, I found that some traders from the Cape of Good Hope had established themselves, from whom I met the most strenuous opposition to my proceeding into the interior. A short time before my arrival some missionaries had visited the bay from the interior, accompanied by Jonquer Africana, the chief of the Namaqua nation. Unfortunately they had left shortly before my arrival.

Finding that these traders would neither supply me with oxen, nor render me any assistance, I endeavoured to send into the country for some pack bullocks, to enable me to reach the missionary station at Jonquer's, where I could procure horses and oxen for my expedition. However, I found that the traders had already got possession of every head of cattle, and none were to be procured but from them. The traders threatened—and I have no doubt that they would carry their threats into execution—to send to the chiefs through whose country I was to pass, to tell them that I was coming with arms and armed men to take their country from them, and advise them not to let me proceed. Their object in opposing me is that they are unwilling that the capabilities of the country should be known, in order that they may enjoy undisturbed the lucrative trade with the interior.

After many fruitless attempts, I at last imagined that all difficulties were overcome when I heard that a missionary had arrived at the trading post, accompanied by several chiefs, who had waggons and oxen with them.

I had already engaged an interpreter, the Damara slave who was purchased by Sir J. Alexander in his expedition and educated in England. Through him I communicated with the chiefs, who at once agreed to supply me with a waggon and oxen, and their own escort to proceed as far as the kraal of the head chief, where I might obtain oxen and horses for my journey to the northeast. On the eve of my departure, I heard to my great astonishment that Mr. Tyndal, the missionary, had used his influence with the chief Amrol to prevent my proceeding; indeed before his arrival, he had heard from a native that I was at Walwich Bay and about to proceed into the interior, when, although he did not know that was my object, he advised the chiefs to prevent my proceeding.

I at once saw the missionary, who acknowledged that he had advised Amrol not to sanction my going, and said that as I was not sent by the government, but was a private individual on my own resources, he would advise the chief to that effect. Such is the influence which the missionaries have over this old chief that he put a stop to my obtaining assistance from the other chiefs, which rendered it impossible that I could proceed. I afterwards ascertained that the missionaries are all directly, or indirectly, connected with these traders, who indeed were established by them as a depôt for provisions to supply the stations in the interior, and also as an outlet for the goods collected from the natives by them, in their double capacity of merchant missionaries.

The opportunity lost was doubly to be regretted, as on the return of these chiefs, Africana was going into the Damara country, to the northeast of the Swatrop, to negociate a treaty of peace with the king of that nation, and therefore my entrance into their country would have been under good auspices. Thus my project was thwarted by the very people to whom I confidently looked for assistance. No offers I made to the chief would induce him to sell me any oxen, and all my efforts to procure any were of no avail, so that I was most reluctantly compelled to give up all hopes of penetrating from that point, which I am satisfied is the most practicable on the coast, and affords greater facilities for travelling than any other.

I examined the Swatrop, or Somerset River, which is forty miles to the north of the Kuisip [Kuiseb], which runs into Walwich Bay. The Swatrop was not visited by Sir J. Alexander, although it was by far the best route he could have followed on his return.

When it flows, it must be a considerable river—the mouth being 500 yards wide; and it must *once* have flowed with great force, having worn its way through rocks of granite. Its mouth is blocked by a bar of sandy beach, and covered with reeds and flags. A species of hemlock grows in its bed, which, to twenty miles from its mouth, is dry. Water is, however, easily procured a few inches from the surface. Passing the first twenty miles, there are large pools and abundant pasture for many thousand head of cattle, which increase the further you proceed to the eastward.

It is by the route of the Swatrop that the natives proceed to and from the interior, it being perfectly practicable for oxen and waggons. It runs nearly due east. From its source (which, according to the natives, is in a mountainous country) to its mouth, a distance of 300 miles, it passes through a succession of fertile plains, lofty hills, and sandy deserts. Seventy miles from the seacoast, the desert changes into plains of fine pasture, which increases in fertility the further you advance, until, at the village where Africana resides, the country is rich and fertile, covered with flowers and a luxuriant vegetation. In its course to the sea, it has worn its way through lofty granite rocks, which on its north bank stretch away in a perfect level for many miles. . . .

I received some information of the country to the northeast from my interpreter, who had been to the source of the Swatrop, and from the chiefs.

The true country of the Damaras extends northward and eastward of the Swatrop, and far surpasses that of the Namaquas. The physical difference between the two people sufficiently proves this: the Namaquas being a poor, undersized race, whilst the Damaras are the finest negroes I have ever seen. Numerous small rivers run from the northward to eastward; and one great water they describe, where are plenty of canoes, and the inhabitants are very wild, with long hair. This exactly agrees with information I received from a Portuguese, who had been far into the interior from Benguela, on slaving expeditions, who told me he had seen some slaves, who were brought from a large lake or river, who were copper coloured, with long, straight hair. The Damaras of the northeast also wear ornaments of gold, which I have myself seen. Their country abounds in cattle, ivory, &c. They are ignorant of the use of firearms, which have always been kept out of the interior, by the policy of the Portuguese slave dealers.

This country supplies at least two-thirds of the slaves taken from the coast of Africa. They are constantly at war with each other, their great object being to obtain prisoners, whom they sell to people who trade between the Portuguese settlements and their own country. The Damaras have reported that amongst a tribe not a very great distance east of the source of the Swatrop, there have been long residing some very aged white people, who were made prisoners many years since, somewhere on the eastern coast.

My intention was to visit the country of the lakes, or rather where they are said to exist, and the sources of the Zambezi, down which river it would have been easy to proceed to the Portuguese settlement of Sofala, in the Mozambique. The natives all speak of a *water country* to the northeast, which must either be the Zambezi, or the lake called Nunmoor.

I induced the master of a vessel which was leaving the coast to proceed down it to the latitude of Nourse's River, which was discovered by the *Espiegle*, in 1823. This river rises in the heart of the unexplored country north of the parallel of the Tropic of Capricorn, and would be a most important outlet, if a trade were opened with that region. At St. Helena I received an account of it from Capt. Stenning, of the barque *John Cock*, whom I had requested to examine its mouth. I must here observe, that from the period of its first discovery it has never been revisited; and even whalers and sealers, who constantly visit the coast, are utterly ignorant of its existence, notwithstanding that fresh water is an object of the greatest importance to them, and most difficult to be obtained. Capt. Stenning reported, that being in lat. 17° 50′ south, he was close in shore (April), and had an excellent view of the river, which was *open*, and running with strength. Its entrance was 400 or 500 yards in width, and had sufficient water to allow a *large boat* to pass the bar.

North of the Swatrop I saw the first change in the nature of the rocks. . . .

The myrrh plant was the only plant I saw of any value; indeed, it is the only symptom of vegetation in the desert. It is found in a space of about thirty square miles, in the country inland from Ichabo, and is very abundant. I learned from the natives that it is of a better quality further from the coast. In March the plant was destitute of leaves, but gum was exuding plentifully from it. An ounce might be extracted from each plant. In appearance, it is low and scrubby, growing in the bare (mica) land.

Near Walwich Bay, the few natives who inhabit the valley of the Kuisip subsist entirely on a species of melon, or prickly pear, which they call narras. It is curious that it is only found in a very circumscribed tract of desert country, frequented by the Namaquas in their visits to the coast. The plant is a spreading, prickly bush, with small leaves and yellow flowers. It bears fruit throughout the year, which may be gathered from the same stem in every stage of growth, from the bud to the ripe fruit.

In the lagoon at the head of the bay are large beds of samphire, which, either dressed, or as salad, affords an excellent antiscorbutic vegetable. It also grows in the mouth of the Swatrop.

Walwich Bay forms the safest harbour from the Cape to the Equator, being sheltered from all winds, and having excellent anchorage. . . .

Some jawbones of whales, which are sticking upright in the sand, marking the spot where some sailors were buried many years ago, who were killed by the natives, appear like masts of ships. The pelicans, standing on the point, in bands of fifteen or twenty, resemble a troop of giants; and the crimson flamingoes running over the sand in large flocks, a battalion of infantry; whilst the surf dashing on the beach, is seen refracted high in air like the flickering light of the aurora borealis. . . .

The lagoon at the head of the bay is generally covered with water to the depth of two or three feet, and is the resort of countless myriads of seafowl, pelicans, flamingoes, plovers, &c.

Wishing one day to secure some specimens of these birds, I took up my quarters for the night under the lee of a heap of whale bones, on the verge of the lagoon. When the moon rose, I found myself in the midst of vast flocks of gulls and other birds, which were roosting on the level sand, a band of pelicans being so close to me that I could have almost touched them as I lay. As the first streak of grey appeared over the eastern sand hills, I turned out of my lair, where, by the bye, I was disturbed during the night by two scorpions, which I actually killed as they ran up my leg in the trousers. Partly concealed by a small hillock of sand, I had leisure to observe a most extraordinary scene. The tide receding, had left a large space of sandy mud uncovered, which was literally alive with birds. Here, as morning dawned, long lines of flamingoes, pelicans, gulls, cormorants, and other birds continued to pour their countless numbers, until the lagoon was covered with a perfect carpet of birds. Innumerable plovers hovered over the mass, striving to introduce themselves into the interstices, and making the air resound with their shrill piping.

In a pool a few feet from me several hundred enormous pelicans had taken their station. Here, amid the uproar of a million throats, they quietly fed, and when the sun appeared, removed to a hillock, where, lazily stretching their wings, they enjoyed the warm rays.

The flamingoes, however, disturbed by the voracious cormorants, who were tilting and jostling against their long legs, testified their displeasure by loud croakings, spreading their wings and displaying their beautiful crimson plumage, now rising in a cloud, and again settling amongst the thick phalanx of black cormorants. The poor gulls were sadly knocked about, their short legs and sluggish gait being much out of place among their taller and more active competitors.

I fired a ball from my rifle over the throng, but the report was lost amid the uproar. The pelicans which were close to me raised their heads and stretched their wings, but quickly resumed their former dignified position, testifying no alarm at my propinquity. Three or four piebald crows were hopping and cawing around me so tame that they readily took pieces of biscuit which I placed at my feet. As the tide flowed, gradually narrowing the space occupied by the birds, they became jammed into a compact mass, fighting and screaming in a manner that beggars description. When they appeared inextricably confused, I rose to bring their meal to a conclusion. The scene which ensued was most amusing. I was actually striding amongst the cormorants before they paid the slightest attention to my appearance.

The flamingoes, higher than the rest, were the first to observe the intrusion. I was amongst them when they took the alarm, when, first raising their heads and uttering warning cries to the rest, they rose in a cloud of crimson. A shot and a shout disturbed the greedy cormorants, who with deafening clamor rose in confusion, followed by the gulls and plovers. The heavy-flying flamingoes were first charged by the mass, throwing them at once into disorder, but when once extricated, their distinct clouds of crimson, white, and black floated slowly away. Last of the rout, the pelicans in a band of at least a thousand brought up the rear, skimming slowly over the pools and resettling at a short distance, where they allowed me to approach and select a victim.

A curious species of shark is found in Walwich Bay; it is about ten feet in length, resembling in size and shape the common shark, but covered with numerous light coloured spots of the size of a shilling. Out of each spot grows a sharp triangular spike not unlike a shark's tooth, and exceedingly sharp. The bay swarms with them, and they delight in frequenting the shallows of the beach, where they often strand themselves. They are not voracious, for I have frequently bathed amongst them with impunity.

[Thus ends Ruxton's article. Baffled in his efforts to penetrate

103

the interior of South Africa, he soon returned to Britain. We have no account of his voyage home.

"Before Leaving Africa," writes Ruxton's friend, Dr. Richard King,[4] "Mr. Ruxton made himself acquainted with the manners and customs of the natural inhabitants of the almost inaccessible valleys of Snewburg [Sneeuwberg], Nieuwveld, and the desolate tracts of Karoo, or desert, extending from the northern boundary of the Cape Colony northward nearly to the Tropic. He contributed to the Ethnological Society [of London, at its meeting of November 26, 1845] an able paper on this interesting people, known as Bushmen, a race of human beings existing on locusts and the larvae of insects, food sought by them as a luxury, and deemed the greatest blessing—what to the rest of mankind is a plague and a pestilence. Desolate and forlorn as is the condition of these poor creatures, Mr. Ruxton describes his intercourse with them to be favourable to their morals, and adds, 'Well may they be now called outcasts, when it is a matter of history that, in 1652, when the Dutch took possession of the Cape, they had large herds of cattle, which the *whites* first obtained by barter, and ultimately by force, a system of persecution which drove them from desert to desert, "their hand raised against every man, and every man's against them." '

"Nothing daunted by the peril of his first adventure in Africa, and still having the same conception of his 'daring project of traversing Africa in the parallel of the southern tropic,' he asked again and again from Her Majesty's Government some little assistance to enrich his private resources, which ended in the application being referred to the Geographical Society for its opinion, and that opinion being filed in the archives of the Colonial Office—an opinion, be it said, equally to the credit of the Society and of Mr. Ruxton—expressed, without loss of time, strongly in its favour. Delay followed delay, which our adventurous traveller could no more brook than those who have trodden before him the same crooked path, destined, like himself, to perform great works with little means, but that the government was incapable of appreciating the rich storehouse it resolved to lay waste, and he consequently withdrew from the field of research in Africa."]

[4] Dr. King, 1811–76, was a medical man, Arctic explorer, naturalist, and author. He was the principal founder of the Ethnological Society of England, and its first secretary, in 1844. For a biographical sketch of King, see the *Dictionary of National Biography*, 1892.

The quotation used here is from Dr. King's excellent biographical sketch of Ruxton, *loc. cit.*

CHAPTER 6

Travels in Mexico, 1846

[B]ECOMING WEARY of official delays and disgusted with lack of support for the proposed further exploration of South Africa, Ruxton abandoned the project and looked elsewhere for service and adventure. The outbreak of the Mexican War afforded an opportunity.

Ruxton's journey to and through Mexico while the war was on has caused some speculation as to his motives and purpose. Some there are who think he was on a secret mission, possibly as a spy for the British government; and the belligerent attitude towards the United States expressed in his Oregon pamphlet (1846) would seem to give some credence to the theory. Also, there is his refusal—in his book *Adventures in Mexico and the Rocky Mountains*—to explain why he was visiting Mexico in wartime. In the Preface to this volume he writes: "It is hardly necessary to explain the cause of my visiting Mexico in such an unsettled period; and I fear that circumstances will prevent my gratifying the curiosity of the reader, should he feel any on that point." This would seem further to envelop the venture in an air of mystery.

But after thus rebuffing the curious and suspicious, he continues his Preface in a more mollifying vein:

"This little work is merely what its title professes it to be, 'The Rough Notes of a Journey through Mexico, and a Winter spent amongst the wild scenes and wilder characters of the Rocky Mountains,' and has no higher aim than to give an idea of the difficulties and hardships a traveller may anticipate, should he venture to pass through it and mix with its semi-barbarous and uncouth people, and to draw a faint picture of the lives of those hardy pioneers of civilisation whose lot is cast upon the boundless prairies and rugged mountains of the Far West."

But he did have an objective other than travel, observations, and adventure. This further mission was revealed after he had travelled the length of Mexico and had reached the American military forces and the commercial caravan traders in New Mexico. He presented himself to them in the role of a representative of British commercial and diplomatic interests, and by this time he had also assumed service as a commercial agent for the Mexican government. This position is revealed by Lieutenant J. W. Abert of the American Army, in his contemporary report of meetings and conversations with Ruxton.[1]

Our British traveller cannot be called a spy, for he made no attempt to conceal his identity, and on all necessary and suitable occasions presented his passport and official credentials.[2] The fact that he carried a rather large quantity of coin—some three thousand dollars was stolen from him at Guajoquilla, in North Mexico, and then re-

---

[1] Abert writes (November 29, 1846): "Mr. Ruxton brought a paper from the English minister, desiring all American officers to extend every facility to English traders on their route to Chihuahua; also other papers, in which it was stated that traders of all nations would be permitted free egress, even Americans, provided they came with Mexican drivers. . . .

"[December 1.] This morning Mr. Kerford's train moved down the river, and formed camp near 'Fray Cristobal,' which is 15 miles below. Mr. Kerford is an Englishman, and having an English passport, is very anxious to go on to Chihuahua, as well as Señor Algier, who is protected by a Spanish passport. The coming of Mr. Ruxton, with letters assuring foreigners that their property would be protected, has made many of the traders very anxious to proceed, for some of them have as much as 150,000 dollars worth of goods at stake. . . .

"[December 4.] Today Captain Walton rode down, and expressed his positive determination to prevent any one from going to Chihuahua until Colonel Doniphan should arrive. This evening, however, all the traders assembled and drew up a letter to Captain Walton, desiring that Mr. Kerford should be allowed to proceed. His goods have come through the United States from England, in the original packages, and have been, thus far, free of duty; and now, if they are brought into competition with the goods of the other traders, it will be ruinous to them; but if Mr. K. is allowed to proceed at once, he will pass on through Chihuahua towards Zacatecas and Durango. As he has an immense stock of goods, this arrangement was greatly desired. . . .

"[December 8.] In the evening, Mr. Houck, Mr. Kerford, Mr. Harmony, El Señor Algier, and El Señor Porros, arrived at our camp; they were going up to see Captain Walton, in order to make a more formal representation." From "Report of Lieut. J. W. Abert, of his Examination of New Mexico," in *Notes of a Military Reconnaissance, from Fort Leavenworth, in Missouri, to San Diego, in California, House Exec. Doc. 41*, 30 Cong., 1 sess., 502, 504–505.

[2] F. E. Voelker, in his excellent article, "Ruxton of the Rocky Mountains," in the Missouri Historical Society *Bulletin*, V, 79–90, presents Ruxton in the role indicated here, and marshals the source materials in substantiation of the appraisal.

covered[3]—is evidence that he was in position to influence officials and obtain considerations beyond his own personal needs. He was undoubtedly able to give valuable aid and advice to those British subjects he encountered who were engaged in the caravan traffic over the Santa Fé Trail to Mexico. Some of these merchants were carrying, as Ruxton later tells us, original package goods that had gone through the United States without payment of customs duties.

Aside from his diplomatic and commercial mission, Ruxton's venture into Mexico and the Rocky Mountains was largely motivated by his keen desire to visit these strange remote lands, hunt in the wilderness of the American West, and subsequently write about his experiences and observations.

The account of Ruxton's travels of 1846–47, as given here in Chapters six through sixteen, is taken from his book, *Adventures in Mexico and the Rocky Mountains* (London, 1847). In this present chapter and the succeeding one, Ruxton's main story and impressions are given through selected extracts from the first 150 pages of the book. Thereafter his writing is quoted in full, except that his chapter headings are not retained.

Ruxton's Preface is as follows:]

Some apology, I am aware, is necessary for offering so meagre an account of Mexico as that which is set before the reader in the following pages. In justice to myself, however, I may state that all the notes and memoranda of the country I passed through, as well as several valuable and interesting documents and MSS connected with the history of Northern Mexico and its Indian tribes, which I had collected, were unfortunately destroyed (with the exception of my rough notebook) in passing the Pawnee Fork of the river Arkansa, as I have mentioned in the body of this narrative; and this loss has left me no alternative but to give a brief outline of my journey, which, bare as it may be, I prefer to lay before the reader in its present shape, rather than draw at hazard from the treacherous notebook of memory, or the less reliable source of a fertile imagination.

[Then follow the two paragraphs already quoted above.]

With a solitary exception I have avoided touching upon American subjects; not only because much abler pens than mine have done that country and people more or less justice or injustice, and I wish to attempt to describe nothing that other English travellers have writ-

[3] See below, in Chapter 7.

ten upon before, and to give a rough sketch of a very *rough* journey through comparatively new ground—but, more than all, for the reason that I have, on this and previous visits to the United States, met with such genuine kindness and unbounded hospitality from all classes of the American people, both the richest and the poorest, that I have not the heart to say one harsh word of them or theirs, even if I could or would.

Faults the Americans have—and who have not? But they are, I maintain, failings of the head and not of the heart, which nowhere beats warmer, or in a more genuine spirit of kindness and affection, than in the bosom of a citizen of the United States.

Would that I could say as much of the sister people. From south to north I traversed the whole of the Republic of Mexico, a distance of nearly two thousand miles, and was thrown amongst the people of every rank, class, and station; and I regret to have to say that I cannot remember to have observed one single commendable trait in the character of the Mexican; always excepting from this sweeping clause the women of the country, who, for kindness of heart and many sterling qualities, are an ornament to their sex, and to any nation.

If the Mexican possesses one single virtue, as I hope he does, he must keep it so closely hidden in some secret fold of his sarape as to have escaped my humble sight, although I travelled through his country with eyes wide open, and for conviction ripe and ready.[4] I trust, for his sake, that he will speedily withdraw from the bushel the solitary light of this concealed virtue, lest before long it be absorbed in the more potent flame which the Anglo-Saxon seems just now disposed to shed over benighted Mexico.

[On July 2, 1846, Ruxton sailed from Southampton for Mexico. A voyage of six days brought him to Madeira and thirteen more to Barbados. After short visits to Grenada, Santo Domingo, and Jamaica, he came to Cuba,] the most brilliant jewel in the crown of Spain. This, the last of their once magnificent dependencies, they may well guard with watchful eye; for not only do the colonists most cordially detest the mother country, and only wait an opportunity to throw off the yoke, but already an unscrupulous and powerful neighbour "of the north" casts a longing eye towards this rich and beautiful island. . . .

The day after our departure from Havana we overtook a small steamer under the British flag, which was pronounced to be the *Arab*,

4 Ruxton's attitude towards the Mexicans seems unduly hostile and his appraisal unfair.

having on board the ex-President of Mexico, General Santa Anna. As she signalled to speak, we bore down upon her, and running along-side, her captain hailed to know if we would take on board four passengers; which was declined, our skipper not wishing to compromise himself with the American blockading squadron at Vera Cruz, by carrying Mexican officers. We had a good view of Santa Anna, and his pretty young wife, who, on hearing our decision, stamped her little foot on the deck, and turned poutingly to some of her suite. It seemed that the *Arab* had disabled her machinery, and was making such slow progress that Santa Anna was desirous of continuing the trip in the *Medway*. He was provided with a passport from the government of the United States to enable him to pass the blockade; which very questionable policy on the part of that government it is difficult to understand, since they were well aware that Santa Anna was bitterly hostile to them, whatever assurances he may have made to the contrary, and at the same time was perhaps the only man whom the Mexican army would suffer to lead them against the American troops.[5]

On the fifth morning after leaving Havana . . . [Ruxton reached Vera Cruz.] The city is well planned, surrounded by an adobe wall, with wide streets crossing each other at right angles. There are also several large and handsome buildings fast mouldering to decay. One hundred years ago a flourishing commercial city, like everything in Spanish America, it has suffered from the baneful effects of a corrupt, impotent government. Now, with a scanty population, and under the control of a military despotism, its wealth and influence have passed away. . . . Everywhere stalks the *sopilote*, "turkey buzzard," sole tenant of the streets, feeding on the garbage and carrion which abound in every corner. . . . These disgusting birds are, however, useful scavengers, and, performing the duty of the lazy Mexicans, are therefore protected by law. . . .

On the sixteenth of August the castle, with a salvo of artillery, announced the approach of the steamer having on board the illustrious ex-President—General Santa Anna. . . . Don Antonio Lopez de Santa Anna is a hale-looking man between fifty and sixty, with an Old Bailey countenance and a very well built wooden leg. The Señora, a pretty girl of seventeen, pouted at the cool reception, for not one

[5] The folly of the United States in accepting the promise of Santa Anna and giving him a passport into Mexico was soon apparent. The former president of Mexico was no sooner back in his country that he repudiated his promise and began raising an army to fight the United States.

viva was heard; and her mother, a fat, vulgar old dame, was rather unceremoniously congeed from the procession, which she took in high dudgeon. The General was dressed in full uniform, and looked anything but pleased at the absence of everything like applause, which he doubtless expected would have greeted him. His countenance completely betrays his character: indeed, I never saw a physiognomy in which the evil passions, which he notoriously possesses, were more strongly marked. Oily duplicity, treachery, avarice, and sensuality are depicted in every feature, and his well-known character bears out the truth of the impress his vices have stamped upon his face. In person he is portly, and not devoid of a certain well-bred bearing which wins for him golden opinions from the surface-seeing fair sex, to whom he ever pays the most courtly attention. . . .

He declares his determination to prosecute to the last the war with the United States, and his willingness to sacrifice his life and fortune in defence of his country. . . .

Two or three days after my arrival in Vera Cruz, suspicious rumours of vomito [a dreaded disease] reached my ears, and caused me to pack my traps; and having determined to ride to Jalapa, instead of travelling by the lumbering *diligencia* [stagecoach], my hospitable entertainers, on learning my intention, immediately made arrangements for a supply of cavalry, and placed me under the charge of a confidential servant of the house, who was to pilot me to Jalapa. . . .

[After traversing *tierra caliente*, "the hot country," or lowlands, they ascended to] beautiful Jalapa, embosomed in mountains and veiled by cloud and mist.

Jalapa, the population of which is nearly 17,000, is situated at the foot of Macultepec, at an elevation of 4,335 feet above the level of the sea. . . .

Near Jalapa are two or three cotton factories, which I believe pay well. They are under the management of English and Americans. The girls employed in the works are all Indians or mestizas, healthy and good-looking. . . .

[Reports of robbers on the road to Puebla caused concern.] Such being the satisfactory state of affairs, before starting on this dangerous expedition, and particularly as I carried all my baggage with me (being too old a soldier ever to part with that), assisted by mine host Don Juan, I had a minute inspection of arms and ammunition, all of which were put in perfect order. One fine morning, therefore, I took my seat in the *diligencia*, with a formidable battery of a double-barrel rifle, a ditto carbine, two brace of pistols, and a blunder-buss. Blank were the faces of my four fellow-passengers when I entered thus equipped. . . .

However, we reached Puebla safe and sound, and drove into the yard of the Fonda de las Diligencias, where the coach and its contents were minutely inspected by a robber-spy, who, after he had counted the passengers and their arms, immediately mounted his horse and galloped away. This is done every day, and in the teeth of the authorities, who wink at the cool proceeding. . . .

Puebla, the capital of the intendancy of that name, is one of the finest cities in Mexico. Its streets are wide and regular, and the houses and public buildings are substantially built and in good taste. The population, which is estimated at between 80,000 and 100,000, is the most vicious and demoralized in the republic. . . .

We left Puebla early in the morning, and, as day broke, a scene of surpassing beauty burst upon us. The sun rising behind the mountains covered the sky with a cold silvery light, against which the peaks stood out in bold relief, whilst the bases were still veiled in gloom. The snow-clad peak of Orizaba, the lofty Popocatepetl, "the hill that smokes," and Iztaccihuatl, "the white woman," lifted their heads now bright with the morning sun. . . .

Passing through a beautiful country, we reached Río Frío, a small plain in the midst of the mountains, and *muy mal punto* for the robbers, as the road winds through a pine forest, into which they can escape in case of repulse. The road is lined with crosses, which here are veritable monuments of murders perpetrated on travellers. . . . We soon after crested the ridge of the mountain, and, descending a winding road, turned an abrupt hill, and, just as I was settling myself in the corner for a good sleep, my arm was seized convulsively by my opposite neighbour, who, with half his body out of the window, vociferated: "*¡'Hi está, 'hi está, mire, por Dios, mire!*"—Look out, for God's sake! there it is. Thinking a *ladrón* [highwayman] was in sight, I seized my gun, but my friend, seeing my mistake, drew in his head, saying, "*¡No, no, Méjico, Méjico, la ciudad!*"

To stop the coach and jump on the box was the work of a moment; and, looking down from the same spot where probably Cortez stood three hundred years ago, before me lay the city and valley of Mexico, bathed by the soft flooding light of the setting sun.

He must be insensible indeed, a clod of clay, who does not feel the blood thrill in his veins at the first sight of this beautiful scene. . . .

The first impression which struck me on seeing the valley of

Mexico was the perfect, almost unnatural, tranquility of the scene. The valley, which is about sixty miles long by forty in breadth, is on all sides enclosed by mountains. . . .

On entering the town, one is struck with the regularity of the streets, the chaste architecture of the buildings, the miserable appearance of the population, the downcast look of the men, the absence of ostentatious display of wealth, and the prevalence of filth which everywhere meet the eye. On every side the passenger is importuned for charity. Disgusting lepers whine for *clacos;* maimed and mutilated wretches, mounted on the backs of porters, thrust out their distorted limbs and expose their sores, urging their human steeds to increase their pace as their victim increases his to avoid them. . . .

Mexico is the headquarters of dirt. The streets are dirty, the houses are dirty, the men are dirty and the women dirtier, and everything you eat and drink is dirty. . . .

The cathedral is a fine large building of incongruous architecture. The interior is rich in silver and gold candlesticks and ornaments of precious metals. It is far inferior to the churches of Catholic Europe. . . . The interior is dark and gloomy, with the usual amount of tinsel and tawdry. . . .[6]

There is little or nothing in the shape of sight-seeing in Mexico. The national museum is worth a visit, as it contains a good collection of Mexican antiquities, of a light and trivial character, however. I have seen no Aztecan remains which impress me with the most distant idea that the ancient Mexicans possessed any of the arts of civilization, or were further advanced than many other nations of ingenious savages, who work in stones and feathers. In the working of stones they were certainly clever, and the wonder is, with the rude instruments they possessed, how they could fashion into any shape the brittle materials they made use of. . . .

Tacubaya is the Richmond of Mexico: villas and country residences abound, where the aristocracy resort during the hot months. The road passes the great aqueduct which supplies the city with water from a spring in Chapultepec. . . . I visited the hill of Chapultepec, celebrated as being the site of Montezuma's palace, on which, towards the close of the seventeenth century, the viceroy Gálvez erected a huge castle, the remains of which are now occupied by the military school.[7]

[6] This great cathedral, although it hardly compares with the best in Europe, is outstanding in America. It occupies one side of the Zocolo, or plaza, and is a principal show place of the city.

Far more interesting than the apocryphal tradition of the Indian's palace, the viceroy's castle, or the existing eyesore, is the magnificent grove of cypress, which outlives all the puny structures of man, and, still in the prime of strength and beauty, looks with contempt on the ruined structures of generation after generation which have passed away. . . .[8]

The private houses of Mexico are well built and commodious. The exteriors of many are chastely and most beautifully decorated, and the rooms are lofty and well proportioned. . . .

The hotels are few and wretchedly bad. The best is La Gran Sociedad, under the same roof with the theatre Nacional, now rechristened of Santa Anna. This is the grand theatre, and is rather a good house, with a company of Spanish comedians. There is also a smaller one, devoted to light comedy and vaudeville. The performers are generally from Havana, and occasionally a "star" arrives from Old Spain.

The streets of Mexico at night present a very animated appearance. In the leading thoroughfares the *tortilleras* displaying their tempting viands, illuminated by the blaze from a *brazero*, which serves to keep the *tortillas* and chile colorado in a proper state of heat. . . .

Red-petticoated *poblanas*, *reboso* wrapped, display their little feet and well-turned ankles as they cross the gutters; and, cigar in mouth, they wend their way to the fandangos of the Barrio de Santa Anna. From every pulque shop is heard the twanging of guitars, and the quivering notes of the *cantadores*, who excite the guests to renewed potations by their songs in praise of the grateful liquor. The popular chorus of one of these is:

> *¿Sabe que es pulque?*
> *¡Licor divino-o!*
> *Lo beben los ángeles*
> *En el sereno-o.*

> *Know ye what pulque is?*
> *Liquor divine!*
> *Angels in heaven*
> *Prefer it to wine.*

[7] Much of the castle of Chapultepec (Grasshopper) is now a historical museum, with the rooms and furnishings of Emperor Maximilian and Carlota as outstanding attractions.

8. The great trees and beautiful woodland park are still admired by modern visitors.

113

Those philosophical strangers who wish to see "life in Mexico" must be careful what they are about, and keep their eyes skinned, as they say in Missouri. . . .

[Ruxton dressed himself as a Mexican and made a round of some amusement places. He visited a pulque shop.]

It was soon known that a foreigner was in the room. In spite of my dress and common sarape, I was soon singled out. Cries of "*Extranjero, Tejano, Yanqui, burro,*" saluted me; I was a Texan, a Yankee, and consequently burro—a jackass. The crowd surrounded me, women pushed through the throng, *a ver el burro*—to look at the jackass—and threats of summary chastisement and ejection were muttered. Seeing that affairs began to look cloudy, I rose, and, placing my hand on my heart, assured the *caballeros y las señoritas* that they laboured under a slight error: that, although my face was white, I was no Texan, neither was I Yankee or a jackass, but "*Ynglés, muy amigo a la república*"— an Englishman, having the welfare of the republic much at heart— and that my affection for them, and hatred of their enemies, was something too excessive to express: that to prove this, my only hope was that they would do me the kindness to discuss at their leisure half an arroba of pulque, which I begged then and there to pay for, and present to them in token of my sincere friendship.

The tables were instantly turned: I was saluted with cries of "*¡Viva el Ynglés! ¡Que meueren los Yanquis! ¡Vivan nostros y pulque!*"—Hurrah for the Englishman! Death to the Yankees! Long live ourselves and pulque! The dirty wretches thronged round me to shake my hand, and semidrunken *poblanas* lavished their embraces on *el güero*. I must here explain that, in Mexico, people with fair hair and complexions are called *güero, güera;* and from the caprice of human nature, the *güero* is always a favourite of the fair sex: the same as, in our country, the olive-coloured foreigners with black hair and beards are thought "such loves" by our fair countrywomen. The *güero*, however, shares this favouritism with the genuine unadulterated negro, who is also greatly admired by the *Mejicanas*. . . .

Society in Mexico, although good, is not much sought after by the foreign residents, who have that resource amongst themselves; neither do the Mexicans themselves care to mix with those out of their own circle. The Mexican ladies are totally uneducated, and in the presence of foreigners, conscious of their inferiority, are usually shy and reserved. . . . As for their personal attractions, I will say, that, although not distinguished for beauty, I never once remember to have seen a really ugly woman. Their brilliant eyes make up for any deficiency of feature, and their figures, uninjured by frightful stays, are full and voluptuous. Now and then, moreover, one does meet with a perfectly beautiful creature; and when a Mexican woman does combine such perfection, she is "some pumpkins," as the Missourians say when they wish to express something superlative in the female line. . . .

After I had been a few days in Mexico I made preparations for my journey to the north. In my search for horses and mules I paid a visit to the horse-dealing establishment of one Smith, a Yankee, and quite a character, who is making a fortune in the trade of horseflesh. His stables are filled with nags of all sorts and sizes, and amongst them were some of General Taylor's troop horses, belonging to a detachment of dragoons which was captured by the Mexicans on the Río Grande. . . .

I selected and purchased two horses from his stud, and better animals never felt a saddle: one [Panchito] I rode upwards of 3,000 miles, and brought it to the end of the journey without flinching; the other, a little blood-horse from the *tierra caliente*, with a coat as fine as silk, I was obliged to part with before entering the intemperate climate of New Mexico, where the cold would have quickly killed it. For mules I visited the Barrio de Santa Anna, the headquarters of the arriero, where I soon provided myself with those useful animals.

The greatest difficulty was to procure servants, who were unwilling to undertake a journey of such length, New Mexico being here quite a terra incognita, and associated with ideas of wild beasts and wilder Indians, and horrors of all sorts. I at length hired a *mozo* to proceed with me as far as Durango, 550 miles from Mexico, and considered the ultima Thule of civilization. He was a tall shambling Mexican, from Puebla; his name, as usual, Jesús María. His certificate of character announced him to be *muy hombre de bien*—very respectable, faithful, and a good road-servant. His wages were one dollar a day and his food—*un peso diario y la comida*—or nearly eighty pounds a year of sterling money.

I was so fortunate as to become acquainted with a young Spaniard who was about to start for the mines of Guadaloupe y Calvo; and as our road as far as Durango was the same, we agreed to travel in company, which was as agreeable on the score of companionship as it was advantageous in point of security against the attacks of robbers, who, in large bands, infest this road. . . .

On the fourteenth of September, just as a salvo of artillery announced the entrance of Santa Anna into the city, our cavalcade, consisting of upwards of twenty horses and mules, packed and loose, sallied out of the north gate, and entered a large common outside the city. . . .

With mules, the first day's start is invariably a scene of the greatest confusion. The animals are wild, the packsaddles have always something wanting, and the *mozos* half drunk and helpless. In a few days, however, everything is shipshape; the mules become as docile as dogs, are packed well and quickly, and proceed along the road in regular order. . . .

To avoid the water-covered plains we took the mountain road, passing through a tract of country covered with lava and scoria, with wild and picturesque scenery. . . .

As we were slowly traversing the rocky sierra, we descried, a few hundred yards ahead of us, a band of seven horsemen drawn up across the road. One of my companion's servants, who had been many years a smuggler on this road, instantly recognised them as a well-known band of robbers; we therefore, as their object was plain, collected our *mulada* into a compact body, and, distributing our party of six, half on each side, we unslung our carbines, threw the flaps off our holsters, and steadily advanced, the Spaniard and myself in front, with our pieces cocked and ready for service. The robbers, however, saw at a glance that two of us were foreigners, for whom and their arms they have a great respect, and, wheeling quickly on one side of the road, they hitched their ready lassos on the horns of their saddles, and, remaining in line, allowed us to pass, saluting us with "*¡Adiós, caballeros, buen viaje!*"—a pleasant journey to you—the leader inquiring of one of the *mozos*, as he passed, whether the *diligencia* was on the road and had many passengers?

They were all superbly mounted, and well armed with carbine, sword, and pistols; and each had a lasso hanging on the horn of his high-peaked saddle. "*Adiós, amigos,*" we said, as we passed them, "*y buena fortuna*"—and good luck this fine morning.

[After five days of travel from Mexico City] . . . we entered a magnificent plain enclosed by mountains, and arrived at Querétaro at two in the afternoon, distant from San Juan del Río forty miles, it being the first town of size or note we had yet seen since leaving Mexico [City].

Querétaro, the chief city of the department of that name, is well built, and contains many handsome churches and other buildings. Its population is over forty thousand, twelve thousand of whom are Indians. It is surrounded by beautiful gardens and orchards, which produce a great quantity of fruit for the market of the capital. It has several cloth factories, which employ a considerable number of Indians, but are not in a very flourishing state. An aqueduct of stone conveys water to the city from some springs in the neighbourhood. Its chief trade is in the manufacture of cigars of the tobacco of the country.

The tobacco, as in France and Spain, is a government monopoly. . . .

The cigars of Querétaro are of a peculiar shape, about three inches long, and square at both ends. To one accustomed to the tobacco of the Havana the pungent flavour of the Querétaro cigars is at first disagreeable, but in a short time the taste acquired for this peculiar raciness renders all other tobacco insipid and tasteless. Excellent pulque is made here; and a beverage called *colinche*, expressed from the juice of the tuna (fruit of the prickly pear), I tasted for the first time. It is of blood-red colour, but of sharp and pleasant flavour.

As we were now in the land par excellence of pulque, the drink of thirsty angels, a short description of this truly national liquor and its manufacture will not be out of place. The maguey, American aloe —*Agave Americana*—is cultivated over an extent of country embracing 50,000 square miles. In the city of Mexico alone the consumption of pulque amounts to the enormous quantity of eleven millions of gallons per annum, and a considerable revenue from its sale is derived by government. The plant attains maturity in a period varying from eight to fourteen years, when it flowers; and it is during the stage of inflorescence only that the saccharine juice is extracted. The central stem which encloses the incipient flower is then cut off near the bottom, and a cavity or basin is discovered, over which the surrounding leaves are drawn close and tied. Into this reservoir the juice distils, which otherwise would have risen to nourish and support the flower. It is removed three or four times during the twenty-four hours, yielding a quantity of liquor varying from a quart to a gallon and a half.

The juice is extracted by means of a syphon made of a species of gourd called *acojote*, one end of which is placed in the liquor, the other in the mouth of a person, who by suction draws up the fluid into the pipe and deposits it in the bowls he has with him for the purpose. It is then placed in earthen jars, and a little old pulque—*madre de pulque*—is added, when it soon ferments, and is immediately ready for use. The fermentation occupies two or three days, and when it ceases the pulque is in fine order.

Old pulque has a slightly unpleasant odour, which heathens have likened to the smell of putrid meat; but, when fresh, is brisk and sparkling, and the most cooling, refreshing, and delicious drink that ever was invented for thirsty mortal; and when gliding down the dust-dried throat of a wayworn traveller, who feels the grateful liquor distilling through his veins, is indeed the "*licor divino*," which Mexicans assert, is preferred by the angels in heaven to ruby wine. . . .

I had intended to remain a day or two in Querétaro, but the town was so crowded with soldiers of the "liberating army," and the accommodation for man and beast at the *mesones* was so execrable, that I determined to proceed at once. . . .

We entered Celaya by a handsome bridge over the Lerma. Inscribed on a stone let into the parapet is a notice to travellers that the good people of Celaya erected this bridge "*por el beneficio de los viajeros*"—for the benefit of the wayfarer—which fact they take care shall not be forgotten.[9] Like all Mexican towns, Celaya is full of churches and *léperos*, and a conspicuous object is the large *colecturía*, a building where the tithes of corn and fruits belonging to the Church are kept. In most villages the *colecturía* stands side by side with the *iglesia* [church], and is invariably the larger building of the two. . . .

The trade of the town consists in the manufacture of saddles, bridles, and articles of leather required for the road. Population about 7,000. Grain of all kinds is most prolific and abundant in the plains of Celaya, and horses and mules are bred in considerable numbers. The distance from Querétaro is thirty-seven miles.

[September] 20th. Leaving Celaya, we passed over a wild and but partially cultivated country, leaving Salamanca on the left. Hares of very large size, and tame as dogs, abound on these plains, and our march today was enlivened by an incessant popping of carbines and rifles. In one patch of mezquit, a thorny shrub very common on the plains, I counted seventy hares in a little glade not one hundred yards square, and they were jumping out of the grass at every step of our animals. We breakfasted at a little Indian village called La Xuage. . . .

The farther we advanced from Mexico the more curious became the provincials in examining *los extranjeros* and their equipments. Our hostess in La Xuage, after she had served the eggs and frijoles, rushed to all her female acquaintance with the news that two strangers were in her house, and *por Dios* that they should come and see the *güero*. As a *güero* I was an object of particular attention. I was examined from head to foot, and the hostess took upon herself to show me off

[9] It was a pleasure in 1947 to cross the bridge and read the same inscription which Ruxton had noted 101 years before.

as a jockey would a horse. My hair was exposed to their wonder and admiration; and, "*Mire*," added my exhibitor, taking me by the moustache, "*mire sus bigotes, son güeros también*"—and do look here, if his *bigotes* are not *güeros* too. "*¡Válgame Dios!*"

Nothing excited the curiosity and admiration of the men so much as the sight of my arms. My double rifle, and servant's double-barreled short carbine and pistols, were handled, and almost worshipped. *Armas tan bonitas* they had never seen. With such weapons, they all agreed, neither Indian nor Texan, nor *el demonio* himself, was to be feared. . . .

After a long journey of nearly fifty miles through an uninteresting country, we arrived at the solitary rancho of Temascatéo, standing alone in a large uninhabited plain. . . .

Mine host of Temascatéo was the beau ideal of a *ventero*. Fat and pulque lined, his heavy head, with large fishy eyes, almost sank into his body, his neck, albeit of stout proportion, being inadequate to support its enormous burden. . . . Asking me all the news of the war, he remarked that *los Tejanos*, as the Americans are called here, were very bad Indians and cannibals; that it was horrible to think of such people taking the country. Much better, he said, if the English, who, he had heard, were a very strong and rich nation, with "*muy poco desorden en su gobierno*"—very little disorder in its government—were to take it; and as England was "*poco mas allá de Méjico*"—only a little the other side of Mexico—in fact, a neighbour, it would not be so bad. . . .

[On September 22, Ruxton travelled the twenty-four miles to Silao and spent most of the day looking for mules.]

After rejecting a hundred at least which were brought for my inspection, I purchased a *tronco*—a pair—of Californian mules, than which no better ever carried saddle or aparejo. This pair, with the two horses I brought with me from Mexico, were the most perfectly enduring animals I ever travelled with. No day was too long, no work too hard, no food too coarse for them. One of the mules, which, from her docility and good temper, I promoted to be my hunting mule, was a short, stumpy animal, with a very large head and long flapping ears. Many a deer and antelope I killed off her back; and, when hunting, I had only to dismount and throw down the lariat on the ground, and she would remain motionless for hours until I returned. These mules became so attached to my horse Panchito, that it was nearly impossible to separate them; and they would follow me like dogs when mounted on his back. They both crossed the grand prairies with me to the Missouri; and when compelled to part them from poor Panchito, I thought their hearts would have broken.

In the *mesón* of Silao we were literally besieged by representatives from every shop in the town, who poured upon us, offering their wares for sale, and every imaginable article required for "the road." This is the custom in all the towns, and shows the scarcity of regular custom. No sooner does a stranger enter a *mesón* than to it flock venders of saddles, bridles, bits, spurs, whips, alforjas, sarapes for yourself, *rebosos* for your ladye-love, sashes, sombreros, boots, silks, and velvets (cotton), and goods of every kind that the town affords. Besides these, Indian women and girls arrive with baskets of fruit—oranges, lemons, grapes, chirimoyas, batatas, platanos, plantains, *camotes, granaditas, mameyes,* tunas, pears, apples, and fruit of every description. Pulque and *colinche* sellers are not wanting, all extolling their goods and pressing them on the unfortunate traveller at the same moment, while *léperos* whine and pray for alms, and *lavanderas* for your clothes to wash, the whole uniting in such a Babel-like din as outbeggars description. Rid yourself of these, and gangs of a more respectable class throng the door for the express purpose of staring; and this is a most ill-bred characteristic of Mexican manners, and one of the greatest of the many annoyances which beset a traveller. Silao is notorious for its population of thieves and robbers, who, it is the boast of the place, are unequaled in audacity as well as dexterity. I saw a striking instance of this. A man entered the corral of the *mesón* and unblushingly offered for sale a pair of wax candles which he had just stolen from a church, boasting of the deed to his worthy companions, who quite approved the feat.

Silao is on the borders of the departments of Guanaxuato and Jalisco, and contains about 5,000 inhabitants. The plains in the vicinity produce abundantly wheat, maize, frijoles, barley, &c., and the soil is admirably adapted for the growth of cotton, tobacco, and cochineal. . . .

22nd. From Silao to La Villa de León the eye looks in vain for signs of cultivation. On these vast plains day after day we met no other travellers than the *arrieros* with their *atajos* of mules from Durango, Zacatecas, and Fresnillo. . . .

23rd. From León the road ascends a sierra, from the top of which is a magnificent view of the plains of Silao. The mule path by which we descended is rough and dangerous, and we had to wait on the summit of the sierra until day dawned before we could with safety undertake the descent. The whole country exhibits traces of volcanic origin. . . . Lagos lies at the foot of another sierra, with a lake in the distance, and seen from this elevation the prospect is very beautiful. . . .

It was a *día de fiesta,* and when we entered Lagos we found the population in great excitement, as on the morrow a *función de toros,* a "bullfight," was to take place, and the *feria,* "annual fair," commenced that very night.

The rancheros with their wives and daughters were pouring into the town from far and near, and we had met on the road many families on their way to the fair, forming a very picturesque cavalcade. First the ranchero himself, the pater familias, in glossy sombrero with its gold or silver rolls, *calzoneras* glittering with many buttons, and snow-white drawers of Turkish dimensions, mounted on a showy horse gaily caparisoned, and bearing on its croup the smiling, smirking dame in span-new *reboso* and red or yellow *enagua.* Next a horse-load or two of *muchachitas,* their brown faces peeping from the *reboso,* showing their black eyes and white teeth, as, shining with anticipated delight of the morrow's festivities, and in a state of perfect happiness and enjoyment, they return their acknowledgments to the compliments of the passing *caballeros.* These, in all the glory of Mexican dandyism, armed with *escopeta* and *machete* (sword), and the ever-ready lasso hanging from the saddlebow, escorted the party caracolling along on their prancing steeds.

The *diques*—streams which run through the streets—were full of women and girls undergoing preparatory ablution, and dressing their long black hair with various unguents at the side of the water. Pedlers were passing from house to house offering for sale gaudy ornaments to the women, earrings of gold and silver and coloured glass, beads of coral and shell from California, amulets and love-charms from the capital, indulgences for peccadilloes committed on the morrow, and suitable for the occasion, the which were in great demand. . . .

24th. We left Lagos for La Villa de la Encarnación, through a barren and uninteresting country, destitute of trees, and the vegetation sparse and burned up. The road was up and down sierras the whole day, scattered with *nopal* and prickly pear; the heat tremendous, and the sun's rays, reverberated from the rocky sierra, fiery and scorching. . . .

25th. To Aguas Calientes, a very pretty town, with some handsome buildings. We met a gipsying or pic-nic party on the road, mounted on *borricos,* with a mule packed with comestibles. A bevy of very pretty girls brought up the rear, under the escort of half a dozen exquisites of the town, got up in the latest fashion of the capital. Their monopoly of such a fair troop was not to be borne, and with tolerable impudence we stopped the party. The dandies, from our sunburnt and road-stained appearance and bristling arms, at once set us down as robbers, and without more ado turned their donkeys and retreated, leaving us masters of the field and the fair. With them our peace was soon made, and we received a pressing invitation to join the party, which, however, we were fain to decline, as our horses were sorely tired. They laughed heartily at the panic of their gallant escort, who were huddled together at a little distance, not knowing whether to advance or retreat. I sent my *mozo* to them to say that the ladies required their presence; and we rode on to the town, where we found our *mulada* arrived and waiting our approach. . . .

25th. [*sic*] To the hacienda of La Punta, in a large plain where are several other plantations, and two rancherias celebrated as being the abode of a band of robbers called *picos largos*, "long-bills." In this day's journey of forty miles one of the horses died from fatigue and heat, and two others were scarcely able to finish the day's journey.

26th. To Zacatecas, through wild uncultivated plains and sierras. On the road we passed some abandoned copper mines, where an old Indian was picking for stray pieces of ore, of which a dream had promised the discovery.

CHAPTER 7

A Journey Through North Mexico

Z ACATECAS, a populous city of between 30,000 and 40,000 inhabitants, is in the midst of one of the most valuable mining districts in Mexico. The country round it is wild and barren, but the rugged sierras teem with the precious metals. Near the town are several lakes or lagunes, which abound in muriate and carbonate of soda. The town itself is mean and badly built, the streets narrow and dirty, and the population bear a very bad character; which indeed is the case in all the mining towns in the country, which is but natural from the very nature of their employment.

From this point the *novedades* [news] poured upon us daily: "*¡Los Indios, los Indios!*" was the theme of every conversation. Thus early (it was a very early Indian season this year and the last) they had made their appearance in the immediate vicinity of Durango, killing the *paisanos*, and laying waste the haciendas and ranchos; and it was supposed they would penetrate even farther into the interior. What a *cosa de Méjico* is this fact! Five hundred savages depopulating a *soi-disant* civilised country, and with impunity!

27th. The road from Zacatecas to Fresnillo lies through a wild uncultivated country without inhabitants. We met a *conducta* from the mines of Fresnillo, bearing bars of silver to the mint at Zacatecas. The waggon in which it was carried was drawn by six mules galloping at their utmost speed. Eight or ten men, with muskets between their knees, sat in the waggon, facing outwards, and as many more galloped alongside, armed to the teeth. Bands of robbers, three or four hundred strong, have been known to attack *conductas* from the mines, even when escorted by soldiers, engaging them in a regular stand-up fight.

Fresnillo is a paltry dirty town, with the neighbouring sierra honeycombed with mines, which are rich and yield considerable profits. A share which the government had in these mines yielded an annual revenue of nearly half a million dollars; but that short-sighted vampire, which sucks the blood of poor Mexico, eager to possess all the golden eggs at once, sold its interest for less than one year's income. *Cosa de Méjico*, here as everywhere!

We were here very kindly invited to take up our abode during our stay, in the hacienda of the mines; the administrator of which is an American, and the officers mostly Spaniards. Enjoying their hospitality, we spent two or three days very pleasantly, and were initiated into all the mysteries of mining. The process of extracting the metal from the ore is curious in the extreme, but its description would require more science than I possess, and more space than I am able to afford. Two thousand mules are at daily work in the *hacienda de beneficios*, and 2,500 men are employed in the mines. From this an idea may be formed of the magnitude of the works. The main shaft is 1200 feet in depth, and a huge engine is constantly employed removing water from the mines. This vast mass of machinery appeared to take care of itself, for I saw neither engineers nor others in the engine house. There are many Cornishmen employed in the mines, who drink and fight considerably, but withal find time to perform double as much work as the Mexicans. The patio, or yard, of the *hacienda de beneficios*, where the porphyritic crushing-mills are at work, contain 32,000 square yards. In undergoing one process, the crushed ore, mixed with copper and salt, is made into enormous mud puddings, and trodden out by mules, which are back deep in the paste; indeed, the whole process of the *beneficio*, a purely chemical one, is most curious and worthy of attention. . . .

On the thirtieth we left Fresnillo, having a journey of fifty-five miles before us to Zaina. The country is desolate and totally uncultivated, excepting here and there where a solitary hacienda or rancho is seen; these are all fortified, for we were now entering the districts which are annually laid waste by the Comanches. The haciendas are all surrounded by walls and flanked with towers loopholed for musketry. A man is always stationed on an eminence in the vicinity, mounted on a fleet horse, on the lookout for Indians; and on their approach a signal is given, and the *peones*, the labourers employed in the milpas [cornfields], run with their families to the hacienda, and the gates are then closed and preparations made for defence.

This morning I gave my horse Panchito a run, *suelto*, amongst the mules and loose animals, mounting Bayou Lobo, the *tierra caliente* horse which gave my *mozo* so severe a fall the day we left the capital.

I had dismounted to tighten the girths a short time after leaving Fresnillo, and before daylight, when, on remounting, the animal as usual
set off full gallop, and, being almost imprisoned in my sarape, which
confined my arms and legs, in endeavouring to throw my right leg
over the saddle I pitched over on the other side and fell upon the top
of my head, at the same moment that the horse kicked out and struck
with great force on my left ear. I lay in the road several hours perfectly insensible; my servant imagined I was dead, and, dragging me
on one side, rode on to overtake the Spaniard. However, showing
signs of life, they placed me again in the saddle, and I rode on for
several hours in a state of unconsciousness. My jaw was knocked on
one side, and when I recovered I had hard work to pull it into its
former position: for days, however, I was unable to open it further
than to admit a fork or a spoon; and as I had to ride forty-five miles
the same day that I met with the accident, and under a burning sun,
I thought myself fortunate in not being disabled altogether.

Zaina is a very pretty little town surrounded with beautiful gardens. It is an isolated spot, and has little or no communication with
other towns.

Oct. 1st. To Sombrerete, distance thirty-four miles. The country became wilder, with less fertile soil, and entirely depopulated, as
much from fear of Indians as from its natural unproductiveness.
Sombrerete was once a mining place of some importance, and the
Casa de la Diputación de Mineria, a large handsome building, is conspicuous in the town. The sierra is still worked, but the veins are not
productive. The *veta negra de Sombrerete*, the famous black vein of
Sombrerete, yielded the greatest *bonanzas* of any mine on the continent of America. It is now exhausted.

2nd. We left the usual road and struck across the country to
the hacienda de San Nicolás, as I was desirous of passing through the
tract of country known as the Mal País, a most interesting volcanic
region, a perfect terra incognita even to Mexicans; and as to travellers,
such *rarae aves* are as little known in these parts as in Timbuctoo. We
journeyed through a perfect wilderness of sierra, and chaparral thickly covered with *nopales* and mezquit, which now became the characteristic tree. The high rank grass was up to our horses' bellies, and,
matted with the bushes of mezquit and prickly pear, was difficult
to make our way through. Hares and rabbits, and javali, a species of
wild hog, abounded, with quail and partridge, and many varieties of
pigeons and doves. . . .

The hacienda de San Nicolás is one of those enormous estates which abound in every part of Mexico, and which sometimes contain sixty or eighty square miles of land. Of course not a hundredth part is under cultivation; but on some, immense herds of horses, mules, and cattle roam almost wild, or rather *did* roam, for the Indians have carried off incredible numbers. The hacienda itself is generally surrounded by the huts of the *peones*. The labourers who are employed on the plantation exist in a kind of serfdom to the owners, and their collection of adobe hovels forms almost a town of itself. The *haciendados* live in almost feudal state, having their hundreds of retainers, and their houses fortified to repel the attacks of Indians or other enemies. . . .

3rd. Our road lay through the Mal Pais—the evil land, as volcanic regions are called by the Mexicans—which has the appearance of having been, at a comparatively recent period, the theatre of volcanic convulsions of an extraordinary nature. . . . In the lonely regions of the Mal Pais, the superstitious Indian believes that demons and gnomes, and spirits of evil purposes have their dwelling places, whence they not unfrequently pounce upon the solitary traveller, and bear him into the cavernous bowels of the earth. . . .

We arrived at the rancho of La Punta in the afternoon, in time to witness the truly national sport of the *coléa de toros*—in English, bull-tailing—for which some two or three hundred rancheros were assembled from the neighbouring plantations.

This rancho, in the fall of last year, was visited by the Comanches, who killed several of the unfortunate *peones*, whom they caught in the road and at work in the milpas, and carried off all the stock belonging to the farm. On the spot where the rancheros were killed and scalped, crosses are erected, and the little piles of stones, which almost bury them, testify to the numerous Ave Marías and Pater Nosters which their friends have uttered when passing, in prayer for their souls in purgatory, and for each prayer have deposited at the foot of the cross the customary stone. . . .

In a large corral, at one end of which was a little building, erected for the accommodation of the lady spectators, were enclosed upwards of a hundred bulls. Round the corral were the horsemen, all dressed in the picturesque Mexican costume, examining the animals as they were driven to and fro in the enclosure, in order to make them wild for the sport—*alzar el coraje*. The ranchero himself, and his sons, were riding amongst them, armed with long lances, separating from the herd, and driving into another enclosure, the most active bulls. When all was ready, the bars were withdrawn from the entrance of the corral, and a bull driven out, who, seeing the wide level plain before him, dashed off at the top of his speed. With a shout, the horsemen pursued the flying animal, who, hearing the uproar behind him, redoubled his speed. Each urges his horse to the utmost, and strives to take the lead and be the first to reach the bull. In such a crowd, of course, first-rate horsemanship is required to avoid accidents and secure a safe lead. For some minutes the troop ran on in a compact mass—a sheet could have covered the lot. Enveloped in a cloud of dust, nothing could be seen but the bull, some hundred yards ahead, and the rolling cloud. Presently, with a shout, a horseman emerged from the front rank; the women cried "!viva!" as, passing close to the stage, he was recognized to be the son of the ranchera, a boy of twelve years of age, sitting his horse like a bird, and swaying from side to side as the bull doubled, and the cloud of dust concealed the animal from his view. "¡Viva Pepito! viva!" shouted his mother, as she waved her reboso, to encourage the boy; and the little fellow struck his spurs into his horse and doubled down to his work manfully. But now two others are running neck and neck with him, and the race for the lead, and the first throw, is most exciting. The men shout, the women wave their rebosos and cry out their names: "¡Alza —Bernardo—Por mi amor, Juan María—Viva Pepitito!" they scream in intense excitement. The boy at length loses the lead to a tall fine-looking Mexican, mounted on a fleet and powerful roan stallion, who gradually, but surely, forges ahead. At this moment the sharp eyes of little Pepe observed the bull to turn at an angle from his former course, which movement was hidden by the dust from the leading horseman. In an instant the boy took advantage of it, and wheeling his horse at a right angle from his original course, cut off the bull. Shouts and vivas rent the air at sight of this skilful manoeuvre, and the boy, urging his horse with whip and spur, ranged up to the left quarter of the bull, bending down to seize the tail, and secure it under his right leg, for the purpose of throwing the animal to the ground. But here Pepe's strength failed him in a feat which requires great power of muscle, and in endeavouring to perform it he was jerked out of his saddle, and fell violently to the ground, stunned and senseless. At least a dozen horsemen were now striving hard for the post of honour, but the roan distanced them all, and its rider, stronger than Pepe, dashed up to the bull, threw his right leg over the tail, which he had seized in his right hand, and, wheeling his horse suddenly outwards, upset the bull in the midst of his career, and the huge animal rolled over and over in the dust, bellowing with pain and fright.

This exciting but dangerous sport exhibits the perfect horsemanship of the Mexicans to great advantage. Their firm yet graceful seat
excels everything I have seen in the shape of riding, and the perfect
command which they have over their horses renders them almost a
part of the animals they ride. Their seat is quite different from the
"park-riding" of Mexico. The sport of *coléa* lasts as long as a bull
remains in the corral, so that at the conclusion, as may be imagined,
the horses are perfectly exhausted.

Another equestrian game is *el gallo*—the cock. In this cruel sport,
an unfortunate rooster is tied by the legs to a tree, or to a picket
driven in the ground, with its head or neck well greased. The horsemen, starting together, strive to be the first to reach the bird, and,
seizing it by the neck, to burst the thongs which secure it, and ride
off with the prize. The well-greased neck generally slips through
the fingers of the first who lay hold of it; but as soon as one is in
possession, he rides off, pursued by the rest, whose object is to rescue
the fowl. Of course in the contest which ensues the poor bird is torn
to pieces, the scraps of the body being presented by the fortunate pos-
sessors as a *gâge d'amour* to their mistresses. . . .

Oct. 4th. At daybreak we came to a river, which in the absence
of a ferry, we swam with all our animals, both packed and loose. We
passed through a flat country, entirely inundated, and alive with geese
and gruyas. The latter bird, of the crane species, is a characteristic
feature in the landscape of this part of Mexico. The cornfields are
visited by large flocks,`and as they fly high in the air, their peculiar
melancholy note is constantly heard, both in the day and night, booming over the plains.

Durango, the metropolis of northern Mexico, is situated near the
root of the Sierra Madre, at the northwestern corner of a large plain,
poorly cultivated and sparsely inhabited. It is a picturesque city, with
two or three large churches and some government buildings "fair to
the eye but foul within," with a population of eighteen thousand,
seventeen thousand of whom are rogues and rascals. Like all other
Mexican cities, it is extremely dirty in the exterior, but the houses are
clean and tidy within, always excepting government buildings. It is
celebrated for its scorpions and bad pulque, and the enormous mass
of malleable iron which rises isolated in the plain, about three miles
from the town. . . .

Durango is distant from the city of Mexico 500 miles in a due
course, or as the bird flies. . . .

Snow falls here occasionally, and the mercury is sometimes seen below the freezing point. For the greater part of the year, however, the heat is excessive, when a low intermittent fever is prevalent, but rarely fatal.

Durango is the seat of a bishopric, and the worthy prelate lately undertook a journey to Santa Fé, in New Mexico, which progress created a furore amongst the devout; and the good old man was glad to return with any hem to his garment, so great was the respect paid to him. That he escaped the Apaches and Comanches is attributed to a miracle: the unfaithful assign the glory to his numerous escort—¿Quién sabe? . . .

There is an English merchant in Durango, and one or two Germans and Americans. Their hospitality is unbounded. There is also a mint, the *administrador* of which is a German gentleman, who has likewise established a cotton factory near the city, which is a profitable concern; *y de más*—and moreover—*las Durangüenas son muy halagüeñas*—the ladies of Durango are very pretty.

I stayed in the house of the widow of a *gachupín*, whose motherly kindness to me, and excellent cooking taught her by her defunct *esposo*, is one of the most pleasurable *memorias* I bear with me from Mexico, where a bastard and miserable imitation of the inimitable Spanish cuisine exists in all its deformity. . . .

The city of Durango may be considered as the ultima Thule of the civilised portion of Mexico. Beyond it, to the north and northwest, stretch away the vast uncultivated and unpeopled plains of Chihuahua, the Bolsón de Mapimí, and the arid deserts of the Gila. In the oases of these, wild and hostile tribes of Indians have their dwelling places, from which they continually descend upon the border settlements and haciendas, sweeping off the herds of horses and mules, and barbarously killing the unarmed peasantry. . . . The Apaches, whose country borders upon the department of Durango, are untiring and incessant in their hostility against the whites; and, being near neighbours, are enabled to act with great rapidity and unawares against the haciendas and ranchos on the frontier. They are a treacherous and cowardly race of Indians, and seldom attack even the Mexicans save by treachery and ambuscade. . . . The animals they have stolen in Durango and Chihuahua they find a ready market for in New Mexico and Sonora; and this traffic is most unblushingly carried on, and countenanced by the authorities of the respective states.

But the most formidable enemy, and most feared and dreaded by the inhabitants of Durango and Chihuahua, are the warlike Comanches, who, from their distant prairie country beyond the Del Norte and Río Pecos, at certain seasons of the year, and annually, undertake regularly organised expeditions into these states, and frequently far into the interior (as last year to the vicinity of Sombrerete), for the purpose of procuring animals and slaves, carrying off the young boys and girls, and massacring the adults in the most wholesale and barbarous manner.

So regular are these expeditions, that in the Comanche calendar the month of September is known as the "Mexico moon," as the other months are designated the buffalo moon, the young bear moon, the corn moon, &c. . . .

In the fall of last year, 1845, and at the present moment, 1846, the Indians have been more audacious than ever was known in previous years. It may be that in the present instance they are rendered more daring by the knowledge of the war between the United States and Mexico, and the supposition that the troops would consequently be withdrawn from the scene of their operations. They are now (September) overrunning the whole department of Durango and Chihuahua, have cut off all communication, and defeated in two pitched battles the regular troops sent against them. Upwards of ten thousand head of horses and mules have already been carried off, and scarcely has a hacienda or rancho on the frontier been unvisited, and everywhere the people have been killed or captured. The roads are impassable, all traffic is stopped, the ranchos barricaded, and the inhabitants afraid to venture out of their doors. The posts and expresses travel at night, avoiding the roads, and intelligence is brought in daily of massacres and harryings. . . .

As Durango may be called the limit of Mexico proper and its *soi-disant* civilization, it may not be out of place to take a hasty glance at the general features of the country, the social and moral condition of the people, and the impressions conveyed to my mind in my journey through it.

There are many causes, physical and moral, which prevent Mexico from progressing in prosperity and civilization. . . .

The entire population is about eight millions, of which three-fifths are Indians, or of Indian origin, and Indios Bravos, or barbarous tribes; the remainder of Spanish descent. This population is scattered over an area of 1,312,850 square miles, in departments widely separated, and having various and distinct interests, the intercommunication insecure, and a large proportion in remote regions, beyond the care or thought of an impotent government. . . .

I believe the capabilities of the whole country to be much over-rated, although its mineral wealth alone must always render it of great importance. . . .

The Mexicans, as a people, rank decidedly low in the scale of humanity. They are deficient in moral as well as physical organization. . . .

The present would-be republican form of government is not adapted to such a population as exists in Mexico, as is plainly evident in the effects of the constantly recurring revolutions. Until a people can appreciate the great principles of civil and religious liberty, the advantages of free institutions are thrown away upon them. A long minority has to be passed through before this can be effected; and in this instance, before the requisite fitness can be attained, the country will probably have passed from the hands of its present owners to a more able and energetic race. On the subject of government I will not touch: I maintain that the Mexicans are incapable of *self*-government, and will always be so until regenerated. The separation from Spain has been the ruin of the country, which, by the by, is quite ready to revert to its former owners; and the prevailing feeling over the whole country, inclines to the re-establishment of a monarchial system. . . .

The population is divided into but two classes—the high and the low: there is no intermediate rank to connect the two extremes, and consequently the hiatus between them is deep and strongly marked. The relation subsisting between the peasantry and the wealthy *hacien-dados*, or landowners, is a species of serfdom, little better than slavery itself. Money, in advance of wages, is generally lent to the peon or labourer, who is by law bound to serve the lender, if required, until such time as the debt is repaid; and as care is taken that this shall never happen, the debtor remains a bondsman to the day of his death.

Law or justice hardly exists in name even, and the ignorant peas-antry, under the priestly thraldom which holds them in physical as well as moral bondage, have neither the energy nor courage to stand up for the amelioration of their condition, or the enjoyment of that liberty which it is the theoretical boast of republican governments their system so largely deals in, but which, in reality, is a practical falsehood and delusion.

On the tenth I left Durango for Chihuahua and New Mexico, taking with me the *mozo* I have before mentioned as bearing any-thing but a good character. The first day's march led through a wild uncultivated country, with large plains of excellent pasture, but not a symptom of cultivation. We stopped at night at the hacienda of El Chorro, a little hamlet of adobe huts surrounding the *casa grande* of the plantation. . . .

11th. To the rancho of Los Sauces—the willows. The plains today were covered with cattle, and horses and mules. . . .

12th. To the rancho of Yerbaniz, through the same uncultivated plains, surrounded by sierras, and passing by a ridge from one into another, each being as like the other as twins. For a thousand miles the aspect of these plains never varied, and the sketch of the plain of Los Sauces would answer for the plain of El Paso, and every intermediate one between Durango and New Mexico. At daybreak this morning I descried three figures, evidently armed and mounted men, descending a ridge and advancing towards me. As in this country to meet a living soul on the road is perhaps to meet an enemy thirsting for your property or your life, I stopped my animals, and uncovering my rifle, rode on to reconnoitre. The strangers also halted on seeing me, and, again moving on when they saw me alone, we advanced, cautiously and prepared, towards each other. As they drew near I at once saw by the heavy rifle which each carried across his saddlebow that they were from New Mexico, and that one was a white man. He proved to be a German named Spiers,[1] who was on his way to the fair of San Juan with a caravan of nearly forty waggons loaded with merchandise from the United States. He had left the frontier of Missouri in May, crossing the grand prairies to Santa Fé, and, learning that his American teamsters would not be permitted to enter Durango, he had ridden on in advance to obtain permission for their admittance. His waggons had been nearly six months on the road, travelling the whole time, and were now a few miles behind them. He gave a dismal account of the state of the country through which I was about to pass. The Comanches were everywhere, and two days before had killed two of his men; and not a soul ventured out of his house in that part of the country. He likewise said it was impossible that I could reach Chihuahua alone and urged me strongly to return. The runaway governor of New Mexico, General Armijo,[2] was travelling in

---

[1] This was Albert Speyer, a well-known trader of the Southwest. He was a native of Prussia, who came to the United States and engaged in trade over the Santa Fé Trail. He had hurried his wagon train across the plains ahead of the American troops, pushing on to Chihuahua, and deep into Mexico. He sold goods at Durango and at the Fair of San Juan de los Lagos. J. J. Webb, who accompanied Speyer on this trip, tells of meeting Ruxton.—*Adventures in the Santa Fé Trade, 1844–1847* (Ralph P. Bieber, ed.), 238–40.

company with his caravan, on his way to Mexico, to give an account of shameful cowardice in surrendering Santa Fé to the Americans without a show of resistance.

A little farther on I saw a long line of waggons, like ships at sea, crossing a plain before me. They were all drawn by teams of eight fine mules, and under the charge and escort of some thirty strapping young Missourians, each with a long heavy rifle across his saddle. I stopped and had a long chat with Armijo, who, a mountain of fat, rolled out of his American dearborn, and inquired the price of cotton goods in Durango, he having some seven waggonloads with him, and also what they said, in Mexico, of the doings in Santa Fé, alluding to its capture by the Americans without any resistance. I told him that there was but one opinion respecting it expressed all over the country —that General Armijo and the New Mexicans were a pack of arrant cowards, to which he answered, "¡Adios! They don't know that I had but seventy-five men to fight three thousand. What could I do?" Twenty-one of the teamsters belonging to this caravan had left it a few days previously, with the intention of returning to the United States by the way of Texas. What became of them will be presently narrated.

After leaving the caravan I saw a herd of *berendos* (antelope) in the plain, but was unable to get within shot, the ground being destitute of cover and the animals very wild. We were now in the country of large game, deer and antelope being abundant in the plains, and bears occasionally met with in the sierras.

This night I encamped near a rancho, being refused admittance into the building, and picqueted my animals around the camp. . . .

The ranchos and haciendas in Durango and Chihuahua are all enclosed by a high wall, flanked at the corners by circular bastions loopholed for musketry. The entrance is by a large gate, which is closed at night; and on the *azotea*, or flat roof of the building, a sentry is constantly posted day and night. Round the corral are the dwellings of the *peones;* the *casa grande*, or proprietor's house, being generally at one end, and occupying one or more sides of the square. In this instance I was refused admittance into the enclosure—for what reason I do not know. . . .

13th. To La Noria Perdizenia, forty miles; the country getting more wild and desolate, and entirely destitute of water. Not a sign of habitation, or a human being on the road. . . .

[2] For an account of Governor Manuel Armijo's varied career, see R. E. Twitchell, *Leading Facts of New Mexican History.*

When I arrived at La Noria, I rode into the square and found the inhabitants in the greatest alarm and dismay. They had been expecting the Indians for some days, as they had already committed several atrocities in the neighbouring ranchos. The women were weeping and flying about in every direction, hiding their children and valuables, barricading the houses, and putting what few arms they could collect in the hands of the reluctant men. As I rode through the village seeking a corral for my animals, a woman ran out of a house and begged me to enter, offering her stable, and corn, and straw for the beasts, and the best her house afforded for myself. I gladly accepted her hospitality and followed her into a neat, clean little house, with a corral full of fig trees and grapevines, and a large yard with a pond of water in the centre, and a stack of *hoja* at one end, promising well for the comfort of the tired animals.

"Ah!" she exclaimed on my entering, "*gracias a Dios*, I have someone to protect the lone widow and her fatherless children. If the savages come now, I don't care, since we have good arms in the house, and those *qui saben manejarlos*—who know how to use them."

. . .

The next morning I resumed my journey, much to the surprise of the people of La Noria, who looked upon us as lost, and, crossing the Nasas beyond the hacienda of El Conejo (the rabbit), intended to go on some leagues farther, when I met some waggons belonging to a Frenchman of Chihuahua; and, as he was brimful of *novedades*, I returned and camped with them near the hacienda, to hear the news. The Comanches, he said, were in great force beyond the village of El Gallo, and were killing and slaying in every direction. They had, a few days before, attacked a company of bullfighters under a *gachupín* named Bernardo, on their way to the fair of El Valle de San Bartólomo, killing seven of them and wounding all the others. They had also had a fight with the troops at the Río Florido, killing seventeen and wounding many more.

On the sixteenth I reached El Gallo (the cock), where the Indians three days before had killed two men belonging to Spiers' caravan, within a hundred yards of the village. The road from El Conejo for forty miles passes through a most dismal country, and was crossed several times by the Indian trail. I had now to keep a sharp lookout, as there was no doubt that they were in the neighbourhood, and presently I had ocular proof of their recent presence. We were passing through a chaparral of mezquit, where the road passes near a point of rocks, on which were seated hundreds of *sopilotes* [buzzards].

About a dozen of these birds flew up from the side of the road, and, turning my horse to the spot, I found they had been collected on the dead body of a Mexican, partly stripped, and the breast displaying several ghastly wounds. The head had been scalped, and a broken arrow still remained buried in the face, or rather what remained of it, for the eyes and part of the brain had been already picked out by the *sopilotes*, and a great part of the body devoured. . . .

I stayed at El Gallo in the house of a farmer who had lost three sons by the Indians within a few years. Two of their widows, young and handsome, were in the house, and he himself had been severely wounded by them on several occasions. Their corn was now ready for cutting, but they were afraid to venture outside the village, and procured enough for their daily consumption by collecting together all the villagers and proceeding to the fields in a body to bring in a supply. I remained here for two days, as one of my mules was seriously lame, during which time my chief occupation was sitting with the family, shelling corn, and *platicando* (chatting). In the evening a guitar was brought, and a fandango got up for my especial amusement. . . .

While here I assisted in the erection of two wooden crosses on the spot where Spiers' men were killed by the Comanches three days before. They had remained behind the caravan to bring some bread that was baking for the party, when just outside the town they were set upon by the Indians and killed.

In Durango and the neighbouring state of Chihuahua, the rancherias are supplied with such simple goods as they require by small traders, resident in the capitals of these states, who trade from one village to another with two or three waggons, which, when their goods are sold, they freight with supplies for the cities or the mines. These traders are all foreigners—French, Germans, English, and Americans; and their adventures and hairbreadth escapes, while passing through the country overrun by Indians, are often most singular and exciting. Their arrivals in the villages are always welcome, as then the *muchachas* make their purchases of *rebosos* and gay *enaguas*, and the *majos*, their sarapes and sashes.

The night before my departure from El Gallo, I was sitting in the corral *platicando*, while all the family were busy as usual corn-shelling, when a loud voice was heard, a cracking of whips, and cries of wo-ha wo-ha-a wo-o-h-ha!

"*¡Extranjeros!*" exclaimed one of the girls.

"*¡Los Tejanos!*" exclaimed another.

"*Los carros*—the waggons," said Don José, and I threw my sarape over my shoulder, and, proceeding to the open space in the centre of the village, dignified by the name of plaza, found four waggons just arrived, and the teamsters unhitching the mules. They proved to be the caravan of one Davy Workman, an Englishman by birth, but long resident in, and a citizen of, the United States; a tall, hard-featured man, and most determined in look, as he was known to be in character —*un hombre muy bien conocido*, as my *patrón* informed me. By this arrival more *novedades* were brought, and ¡*los Indios, los Indios!* were on everybody's tongue.

Señor Ángel, my *mozo*, here openly rebelled, and refused to proceed farther; but a promise of a few extra dollars at length induced him to agree to accompany me as far as Mapimí, sixty-five miles from El Gallo, and situated on what is called the frontier.

From El Gallo to Mapimí a mule track leads the traveller through a most wild and broken country, perfectly deserted; rugged sierras rising from the mezquit-covered plains, which are sterile and entirely destitute of water. . . .

I had resolved to pass through this part of the country, although far out of the beaten track, in order to visit El Real de Mapimí, a little town, near a sierra which is said to be very rich in ore; and also for the purpose of travelling through a tract of country laid waste by the Comanches. . . .

It was ten at night when we reached Mapimí. . . . The mules and horses properly cared for, I rolled myself in my blanket in the middle of the street, and went supperless to sleep, after a ride of sixty-five miles.

El Real de Mapimí is situated on a plain at the foot of a mountain called, from its supposed resemblance to a purse, the Bolsón de Mapimí. . . . My impression is that the mines of Mapimí, if properly worked, would be the most productive in the country; and the transportation of machinery, by way of the Río Grande and Monclova, would be practicable, and attended with comparatively little expense. The town itself is merely a collection of adobe houses, and, with the exception of a cotton factory, the superintendent of which is an Englishman, possesses no trade of any description. . . . Between Mapimí and Chihuahua is a large unpeopled tract of country called the *travesía;* it once possessed several thriving villages and ranchos, now deserted and in ruins, where the Indians resort during their incursions, and leave their tired animals to be recruited in the pastures which have sprung up on the once cultivated fields, removing them on their return. . . .

Here I gave my *mozo*, Ángel, his *congé*, and picked up, much to my astonishment, a little Irishman, who had been eighteen years in Mexico, during which time he had passed over nearly the whole republic, excepting New Mexico. He had lost all traces of his Milesian descent, being in character, manners, and appearance a perfect Mexican, and had almost forgotten his own language. Indians, moreover, had no terrors for him, and he at once agreed to accompany me to Chihuahua. . . .

One event occurred in Mapimí which annoyed me excessively. The night of my arrival, my animals, I fear, were rather scantily supplied with corn; and to revenge the slight, the mules ate the tail of my beautiful Panchito to the very dock—a tail which I had tied, and combed, and tended with the greatest care and affection. In the morning I hardly recognised the animal. . . . The tails of the mules were at the end of my journey picked like a bone, for whenever their supper was poor, they immediately fell to work on each other's tails. . . .

On the twenty-third I left Mapimí, the whole population, I do believe, turning out to see me put my head in the lion's mouth. For thirty-six miles we travelled through an arid chaparral, when, towards sunset, we entered into a more open plain, where we saw the ruined houses of Jarral Grande. The houses had been built round a large open space covered with grass, each one standing in a garden. At the entrance of the village, and scattered along the road, was a perfect forest of crosses, many of them thrown down or mutilated by the Indians. The houses were most of them tumbling to pieces, but some were still entire. The gardens, overrun with a wilderness of weeds, still contained flowers, and melon vines crept from the enclosures out into the green. In one house that I entered, a hare was sitting on the threshold, and some leverets were inside; and on the flat *azotea* of another sat a large cat. The walls, too, of the ruined houses were covered with creepers, which hung from the broken roofs and about the floors. . . .

We took the animals down to the arroyo near the village, and, rifle in hand, watched them as they drank. In the sand at the edge of the stream were numerous marks of horses' feet and mocassin tracks fresh and recent. The Indians had been there that morning, and might very probably return, so it behooved us to be on the watch. We therefore picqueted the mules and horses in the open space in the middle of the village, while we ourselves retreated to the shelter and shadow of a house within pistol-shot, whence we could command all the approaches to the green without being ourselves seen, one standing sentry while the other slept. . . .

We were in our saddles before sunrise, and with great difficulty made our way in the dark through the thick chaparral. On approaching a stream called Arroyo de los Indios, or Indian River, I had been warned to be on the lookout, as that stream was a favourite stopping-place of the Indians. . . .

We had another night of watchfulness, or rather half a night, for shortly after midnight we again packed the mules and started. This I did on account of the greater security of travelling at night, and in order to reach Jarral Chiquito, if possible, before sunrise, when, if Indians had been encamped there, as was more than probable, we might escape before we were observed. The distance from Jarral Grande to Arroyo de los Indios was forty miles, and from that river to Jarral Chiquito, or Little Jarral, the same. The latter place was also a noted stopping-place of the Indians. . . .

We reached Jarral Chiquito shortly after sunrise, and I rode on to reconnoitre. No Indians were there, but plenty of "sign." The village was situated on a hill, near a small spring of salitose water, round which grows a clump of cottonwoods, a species of poplar (alamo). The village had been entirely burned by the Indians, with the exception of one house which was still standing, the roof of which they had torn off, and from the upper walls had shot down with arrows all the inmates. Inside were the skeleton of a dog and several human bones. A dreary stillness reigned over the whole place, unbroken by any sound save the croaking of a bullfrog in the spring, round which we encamped for a few hours. At noon we again started, and travelled on till nearly dark, when we encamped in the middle of a bare plain, without water for the animals or wood with which to make a fire. . . .

On the twenty-sixth at daybreak we were packed and off, and, after a journey of forty miles, to our great satisfaction we struck the settlements of Guajoquilla. . . .

Guajoquilla is a pretty, quaint little town, with its whitewashed adobe houses, and looking clean and neat. The arrival of strangers, and in such an extraordinary garb, and moreover evidently from the *travesía* and Mapimí, created no little sensation. The people flocked round me, inquiring the *novedades*, and how I had escaped the Indians. . . .

I had hardly dismounted when a tall, gaunt figure elbowed its way through the admiring crowd, and seizing my hand, exclaimed,

"Thank God, here's a countryman at last!" and burst into tears. Regarding him with astonishment, I perceived at once that he was an American, and, by his dress of well-worn homespun, evidently a Missourian, and one of the teamsters who accompany the Santa Fé caravans from the United States. He quickly told me his story. He was one of the twenty-one Americans who, as I have before mentioned, left Mr. Spiers' caravan some thirty or forty days before, intending to proceed across the country to the United States, by way of Texas. They had purchased horses and mules at the hacienda of La Sarca, and, without a guide, and knowing nothing of the nature of the country they had to traverse, had entered a tract between the Bolsón of Mapimí and the sierras of El Diablo, which is entirely destitute of game and water. Here their animals had nearly all died; and themselves, separating in small parties, had vainly searched for water, remaining for eight days with no other sustenance than the blood of mules, and reduced to the most revolting extremities to assuage their burning thirst. The man before me and another had found their way to a hole of water after several days' travel, near which some *pastores* (shepherds) were tending a large flock of sheep, and these men had brought them into Guajoquilla. According to his account, the others must long ere this have perished, for when he left them they were prostrate on the ground, unable to rise, and praying for death. In the hope of recovering some of their effects, his companion, after recruiting his strength, had started back to the spot with some Mexicans, but, meeting a party of Comanches, they had returned without reaching the place. The next day, however, some *vaqueros* entered the town bearing six or seven Americans behind their saddles, and towards the evening two more were brought in, making eleven in all who had arrived. Such miserable, emaciated creatures it has never been my lot to see. With long hair and beards, and thin cadaverous faces, with the cheek-bones projecting almost through the skin, and their mouths cracked with the drought, they dismounted before my door, weak and scarcely able to stand; most of them had entirely lost their voices, and some were giddy and light-headed with the sufferings they had endured. From their account I had no doubt that ten of their party were perishing in the sierra, or most probably had already expired; for they were entirely exhausted when the last of those who had arrived left the spot where they had been lying. After ordering my servant to make a large quantity of strong soup for the poor fellows, and providing for their immediate wants, I proceeded to the alcalde of the place and told him the story. He at once agreed with me that some steps must be taken to rescue the sufferers if still alive, but he doubted if the people in the town would undertake the expedition....

Determined to go myself in search of the Americans, I beat up for volunteers, and soon got four or five rancheros, who were mounted and armed by the prefect, to agree to accompany me. Eight of the Americans were also sufficiently recovered the next day to be of the party; and about noon we started, sixteen in number, well armed and mounted. The alcalde, before we left, informed the Americans that, although prisoners, he did not hesitate to allow them to proceed under my command, as I had made myself answerable for their return.

Taking an easterly course, we crossed a sierra and entered upon a broken country dotted with groves of mezquit and palms, and intersected by numerous ravines and cañons. About ten at night we halted for an hour to allow our horses to feed on the damp grass, as there was no water, and afterwards continued our journey at as rapid a rate as the nature of the country would admit. All night we passed through a wild and perfectly desert tract, crossing rough sierras and deep ravines. A large and recent Indian trail crossed the country from north to south, which my Mexican guide said was the main road of the Comanches into the interior. At sunrise we reached a little hole of water, and a few feet beyond it lay the body of a mule which two of the Americans had killed for its blood, not knowing that water was within a few feet of them. No sooner had they gorged themselves with the hot blood than they discovered the pool, but were so sickened with their previous draught as to be unable to drink. Here we allowed our animals to fill themselves, and immediately rode on without resting. . . .

Towards evening, after travelling rapidly all the day, we approached the spot where the Americans had left their companions, and I caused the party to separate and spread out, to look for tracks of men or horses. Shortly after, one of them stopped and called me to his side. He had discovered the body of a horse which they had left alive when they had last seen their companions. Its swollen tongue and body showed that the poor animal had died from excessive thirst, and was a bad omen of our finding the men alive. A few yards farther on lay another, which had died from the same cause. Presently we reached the spot, and found guns, and blankets, and ammunition, but no signs of the lost men. The ground, hard and rocky, afforded no clue to the course they had followed, but it was evident that they must have taken an opposite course to that from which we had just come, or we must have seen their tracks in the plains. The horses had been dead at least three days, and had evidently been turned loose to shift for themselves, as they were without ropes. No doubt remained in my mind as to their fate. . . .

After an ineffectual search we were obliged to turn back, as our animals had been nearly thirty hours without eating, and were almost exhausted; and here there was no grass or herbage of any description. . . .

About four in the afternoon next day we rode into Guajoquilla, and, before I had dismounted, Don Augustin Garcia, the prefect, followed by a crowd, accosted me:

"*¿Qué novedades?*" he asked.

"Nothing," I answered.

"*Pues aquí tiene usted muchas*—Well, here we have plenty of bad news for you. The robbers have broken into your room, and stolen all your baggage."

"*Pues,*" I answered, "*si no hay remedio*—if it can't be helped, it can't."

My servant now made his appearance, with a face as white as a sheet; I had given him strict orders, when I started, on no account to leave the house until my return. The night before, however, he had been induced by the robbers to go to a fandango, where they locked him in a room for several hours with a party of men and women drinking and dancing. When he returned to the house, he found the door of my room, which was entered from the street, open, and thinking that I had returned, he went into the house, and, awakening the women, asked them when I had come back. They told him that I was not yet returned, and he replied, "He must be, for his door was wide open."

At this point, out jumped the *patrona* from her bed. "*¡Ladrones, ladrones!*" she cried out, instantly guessing what had happened. Striking a light, the whole household entered my room and found it stripped of everything. They had actually carried off the matting of my packsaddles; trunks and saddles, guns, pistols, sword, and all were gone; and in one of the packs were some three thousand dollars, so they had made a good night's work of it. My servant was in despair; his first idea was to run, for I would kill him, he said, as soon as I arrived. The old *patrona* did not lose her presence of mind; she rushed to her *sala*, and snatched from the wall a little image of el Niño de Atocha, a juvenile saint of extraordinary virtue. Seizing my distracted *mozo* by the shoulders, she forced him on his knees, and, surrounded by all the women of the family, vowed to the uplifted saint three masses, the cook on her part a penance, and my servant a mass likewise, if the stolen goods were recovered, besides scores of Pater Nosters, dozens of Ave Marías, &c. &c. Having done this, as she told me when giving a history of the affair, her heart became calm; the blessed child of Atocha had never deserted her, a lone widow, with only a *buellada* of two hundred cattle to depend upon, and her husband killed by the *bárbaros;* and she felt assured that by the saint's means the things would be recovered. The scandal, she said, the *infamia* of the robbery taking place in her house! and a stranger too to be plundered, *lejos de su patria y sus amigos ¡ay qué lástima, qué infamia!*—far from his country and his friends; what an atrocity!

The prefect, Don Augustin, was soon on the scent; one man was already suspected, who had been seen in front of the house late on the night of the robbery, and passing by frequently, had attracted the attention of my *patrona.* My *mozo,* pistol in hand, went to the house of this man and collared him, and when I arrived had already lodged him in the *calabozo.* Two others were shortly after taken on suspicion of being accomplices.

"*No hay cuidado*—there is no fear," said Don Augustin; "we'll get everything back; I have put them to the torture, and they have already confessed to the robbery."

My servant, who witnessed the operation, said it was beautiful to see the prefect screwing a confession out of them. Their necks and feet were placed in two different holes, which, by means of a screw, were brought together until every muscle of the body and limbs was in a frightful state of tension, and the bones almost dislocated. At length they divulged where one trunk was concealed, and then another, and after two or three faintings, one article after another was brought to light. In the intervals the prefect rushed to me, wiping the perspiration from his forehead.

"*No hay cuidado, no hay cuidado;* we'll have everything out of them. They have just now fainted off, but when they recover they shall be popped in again."

At last everything was recovered but a small dirk knife with a mother-of-pearl handle, which defied screwing, and I begged Don Augustin not to trouble himself about it, as everything else was safe. But, "No," he said, "*no hay cuidado, no hay cuidado;* we'll have everything out of them; strangers must not be robbed with impunity in my prefecture." However, it took another violent screw, and the poor wretch, with eyes starting out of his head, cried out at last to stop, and pulled out of his pocket the missing knife, which he had doubtless determined to keep, on the principle of having "something for his money." . . .

When everything had been brought back, my good old *patrona* rushed to me with el Santo Niño de Atocha, which she begged me to kiss, at the same time hanging it in my room to protect it from another spoliation. That evening I was sitting at the door, enjoying a chat with the *señoritas de la casa,* and a *cigarro,* when I saw a figure, or rather the trunk, of a woman, moving along on what appeared to be the stumps of legs, enveloped in a cloud of dust, as she slowly crept along the road. She passed three or four times, going and returning upwards of a hundred yards, and earnestly praying the while. "*Por Dios,*" I asked one of the girls—"for God's sake, what's this?"

"*Es Dolores, la cocinera*—It's Dolores, the cook—performing penance," was the answer, and her vow instantly recurred to me. The poor old body had vowed to walk so many hundred yards on her knees in the public streets, repeating at the same time a certain number of Ave Marías, if the credit of the family was restored by the discovery of the thief and the recovery of my property.

I had a large pot of soup kept always on the fire, to which the half-starved Americans had access whenever they felt inclined, and, as I was sitting at the door, several of them passed into the house, brushing by the *muchachas* without the usual "*con su licencia,*" much to the indignation of the ladies.

It is a general impression amongst the lower classes in Mexico, that the Americans are half savages, and perfectly uncivilised. The specimens they see in Northern Mexico are certainly not remarkably polished in manners or appearance, being generally rough backwoodsmen from Missouri. They go by the name of "burros," jackasses, and have the reputation of being infidels who worship the devil, &c. I was trying to explain to my female friends that the Americans were a very civilised people, and a great portion of them of the same religion as their own, but they scouted the idea; the priests had told them the contrary, and now they saw with their own eyes that they were burros.

"*Ni saludan las mujeres,*" indignantly exclaimed a dark beauty, as a conclusive argument—they do not even salute the women when they pass—as, just at that moment, a Missourian, six feet high in his mocassins, stepped over her head as she sat on the sill of the gate.

"*Ni saludan las mujeres,*" she repeated; "you see it yourself. *Ah, no, por Dios, son burros, y muy sin vergüenzas*"—they are jackasses,

and entirely without shame. "*¡Válgame Dios, qué hombres tan fieros!*"
—what wild men they are. . . .

On the third of November, I left Guajoquilla, under the escort
of ten thousand blessings heaped upon me by my kindhearted hostess
and her family, and under the especial protection of the holy infant
of Atocha. We left after dark, as, on account of the *novedades*, it was
deemed not only prudent, but indispensable to safety, to travel in the
night. . . . A little after sunrise we reached the rancho of La Remada,
where was a detachment of troops to protect the people from the
Indians; and we halted here, to feed the animals, for two or three
hours, after which we resumed our journey to Santa Rosalía. . . .

I put up in the house of an American who has a little "dry-
goods" store in the town, and in the middle of the night was called
up by a violent knocking at the gate. As the mob had been talking
of revenging themselves for the defeat sustained by the Mexican
troops at Monterey the other day, by sacking the two unfortunate
little stores belonging to Americans, my host thought his time was
come, but, resolving to die game, came to me to assist in defending
the house. We therefore carried all the arms into the store and placed
them on the counter, which served as a parapet for our bodies. The
door of the shop opened into the street, and behind it we could hear
the clanking of swords and other warlike noises. Presently a loud
knock and voice exclaimed, "*Abra la puerta.*"

"*¿Quién es?*" I asked—Who is it?

No answer; but "*Abra la puerta!*"—open the door—was repeated.

However, finding that we paid no attention to the request, another summons was tried, with the addition of "*en el nombre del
General*—in the name of the General—who has sent me, his *ayudante*,
to speak with the master of this house."

With this "open sesame" we unbarred the door to the General's
aide-de-camp, a ferocious-looking individual with enormous moustache and clattering sabre.

"Where," he asked, in an authoritative voice, "is this American
spy who entered the town to-day and concealed himself in this
house?" No answer. Question repeated with like effect. The mous-
tached hero grinned with rage, and turned to his followers, saying,
"You see this"; and then, turning to us, said, "It is the General's order
that every foreigner in this house immediately attend at his quarters,
where you will answer for harbouring a spy," turning to the master
of the house.

We speedily donned our clothes and appeared at the house of

the General, who was sitting in a room waiting our arrival. Without waiting for any explanation, I immediately presented my credentials, saying, "*Hí tiene usted, mi General, mis pasapuertas y carta de securidad,*" which, to the dissatisfaction of the *ayudante*, after glancing at, he returned with a low bow, and many apologies for disturbing me at so late an hour. . . .[3]

Leaving Santa Rosalía on the fifth, we proceeded to Los Saucillos, a small Indian village, the population of which is entirely employed in mining on their own account. It is situated on the Conchos, here a broad but shallow stream, which runs into the Del Norte above the presidio of that name; this village is thirty-six miles from Santa Rosalía. . . .

On the sixth we made a short day's journey to San Pablo, a little town on a confluent of the Conchos, in the midst of a marshy plain. . . .

On the seventh, leaving San Pablo, I met a caravan of waggons from Chihuahua, with a number of officers and families, who were leaving that city from fear of the Americans, who were reported to be on their way to attack it. Amongst the party was the celebrated Andalucian matador Bernardo, who with his troop of bullfighters had been lately attacked by the Indians, and nearly all of them killed— himself escaping after a desperate sword-fight and many severe wounds. . . .

The next morning, at sunrise, we started for Chihuahua, crossing a plain abounding with antelope, and reached that city about two o'clock. The first appearance of the town from a neighbouring hill is extremely picturesque, its white houses, church spires, and the surrounding gardens affording a pleasing contrast to the barren plain which surrounds it. I was most hospitably received by an English family resident in the town, who have the exclusive management of the mint and the numerous mines in the neighbourhood. In this remote and but semicivilised city, I was surprised to find that they had surrounded themselves with all the comforts, and many of the luxuries, of an English home; and the kindness I here experienced almost spoiled me for the hardships and privations I met with in my subsequent journey.

[3] British credentials carried great respect in Mexico.

CHAPTER 8

From Chihuahua to El Paso

CHIHUAHUA, the capital city of the state or department of that name, was built towards the close of the seventeenth century, and therefore cannot boast of such antiquity even as the more remote city of Santa Fé. Its population is between eight and ten thousand permanent inhabitants, although it is the resort of many strangers from New Mexico, California, and Sonora. The cathedral, which is considered by the American traders one of the finest structures in the world, is a large building in no style of architecture, but with rather a handsome façade, embellished with statues of the twelve apostles.

Opposite the principal entrance, over the portals which form one side of the square, were dangling the grim scalps of one hundred and seventy Apaches, who had lately been most treacherously and inhumanly butchered by the Indian hunters in the pay of the state. The scalps of men, women, and children, were brought into the town in procession, and hung as trophies, in this conspicuous situation, of Mexican valour and humanity!

The unfinished convent of San Francisco, commenced by the Jesuits prior to their expulsion from the country, is also a conspicuous mass of masonry and bad taste. It is celebrated as having been the place of confinement of the patriot Hidalgo, the Mexican Hampden, who was executed in a yard behind the building in 1811. A monument to his memory has been erected in the Plaza de Armas, a pyramid of stone, with an inscription eulogistic of that *one* honest Mexican.

The town also boasts a *casa de moneda*, or mint, under the management of an English gentleman, where silver, gold, and copper are coined, and an *aduana*, or customhouse. An aqueduct conveys water to the city from the neighbouring stream, the work of the former Spanish government; it is small, and badly constructed.

146

The shops are filled with goods of the most paltry description, brought mostly from the United States by way of Santa Fé. The cotton goods called "domestics" in the United States are, however, of good quality, and in great demand. Traders arriving in Chihuahua either sell their goods in bulk to resident merchants, or, opening a store, retail them on their own account; but the latter method occasions great delay and inconvenience, the payments being made in copper and small coins, which it is difficult to exchange for gold, and are not current out of the state.

The trade between the United States and Santa Fé and Chihuahua presents a curious feature in international commerce. The capital embarked in it must exceed a million of dollars, which, however, is subject to great risks, not only on account of the dangers to be apprehended in passing the vast prairies, both from Indian attacks and the loss of animals by the severity of the climate, but from the uncertainty of the laws in force in remote departments of Mexico with regard to the admission of goods and the duties exacted on them.

It appears that in the "port" of Santa Fé the ordinary *derechos de arancel*, or customs duties, have been laid aside and a new tariff substituted, by the late Governor Armijo, who, instead of levying the usual ad valorem duties on goods imported from the United States, established the system of exacting duties on "waggonloads," without reference to the nature of the goods contained in them, each waggon paying five hundred dollars, whether large or small. The injustice of such an impost was apparent, since the merchant, who carried an assortment of rich and valuable goods into the interior of the country for the fair of San Juan and the markets of the capital and larger cities, paid the same duty as the petty trader on his waggonload of trumpery for the Santa Fé market.

Moreover, the revenue of the customs must have suffered in an equal ratio, for the traders, to avoid the duties, crowded two or more ordinary waggonloads into one huge one and thus saved the duties on two waggons. Notwithstanding this, however, the system still prevails, much to the dissatisfaction of those who, in the former state of things, could, by the skilful application of a bribe, pass any amount of goods at almost nominal expense.

The state of Chihuahua produces gold, silver, copper, iron, saltpetre, &c.; indeed, it is productive in mineral wealth alone, for the soil is thin and poor, and there is everywhere a great scarcity of water. It is, moreover, infested with hostile Indians, who ravage the whole country and prevent many of its most valuable mines from being worked. These Indians are the Apaches, who inhabit the ridges and plains of the Cordillera, the Sierra Madre on the west, and the tracts between the Conchos and Del Norte on the east, while scattered tribes roam over all parts of the state, committing devastations on the ranchos and haciendas, and depopulating the remote villages.

For the purpose of carrying on a war against the daring savages, a species of company was formed by the Chihuahueños, with a capital raised by subscription. This company, under the auspices of the government, offered a bounty of fifty dollars a scalp, as an inducement to people to undertake a war of extermination against the Apaches. One Don Santiago Kirker,[1] an Irishman, long resident in Mexico, and for many years a trapper and Indian trader in the Far West, whose exploits in Indian killing would fill a volume, was placed at the head of a band of some hundred and fifty men, including several Shawanee and Delaware Indians, and sent *en campaña* against the Apaches. The fruits of the campaign were the trophies I saw dangling in front of the cathedral.

In the month of August, the Apaches being then *en paz* with the state, entered, unarmed, the village of Galeana, for the purpose of trading. This band, which consisted of a hundred and seventy, including women and children, was under the command of a celebrated chief, and had no doubt committed many atrocities on the Mexicans; but at this time they had signified their desire for peace to the government of Chihuahua, and were now trading in good faith, and under protection of the faith of treaty. News of their arrival having been sent to Kirker, he immediately forwarded several kegs of spirits, with which they were to be regaled, and detained in the village until he could arrive with his band. On a certain day, about ten in the morning, the Indians being at the time drinking, dancing, and amusing themselves, and *unarmed*, Kirker sent forward a messenger to say that at such an hour he would be there.

The Mexicans, when they saw him approach with his party, suddenly seized their arms and set upon the unfortunate Indians, who, without even their knives, attempted no resistance, but, throwing

[1] James Kirker, born in Belfast, Ireland, December 2, 1793, came to America at the age of seventeen. He went to St. Louis, entered the Western fur trade, and journeyed to New Mexico. His fame as an Indian fighter led to his employment by the Chihuahua officials to wage a war of extermination against the Apaches. Late in 1846, Kirker joined Colonel A. W. Doniphan's forces near El Paso and acted as scout, guide, and interpreter for the American troops. In 1849 he acted as guide to California-bound gold seekers. See notes by Ralph P. Bieber in Vols. 3. 5, and 7 of "The Southwest Historical Series."

themselves on the ground when they saw Kirker's men surrounding them, submitted to their fate. The infuriated Mexicans spared neither age nor sex; with fiendish shouts they massacred their unresisting victims, glutting their long pent-up revenge of many years of persecution. One woman, big with child, rushed into the church, clasping the alter and crying for mercy for herself and unborn babe. She was followed, and fell pierced with a dozen lances; and then—it is almost impossible to conceive such an atrocity, but I had it from an eyewitness on the spot not two months after the tragedy—the child was torn alive from the yet palpitating body of its mother, first plunged into the holy water to be baptized, and immediately its brains were dashed out against a wall.

A hundred and sixty men, women, and children were slaughtered, and, with the scalps carried on poles, Kirker's party entered Chihuahua—in procession, headed by the Governor and priests, with bands of music escorting them in triumph to the town.

Nor is this a solitary instance of similar barbarity, for on two previous occasions parties of American traders and trappers perpetrated most treacherous atrocities on tribes of the same nation on the river Gila. The Indians, on their part, equal their more civilised enemies in barbarity; and such is the war of extermination carried on between the Mexicans and Apaches.

But to return to Chihuahua. The state, which comprises an area of 107,584 square miles, contains only 180,000 inhabitants—and this is probably an exaggerated estimate—or not two inhabitants to the square mile. Of this vast territory not twenty square miles are under cultivation, and at least three-fifths is utterly sterile and unproductive. The city of Chihuahua is distant from Mexico, in a direct line, 1,250 miles, and from the nearest seaport, Guaymas, in the Gulf of California, over an almost impracticable country, 600 miles. Thus its isolated position, and comparative worthlessness to Mexico, are apparent.

Chihuahua is a paradise for sportsmen. In the sierras and mountains are found two species of bears—the common black bear or American bear, and the grizzly bear of the Rocky Mountains. The last are the most numerous, and are abundant in the sierras in the neighbourhood of Chihuahua. The *carnero cimarron*—the big-horn or Rocky Mountain sheep—is also common on the Cordillera. Elk, black-tailed deer (*cola prieta*, a large species of the fallow deer), the common red deer of America, and antelope abound on all the plains and sierras. Of smaller game, peccaries (javali), also called *cojamete*,

149

hares, and rabbits are everywhere numerous; and beavers are still found in the Gila, the Pecos, the Del Norte, and their tributary streams. Of birds—the *faisán*, commonly called *paisano*, a species of pheasant: the quail, or rather a bird between a quail and a partridge, is abundant; while every variety of snipe and plover is found on the plains, not forgetting the *gruya*, of the crane kind, whose meat is excellent. There are also two varieties of wolf—the white, or mountain wolf; and the coyote, or small wolf of the plains, whose long-continued and melancholy howl is an invariable adjunct to a Mexican night encampment.

But, perhaps, in all departments of natural history the entomologist would find the plains of Chihuahua most prolific in specimens. I have counted seventy-five varieties of grasshoppers and locusts, some of enormous size and most brilliant and fantastic colours. There is also an insect peculiar to this part of Mexico—at least I have not met with it excepting on the plains of Durango and Chihuahua, neither have I met with more than one traveller who has observed it, although it is most curious and worthy of attention.

This insect is from four to six inches in length, and has four long and slender legs. The body appears to the naked eye to be nothing more than a blade of grass, without the slightest muscular action or appearance of vitality, excepting in the antennae, which are two in number, and about half an inch in length. They move very slowly on their long legs, and resemble a blade of grass being carried by ants. I saw them several times before examining them minutely, thinking that they were in fact bits of grass. I heard of no other name for them than the local one of *zacateros*, from *zacate* (grass); and the Mexicans assert that if horses or mules swallow these insects, they invariably die.[2]

Of bugs and beetles there is endless variety—including the *cocuyo* or lantern bug, and the tarantula.

Of reptiles those most frequently met with are the rattlesnake and copperhead, both of which are poisonous. The scorpion is common all over the republic, and its sting is sometimes fatal to children or persons of inflammable temperament. The cameleon abounds in the plains, a grotesque, but harmless and inoffensive animal. It always assimilates its colour to that of the soil where it is found. The cameleon is the "horned frog" of the prairies of America.

The characteristic shrub on the plains of Chihuahua is the mez-

[2] Since writing the above, I find that this insect is noticed in Clavigero, who calls it, on the authority of Hernandez, *quauhmecatl*, a Mexican name; therefore it is probable that it is also found in Southern Mexico. Ruxton's note.

quit—a species of acacia, which grows to the height of ten or twelve feet. The seeds, contained in a small pod, resemble those of the laburnum, and are used by the Apaches to make a kind of bread or cake, which is sweet and pleasant to the taste. The wood is exceedingly hard and heavy.[3] This constantly recurring and ugly shrub becomes quite an eyesore to the traveller passing the mezquit-covered plains, as it is the only thing in the shape of a tree seen for hundreds of miles, excepting here and there a solitary alamo or willow, which overhangs a spring, and which invariably gives a name to the rancho or hacienda which may generally be found in the vicinity of water. Thus day after day I passed the ranchos of El Sauz, Los Sauzes, Los Sauzillos—the willow, the willows, the little willows—or El Alamo, Los Alamitos—the poplar, the little poplars. The last is the only timber found on the streams in Northern Mexico, and on the Del Norte and the Arkansa it grows to a great size.

Chihuahua at this time was in a state of considerable ferment, on account of the anticipated advance of the Americans upon the city from New Mexico. That department had been occupied by them without opposition, Governor Armijo and his three thousand heroes scattering before the barbarians of the north, as they please to call the Americans, without firing a shot. A body of troops had now advanced to the borders of the department, and were known to be encamped on the Río del Norte, at the entrance of the Jornada del Muerto—the deadman's journey—a tract of desert, without wood or water, which extends nearly one hundred miles across a bend of the river; and a journey across which is dreaded by the Mexicans, not only on account of these natural difficulties, but from the fact of its being the haunt of numerous bands of Apaches, who swoop down from the sierras upon travellers, who, with their exhausted animals, have but little chance of escape.

In rear of the American troops was the long-expected *caravana* of upwards of two hundred waggons, destined for Chihuahua and the fair of San Juan. These, entering Santa Fé with the troops, had of course paid no duty in that port of entry, and it was a great object with the Governor of Chihuahua that they should proceed to that city and pay the usual duties to him, which otherwise would have been payable to the customhouse of Santa Fé. The government being entirely without funds, and anxious to raise and equip a body of troops to oppose the advance of the Americans, the arrival of the caravan would have been most opportune, since, at the usual rate of

[3] From the mezquit exudes gum Arabic. Ruxton's note.

duties, viz. five hundred dollars for each waggon, the amount to be received by the government would exceed one hundred thousand dollars.

However, the merchants, particularly the Americans, were reluctant to trust their property to the chances of Mexican honour, not knowing how they might be treated under the present circumstances of war; and having neglected to profit by the permission of General Kearney, who then commanded the United States troops, to proceed to their destination, now that that officer had advanced to California and the command had devolved on another, they were ordered to remain in rear of the troops and not to advance excepting under their escort. The commanding officer deemed it imprudent to allow such an amount of the sinews of war to be placed in the hands of the enemy, to be used against the Americans. That this was very proper under the circumstances there could be no gainsaying, but at the same time there was a very large amount of property belonging to English merchants and others of neutral nations, who were suffering enormous losses by the detention of their goods; and as no official notification had been given of the *blockade* of the frontier town of Santa Fé, this prohibition to proceed was considered unjust and arbitrary. My opinion, however, is, that the officer in command of the United States troops was perfectly justified in the course he pursued, knowing well the uses to which the money thus obtained would have been applied.

In order to keep the enemy in ignorance of the state of affairs in Chihuahua, no one had been permitted to leave the state for some months; and when it was known that I had received a carte blanche from Don Ángel Trias, the governor, to proceed where I pleased, I was from this circumstance invested with all kinds of official dignities by the population. As it was known that I was the bearer of sundry dispatches from the Governor to the Americans, I was immediately voted to be *comisionado* on the part of the Mexican government to treat for peace, or I was *un coronel Ynglés*, bound to Oregon to settle the difference respecting that disputed territory. The mysterious fact of an Englishman travelling through the country at such a time, and being permitted to proceed *al norte*, which permission their most influential citizens had been unable to obtain, was sufficient to put the curious on the *qui vive*; and when on the morning of my departure an escort of soldiers was seen drawn up at my door, I was immediately promoted to be "somebody." This escort—save the mark! —consisted of two or three dragoons of the regiment of Vera Cruz, which had been several years in Santa Fé, but had run away with the Governor on the approach of the Americans, and were now stationed at Chihuahua. Their horses—wretched, half-starved animals—were borrowed for the occasion; and the men, refusing to march without some provision for the road, were advanced their *sueldo* by a patriotic merchant of the town, who gave each a handful of copper coins, which they carefully tied up in the corners of their sarapes. Their dress was original and uniform—in rags. One had on a dirty broad-brimmed straw hat, another a handkerchief tied round his head. One had a portion of a jacket; another was in his shirt-sleeves, with overalls, open to the winds, reaching a little below the knees. All were bootless and unspurred. One had a rusty sword and lance, another a gun without a hammer, the third a bow and arrows. Although the nights were piercingly cold, they had but one wretched, tattered sarape of the commonest kind between them, and no rations of any description.

These were regulars of the regiment of Vera Cruz. I may as well here mention that, two or three months after, Colonel Doniphan, with nine hundred volunteers, marched through the state of Chihuahua, defeating on one occasion three thousand Mexicans with great slaughter, and taking the city itself, without losing *one man* in the campaign.

At Sacramento the Mexicans entrenched themselves behind formidable breastworks, having ten or twelve pieces of artillery in battery, and numbering at least three thousand. Will it be believed that these miserable creatures were driven from their position, and slaughtered like sheep, by nine hundred raw backwoodsmen, who did not lose *one single man* in the encounter?[4]

On the tenth of November I left Chihuahua, bound for the capital of New Mexico. Passing the Rancho del Sacramento, where, a few months after, the Missourians slaughtered a host of Mexicans, we entered a large plain well covered with grass, on which were immense flocks of sheep. A coyote lazily crossed the road, and, stopping within a few yards, sat down upon its haunches, and coolly regarded us as we passed. Panchito had had a four days' rest and was in fine condition and spirits, and I determined to try the mettle of the wolf; the level plain, with its springy turf, offering a fine field for a course.

---

[4] The Battle of Sacramento, February 28, 1847, occurred near the Rancho of Sacramento, some sixteen miles north of the city of Chihuahua. Colonel A. W. Doniphan's troops, escorting a trading caravan of about 315 wagons, won a brilliant victory over superior Mexican forces. See J. H. Smith, *The War with Mexico* (1919), I, 303–13.

Cantering gently at first, the coyote allowed me to approach within a hundred yards before he loped lazily away; but finding I was on his traces, he looked round, and, gathering himself up, bowled away at full speed. Then I gave Panchito the spur, and, answering it with a bound, we were soon at the stern of the wolf. Then, for the first time, the animal saw we were in earnest, and, with a sweep of his bushy tail, pushed for his life across the plain. At the distance of two or three miles a rocky ridge was in sight, where he evidently thought to secure a retreat, but Panchito bounded along like the wind itself, and soon proved to the wolf that his race was run. After trying in vain to double, he made one desperate rush, upon which, lifting Panchito with rein and leg, we came up and passed the panting beast, when, seeing that escape was impossible, he lay down, and, with sullen and cowardly resignation, curled up for the expected blow, as pistol in hand I reined up Panchito at his side. However, I was merciful and allowed the animal to escape.

At ten at night I arrived at the hacienda of El Sauz, belonging to the governor of Chihuahua, Don Ángel Trias.[5] It was enclosed with a high wall, as a protection from the Indians, who, a short time before, had destroyed the cattle of the hacienda, filling a well in the middle of the corral with the carcases of slaughtered sheep and oxen. It was still bricked up.

The next day we proceeded to another hacienda, likewise called after the willows, Los Sauzillos. Passing a large plain, in the midst of which stood a lone poplar, wolves were continually crossing the road, both the coyote and the large grey variety. I was this day mounted upon the *alazán* which I had purchased at Guajoquilla. We were within sight of our halting-place for the night, when the horse, which had carried me all day without my having had recourse to whip or spur, suddenly began to flag, and I noticed that a profuse perspiration had broken out on its ears and neck. I instantly dismounted, and perceived a quivering in the flank and a swelling of the belly. Before I could remove the saddle the poor beast fell down, and although I opened a vein and made every attempt to relieve it, it once more rose

[5] Governor Trias was second in command of Mexican forces at the Battle of Sacramento. James J. Webb, Santa Fé trader, wrote of him: "He was an unprincipled tyrant in all his bearing towards his own people in an inferior position, and considered all foreigners (especially Americans) as only worthy of his contempt. . . . . [He] spent some time in the United States and also traveled extensively in Europe. . . . . [He] could speak English fluently and (I understood) also French and German. I never heard an American speak of him with respect, and there was no love lost."—*Op. cit.,* 225.

"*Mountain man preparing supper*"
(A. J. Miller)

"Trappers' encampment"
(A. J..Miller)

From the Porter collection

to its legs and, spinning round in the greatest apparent agony, fell dead to the ground.

The cause of its death was that my servant, contrary to my orders, had given the animals young corn the night before, which food is often fatal to horses not accustomed to feed on grain.

This rancho is situated on the margin of a lake of brackish water, and we found the people actual prisoners within its walls, the gates being closed, and a man stationed on the *azotea* with a large wall-piece, looking out for Indians. At night a large fire was kindled on the roof, the blaze of which illuminated the country far and near. Not a soul would venture after sunset outside the gate, which the major-domo, a *gachupín*, refused to open to allow my servant to procure some wood for a fire to cook my supper, and we had to content ourselves with one of corncobs, which lay scattered about the corral.

On the twelfth, passing Encinillas, a large hacienda belonging to Don Ángel Trias, we encamped on the banks of an arroyo, running through the middle of a plain, walled by sierras, where the Apaches have several villages. This being very dangerous ground, we put out the fire at sunset and took all precautions against surprise. The animals fared badly, the grass being thin and burned up by the sun, and what little there was being of bad quality.

The next day we reached the small village of El Carmen, and, camping by a little thread of a rivulet outside of the town, were surrounded by all the loafers of the village. The night was very cold, and our fire, the fuel for which we purchased, was completely surrounded by these idle vagabonds. At last, my temper being frozen out of me, I went up to the fire and said, "*Señores*, allow me to present you with three rials, which will enable you to purchase wood for two fires; this fire I will be obliged to you if you will allow myself and fellow travellers to warm ourselves by, as we are very cold; and also, with your kind permission, wish to cook our suppers by it." This was enough for them; a Mexican like a Spaniard, is very sensitive, and the hint went through them. They immediately dispersed, and I saw no more of them the remainder of the evening.

Near El Carmen is a pretty little stream, fringed with alamos, which runs through a wild and broken country of sierras. The plains, generally about ten to twenty miles in length, are divided from each other by an elevated ridge, but there is no perceptible difference in the elevation of them from Chihuahua to El Paso. The road is level excepting in crossing these ridges, and hard everywhere except on the marshy plain of Encinillas, which is often inundated. This lake has no outlet and is fed by numerous small streams from the sierras; its length is ten miles, by three in breadth. The marshy ground around the lake is covered with an alkaline efflorescence called *tezquite*, a substance of considerable value. The water, impregnated with salts, is brackish and unpleasant to the taste, but in the rainy season loses its disagreeable properties.

On the fourteenth we travelled sixty miles, and camped on a bare plain without wood or water, the night being so dark that we were unable to reach Carrizal, although it was but a few miles distant from our encampment. The next morning we reached the village, where I stopped the whole day, during an extraordinary hurricane of wind, which rendered travelling impossible. We had been on short commons for two days, as the hungry escort had devoured my provisions, but here I resolved to have a feast, and, setting all hands to forage, on return we found our combined efforts had produced an imposing pile of several yards of beef (for here the meat is cut into long strips and dried), onions, chiles, frijoles, sweet corn, eggs, &c. An enormous olla was procured, and everything was bundled pell-mell into it, seasoned with pepper and salt and chile.

To protect the fire from the hurricane that was blowing, all the packs and saddles were piled round it, and my servant and the soldiers relieved each other in their vigilant watch of the precious compound, myself superintending the process of cooking. Our appetites, ravenous with a fast of twenty-four hours, were in first-rate order, but we determined that the pot should be left on the fire until the savoury mess was perfectly cooked. It was within an hour or two of sunset, and we had not yet broken our fast. The olla simmered, and a savoury steam pervaded the air. The dragoons licked their lips, and their eyes watered—never had they had such a feast in perspective; for myself, I never removed my eyes from the pot, and had just resolved that, when the *puro* in my mouth was smoked out, the puchero would have attained perfection. At length the moment arrived; my *mozo*, with a blazing smile, approached the fire, and with guarded hands seized the top of the olla and lifted it from the ashes.

"*¡Ave María Purísima! ¡Santísima Virgen!*" broke from the lips of the dragoons; "*¡Mil carajos!*" burst from the *heart* of the *mozo;* and I sank almost senseless to the ground. On lifting the pot the bottom fell out, and splash went everything into the blazing fire. *¡Válgame Dios!* what a moment was that! Stupified, and hardly crediting our senses, we gazed at the burning, frizzling, hissing remnants, as they were consuming before our eyes. Nothing was rescued, and our elaborate feast was simplified into a supper of frijoles and chile colorado, which, after some difficulty, we procured from the village.

The next morning we started before daylight, and at sunrise watered our animals at the little lake called Laguna de Patos, from the ducks which frequent it; and at midday we halted at another spring, the Ojo de le Estrella—star spring—where we again watered them, as we should be obliged to camp that night without water. We chose a camping-ground in a large plain covered with mezquit, which afforded us a little fuel—now become very necessary, as the nights were piercingly cold. As we had been unable to procure provisions in Carrizal, we went to bed supperless, which was now a very usual occurrence. My animals suffered from the cold, which, coming as they did from the *tierra caliente*, they felt excessively, particularly a little blood horse with an exceedingly fine coat. I was obliged to share my blankets with this poor animal, or I believe it would have died in the night.

Just at daybreak the next morning I was riding in advance of the party, when I met a cavalcade of horsemen whose wild costume, painted faces, and arms consisting of bows and arrows, made me think at first that they were Indians. On their part, they evidently did not know what to make of me, and halted while two of them rode forward to reconnoitre. I quickly slipped the cover off my rifle and advanced. Seeing my escort following, they saw we were *amigos;* but the nearer they approached me, the more certain was I that they were Apaches, for they were all in Indian dress, and frightfully painted. I was as nearly as possible shooting the foremost, when he exclaimed in Spanish, "*¡Adiós, amigo! ¿qué novedades hay?*" and I then saw a number of mules, packed with bales and barrels, behind him. They were Paseños, on their way to Chihuahua, with *aguardiente*, raisins, and fruit; and shortly after passing them, I found in the road a large bag of *pasas* or raisins, which I pounced upon as a great prize, and, sitting at the roadside, devoured the fruit with great gusto, as this was our second day of banyan. This bag lasted for many days. I found the raisins a great improvement to stews, &c., and we popped a handful or two into every dish.

At ten o'clock we reached a muddy hole of water, entirely frozen—my animals refusing to drink, being afraid of the ice after we had broken it. The water was as thick as pea soup; nevertheless we filled our *huages* with it, as we should probably meet with none so good that day. Towards sunset we passed a most extraordinary mountain of loose shifting sand, three miles in breadth, and, according to

157

the Paseños, sixty in length. The huge rolling mass of sand is nearly destitute of vegetation, save here and there a bunch of greasewood half-buried in the sand. Road there is none, but a track across is marked by the skeletons of dead bodies of oxen, and of mules and horses, which everywhere meet the eye. On one ridge the upper half of a human skeleton protruded from the sand, and bones of animals and carcases in every stage of decay. The sand is knee deep, and constantly shifting, and pack animals have great difficulty in passing. After sunset we reached a dirty, stagnant pool, known as the Ojo de Malayuca; but, as there was not a blade of grass in the vicinity, we were compelled to turn out of the road and search over the arid plain for a patch to camp in. At last we succeeded in finding a spot, and encamped, without wood, water, or supper, being the second day's fast. The next day, passing a broken country, perfectly barren, we struck into the valley of El Paso, and for the first time I saw the well-timbered bottom of the Río Bravo del Norte.[6] Descending a ridge covered with greasewood and mezquit, we entered the little village of El Paso,[7] with its vineyards and orchards and well-cultivated gardens lying along the right bank of the river.

On entering the plaza I was immediately surrounded by a crowd, for my escort had ridden before me and mystified them with wonderful accounts of my importance. However, as I did not choose to enlighten them as to my destination or the object of my journey, they were fain to rest satisfied with the egregious lies of the *dragones*. In the plaza was a little guardhouse, where a ferocious captain was in command of a dirty dozen or two of *soldados*. This worthy, to show his importance, sent a sergeant to order my instant attendance at the guardroom. In as many words I told the astonished messenger to tell his officer "to go to the devil," to his horror, and the delight of the surrounding crowd. The answer was delivered word for word, but I heard no more from the military hero. My next visitor was the *prefecto*, who is an important personage in a small place. That worthy, with a dignified air, asked in a determined tone—as much as to say to the crowd, "See how soon I will learn his business"—

"*¿Por 'ónde pasa usted, caballero?*"—Where are you bound?

"*Por Santa Fé y Nuevo Méjico,*" I answered.

[6] This river, also called the Río Grande del Norte (Great River of the North), later became generally known as the Río Grande.

[7] This was not the present El Paso, Texas, but the village across the river that was later rechristened Ciudad Juárez. Its present name honors Benito Juárez, famous Mexican patriot and president.

"*No, señor,*" he immediately rejoined, "this cannot be permitted: by the order of the Governor no one is allowed to go to the north; and I must request, moreover, that you exhibit your passport and other *documentos.*"

"'*Hí lo tiene usted*"—here you have it—I answered, producing a credential, which at once caused the hat to fly from his head, and an offer of himself, *su casa, y todo lo que tiene, a mi disposición*—his house, and all in it, at my disposal. However, all his munificent offers were declined, as I had letters to the *cura,* a young priest named Ortiz, whose unbounded hospitality I enjoyed during my stay.

CHAPTER 9

Up the Río Grande

L Paso del Norte, so called from the ford of
that river, which is here first struck and crossed on the way to New
Mexico, is the oldest settlement in Northern Mexico, a mission having
been established there by el padre Fray Augustin Ruiz, one of the
Franciscan monks who first visited New Mexico, as early as the close
of the sixteenth century (about the year 1585). Fray Ruiz, in company with two others, named Venabides and Marcos, discovering in
the natives a laudable disposition to receive the word of God and
embrace *la santa fé Católica*, remained here a considerable time,
preaching by signs to the Indians, and making many miraculous con-
versions. Eventually, Venabides having returned to Spain and given
a glowing account of the riches of the country and the *muy buen
índole*—the very proper disposition of the aborigines—Don Juan
Oñate was dispatched to conquer, take possession of, and govern the
remote colony, and on his way to Santa Fé established a permanent
settlement at El Paso. Twelve families from Old Castile accompanied
Oñate to Nuevo Méjico to form a colony, and their descendants still
remain scattered over the province.[1]

Several years after, when the Spanish colonists were driven out
of New Mexico, they retreated to El Paso, where they erected a forti-

[1] The statements here are erroneous. Father Ruiz, usually known by the
name Rodríguez, journeyed in 1581 into New Mexico, where he became a missionary martyr. He did not establish a mission in the El Paso district. See Twitchell, *op. cit.*, I, 255–56; and G. P. Hammond and A. Rey (eds.), *The Gallegos
Relation of the Rodríguez Expedition to New Mexico* (1927).

Nor did Oñate, on his way northward to found New Mexico in 1598, establish a settlement here. The first establishment in the vicinity of El Paso was the
convent of Guadalupe, started by Garcia de Zuñiga in 1659. The town of El Paso
(Ciudad Juárez) was founded in 1682 by the New Mexicans who fled the Popé
uprising of 1680.—Twitchell, *op. cit.*, I, 367.

fication and maintained themselves until the arrival of reinforcements from Mexico. The present settlement is scattered for about fifteen miles along the right bank of the Del Norte, and contains five or six thousand inhabitants. The plaza, or village, of El Paso, is situated at the head of the valley, and at the other extremity is the presidio of San Eleazario. Between the two is a continued line of adobe houses, with their plots of garden and vineyard.

The farms seldom contain more than twenty acres, each family having a separate house and plot of land.

The Del Norte is dammed about a mile above the ford, and water is conveyed by an *acequia madre*—main canal—to irrigate the valley. From this *acequia*, other smaller ones branch out in every direction, until the land is intersected in every part with dikes, and is thus rendered fertile and productive.

The soil produces wheat, maize, and other grains, and is admirably adapted to the growth of the vine, which is cultivated here, and yields abundantly; and a wine of excellent flavour is made from the grapes. Brandy of a tolerable quality is also manufactured, and, under the name of *aguardiente del Paso*, is highly esteemed in Durango and Chihuahua. Under proper management wine-making here might become a very profitable branch of trade, as the interior of Mexico is now supplied with French wines, the cost of which, owing to the long land-carriage from the seaports, is enormous, and wine might be made from the Paso grape equal to the best growths of France or Spain. Fruits of all kinds, common to temperate regions, and vegetables, are abundant and of good quality.

The river bottom is timbered with cottonwoods, which extend a few hundred yards on each side of the banks. The river itself is here a small turbid stream, with water of a muddy red, but in the season of the rains it is swollen to six times its present breadth, and frequently overflows the banks. It is of fordable depth in almost any part; but, from the constantly shifting quicksands and bars, is always difficult, and often dangerous, to cross with loaded waggons. It abounds with fish and eels of large size. The houses of the Paseños are built of the adobe, and are small, but clean and neatly kept. Here, as everywhere else in Northern Mexico, the people are in constant fear of Indian attacks, and, from the frequent devastations of the Apaches, the valley has been almost swept of horses, mules, and cattle. The New Mexicans too, disguised as Indians, often plunder these settlements (as occurred during my visit, when two were captured) and frequently accompany the Apaches in their raids on the state of Chihuahua—*cosas de Méjico*.

At this time the Paseños had enrolled themselves into a body of troops termed *auxiliares*, seven hundred strong; but in spite of them the Apaches attacked a *mulada* at the outskirts of the town, and, but for the bravery of two negroes, runaway slaves from the Cherokee nation, would have succeeded in carrying off the whole herd; this was during my stay in this part of the country. One of the herders was killed, but the negroes, when the animals were already in the hands of the Indians, seized their rifles and came to the rescue, succeeding in recapturing the *mulada*.

At El Paso I found four Americans, prisoners at large. They had arrived here on their way to California, with a mountain trapper as their guide, who, from some disagreement respecting the amount of pay he was to receive, thought proper to revenge himself by denouncing them as spies, and they were consequently thrown into prison. It being subsequently discovered that the informer had committed the most barefaced perjury, these men were released, and the denouncer confined in their stead—quite an un-Mexican act of justice. However, as they had arrived unprovided with passports, they were detained as prisoners, although permitted to go at large about the place, living, or rather existing, on charity. Their baggage had been taken from them, their animals sold, and they were left to shift for themselves. I endeavoured to procure their liberty, by offering to take them with me and guarantee their good conduct while in the country, and also that they would not take up arms against the Mexicans; but this having no effect, and as the poor fellows were in a wretched condition, I advised them to run for it, promising to pick them up on the road and supply them with the necessary provision, and cautioning them at the same time to conceal themselves in the daytime, travelling at night, and on no account to enter the settlements. They disappeared from El Paso the same night, and what became of them will be presently shown.

On the nineteenth I left the Paso with an escort of fifteen *auxiliares*, a ragged troop, with whom to have marched through Coventry would have broken the heart of Sir John Falstaff. Armed with bows and arrows, lances, and old rusty *escopetas*, and mounted on miserable horses, their appearance was anything but warlike, and far from formidable. I did my best to escape the honour, knowing that they would only be in my way, and of not the slightest use in case of Indian attack; but all my protestations were attributed to modesty, and were overruled, and I was fain to put myself at the head of the band of valiant Paseños, who were to escort me to the borders of the state of

Chihuahua. One of them, a very old man, with a long lance which he carried across his saddlebow, and an old rusty bell-mouthed *escopeta*, attached himself particularly to me, riding by my side and pointing out the points—the *mal puntos*—whence the Apaches usually made their attacks. He had, he told me, served all through the War of Independence, "*y por el Rey*"—for the king—he added, reverently doffing his hat at the mention of the king. He was a loyalist heart and soul. "*¡Ojalá por los días felices del reyno!*"—alas for the happy time when Mexico was ruled by a king!—was his constant sighing exclamation. A doblon, with the head of Carlos Tercero, hung round his neck, and was ever in his hand, being reverently kissed every few miles. He was, he said, *medio tonto*—half-crazy—and made verses, very sorry ones, but he would repeat them to me when we arrived in camp.

Leaving El Paso, we travelled along the rugged precipitous bank of the river, crossing it about three miles above the village, and, striking into a wild barren-looking country, again made the river about sunset, and encamped in the bottom, under some very large cottonwoods, at a point called Los Alamitos—the little poplars—although they are enormous trees. We had here a very picturesque camp. Several fires gleamed under the trees, and round them lay the savage-looking Paseños, whilst the animals were picqueted round about. Several deer jumped out of the bottom when we entered, and on the banks of the river I saw some fresh beaver "sign."

The next day, halting an hour at the Brazitos, an encamping-ground so called, and a short time afterwards passing the battle-ground where Doniphan's Missourians routed the Mexicans,[2] we saw Indian sign on the banks of the river, where a considerable body had just crossed. A little farther on we met a party of seven soldiers returning from a successful hunt after the Americans who had escaped from the Paso. These unfortunates were sitting quietly behind their captors, who had overtaken them at the little settlement of Doñana, which they foolishly entered to obtain provisions.

Doñana is a very recent settlement of ten or fifteen families,[3] who, tempted by the richness of the soil, abandoned their farms in the valley of El Paso, and have here attempted to cultivate a small tract in the very midst of the Apaches, who have already paid them several visits and carried off or destroyed their stock of cattle. The

[2] The Brazito engagement occurred Christmas afternoon, 1846. Seven of Doniphan's men were slightly wounded; the Mexican loss was one howitzer captured and about one hundred men killed or wounded.—Smith, *op. cit.*, I, 302.

[3] Doñana was founded in 1842.

163

huts are built of logs and mud, and situated on the top of a tabular bluff which looks down upon the river bottom.

The soil along this bottom, from El Paso to the settlements of New Mexico, is amazingly rich, and admirably adapted for the growth of all kinds of grain. The timber upon it is cottonwood, dwarf oak, and mezquit, under which is a thick undergrowth of bushes. Several attempts have been made to settle this productive tract, but have all of them failed from the hostility of the Apaches. Should this department fall into the hands of the Americans, it will soon become a thriving settlement; for the hardy backwoodsman, with his axe on one shoulder and rifle on the other, will not be deterred by the savage, like the present pusillanimous owners of the soil, from turning it to account.

The next day we encamped at San Diego, the point where the traveller leaves the river and enters upon the dreaded Jornada del Muerto—the journey of the dead man.[4] All the camping and watering places on the river are named, but there are no settlements, with the exception of Doñana, between El Paso and Socorro, the first settlement in New Mexico, a distance of 250 miles.

At San Diego we saw more Indian signs, the consequences of which was that my escort reported their horses to be exhausted and unable to proceed; so, nothing loth, I gave them their *congé*, and the next morning they retraced their steps to El Paso, leaving me with my two servants to pass the Jornada. I was now at the edge of this formidable desert, where along the road the bleaching bones of mules and horses testify to the dangers to be apprehended from the want of water and pasture, and many human bones likewise tell their tale of Indian slaughter and assault.

I remained in camp until noon, when for the last time we led the animals to the water and allowed them to drink their fill; we then mounted, and at a sharp pace struck at once into the Jornada. The road is perfectly level and hard, and over plains bounded by sierras. *Palmillas* and bushes of sage (artemisia) are scattered here and there, but the mezquit is now becoming scarce, the *tornilla* or screw-wood taking its place; farther on this wood ceases, and there is then no fuel to be met with of any description. Large herds of antelope bounded past, and coyotes skulked along on their trail, and prairie-dog towns were met every few miles, but their inmates were snug in their winter

---

[4] The famous Jornada del Muerto was a direct route that avoided the deep canyon of the Río Grande and its wide bend to the west. The Jornada was about ninety miles long.

quarters, and only made their appearance to bask in the meridian sun. Shortly after leaving San Diego we found water in a little hole called El Perillo—the little dog—but our animals, having so lately drunk, would not profit by the discovery, and we hurried on, keeping the pack animals in a sharp trot. Near the Perillo is a point of rocks which abuts upon the road, and from which a large body of Apaches a few years since pounced upon a band of American trappers and entirely defeated them, killing several and carrying off all their animals. Behind these rocks they frequently lie in ambush, shooting down the unwary traveller, whose first intimation of their presence is the puff of smoke from the rocks, or the whiz of an arrow through the air. One of my *mozos*, who was a New Mexican and knew the country well, warned me of the dangers of this spot, and before passing it I halted the mules and rode on to reconnoitre; but no Apache lurked behind it, and we passed unmolested.

About midnight we stopped at the Laguna del Muerto—the deadman's lake—a depression in the plain, which in the rainy season is covered with water, but was now hard and dry. We rested the animals here for half an hour, and, collecting a few armfuls of artemisia, attempted to make a fire, for we were all benumbed with cold; but the dry twigs blazed brightly for a minute, and were instantly consumed. By the temporary light it afforded us we discovered that a large party of Indians had passed the very spot but a few hours, and were probably not far off at that moment, and, if so, they would certainly be attracted by our fire, so we desisted in our attempts. The mules and horses, which had travelled at a very quick pace, were suffering, even thus early, from want of water, and my horse bit off the neck of a *huage*, or gourd, which I had placed on the ground, and which the poor beast by his nose knew to contain water. However, as there was not a vestige of grass on the spot, after a halt of half an hour, we again mounted and proceeded on our journey, continuing at a rapid pace all night. At sunrise we halted for a couple of hours on a patch of grass which afforded a bite to the tired animals, and about three in the afternoon had the satisfaction of reaching the river at the watering-place called Fray Cristóval, having performed the whole distance of the Jornada, of ninety-five, or, as some say, one hundred miles, in little more than twenty hours.

The plain through which the Deadman's Journey passes is one of a system, or series, which stretch along the tableland between the Sierra Madre, or main chain of the Cordillera, on the west, and the small mountain chain of the Sierra Blanca and the Órganos, which form the dividing ridge between the waters of the Del Norte and the Río Pecos. Through this valley, fed by but few streams, runs the Del Norte. Its water, from the constant abrasion of the banks of alluvial soil, is very muddy and discoloured, but nevertheless of excellent quality, and has the reputation at El Paso of possessing chemical properties which prevent diseases of the kidneys, stone, &c. &c.

The White Mountain and the Órganos are singularly destitute of streams, but on the latter is said to be a small lake, in the waters of which may be seen the phenomenon of a daily rise and fall similar to a tide. They are also reported to abound in minerals, but, from the fact of these sierras being the hiding-places of Apaches, they are never visited excepting during a hostile expedition against these Indians, and consequently in these excursions but little opportunity is afforded for an examination of the country. The sierras are also celebrated for medicinal herbs of great value, which the Apaches, when at peace with the Paseños, sometimes bring in for sale.

Indeed, from the accounts which I have received from the people of these mountains, I should judge them to be well worthy of a visit, which, however, would be extremely hazardous on account of the hostility of the Indians and the scarcity of water. Their formation is apparently volcanic, and—judging from the nature of the plains, which in many places are strewed with volcanic substances and exhibit the bluffs of tabular form, composed of basaltic lava, known by the name of mesas (tables)—the valley must at one time have been subjected to volcanic agency.

Staying at Fray Cristóval but one night, I pushed on to the ruins of Valverde,[5] a long-deserted rancheria, a few miles beyond which was the advanced post of the American troops. Here, encamped on the banks of the river in the heavy timber, I found a great portion of the caravan which I have before mentioned as being en route to Chihuahua, and also a surveying party under the command of Lieutenant Abert,[6] of the United States Topographical Engineers. Being entirely out of provisions, and my camp hungry, the next morning I mounted my hunting mule and crossed the river, which was partially

[5] Later to be the scene of one of the important engagements in Colonel Sibley's Texan invasion of New Mexico—the Battle of Valverde, February 21, 1862.

[6] Lieutenant J. W. Abert of the Topographical Engineers, attached to the Army of the West, tells of Ruxton's arrival at the camp of the Engineers on November 28, 1846. Abert gives the war news brought by Ruxton and reveals something of Ruxton's role and mission not given by the young English traveller. See Note 1, Chapter 6, above.

frozen, to look for deer in the bottom. Thanks to my mule, as I was passing through a thicket I saw her prick her ears and look on one side, and, following her gaze, descried three deer standing under a tree with their heads turned towards me. My rifle was quickly up to my shoulder, and a fine large doe dropped to the report, shot through the heart. Being in a hurry, I did not wait to cut it up, but threw it onto my mule, which I drove before me to the river. Large blocks of ice were floating down, which rendered the passage difficult, but I mounted behind the deer and pushed the mule into the stream. Just as we had got into the middle of the current a large piece of ice struck her, and, to prevent herself being carried down the stream, she threw herself on her haunches, and I slipped over the tail, and head over ears into the water. Rid of the extra load, the mule carried the deer safely over and trotted off to camp, where she quietly stood to be unpacked, leaving me, drenched to the skin, to follow after her.

The traders had been lying here many weeks, and the bottom where they were encamped presented quite a picturesque appearance. The timber extends half a mile from the river, and the cottonwood trees are of large size, without any undergrowth of bushes. Amongst the trees, in open spaces, were drawn up the waggons, formed into a corral or square, and close together, so that the whole made a most formidable fort, and, when filled with some hundred rifles, could defy the attacks of Indians or Mexicans. Scattered about were tents and shanties of logs and branches of every conceivable form, round which lounged wild-looking Missourians, some cooking at the campfires, some cleaning their rifles or firing at targets—blazes cut in the trees, with a bull's eye made with wet powder on the white bark. From morning till night the camp resounded with the popping of rifles, firing at marks for prizes of tobacco, or at any living creature which presented itself. The oxen, horses, and mules were sent out at daylight to pasture on the grass of the prairie, and at sunset made their appearance, driven in by the Mexican herders, and were secured for the night in the corrals. My own animals roamed at will, but every evening came to the river to drink, and made their way to my camp, where they would frequently stay round the fire all night. They never required herding, for they made their appearance as regularly as the day closed, and would come to my whistle whenever I required my hunting mule. The poor beasts were getting very poor, not having had corn since leaving El Paso, and having subsisted during the journey from that place on very little of the coarsest kind of grass. They felt it the more as they were all accustomed to be fed on grain; and the severe cold was very trying to them, coming as they did, from a tropical climate. My favourite horse, Panchito, had lost all his good looks; his once full and arched neck was now a perfect "ewe," and his ribs and hipbones were almost protruding through the skin; but he was as game as ever, and had never once flinched in his work.

Provisions of all kinds were very scarce in the camp, and the game, being constantly hunted, soon disappeared. Having been invited to join the hospitable mess of the officers of the Engineers, I fortunately did not suffer, although even they were living on their rations, and on the produce of our guns. The traders, mostly young men from the Eastern cities, were fine hearty fellows, who employ their capital in this trade because it combines pleasure with profit, and the excitement and danger of the journey through the Indian country are more agreeable than the monotonous life of a city merchant. The volunteers' camp was some three miles up the river on the other side. Colonel Doniphan, who commanded, had just returned from an expedition into the Navajo country for the purpose of making a treaty with the chiefs of that nation, who had hitherto been bitter enemies of the New Mexicans. From appearances no one would have imagined this to be a military encampment. The tents were in a line, but there all uniformity ceased. There were no regulations in force with regard to cleanliness. The camp was strewed with the bones and offal of the cattle slaughtered for its supply, and not the slightest attention was paid to keeping it clear from other accumulations of filth. The men, unwashed and unshaven, were ragged and dirty, without uniforms, and dressed as, and how, they pleased. They wandered about, listless and sickly looking, or were sitting in groups playing at cards, and swearing and cursing, even at the officers if they interfered to stop it (as I witnessed). The greatest irregularities constantly took place. Sentries, or a guard, although in an enemy's country, were voted unnecessary; and one fine day, during the time I was here, three Navajo Indians ran off with a flock of eight hundred sheep belonging to the camp, killing the two volunteers in charge of them, and reaching the mountains in safety with their booty. Their mules and horses were straying over the country; in fact, the most total want of discipline was apparent in everything. These very men, however, were as full of fight as game cocks, and shortly after defeated four times their number of Mexicans at Sacramento, near Chihuahua.[7]

[7] Lieutenant Ruxton, as an experienced European military man, looked with contempt upon the discipline and management of the American army, but he did recognize the fighting ability of the individual men.

The American can never be made a soldier; his constitution will not bear the restraint of discipline, neither will his very mistaken notions about liberty allow him to subject himself to its necessary control. In a country abounding with all the necessaries of life, and where anyone of physical ability is at no loss for profitable employment; moreover, where, from the nature of the country, the lower classes lead a life free from all the restraint of society, and almost its conventional laws, it is easy to conceive that it would require great inducements for a man to enter the army and subject himself to discipline for the sake of the trifling remuneration, when so many other sources of profitable employment are open to him. For these reasons the service is unpopular, and only resorted to by men who are either too indolent to work, or whose bad characters prevent them seeking other employment.

The volunteering service, on the other hand, is eagerly sought, on occasions such as the present war with Mexico affords, by young men even of the most respectable classes, as, in this, discipline exists but in name, and they have privileges and rights, such as electing their own officers, &c., which they consider to be more consonant to their ideas of liberty and equality. The system is palpably bad, as they have sufficiently proved in this war. The election of officers is made entirely a political question, and quite irrespective of their military qualities, and, knowing the footing on which they stand with the men, they, if even they know how, are afraid to exact of them either order or discipline. Of drill or manoeuvring the volunteers have little or no idea. "Every man on his own hook" is their system in action; and trusting to, and confident in, their undeniable bravery, they "go ahead," and overcome all obstacles. No people know better the advantages of discipline than do the officers of the regular service; and it is greatly to their credit that they can keep the standing army in the state it is. As it is mostly composed of foreigners—Germans, English, and Irish, and deserters from the British army—they might be brought to as perfect a state of discipline as any of the armies of Europe; but the feeling of the people will not permit it; the public would at once cry out against it as contrary to republican notions and the liberty of the citizen.

There is a vast disparity between the officers of the regular army and the men they command. Receiving at Westpoint (an admirable institution) a military education by which they acquire a practical as well as theoretical knowledge of the science of war, as a class they are probably more distinguished for military knowledge than the officers of any European army. Uniting with this a high chivalrous feeling and most conspicuous gallantry, they have all the essentials of the officer and soldier. Notwithstanding this, they have been hitherto an unpopular class in the United States, being accused of having a tendency to aristocratic feeling, but rather, I do believe, from the marked distinction in education and character which divides them from the mass, than any other reason. However, the late operations in Mexico have sufficiently proved that to their regular officers alone, and more particularly to those who have been educated at the much-decried Westpoint, are to be attributed the successes which have everywhere attended the American arms; and it is notorious that on more than one occasion the steadiness of the small regular force, and particularly of the artillery, under their command, has saved the army from most serious disasters.

I remained at Valverde encampment several days in order to recruit my animals before proceeding farther to the north, passing the time in hunting—game, although driven from the vicinity of the camp, being still plentiful at a little distance. Besides deer and antelope, turkeys were very abundant in the river bottom; and, of lesser game, hares, rabbits, and quail were met with on the plain, and geese and ducks in the river.

One day I got a shot at a panther (painter),[8] but did not kill it, as my old mule was so disturbed at the sight of the beast that she refused to remain quiet. The prairie between the Del Norte and the mountain, a distance of twelve or fourteen miles, is broken into gulleys and ravines, which intersect it in every direction. At the bottom of these is a thick growth of coarse grass and greasebushes, where the deer love to resort in the middle of the day. I was riding slowly up one of these cañons, with my rifle across the saddlebow and the reins thrown on the mule's neck, being at that moment engaged in lighting my pipe, when the mule pricked her ears and turned her head to one side very suddenly, giving a cant round at the same time. I looked to the right and saw a large panther, with his tail sweeping the ground, trotting leisurely up the side of the ravine, which rose abruptly from the dry bed of a watercourse, up which I was proceeding. The animal, when it had reached the top, turned round and looked at me, its tiger-like ears erect, and its tail quivering with anger. The mule snorted and backed, but, fearing to dismount, lest the animal should run off, I raised my rifle and fired both barrels at the beast, which, giving a hissing growl, bounded away unhurt.

8 Probably a cougar.

It was, however, dangerous to go far from the camp, as Apaches and Navajos were continually prowling round, and, as I have mentioned, had killed two of the volunteers, and stolen eight hundred sheep.[9] One day, while hunting, I came upon a fire which they had just left, and, as several oxen were lost that night, this party, which, from the tracks, consisted of a man, woman, and boy, had doubtless run them off. I was that day hunting in company with a French Canadian and an American, both trappers and old mountain men, when, at sundown, just as we had built a fire and were cooking our suppers under some trees near the river, we heard the gobble-gobble of an old turkey cock, as he called his flock to roost. Lying motionless on the ground, we watched the whole flock, one after another, fly up to the trees over our heads, to the number of upwards of thirty. There was still light enough to shoot, and the whole flock was within reach of our rifles, but, as we judged that we could not hope for more than one shot apiece, which would only give three birds, we agreed to wait until the moon rose, when we might bag the whole family.

Hardly daring to move, we remained quiet for several hours, as the moon rose late, consoling ourselves with our anticipations of a triumphal entry into camp, on the morrow, with twenty or thirty fine turkeys for a Christmas feast.

At length the moon rose, but unfortunately clouded; nevertheless we thought there was sufficient light for our purpose, and, rifle in hand, approached the trees where the unconscious birds were roosting. Creeping close along the ground, we stopped under the first tree we came to, and, looking up, on one of the topmost naked limbs was a round black object. The *pas* was given to me, and, raising my rifle, I endeavoured to obtain a sight, but the light was too obscure to draw "a bead," although there appeared no difficulty in getting a level. I fired, expecting to hear the crash of the falling bird follow the report, but the black object on the tree never moved. My companions chuckled, and I fired my second barrel with similar result, the bird still remaining perfectly quiet. The Canadian then stepped forth, and, taking a deliberate aim, bang he went.

"*Sacré enfant de Gârce!*" he exclaimed, finding he too had missed the bird; "I aim straight, *mais* light *très* bad, *sacré!*"

Bang went the other's rifle, and bang-bang went my two barrels immediately after, cutting the branch in two on which the bird was sitting, who, thinking this a hint to be off, and that he had sufficiently amused us, flew screaming away. The same compliments were paid

9 Abert tells of the same misfortune, *loc. cit.*, 502.

to every individual, one bird standing nine shots before it flew off; and, to end the story, we fired away every ball in our pouches without as much as touching a feather, the fact of the matter being that the light was not sufficient to see an object through the fine sight of the rifles.

At Valverde my Mexican servant deserted, why or wherefore I could not understand, as he did not even wait for his pay, and carried off no equivalent. I also left here the Mexico-Irishman who had accompanied me from Mapimí. He was already suffering from the severities of the climate, and, being very delicate, I did not think him able to stand a winter journey over the Rocky Mountains. He therefore returned to Chihuahua with one of the traders. From this point to my winter quarters in the mountains I was entirely on my own resources, being unable to hire a servant in whom I could place the least confidence, and preferring to shift for myself, rather than be harassed with being always on the watch to prevent my *fidus Achates* from robbing or murdering me. My animals gave me little or no trouble, and I had now reduced my requa to five, having left at El Paso the *tierra caliente* horse, another having died on the road, and a mule having been lost or strayed on the Del Norte. In travelling I had no difficulty with the pack and loose mules. I rode in front on Panchito, and the mules followed like dogs, never giving me occasion even to turn round to see if they were there; for if, by any accident, they lost sight of the horse, and other animals were near, they would gallop about smelling at each, and often, starting off to horses or mules feeding at a distance, would return at full gallop, crying with terror until they found their old friend. Panchito, on his part, showed equal signs of perturbation if they remained too far behind, as sometimes they would stop for a mouthful of grass, and, turning his head, would recall them by a loud neigh, which invariably had the effect of bringing them up at a hand-gallop.

The greatest difficulty I experienced was in packing the mules, which operation, when on an aparejo, or Mexican packsaddle, is the work of two men, and I may as well describe the process.

The equipment of a pack mule—*mula de carga*—consists first and foremost of the aparejo, which is a square pad of stuffed leather. An idea of the shape may be formed by taking a book and placing it saddle-fashion on any object, the leaves being equally divided, and each half forming a flap of the saddle. This is placed on the mule's back on a *jerga*, or saddlecloth, which has under it a *salea*, raw sheepskin softened by the hand, which prevents the saddle chafing the back. The aparejo is then secured by a broad grass band, which is drawn so tight that the animal appears cut in two, and groans and grunts most awfully under the operation, which to a greenhorn seems most unnecessary and cruel. It is in this, however, that the secret of packing a mule consists; the firmer the packsaddle, the more comfortably the mule travels, and with less risk of being *matada*, literally "killed," but meaning "chafed and cut."

The *carga* is then placed on the top, if a single pack; or if two of equal weight, one on each side, being coupled together by a rope, which balances them on the mule's back; a stout pack rope is then thrown over all, drawn as tight as possible under the belly, and laced round the packs, securing the load firmly in its place. A square piece of matting—*petate*—is then thrown over the pack to protect it from rain, the *tapojos* is removed from the mule's eyes, and the operation is complete. The *tapojos*—blinker—is a piece of thin embroidered leather, which is placed over the mule's eyes before being packed, and, thus blinded, the animal remains perfectly quiet. The *cargador* stands on the near side of the pack, his assistant on the other, hauling on the slack of the rope, with his knee against the side of the mule for a purchase; when the rope is taut, he cries "*Adiós!*" and the packer, rejoining "*Vaya!*" makes fast the rope on the top of the *carga*, sings out "*Anda!*" and the mule trots off to her companions, who feed round until all the mules of the *atajo* are packed.

Muleteering is the natural occupation of the Mexican. He is in all his glory when travelling as one of the *mozos* of a large *atajo*—a caravan of pack mules; but the height of his ambition is to attain the rank of *mayordomo* or *capitán*—the *brigadero* of Castile. The *atajos*, numbering from fifty to two hundred mules, travel a daily distance—*jornada*—of twelve or fifteen miles, each mule carrying a pack weighing from two to four hundred pounds. To a large *atajo* eight or ten muleteers are attached, and the dexterity and quickness with which they will saddle and pack an *atajo* of a hundred mules is surprising. The animals being driven to the spot, the lasso whirls round the head of the muleteer and falls over the head of a particular mule. The *tapojos* is placed over the eyes, the heavy *aparejo* adjusted, and the pack secured, in three minutes. On reaching the place where they purpose to encamp, the packsaddles are all ranged in regular order, with the packs between, and covered with the *petates*, a trench being cut round them in wet weather to carry off the rain. One mule is always packed with the metate—the stone block upon which the maize is ground to make *tortillas,* and the office of cook is undertaken in turn by each of the muleteers. Frijoles and chile colorado comprise their daily bill of fare, with a drink of pulque when passing through the land of the maguey.

On the fourteenth of December the camp was broken up, the traders proceeding to Fray Cristóval, at the entrance of the Jornada, to wait the arrival of the troops, which were about to advance on Chihuahua; and myself, in company with Lieutenant Abert's party,[10] en route to Santa Fé. Crossing the Del Norte, we proceeded on its right bank ten or twelve miles, encamping in the bottom near the new settlement of San Antonio, a little hamlet of ten or twelve log huts, inhabited by *pastores* and *vaqueros*—shepherds and cattle-herders. The river is but thinly timbered here, the soil being arid and sterile; on the bluffs, however, the grass is very good, being the gramma or feather grass, and numerous flocks of sheep are sent hither to pasture from the settlements higher up the stream.

The next day we passed through Socorro, a small wretched place, the first settlement of New Mexico[11] on the river. The houses are all of adobe, inside and out, one story high, and with the usual *azotea* or flat roof. They have generally a small window, with thin sheets of talc (which here abounds) as a substitute for glass. They are, however, kept clean inside, the mud floors being watered and swept many times during the day. The faces of the women were all stained with the fiery red juice of a plant called *alegría,* from the forehead to the chin. This is for the purpose of protecting their skin from the effects of the sun, and preserving them in untanned beauty to be exposed in the fandangos. Of all people in the world the Mexicans have the greatest antipathy to water, hot or cold, for ablutionary purposes. The men never touch their faces with that element, except in their bimonthly shave; and the women besmear themselves with fresh coats of *alegría* when their faces become dirty: thus their counte- nances are covered with alternate strata of paint and dirt, caked, and cracked in fissures. My first impressions of New Mexico were any- thing but favourable, either to the country or the people. The popu- lation of Socorro was wretched looking, and every countenance seemed marked by vice and debauchery. The men appear to have no other employment than smoking and basking in the sun, wrapped in their sarapes; the women in dancing and intrigue. The appearance

---

[10] Abert tells of the journey to Santa Fé, December 15 to 23. *Loc. cit.,* 507–14.
[11] Doñana and El Paso were then considered to be in Chihuahua.

of Socorro is that of a dilapidated brick kiln, or a prairie-dog town; indeed, from these animals the New Mexicans appear to have derived their style of architecture. In every village we entered, the women flocked round us begging for tobacco or money, the men loafing about, pilfering everything they could lay their hands on. As in other parts of Mexico, the women wore the *enagua*, or red petticoat, and *reboso*, and were all bare-legged. The men were some of them clad in buckskin shirts, made by the Indians. Near Socorro is a mining sierra, where gold and silver have been extracted in small quantities. All along the road we met straggling parties of the volunteers, on horse or mule back, and on foot. In every camp they usually lost some of their animals, one or two of which our party secured. The five hundred men who were on the march covered an extent of road of more than a hundred miles—the ammunition and provision waggons travelling through an enemy's country without escort!

On the sixteenth we passed through Limitar, another wretched village, and a sandy, desert country, quite uninhabited, camping again on the Del Norte; and next day, stopping an hour or two at Sabanal, we reached Bosque Redondo, the hacienda of one of the Chaves family, and one of the *ricos* of New Mexico.

The churches in the villages of New Mexico are quaint little buildings, looking, with their adobe walls, like turf stacks. At each corner of the façade half a dozen bricks are erected in the form of a tower, and a centre ornament of the same kind supports a wooden cross. They are really the most extraordinary and primitive specimens of architecture I ever met with, and the decorations of the interior are equal to the promises held out by the imposing outside.

The houses are entered by doors which barely admit a full-grown man; and the largest of New Mexican windows is but little bigger than the ventilator of a summer hat. However, in his rabbit burrow, and with his *tortillas* and his chile, his *ponche*[12] and cigar of *hoja*,[13] the New Mexican is content; and with an occasional traveller to pilfer, or the excitement of a stray Texan or two to massacre now and then, is tolerably happy—his only care being that the river rise high enough to fill his *acequia*, or irrigating ditch, that sufficient maize may grow to furnish him *tortillas* for the winter, and shucks for his half-starved horse or mule, which the Navajos have left, out of charity, after killing half his sons and daughters and bearing into captivity the wife of his bosom.

[12] A pungent tobacco grown in New Mexico. Ruxton's note.
[13] *Hoja*, corn shuck, leaves of Indian corn. Ruxton's note.

We encamped behind the house at Bosque Redondo, for which privilege I asked permission of the proprietor; and who doled us out six pennyworth of wood for our fires, never inviting us into his house, or offering the slightest civility. *Cosas de Méjico.*

On the seventeenth we reached Albuquerque, next to Santa Fé the most important town in the province, and the residence of the ex-Governor Armijo. We found here a squadron of the First United States Dragoons, the remainder of the regiment having accompanied General Kearney[14] to California. We encamped near a large building where the men were quartered; and in the evening a number of them came round the fire, asking the news from the lower country. I saw that some of them had once worn a different-coloured uniform from the sky-blue of the United States Army; and in the evening, as I was walking with some of the officers of the regiment, I was accosted by one, whom I immediately recognised as a man named Herbert, a deserter from the regiment to which I had once belonged. He had imagined that, as several years had elapsed since I had seen him, his face would not have been familiar to me, and inquired for a brother of his who was still in the regiment, denying at first that he had been in the British service.

The settled portion of the province of New Mexico is divided into two sections, which, from their being situated on the Río del Norte, are designated Río Arriba and Río Abajo, or up the river and down the river. Albuquerque is the chief town of the latter, as Santa Fé is of the former as well as the capital of the province.

The town and the estates in the neighbourhood belong to the Armijo family; and the general of that name, and ex-governor, has here a *palacio;* and has also built a barrack, in which to accommodate the numerous escort which always attends him in his progresses to and from his country seat.

The families of Armijo, Chaves, Peréa, and Ortiz are par excellence the *ricos* of New Mexico—indeed, all the wealth of the province is concentrated in their hands; and a more grasping set of people, and more hard-hearted oppressors of the poor, it would be difficult to find in any other part of Mexico, where the rights or condition of the lower classes are no more considered than in civilised countries is the welfare of dogs and pigs.

I had letters to the Señora Armijo, the wife of the runaway governor; but as it was late at night when we arrived, and as I intended

[14] Stephen W. Kearny had led his "Army of the West" to Santa Fé and had continued to California.

to leave the next morning, I did not think it worth while to present them, merely delivering to the *mayordomo* some private letters which had been intrusted to my care from Chihuahua. However, as I passed the windows of the *sala*, I had a good view of the lady, who was once celebrated as the belle of New Mexico. She is now a fat, comely dame of forty, with the remains of considerable beauty, but quite *passée*.

Our halting-place next day was at Bernalillo, a more miserable place than usual; but as I had brought letters to a wealthy *haciendado*, one Julian Peréa, I anticipated an unusual degree of hospitality. On presenting the letter, everything Don Julian possessed was instantly thrown at my feet; but out of the magnificent gift I only selected an armful of wood, from a large yardful, for our fire, and for which he charged me three rials, as well as three more for the use of an empty corral for the animals; we ourselves encamping outside his gate on the damp thawing snow, without receiving the ghost of an invitation to enter his house.

We this day got a first glimpse of one of the spurs of the Rocky Mountains, appearing, far in the distance, white with snow.

On the twentieth we encamped in a pretty valley on the Río Grande, under a high tabular bluff which overhangs the river on the western bank, and on the summit of which are the ruins of an old Indian village. About two miles from our camp was the pueblo of San Felipe, a village of the tribe of Indians known as Pueblos, or Indios Manzos—half-civilised Indians.

During the night our *mulada*, which was grazing at large in the prairie, was stampeded by the Indians. I was lying out some distance from the fire, when the noise of their thundering tread roused me, and, as they passed the fire at full gallop, I at once divined the cause. Luckily for me, Panchito, my horse, wheeled out of the crowd, and, followed by his mules, galloped up to the fire, and came to me when I whistled; the remainder of the *mulada* continuing their flight. The next morning, two fine horses and three mules were missing, and, of course, were not recovered.

The next day we encamped on Galistéo, a small stream coming from the mountains. We had now entered a wild broken country, covered with pine and cedar. A curious ridge runs from east to west, broken here and there by abrupt chasms, which exhibit its formation in alternate strata of shale and old red sandstone. There are here indications of coal, which are met along the whole of this ridge. We encamped on a bleak bluff, without timber or grass, which overlooked the stream. Late in the evening we heard the creaking of a waggon's wheels and the wo-ha of the driver, as he urged his oxen up the sandy bluff. A waggon drawn by six yoke of oxen soon made its appearance, under the charge of a tall raw-boned Yankee. As soon as he had unyoked his cattle, he approached our fire, and, seating himself almost in the blaze, stretching his long legs at the same time into the ashes, he broke out with, "Cuss sich a darned country, I say! Wall, strangers, an ugly camp this, I swar; and what my cattle ull do I don't know, for they have not eat since we put out of Santa Fé, and are darned near giv out, that's a fact; and thar's nothin' here for 'em to eat, surely. Wall, they must just hold on till tomorrow, for I have only got a pint of corn apiece for 'em tonight anyhow, so there's no two ways about that. Strangers, I guess now you'll have a skillet among ye; if yer a mind to trade, I'll just have it right off; anyhow, I'll just borrow it tonight to bake my bread, and, if yer wish to trade, name your price. Cuss sich a darned country, say I! Jist look at them oxen, wull ye!—they've nigh upon two hundred miles to go; for I'm bound to catch up the sogers afore they reach the Pass, and there's not a go in 'em."

"Well," I ventured to put in, feeling for the poor beasts, which were still yoked and standing in the river completely done up, "would it not be as well for you to feed them at once and let them rest?"

"Wall, I guess if you'll some of you lend me a hand, I'll fix 'em right off; tho', darn 'em! they've giv me a pretty darned lot of trouble, they have, darn 'em; but the critturs will have to eat, I b'lieve."

I willingly lent him the aid he required, and also added to their rations some corn, which my animals, already full, were turning up their noses at, and which the oxen greedily devoured. This done, he returned to the fire and baked his cake, fried his bacon, and made his coffee, his tongue all the while keeping up an incessant clack. This man was by himself, having a journey of two hundred miles before him, and twelve oxen and his waggon to look after, but dollars, dollars, dollars was all he thought of. Everything he saw lying about he instantly seized, wondered what it cost, what it was worth, offered to trade for it or anything else by which he might turn a penny, never waiting for an answer, and rattling on, eating, drinking, and talking without intermission; and at last, gathering himself up, said, "Wall, I guess I'll turn into my waggon now, and some of you will, may be, give a look round at the cattle every now and then, and I'll thank you"; and saying this, with a hop, step, and a jump, was inside his waggon and snoring in a couple of minutes.

We broke up camp at daybreak, leaving our friend wo-ha-ing

his cattle through the sandy bottom, and "cussing the darned country" at every step. We crossed several ridges clothed with cedars, but destitute of grass or other vegetation; and passing over a dismal plain descended into a hollow, where lay, at the bottom of a pine-covered mountain, the miserable mud-built Santa Fé; and shortly after, way-worn and travel-stained, and my poor animals in a condition which plainly showed that they had seen some hard service, we entered the city, after a journey of not much less than two thousand miles.

CHAPTER 10

Land of the Pueblos

Santa Fé, the capital of the province of Nuevo Méjico, contains about three thousand inhabitants, and is situated about fourteen miles from the left bank of the Del Norte, at the foot of a mountain forming one of the eastern chain of the Rocky Mountains. The town is a wretched collection of mud houses, without a single building of stone, although it boasts a *palacio*—as the adobe residence of the Governor is called[1]—a long low building, taking up the greater part of one side of the plaza or public square, round which runs a *portal* or colonnade supported by pillars of rough pine. The appearance of the town defies description, and I can compare it to nothing but a dilapidated brick kiln or a prairie-dog town. The inhabitants are worthy of their city, and a more miserable, vicious-looking population it would be impossible to imagine. Neither was the town improved, at the time of my visit, by the addition to the population of some three thousand Americans, the dirtiest, rowdiest crew I have ever seen collected together.

Crowds of drunken volunteers filled the streets, brawling and boasting, but never fighting; Mexicans, wrapped in sarape, scowled upon them as they passed; donkey-loads of *hoja*—corn shucks—were hawking about for sale; and Pueblo Indians and priests jostled the rude crowds of brawlers at every step. Under the *portales* were numerous monte-tables, surrounded by Mexicans and Americans. Every other house was a grocery, as they call a gin or whisky shop, continually disgorging reeling drunken men, and everywhere filth and dirt reigned triumphant.

The extent of the province of New Mexico is difficult to define, as the survey of the northern sections of the republic has never been

[1] The reconstructed Governor's Palace, occupying one side of the plaza, is now a historical museum.

LAND OF THE PUEBLOS

undertaken,[2] and a great portion of the country is still in the hands of the aborigines, who are at constant war with the Mexicans. It has been roughly estimated at six thousand square miles, with a population of seventy thousand, including the three castes of descendants of the original settlers, mestizos, and Indios Manzos or Pueblos; the mestizos, as is the case throughout the country, bearing a large proportion to the Mexico-Spanish portion of the population—in this case as fifty to one.

The Pueblos, who are the original inhabitants of New Mexico, and, living in villages, are partially civilised, are the most industrious portion of the population, and cultivate the soil in a higher degree than the New Mexicans themselves. In these Indians, in their dwellings, their manners, customs, and physical character, may be traced a striking analogy to the Aztecans or ancient Mexicans. Their houses and villages are constructed in the same manner as, from existing ruins, we may infer that the Aztecans constructed theirs. These buildings are of two, three, and even five stories, without doors or any external communication, the entrance being at the top by means of ladders through a trap door in the *azotea*, or flat roof. The population of the different Pueblos scattered along the Del Norte and to the westward of it is estimated at twelve thousand, without including the Moquis, who have preserved their independence since the year 1680.

The general character of the department is extreme aridity of soil, and the consequent deficiency of water, which must ever prevent its being thickly settled. The valley of the Del Norte is fertile, but of very limited extent; and other portions of the province are utterly valueless in an agricultural point of view, and their metallic wealth is greatly exaggerated. From association with the hardy trappers and pioneers of the Far West, the New Mexicans have in some degree imbibed a portion of their enterprise and hardihood; for settlements have been pushed far into the Rocky Mountains, whose inhabitants are many of them expert buffalo-hunters and successful trappers of beaver. The most northern of these[3] is on the Río Colorado, or Red River Creek, an affluent of the Del Norte, rising in the eastern chain of the Rocky Mountains, one hundred miles north of Santa Fé.

[2] Lieutenant Abert, of the U.S.T. Engineers, surveyed the greater portion of New Mexico in 1846. Ruxton's note. [See Abert's excellent description of New Mexico, *loc. cit.*, 440–520.]

[3] This town, on Red River, is now called Questa. It is about twenty miles south of the Colorado border.

Of the many so-called gold mines in New Mexico there is but one which has in any degree repaid the labour of working. This is El Real de Dolores, more commonly known as El Placer, situated eight leagues from Santa Fé, on the ridge of the Sierra Obscura. The gold is mostly found in what is technically called "dust," in very small quantities and with considerable labour. It has perhaps produced, since its discovery in 1828, two hundred thousand dollars, but it is very doubtful if any of these *placeres* would repay the working on a large scale.[4]

It is a favourite idea with the New Mexicans that the Pueblo Indians are acquainted with the existence and localities of some prodigiously rich mines, which in the early times of the conquest were worked by the Spaniards, at the expense of infinite toil and slavery on the part of the Indians; and that, fearing that such tyranny would be repeated if they were to disclose their secret, they have ever since steadily refused to point them out.

It is remarkable that, although existing, from the earliest times of the colonization of New Mexico, a period of two centuries, in a state of continual hostility with the numerous savage tribes of Indians who surround their territory, and in constant insecurity of life and property from their attacks—being also far removed from the enervating influences of large cities, and, in their isolated situation, entirely dependent upon their own resources—the inhabitants are totally destitute of those qualities which, for the above reasons, we might naturally have expected to distinguish them, and are as deficient in energy of character and physical courage, as they are in all the moral and intellectual qualities. In their social state but one degree removed from the veriest savages, they might take a lesson even from these in morality and the conventional decencies of life. Imposing no restraint on their passions, a shameless and universal concubinage exists, and a total disregard of moral laws, to which it would be impossible to find a parallel in any country calling itself civilised. A want of honourable principle, and consummate duplicity and treachery, characterize all their dealings. Liars by nature, they are treacherous and faithless to their friends, cowardly and cringing to their enemies; cruel, as all cowards are, they unite savage ferocity with their want of animal courage; as an example of which, their recent massacre

[4] Abert visited the *placeres*, September 29 to October 1, 1846, and described them in his report, *loc. cit.*, 448–52. Dr. Adolphus Wislizenus also visited them in July, 1846, and gave an excellent description of them in his *Memoir of a Tour to New Mexico, 1846 and 1847*, 29–33.

of Governor Bent[5] and other Americans may be given—one of a hundred instances.

I have before observed that a portion of the population of New Mexico consists of Indians, called Pueblos from the fact of their living in towns, who are in a semi-civilised state, and in whose condition may be traced an analogy to the much exaggerated civilisation of the ancient Mexicans. It is well known that, in the traditions of that people, the Aztecs migrated from the north, from regions beyond the Gila, where they made the first of their three great halts; but it is generally supposed that no traces of their course, or former habitation, existed to the northward of this river. In the country of the Navajos, as well as in the territories of the independent Moqui, are still discoverable traces of their residence, and, as I have before remarked, the Pueblo Indians construct and inhabit houses and villages of the same form and material as the *casas grandes* of the ancient Mexicans; retain many of their customs and domestic arts, as they have been handed down to us, and numerous traces of a common origin.

Amongst many of the religious forms still retained by these people, perhaps the most interesting is the perpetuation of the holy fire, by the side of which the Aztecan kept a continual watch for the return to earth of Quetzalcoatl—the god of air—who, according to their tradition, visited the earth, and instructed the inhabitants in agriculture and other useful arts. During his sojourn he caused the earth to yield tenfold productions, without the necessity of human labour: everywhere corn, fruit, and flowers delighted the eye; the cotton plant produced its woof already dyed by nature with various hues; aromatic odours pervaded the air; and on all sides resounded the melodious notes of singing birds. The lazy Mexican naturally looks back to this period as the "golden age"; and as this popular and beneficent deity, on his departure from earth, promised faithfully to return and revisit the people he loved so well, this event is confidently expected to the present day. Quetzalcoatl embarked, in his boat of rattlesnake skins, on the Gulf of Mexico; and as he was seen to steer to the eastward, his arrival is consequently looked for from that quarter. When the Spaniards arrived from the east, as they resembled the god in the colour of their skin, they were at first gen-

---

[5] Governor Charles Bent, of the trading firm of Bent and St. Vrain, was appointed by General Kearny as the first American governor of New Mexico. He was killed at his home in Taos on January 19, 1847, one of the victims of the uprising.

erally supposed to be messengers from, or descendants of, the god of air.[6]

This tradition is common to the nations even of the far-off north, and in New Mexico the belief is still clung to by the Pueblo Indians, who in a solitary cave of the mountains have for centuries continued their patient vigils by the undying fire; and its dim light may still be seen by the wandering hunter glimmering from the recesses of a cave, when, led by the chase, he passes in the vicinity of this humble and lonely temple.

Far to the north, in the country of the Moquis, the hunters have passed, wonderingly, ruins of large cities, and towns inhabited by Indians, of the same construction as those of the Pueblos, and identical with the *casas grandes* on the Gila and elsewhere.

In the absence of any evidence, traditionary or otherwise, on which to found an hypothesis as to the probable cause of the migration of the Mexicans from the north, I have surmised that it is just possible that they may have abandoned that region on account of the violent volcanic convulsions which, from the testimony of people who have visited these regions, I have no doubt have at a comparatively recent period agitated that portion of the country; and from my own knowledge the volcanic formations become gradually more recent as they advance to the north along the whole tableland from Mexico to Santa Fé. These disturbances may have led to their frequent changes of residence, and ultimate arrival in the south.[7] If their object was to fly from such constantly recurring commotions, their course would naturally be to the south, where they might expect a genial soil and climate, in a direction in which they might also avoid the numerous and warlike nations who inhabited the regions south of their abandoned country. Thus we find the remains of the towns built in the course of their migration, generally in insulated spots of fertility, oases in the vast and barren tracts they were obliged to traverse, which spread from the shores of the Great Salt Lake of the north towards the valley of the Gila, and still southward along the ridges of the Cordillera, which, a continuation of the Andes chain, stretch far away to the southern portion of the country.

[6] The Quetzalcoatl legend aided Cortez in his entry into Mexico. For descriptions and beliefs regarding the "Fair God," see H. I. Priestley, *The Mexican Nation*, and the writings of Prescott, H. H. Bancroft, and Bernal Diaz.

[7] Although, geologically speaking, the volcanic disturbances are "recent," few if any modern ethnologists would accept Ruxton's hypothesis as to the cause of the early migrations.

The Indians of Northern Mexico, including the Pueblos, belong to the same family—the Apache,[8] from which branch the Navajos, Apaches Coyoteros, Mescaleros, Moquis, Yubipias, Maricopas, Chiricaquis, Chemeguabas, Yumayas (the two last tribes of the Moqui), and the Nijoras, a small tribe on the Gila. All these speak dialects of the same language, more or less approximating to the Apache, and of all of which the idiomatic structure is the same. They likewise all understand each other's tongue. What relation this language bears to the Mexican is unknown, but my impression is that it will be found to assimilate greatly, if not to be identical.

The Pueblo Indians of Taos, Pecuris, and Acoma speak a language of which a dialect is used by those of the Río Abajo, including the Pueblos of San Felipe, Sandia, Ysleta, and Jémez. They are eminently distinguished from the New Mexicans in their social and moral character, being industrious, sober, honest, brave, and at the same time peaceably inclined if their rights are not infringed. Although the Pueblos are nominally *Cristianos,* and have embraced the outward forms of *la santa fé Católica,* they yet, in fact, still cling to the belief of their fathers, and celebrate in secret the ancient rites of their religion. The aged and devout of both sexes may still be often seen on their flat housetops, with their faces turned to the rising sun, and their gaze fixed in that direction from whence they expect, sooner or later, the god of air will make his appearance. They are careful, however, not to practise any of their rites before strangers, and ostensibly conform to the ceremonies of the Roman Church.

In the country of the Moquis are the remains of five cities of considerable extent, the foundations and some of the walls of which (of stone) are still standing, and on the sites of some they still inhabit villages, the houses of which are frequently built of materials found amongst the ruins. A great quantity of broken pottery is found wherever these remains exist, the same in form and material as the relics of the same kind preserved in the city of Mexico. The ruins on the Gila, in particular, abound in these remains, and I have been assured that for many miles the plain is strewed with them. There are also remains of *acequias,* or irrigating canals, of great length and depth.

The five pueblos in the Moqui are Orayxa, Masanais, Jongoapi, Gualpi, and another, the name of which is not known. This tribe is,

[8] Ruxton's ethnology has been greatly revised by modern anthropologists. The early Spaniards first applied the general term "Apache" to the wild tribes of the north, and subsequently, as they became better acquainted, applied different names to various subdivisions and to adjacent tribes.

185

curiously enough, known to the trappers and hunters of the mountains as the Welsh Indians.[9] They are, they say, much fairer in complexion than other tribes, and have several individuals amongst them perfectly white, with light hair. The latter circumstance is accounted for by the frequent occurrence amongst the Navajos, and probably the Moquis also, of albinos, with the Indian feature, but light complexions, eyes, and hair.

In connection with this, I may mention a curious circumstance which happened to me, and tends to show that there is some little foundation for the belief of the trappers that the Moqui Indians are descendants of the followers of Prince Madoc.

I happened on my arrival at the frontier of the United States (at Fort Leavenworth) to enter the log hut of an old negro woman, being at the time in my mountain attire of buckskins, over which was thrown a Moqui or Navajo blanket, as it was wet weather. The old dame's attention was called to it by its varied and gaudy colours, and, examining it carefully for some time, she exclaimed, "That's a Welsh blanket; I know it by the woof!" She had, she told me, in her youth, lived for many years in a Welsh family and in a Welsh settlement in Virginia, or one of the Southern states, and had learned their method of working, which was the same as that displayed in my blanket. The blankets and *tilmas* manufactured by the Navajos, Moquis, and the Pueblos are of excellent quality, and dyed in durable and bright colours; the warp is of cotton filled with wool, the texture close and impervious to rain. Their pottery is, as I have before remarked, the same as that manufactured by the Aztecs, painted in bright patterns by coloured earths and the juice of several plants. The dress of the Pueblos is a mixture of their ancient costume with

[9] The idea of Welsh Indians was an early and persistent belief among Western explorers and travellers. The legend is given a thorough review and is traced in scholarly fashion by David Williams in his "John Evans' Strange Journey," in the *American Historical Review*, Vol. LIV (January and April, 1949), 277-95, 508-29. The Mandans of the Dakota region and the Moqui (or Hopi) of Arizona were the tribes most frequently referred to as possibly the "Welsh Indians." John Evans, in 1795-97, came from Wales and made a special journey up the Missouri River to seek Welsh Indians. Despite his ardor, he suffered disappointment. Upon his return he wrote: "In respect of the Welch Indians, I have only to inform you that I could not meet with such a people, and from the intercourse I have had with Indians from latitude 35 to 49 I think you may with safety inform our friends that they have no existence."—Williams, *loc. cit.*, 526.

The legend persisted nonetheless. After the Mormons settled in Utah, Brigham Young sent missionaries to the Moquis in the hope that they might prove to be the "Welsh Indians."

that introduced by the Spaniards. A *tilma,* or small blanket without sleeves, is worn over the shoulder, and their legs and feet are protected by mocassins and leggings of deerskin or woolen stuff. Their heads are uncovered, and their hair long and unconfined, save the centre or scalp lock, which is usually bound with gay-coloured ribbon. The women's dress is the same as that of the squaws of the wild Indians of the prairies, generally covered with a bright-coloured blanket, or a mantle of cloth.

The Pueblo Indians have been more than once the chief actors in the many insurrections which have disturbed this remote province. In 1837 they overturned the government, killing the incapable man at the head of it, as they had done his predecessor, and placing one of their own party at the head of affairs.[10] Recently they rose upon the Americans, who have taken possession of the country, and, in conjunction with the Mexicans, massacred Governor Bent and many others. They were defeated by the American troops in a pitched battle at La Cañada, but defended most gallantly their chief pueblo (of Taos), which was taken and destroyed after a desperate resistance.[11]

Although I had determined to remain some time in Santa Fé to recruit my animals, I was so disgusted with the filth of the town and the disreputable society a stranger was forced into, that in a very few days I once more packed my mules and proceeded to the north, through the valley of Taos.

It was a cold, snowy day on which I left Santa Fé, and the mountain, although here of inconsiderable elevation, was difficult to cross on account of the drifts. My mules, too, were for the first time introduced to snow on a large scale, and, by their careful, mincing steps and cautious movements, testified their doubts as to the security of such a road. The mountain is covered with pine and cedar, and the road winds through the bed of an arroyo, between high banks now buried in the snow. Not a living thing was visible, but once a large grey wolf was surprised on our turning a corner of rock, and in his

[10] The Pueblo insurrectionists killed Governor Pérez and elected a Taos Indian, José Gonzales, governor. Manuel Armijo, who cunningly promoted the rebellion, soon came out as champion of the central government and by suppressing the uprising won the governorship. Americans were sometimes accused of promoting the insurrection, but appear to have had little or no connection with it. For an account of the uprising of 1837, see Twitchell, *op. cit.,* II, 53–67.

[11] A number of Americans, in several villages, were killed in this frenzied uprising, of January 19, 1847. See Twitchell, *op. cit.,* II, 233–43, for one of the many accounts of the affair.

hurry to escape plunged into a snowdrift, where I could easily have dispatched the animal with a pistol, but Panchito was in such a state of affright that nothing would induce him to stand still or approach the spot.

Over ridges and through mountain gorges we passed into a small valley, where the pueblo of Ohuaqui afforded me shelter for the night, and a warm stable with plenty of corn for my animals, a luxury they had long been unaccustomed to.

I was here made welcome by the Indian family, who prepared my supper of frijoles and *atole*, the last *the* dish of New Mexico. It is made of the Indian meal, mixed with water into a thick gruel, and thus eaten—an insipid compound. Far more agreeable is the pinole of the *tierra afuera*, which is the meal of parched maize, mixed with sugar and spices, and of which a handful in a pint of water makes a most cooling and agreeable drink, and is the great standby of the *arrieros* and road-travellers in that starving country.

The *patrona* of the family seemed rather shy of me at first, until, in the course of conversation, she discovered that I was an Englishman. "*Gracias á Dios,*" she exclaimed, "a Christian will sleep with us tonight, and not an American!"

I found over all New Mexico that the most bitter feeling and most determined hostility existed against the Americans, who certainly in Santa Fé and elsewhere have not been very anxious to conciliate the people, but by their bullying and overbearing demeanour towards them, have in a great measure been the cause of this hatred, which shortly after broke out in an organised rising of the northern part of the province, and occasioned great loss of life to both parties.

After supper the women of the family spread the floor with blankets, and every one, myself included, cigar in mouth, lay down—to the number of fifteen—in a space of less than that number of square feet; men, women, and children, all smoking and chattering. Just over my head were roosting several fowls; and one venerable cock every five minutes saluted us with a shrill crow, to the infinite satisfaction of the old Indian, who at every fresh one exclaimed, "*¡Ay, cómo canta mi gallo, tan claro!*—How clear sings my cock, the fine fellow! *¡Válgame Dios, qué paxarito tan hermoso!*—What a lovely bird is this!"

The next day, passing the miserable village of La Cañada, and the Indian pueblo of San Juan, both situated in a wretched, sterile-looking country, we reached El Embudo[12]—the funnel—where I put up in the house of an old Canadian trapper, who had taken to himself a Mexican wife and was ending his days as a quiet ranchero. He appeared to have forgotten the plenty of the mountains, for his pretty daughter set before us for supper a plate containing six small pieces of fat pork, like dice, floating in a sea of grease, hot and red with chile colorado.

We crossed, next day, a range of mountains covered with pine and cedar; on the latter grew great quantities of mistletoe, and the contrast of its bright green and the sombre hue of the cedars was very striking. The snow was melting on the ascent, which was exposed to the sun, and made the road exceedingly slippery and tiring to the animals. On reaching the summit a fine prospect presented itself. The Rocky Mountains, stretching away on each side of me, here divided into several branches, whose isolated peaks stood out in bold relief against the clear, cold sky. Valleys and plains lay between them, through which the river wound its way in deep cañons. In the distance was the snowy summit of the Sierra Nevada, bright with the rays of the setting sun, and at my feet lay the smiling vale of Taos, with its numerous villages and the curiously constructed pueblos of the Indians. Snow-covered mountains surrounded it, whose ridges were flooded with light, while the valley was almost shrouded in gloom and darkness.

On descending I was obliged to dismount and lead my horse, whose feet, balled with snow, were continually slipping from under him. After sunset the cold was intense, and, wading through the snow, my mocassins became frozen, so that I was obliged to travel quickly to prevent my feet from being frostbitten. It was quite dark when I reached the plain, and the night was so obscure that the track was perfectly hidden, and my only guide was the distant lights of the villages. Coming to a frozen brook, the mules refused to cross the ice, and I spent an hour in fruitless attempts to induce them. I could find nothing at hand with which to break the ice, and at length, half frozen, was obliged to turn back and retrace my steps to a rancho, which the Indian boy who was my guide said was about a mile distant. This I at length reached, though not before one of my feet was frostbitten, and my hands so completely numbed by the excessive cold that I was unable to unpack the mules when I got in. To protect the poor animals from the cold, as there was no stable to place them in, I devoted the whole of my bedding to cover them, reserving to myself only a sarape, which, however, by the side of a blazing wood

[12] These three villages are shown on the Abert and Peck map, which accompanies the Abert account, *loc. cit.*, 548.

fire, was sufficient to keep me warm. The good lady of the house sent me a huge bowl of *atole* as I was engaged in clothing the animals, which I offered to Panchito as soon as the messenger's back was turned, and he swallowed it, boiling hot as it was, with great gusto.

The next morning, with the assistance of some rancheros, I crossed the stream, and arrived at Fernández,[13] which is the most considerable village in the valley.

El Valle de Taos is situated about eighty miles to the northward of Santa Fé, on the eastern side of the Del Norte. It contains several villages or rancherias, the largest of which are estimated at eight thousand, including the Pueblo Indians. The soil is exceedingly fertile, and produces excellent wheat and other grain. The climate being rigorous, and the summers short, fruit does not ripen to perfection, but vegetables of all kinds are good and abundant, onions in particular growing to great size and excellent flavour. The climate is colder than at Santa Fé, the thermometer sometimes falling to zero in winter, and seldom rising above 75° in summer; the nights in summer being delightfully cool, but in winter piercingly cold. Although generally healthy, infectious disorders are sometimes prevalent and fatal; and periodical epidemics have on several occasions nearly decimated the inhabitants.

In all maps the valley of Taos is confounded with a city which under that name appears in them, but which does not exist, Fernández being the chief town of the valley, and no such town as *Taos* to be found. The valley derives its name from the Taoses, a tribe of Indians who once inhabited it, and the remains of which inhabit a pueblo under the mountain about seven miles from Fernández.[14] Humboldt mentions Taos as a city containing 8,900 inhabitants. Its latitude is about 36° 30', longitude between 105° 30' and 106° west of Greenwich, but its exact position has never been accurately determined. The extent of the valley from El Rancho to Arroyo Hondo is seventeen miles, the breadth from the Del Norte to the mountains about the same.

Several distilleries are worked both at Fernández and El Rancho, the latter better known to Americans as The Ranch. Most of them belong to Americans, who are generally trappers and hunters, who having married Taos women have settled here. The Taos whisky, a

[13] Fernández [de Taos] is the village now known as Taos.
[14] The Taos Indian village, mainly in two large communal houses, is located on Taos Creek, about five miles from the town of Taos.

raw fiery spirit which they manufacture, has a ready market in the mountains amongst the trappers and hunters, and the Indian traders, who find the "firewater" the most profitable article of trade with the aborigines, who exchange for it their buffalo robes and other peltries at a "tremendous sacrifice."[15]

In Fernández I was hospitably entertained in the house of an American named Lee,[16] who had for many years traded and trapped in the mountains, but who now, having married a Mexican woman, had set up a distillery and was amassing a considerable fortune. He gave me a pressing invitation to stop the winter with him, which I was well inclined to accept, if I could have obtained good pasture for my animals; that, however, was not to be had, and I continued my journey. A few days after my departure, Lee's house was attacked by the Mexicans, at the time when they massacred Governor Bent[17] in the same village, and himself killed, with every foreigner in the place excepting the brother of Lee,[18] who was protected by the priest and saved by him from the savage fury of the mob.

Bent, as well as Lee, had resided many years in New Mexico, both having wives and children in the country, and were supposed to have been much esteemed by the people. The former was an old trader amongst the Indians, and the owner of Bent's Fort, or Fort William,[19] a trading post on the Arkansa, well known for its hospitality to travellers in the Far West. From his knowledge of the country and the Mexican character, Mr. Bent had been appointed Governor of New Mexico by General Kearney, and it was during a temporary visit to his family in Fernández that he was killed in their

[15] This liquor, known to the American trappers as "Taos lightnin'," was made from wheat.

[16] Stephen Luis Lee was acting sheriff of Taos at the time of the uprising in which he was killed. In 1843, he and Narciso Beaubien, also killed in the uprising, had been given the Sangre de Cristo land grant of over 1,000,000 acres, embracing all of present Costilla County, Colorado.

[17] Charles Bent, son of Silas and Martha Kerr Bent, was born November 11, 1789. In 1828, he journeyed over the Santa Fé Trail and began trade in New Mexico. His long friendship and business dealings with New Mexicans led to his choice as the first American governor of New Mexico, appointed September 22, 1846. For an account of his death, see Twitchell, op. cit., II, 233–35.

[18] General Elliott Lee, brother of Stephen Luis Lee, escaped the massacre.

[19] Bent's Fort, the most important fur-trade post of the Southwest, was built in 1832 and abandoned in 1849. Its site, about ten miles east of La Junta, Colorado, is marked with a granite monument. For data on the fort, see G. B. Grinnell, Old Bent's Fort and Its Builders.

presence, and scalped and mutilated, by a mob of Pueblos and the people of Taos.

William Bent[20] was one of those hardy sons of enterprise with whom America abounds, who, from love of dangerous adventure, forsake the quiet monotonous life of the civilised world for the excitement of a sojourn in the Far West. For many years he traded with Indians on the Platte and Arkansa, winning golden opinions from the poor Indians for his honesty and fair dealing, and the greatest popularity from the hardy trappers and mountaineers for his firmness of character and personal bravery.

Notwithstanding the advice I received not to attempt such a journey at this season, I determined to cross the mountains and winter on the other side, either at the head of Arkansa or Platte, or in some of the mountain valleys, which are the wintering places of many of the trappers and mountain men. I therefore hired a half-breed Pueblo as a guide, who, by the by, was one of the most rascally-looking of rascally Mexicans, and on the first of January was once more on my way.

I left Fernández late in the day, as I intended to proceed only twelve miles to Arroyo Hondo, and there remain for the night. After proceeding a mile or two we came to a stream about thirty feet in breadth and completely frozen. Here the mules came to a stop, and nothing would induce them to attempt to cross. Even the last resource, that of crossing myself on Panchito and pretending to ride away with their favourite, entirely failed, although they ran up and down the bank bellowing with affright, smelling the ice, feeling it with their forefeet, and, throwing up their heads, would gallop to another point, and up and down, in great commotion. At length I had to take a pole, which was opportunely lying near, and break the ice away, having to remove the broken blocks entirely before they would attempt it. With all this, however, my old hunting mule still refused; but, as I knew she would not be left behind, I proceeded on with the rest. At this she became frantic, galloped away from the river, returned, bellowed and cried, and at last, driven to desperation, she made a jump right into the air, but not near the broken place, and came down like a lump of lead on the top of the ice, which, of course, smashed under her weight, and down she went into a deep hole, her head just appearing out of the water, which was "mush" with ice. In this "fix" she remained perfectly still, apparently con-

[20] William Bent, brother of Charles, was the resident proprietor of Bent's Fort on the Arkansas.

scious that her own exertions would be unavailing; and I therefore had to return, and, up to my middle in water, break her out of the ice, expecting every moment to see her drop frozen to death. At last, and with great labour, I extricated her, when she at once ran up to the horse and hinnied her delight at the meeting.

By this time it was pitchy dark, and the cold had become intense; my mocassins and deerskin leggings were frozen hard and stiff, and my feet and legs in a fair way of becoming in the same state. There was no road or track, the snow everywhere covering the country, and my guide had evidently lost his way. However, I asked him in which direction he thought Arroyo Hondo to be, and pushed straight on for it, floundering through the snow and falling into holes and ravines, and at length was brought to a dead halt, my horse throwing himself on his haunches, and just saving his master and himself a fall down a precipice some five hundred feet in depth, which formed one side of the Arroyo Hondo.

The lights of the rancho to which we were bound twinkled at the bottom, but to attempt to reach it, without knowing the road down the ravine, was like jumping from the top of the Monument. However, as I felt I was on the point of freezing to death, I became desperate and charged the precipice, intending to roll down with Panchito, if we could not do better; but the horse refused to move, and presently, starting to one side as I spurred him, fell headlong into a snowdrift some twenty feet in depth, where I lay under him; and, satisfied in my mind that I was *in extremis*, wished myself further from Arroyo Hondo and deplored my evil destiny. Panchito, however, managed to kick himself out; and I, half smothered and with one of my ribs disabled, soon followed his example, and again mounted. We presently came to a little adobe house, and a man, hearing our cries to each other in the dark, came out with a light. To my request for a night's lodging he replied, *"No se puede, no había más que un quartito"*—that there was no room, but one little chamber, but that at the rancho I would be well accommodated. With this hint I moved on, freezing in my saddle, and again attempted to descend, but the darkness was pitchy, and the road a wall. Whilst attempting the descent once more, a light appeared on the bank above us, and a female voice crying out, *"¡Vuélvase amigo, por Dios! que no se baja* —Return, friend, for God's sake! and don't attempt to go down. *Que vengan, pobrecitos, para calentarse*—come, poor fellows, and warm yourselves. *Por 'hí se sube, por 'hí*—this way, this is the way up" —she cried to us, holding up the light to direct our steps. *"¡Ay de mí,*

cómo sufren los pobres viajeros!—alas, what poor travellers suffer!"
—she exclaimed, eying our frozen appearance, and clothes white with
snow; and, still holding up the light, she led the way to her house,
where now, lectured by his wife for his inhospitality, the man who
had sent us away from his door bestirred himself to unpack the mules,
which, with our numbed hands, it was impossible for us to do.

A little shed full of corn shucks (the leaf of the maize, of which
animals are very fond) provided a warm shelter for the shivering
beasts; and having attended to their wants, and piled before them
enough *hoja* for a regiment of cavalry, I entered the house, where
half a dozen women were soon rubbing life into my hands and feet,
which were badly frostbitten, whilst others were busy preparing *atole*
and chile, and making *tortillas* on the hearth.

A white stone marks this day of my journey, when, for the first
time, I met with native hospitality on Arroyo Hondo. In this family,
which consisted of about fifteen souls, six were on their beds suffering from *sarampión*—the measles—which was at the time of my journey carrying off many victims in Santa Fé and Taos Valley. An old
crone was busy decocting simples in a large olla over the fire. She
asked me to taste it, giving it the name of *aceite de vivoras*—rattlesnake oil; and as I expressed my disgust by word and deed at the
intimation, which just saved my taking a gulp, the old lady was convulsed with laughter, giving me to understand that it was not really
viper oil, but was so called—*no más*. This pot, when cooked, was set
on one side, and all the patients, one after the other, crawled from
their blankets and imbibed the decoction from the gourd. One of
the sick was the mother of the family, who had run after us to bring
us back when her husband had told her of our situation—one instance
of the many which I have met of the kindness of heart of Mexican
women.

The next morning we descended into the Arroyo, and even
in daylight the track down was exceedingly dangerous, and to have
attempted it in the dark would have been an act of no little temerity.
On the other bank of the stream was situated a mill and distillery belonging to an American by the name of Turley,[21] who had quite
a thriving establishment. Sheep and goats, and innumerable hogs, ran
about the corral; his barns were filled with grain of all kinds, his mill

[21] Simeon Turley was born in Kentucky in 1807 and came to New Mexico
in 1830, according to a letter of his in the Álvarez Papers, New Mexico Historical
Society. Some of his letters, written to his brother, J. B. Turley, are in the Missouri Historical Society library.

with flour, and his cellars with whisky "in galore." Everything about the place betokened prosperity. Rosy children, uniting the fair complexions of the Anglo-Saxon with the dark tint of the Mexican, gambolled before the door. The Mexicans and Indians at work in the yard were stout, well-fed fellows, looking happy and contented; as well they might, for no one in the country paid so well, and fed so well, as Turley, who bore the reputation, far and near, of being as generous and kindhearted as he was reported to be rich. In times of scarcity no Mexican ever besought his assistance and went away empty-handed. His granaries were always open to the hungry, and his purse to the poor.

Three days after I was there they attacked his house, burned his mill, destroyed his grain and his live stock, and inhumanly butchered himself and the foreigners with him, after a gallant defence of twenty-four hours—nine men against five hundred. Such is Mexican gratitude.

I here laid in a small supply of provisions, flour and dried buffalo meat, and got besides a good breakfast—rather a memorable occurrence. Just as I arrived, a party of Mormons, who had left Colonel Cooke's command on their way to California, and were now about to cross the mountains to join a large body of their people who were wintering on the Arkansa, intending to proceed to California in the ensuing spring, were on the point of starting.[22] There were some twelve or fifteen of them, raw-boned fanatics, with four or five pack mules carrying their provisions, themselves on foot. They started several hours before me; but I overtook them before they had crossed the mountain, straggling along, some seated on the top of the mules' packs, some sitting down every few hundred yards, and all looking tired and miserable. One of the party was an Englishman, from Biddenden, in Kent, an old Peninsular soldier. I asked what could have induced him to have undertaken such an expedition. He looked at me, and, without answering the question, said, "Dang it, if I only once get hoam!"

Arroyo Hondo runs along the base of a ridge of mountain of moderate elevation, which divides the valley of Taos from that of Río Colorado, or Red River, both running into the Del Norte. The trail

---

22 This was a sick detachment, which was separated from the main Mormon Battalion and sent to Pueblo, on the Upper Arkansas. For an account of these Mormons and their coreligionists at the site of Pueblo, Colorado, see L. R. Hafen and F. M. Young, "The Mormon Settlement at Pueblo, Colorado, during the Mexican War," *Colorado Magazine*, Vol. IX, 121–36. See also Daniel Tyler, *A Concise History of the Mormon Battalion in the Mexican War, 1846–1847* (1881).

from one to the other runs through and over the mountain, a distance of about twelve miles. It is covered with pine and cedar and a species of dwarf oak; and numerous small streamlets run through the cañons and gorges. Near these grows plentifully a shrub which produces a fruit called by the mountaineers "serviceberries," of a dark blue, the size of a small grape, and of very pleasant flavour.

My animals, unused to mountain travelling, proceeded very slowly. Every little stream of frozen water was the cause of delay. The mules, on reaching the brink, always held a council of war, smelt and tried it with their forefeet, and bellowed forth their dislike of the slippery bridge. Coronela, my hunting mule, since her mishap at Fernández, was always the first to cross, but I had first to strew the ice with branches, or throw a blanket over it, before I could induce them to pass; and at last, tired of the delays thus occasioned, I passed with the horse, and left the mules to use their own discretion, although not unfrequently half an hour or more would elapse before they overtook me.

All this day I marched on foot through the snow, as Panchito made sad work of ascending and descending the mountain, and it was several hours after sunset when I arrived at Río Colorado, with one of my feet badly frozen. In the settlement, which boasted about twenty houses, on inquiry as to where I could procure a corral and *hoja* for the animals, I was directed to the house of a French Canadian —an old trapper named Laforey—one of the many who are found in these remote settlements, with Mexican wives, and passing the close of their adventurous lives in what to them is a state of ease and plenty; that is, they grow sufficient maize to support them, their faithful and well-tried rifles furnishing them with meat in abundance, to be had in all the mountains for the labour of hunting.

I was obliged to remain here two days, for my foot was so badly frozen that I was quite unable to put it to the ground. In this place I found that the Americans were in bad odour; and as I was equipped as a mountaineer, I came in for a tolerable share of abuse whenever I limped through the village. As my lameness prevented me from pursuing my tormentors, they were unusually daring, saluting me, every time I passed to the shed where my animals were corralled, with cries of "*Burro, burro, ven a comer hoja*—Jackass, jackass, come here and eat shucks. *Anda, coxo, a ver los burros, sus hermanos*—Hallo, game-leg, go and see your brothers, the donkeys"—and at last, words not being found heavy enough, pieces of adobe rattled at my ears. This, however, was a joke rather too practical to be pleasant; so, the next time I limped to the stable, I carried my rifle on my shoulder, which was a hint never to be mistaken by Mexican, and hereafter I passed with impunity. However, I was obliged to watch my animals day and night, for, as soon as I fed them, either the corn was bodily stolen, or a herd of hogs was driven in to feed at my expense. The latter aggression I put a stop to by administering to one persevering porker a pill from my rifle, and promised the threatening crowd that I would have as little compunction in letting the same amount of daylight into them if I caught them thieving the provender; and they seemed to think me in earnest, for I missed no more corn or shucks. I saw plainly enough, however, that my remaining here, with such a perfectly lawless and ruffianly crew, was likely to lead me into some trouble, if, indeed, my life was not in absolute danger, which, from what occurred shortly after, I have now no doubt it was; and therefore I only waited until my foot was sufficiently recovered to enable me to resume my journey across the mountains.

The fare in Laforey's house was what might be expected in a hunter's establishment: venison, antelope, and the meat of the *carnero cimarrón*, the Rocky Mountain sheep, furnished his larder; and such meat (poor and tough at this season of the year), with cakes of Indian meal, either *tortillas* or *gorditas*,[23] furnished the daily bill of fare. The absence of coffee he made the theme of regret at every meal, bewailing his misfortune in not having at that particular moment a supply of this article, which he never before was without, and which I may here observe, amongst the hunters and trappers when in camp or rendezvous, is considered as an indispensable necessary. Coffee, being very cheap in the States, is the universal beverage of the Western people, and finds its way to the mountains in the packs of the Indian traders, who retail it to the mountain men at the moderate price of from two to six dollars the half-pint cup. However, my friend Laforey was never known to possess any, and his lamentations were only intended to soften my heart, as he thought (erroneously) that I must certainly carry a supply with me.

"*Sacré enfant de Gârce*," he would exclaim, mixing English, French, and Spanish into a puchero-like jumble, "*voyez-vous* dat I vas nevare tan pauvre as dis time; mais before I vas siempre avec plenty café, plenty sucre; mais now, God dam, I not go à Santa Fé, God dam, and mountain men dey come aquí from autre côté, drink all my café. Sacré enfant de Gârce, nevare I vas tan pauvre as dis time, God dam.

23 The *tortilla* is a round flat pancake, made of the Indian corn meal; the *gordita* is of the same material, but thicker. Ruxton's note.

I not care comer meat, ni frijole, ni corn, mais widout café I no live. I hunt may be two, three day, may be one week, mais I eat nothin; mais sin café, enfant de Gârce, I no live, parceque me not sacré Espagnol, mais one Frenchman."

Río Colorado is the last and most northern settlement of Mexico, and is distant from Vera Cruz two thousand miles. It contains perhaps fifteen families, or a population of fifty souls, including one or two Yuta Indians, by sufferance of whom the New Mexicans have settled this valley, thus ensuring to the politic savages a supply of corn or cattle without the necessity of undertaking a raid on Taos or Santa Fé whenever they require a remount. This was the reason given me by a Yuta for allowing the encroachment on their territory.

The soil of the valley is fertile, the little strip of land which comprises it yielding grain in abundance, and being easily irrigated from the stream, the banks of which are low. The plain abounds with *alegría*, the plant from which the juice is extracted with which the belles of Nuevo Méjico cosmetically preserve their complexions. The neighbouring mountains afford plenty of large game—deer, bears, mountain sheep, and elk; and the plains are covered with countless herds of antelope, which, in the winter, hang about the foot of the sierras, which shield them from the icy winds.

No state of society can be more wretched or degrading than the social and moral condition of the inhabitants of New Mexico: but in this remote settlement, anything I had formerly imagined to be the *ne plus ultra* of misery, fell far short of the reality:—such is the degradation of the people of the Río Colorado. Growing a bare sufficiency for their own support, they hold the little land they cultivate, and their wretched hovels, on sufferance from the barbarous Yutas, who actually tolerate their presence in their country for the sole purpose of having at their command a stock of grain and a herd of mules and horses, which they make no scruple of helping themselves to, whenever they require a remount or a supply of farinaceous food. Moreover, when a war expedition against a hostile tribe has failed, and no scalps have been secured to ensure the returning warriors a welcome to their village, the Río Colorado is a kind of game preserve, where the Yutas have a certainty of filling their bag if their other covers draw blank. Here they can always depend upon procuring a few brace of Mexican scalps, when such trophies are required for a war dance or other festivity, without danger to themselves, and merely for the trouble of fetching them.

Thus, half the year, the settlers fear to leave their houses, and their corn and grain often remain uncut, the Indians being near: thus the valiant Mexicans refuse to leave the shelter of their burrows even to secure their only food. At these times their sufferings are extreme, being reduced to the verge of starvation; and the old Canadian hunter told me that he and his son entirely supported the people on several occasions by the produce of their rifles, while the maize was lying rotting in the fields. There are sufficient men in the settlement to exterminate the Yutas, were they not entirely devoid of courage; but, as it is, they allow themselves to be bullied and ill-treated with the most perfect impunity.

Against these same Indians a party of a dozen Shawnee and Delaware trappers waged a long and most destructive war, until the last of the Yutas were fain to beg for peace, after losing many of their most famous warriors and chiefs. The cowardly Mexicans, however, have seldom summoned courage to strike a blow in their own defence, and are so thoroughly despised by their savage enemies that they never scruple to attack them, however large the party, or in spite of the greatest disparity in numbers between them.

On the third day, the inflammation in my frostbitten foot having in some measure subsided, I again packed my mules, and, under a fusillade of very hard names from the *pelados*, turned my back on Mexico and the Mexicans.

Laforey escorted me out of the settlement to point out the trail —for roads now had long ceased—and, bewailing his hard fate in not having "plenty *café avec sucre*, God dam," with a concluding *enfant de Gârce*, he bid me good by, and recommended me to mind my hair— in other words, look out for my scalp. Cresting a bluff which rose from the valley, I turned in my saddle, took a last look of the adobes, and, without one regret, cried, "*¡Adiós, Méjico!*"

I had now turned my back on the last settlement, and felt a thrill of pleasure as I looked at the wild expanse of snow which lay before me, and the towering mountains which frowned on all sides, and knew that now I had seen the last—for some time at least—of civilised man under the garb of a Mexican sarape.

CHAPTER II

The Upper Arkansa

O<small>UR</small> COURSE on leaving Red River was due north, my object being to strike the Arkansa near its headwaters on the other side of the Rocky Mountains, and follow as near as possible the Yuta trail, which these Indians use in passing from the Del Norte to the Bayou Salado,[1] on their annual buffalo hunts to that elevated valley.

Skirting a low range of mountains, the trail passes a valley upwards of fifty miles in length,[2] intersected by numerous streams (called creeks by the mountain men), which rise in the neighbouring highlands, and fall into the Del Norte, near its upper waters. Our first day's journey, of about twenty-five miles, led through the uplands at the southern extremity of the valley. These are covered with pine and cedar, and the more open plains with bushes of wild sage, which is the characteristic plant in all the elevated plains of the Rocky Mountains. On emerging from the uplands, we entered a level prairie, covered with innumerable herds of antelope. These graceful animals, in bands containing several thousands, trotted up to us, and, with pointed ears and their beautiful eyes staring with eager curiosity, accompanied us for miles, running parallel to our trail within fifty or sixty yards.

The cold in these regions is more intense than I ever remember to have experienced, not excepting even in Lower Canada; and when a northerly wind sweeps over the bleak and barren plains, charged as it is with its icy reinforcements from the snow-clad mountains, it assails the unfortunate traveller, exposed to all its violence, with bloodfreezing blasts, piercing to his very heart and bones.

[1] Salty Marsh. The term was applied to present South Park, Colorado, at the head of the South Platte River. The early name derives from the salt spring and marsh near the southern end of South Park.

[2] San Luis Villey, Colorado, sometimes called the "Roof Garden of America," from its high elevation (about 7,600 feet).

Such was the state of congelation I was in on this day that even the shot-tempting antelope bounded past unscathed. My hands, with fingers of stone, refused even to hold the reins of my horse, who travelled as he pleased, sometimes slueing round his stern to the wind, which was dead ahead. Mattias, the half-breed who was my guide, enveloped from head to foot in blanket, occasionally cast a longing glance from out its folds at the provoking venison as it galloped past, muttering at intervals, "*Jesús, Jesús, qué carne*"—what meat we're losing! At length, as a band of some three thousand almost ran over us, human nature, although at freezing point, could no longer stand it. I jumped off Panchito, and, kneeling down, sent a ball from my rifle into the thick of the band. At the report two antelopes sprang into the air, their forms being distinct against the horizon above the backs of the rest; and when the herd had passed, they were lying kicking in the dust, one shot in the neck, through which the ball had passed into the body of another. We packed a mule with the choice pieces of meat, which was a great addition to our slender stock of dried provisions. As I was "butchering" the antelope, half a dozen wolves hung round the spot, attracted by the smell of blood; they were so tame, and hungry at the same time, that I thought they would actually have torn the meat from under my knife. Two of them loped round and round, gradually decreasing their distance, occasionally squatting on their haunches, and licking their impatient lips, in anxious expectation of a coming feast. I threw a large piece of meat towards them, when the whole gang jumped upon it, fighting and growling, and tearing each other in the furious melee. I am sure I might have approached near enough to have seized one by the tail, so entirely regardless of my vicinity did they appear. They were doubtless rendered more ravenous than usual by the uncommon severity of the weather, and, from the fact of the antelope congregating in large bands, were unable to prey upon these animals, which are their favourite food. Although rarely attacking a man, yet in such seasons as the present I have no doubt that they would not hesitate to charge upon a solitary traveller in the night, particularly as in winter they congregate in troops of from ten to fifty. They are so abundant in the mountains that the hunter takes no notice of them, and seldom throws away upon the skulking beasts a charge of powder and lead.

This night we camped on Rib Creek, the Costilla[3] of the New Mexican hunters, where there was no grass for our poor animals, and

[3] Costilla Creek and the ones subsequently crossed—Culebra and Trinchera —still retain their Spanish names.

the creek was frozen to such a depth that, after the greatest exertions in breaking a hole through the ice, which was nearly a foot thick, they were unable to reach the water. It is a singular fact that during intense cold, horses and mules suffer more from want of water than in the hottest weather, and often perish in the mountains when unable to procure it for two or three days in the frozen creeks. Although they made every attempt to drink, the mules actually kneeling in their endeavours to reach the water, I was obliged to give it them, one after the other, from a small tin cup which held half a pint, and from which the thirsty animals greedily drank. This tedious process occupied me more than an hour, after which there was another hour's work in hunting for wood and packing it on our backs into camp. Before we had a fire going it was late in the night, and almost midnight before we had found a little grass and picqueted the animals; all of which duties at last being effected, we cooked our collops of antelope meat, smoked a pipe, and rolled ourselves in our blankets before the fire. All night long the camp was surrounded by wolves, which approached within a few feet of the fire, and their eyes shone like coals as they hovered in the bushes, attracted by the savoury smell of the roasting venison.

The next day we struck La Culebra, or Snake Creek, where we saw that the party of Mormons had encamped, and apparently halted a day, for more than ordinary pains had been taken to make their camp comfortable, and several piles of twigs, of the sagebrush and rushes, remained, of which they had made beds. However, we were obliged to go farther down the creek, as there was no firewood near the point where the trail crosses it, and there found a sheltered place with tolerable grass, and near an air hole in the ice where the animals could drink. I remarked that in the vicinity of the Mormon camp no watering-place had been made for their animals, and, as we had seen no holes broken in the ice of the creeks we had passed, I concluded that these people had allowed their animals to shift for themselves, the consequences of which negligence were soon apparent in our further advance.

The cold was so intense that I blanketed all my animals, and even then expected that some of the mules would have perished; for it snowed heavily during the night, and the storm ended in a watery sleet, which froze as soon as it fell, and in the morning the animals were covered with a sheet of ice. We ourselves suffered extremely, turning constantly, and rolling almost into the embers of the scanty fire; and towards daybreak I really thought I should have frozen

Antelope
"wonderfully curious" animals, at Independence Rock
(A. J. Miller). Scenes like this were familiar to Ruxton
although his projected trip to this region of the Rockies
was canceled by his death

Acoma
the country and the culture of the Pueblo Indians
deeply interested Ruxton

bodily. My bedding consisted of two blankets—one of them a very thin one, which was all I had between my body and the snow; and the other, first soaked with the sleet and afterwards frozen stiff and hard, was more like a board than a blanket, and was in that state no protection against the cold. It is well known that the coldest period of the twenty-four hours is that immediately preceding the dawn of day. At this time one is generally awakened by the sensation of death-like chill, which penetrates into the very bones; and as the fire is by this time usually extinguished, or merely smouldering in the ashes, the duty of replenishing is a very trying process. To creep out of the blanket and face the cutting blast requires no little resolution; and, if there be more than one person in the camp, the horrible moment is put off by the first roused, in hopes that someone else will awaken and perform the duty. However, should the coughs and hems succeed in rousing all, it is ten to one but that all, with a blank look at the cheerless prospect, cover their heads with the blanket, and with a groan, cuddling into a ball, resettle themselves to sleep, leaving the most chilly victim to perform the office.

The half-frozen animals, standing over their picquet-pins and collapsed with cold, seem almost drawn within themselves, and occasionally approach the fire as close as their lariats will allow, bending down their noses to the feeble warmth, the breath in steaming volumes of cloud issuing from their nostrils, whilst their bodies are thickly clad with a coat of frozen snow or sleet.

Our next camp was on La Trinchera, or Bowl Creek. The country was barren and desolate, covered with sage, and with here and there a prairie with tolerable pasture. Antelope were abundant, and deer and turkeys were to be seen on the creeks. The trail passed, to the westward, a lofty peak[4] resembling in outline that one known as James's or Pike's Peak,[5] which is some two hundred and fifty miles to the north. The former is not laid down in any of the maps, although it is a well-known landmark to the Indians.

The creeks are timbered with cottonwoods, quaking asp, dwarf oak, cedar, and wild cherry, all of small growth and stunted, while the uplands are covered with a dwarfish growth of pines. From Río Colorado we had been constantly followed by a large grey wolf.

[4] Mount Blanca, elevation 14,363 feet.

[5] Dr. Edwin James, with Major S. H. Long's expedition of 1820, was the first white man to climb to the summit of the peak that Z. M. Pike had seen in 1806. Major Long called it James Peak, but Pike's name became permanently attached to the famous mountain, which is near present Colorado Springs.

Every evening, as soon as we got into camp, he made his appearance, squatting quietly down at a little distance, and after we had turned in for the night helping himself to anything lying about. Our first acquaintance commenced on the prairie where I had killed the two antelope, and the excellent dinner he then made, on the remains of the two carcases, had evidently attached him to our society. In the morning, as soon as we left the camp, he took possession, and quickly ate up the remnants of our supper and some little extras I always took care to leave for him. Shortly after, he would trot after us, and, if we halted for a short time to adjust the mule packs or water the animals, he sat down quietly until we resumed our march. But when I killed an antelope and was in the act of butchering it, he gravely looked on, or loped round and round, licking his jaws, and in a state of evident self-gratulation. I had him twenty times a day within reach of my rifle, but he became such an old friend that I never dreamed of molesting him.

Our day's travel was usually from twenty to thirty miles, for the days were very short, and we were obliged to be in camp an hour before sunset, in order to procure wood, and water the animals before dark. Before arriving at the creek where we proposed to camp, I rode ahead and selected a spot where was good grass and convenient water. We then unpacked the mules and horses and immediately watered them, after which we allowed them to feed at large until dark. In the meantime we hunted for firewood, having sometimes to go half a mile from camp, packing it on our shoulders to the spot we intended for our fire, the mule packs and saddles, &c., being placed to windward of it as a protection from the cold blasts. We then cooked supper, and at dark picqueted the animals round the camp, their lariats (or skin ropes) being attached to pegs driven in the ground. After a smoke, we spread our blankets before the fire and turned in, rising once or twice in the night to see that all was safe, and remove the animals to fresh grass when they had cleared the circle round their picquets. Guard or watch we kept none, for after a long day's travel it was too much for two of us to take alternate sentry, thus having but half the night for sleep.

We were now approaching a part of the journey much dreaded by the Indians and New Mexican buffalo hunters, and which is quite another "Jornada del Muerto," or deadman's journey. A creek called Sangre Cristo—blood of Christ—winds through a deep cañon, which opens out at one point into a small circular basin called El Vallecito—

the little valley. It is quite embosomed in the mountains; and down their rugged sides, and through the deep gorges, the wind rushes with tremendous fury, filling the valley with drifted snow, and depositing it in the numerous hollows with which it is intersected. This renders the passage of the Vallecito exceedingly difficult and dangerous, as animals are frequently buried in the snow, which is sometimes fifteen or twenty feet deep in the hollows, and four or five on the level.

This valley is also called by the mountaineers the "Wind-trap," a very appropriate name, as the wind seems to be caught and pent up here the year round, and, mad with the confinement, blows round and round, seeking for an escape.

Wishing to have my animals fresh for the passage of this dreaded spot, I this day made a short journey of fifteen miles, and camped in the cañon about three miles from the mouth of the Wind-trap. The cañon was so precipitous that the only place I could find for our camp was on the side of the mountain, where was tolerably good gramma grass, but a wretched place for ourselves; and we had to burrow out a level spot in the snow before we could place the packs in a position where they would not roll down the hill. The cedars were few and far between, and the snow covered everything in the shape of wood; and as in our last camp my tomahawk had been lost in the snow, I was unable to procure a log, and was fain to set fire to a cedar near which we had laid our packs. The flame, licking the stringy and dry bark, quickly ran up the tree, blazed along the branches in a roar of fire, illuminating the rugged mountain and throwing its light upon the thread of timber skirting the creek which wound along the bottom far beneath.

All night long the wind roared through the cañon, and at times swept the blankets from our chilled bodies with the force of a giant. The mules and horses after dark refused to feed, and, as there was no spot near where we could picquet them, the poor beasts sought shelter from the cruel blasts in the belt of dwarf oak which fringed the creek.

We passed a miserable night, perched upon the mountainside in our lonely camp, and without a fire, for the tree was soon consumed. Our old friend the wolf, however, was still a companion, and sat all night within sight of the fire, howling piteously from cold and hunger. The next morning I allowed the animals a couple of hours after sunrise to feed and fill themselves; and then, descending from our camp, we entered at once the pass into the dreaded Vallecito. A few hundred yards from the entrance lay a frozen mule, half-buried in the snow; and a little farther on another, close to the creek where the Mormons had evidently encamped not two days before.

The Vallecito was covered with snow to the depth of three feet, to all appearances perfectly level, but in fact full of hollows, with fifteen or twenty feet of snow in them. With the greatest difficulty and labour we succeeded in crossing, having to dismount and beat a path through the drifts with our bodies. The pack mules were continually falling, and were always obliged to be unpacked before they could rise. As this happened every score yards, more than half the day was consumed in traversing the valley, which cannot exceed four miles in length.

The mountain rises directly from the north end of the Vallecito, and is the dividing ridge between the waters of the Del Norte and the Arkansa, or Río Napeste of the Mexicans. The ascent to the summit, from the western side, is short, but very steep; and the snow was of such a depth that the mules could hardly make their way to the top. Leading my horse by the bridle, I led the way, and at length, numbed with cold, I reached the summit, where is a level plateau of about a hundred square yards.[6] Attaining this, and exposed to the full sweep of the wind, a blast struck me, carrying with it a perfect avalanche of snow and sleet, full in my front, and knocked me as clean off my legs as I could have been floored by a twenty-four pound shot.

The view from this point was wild and dismal in the extreme. Looking back, the whole country was covered with a thick carpet of snow, but eastward it was seen in patches only here and there. Beside me lay the main chain of the Rocky Mountains, Pike's Peak lifting its snowy head far above the rest; and to the southeast the Spanish Peaks (Cumbres Españolas)[7] towered like twin giants over the plains. Beneath the mountain on which I stood was a narrow valley, through which ran a streamlet bordered with dwarf oak and pine, and looking like a thread of silver as it wound through the plain. Rugged peaks and ridges, snow clad and covered with pine, and deep gorges filled with broken rocks, everywhere met the eye. To the eastward the mountains gradually smoothed away into detached spurs and broken ground, until they met the vast prairies, which stretched far as the eye could reach, and hundreds of miles beyond—a sea of seeming barrenness, vast and dismal. A hurricane of wind was blowing at the time,

[6] The crossing of the range at that time was by Sangre de Cristo Pass, instead of by the modern highway route over Veta Pass.

[7] The Spanish Peaks, or Huajatollas—breasts of the world—lie directly west of present Walsenburg.

and clouds of dust swept along the sandy prairies, like the smoke of a million bonfires. On the mountaintop it roared and raved through the pines, filling the air with snow and broken branches, and piling it in huge drifts against the trees. The perfect solitude of this vast wilderness was almost appalling. From my position on the summit of the dividing ridge I had a bird's-eye view, as it were, over the rugged and chaotic masses of the stupendous chain of the Rocky Mountains, and the vast deserts which stretched away from their eastern bases; while, on all sides of me, broken ridges, and chasms and ravines, with masses of piled-up rocks and uprooted trees, with clouds of drifting snow flying through the air, and the hurricane's roar battling through the forest at my feet, added to the wildness of the scene, which was unrelieved by the slightest vestige of animal or human life. Not a sound, either of bird or beast, was heard—indeed, the hoarse and stunning rattle of the wind would have drowned them, so loud it roared and raved through the trees.

The animals strove in vain to face the storm, and, turning their sterns to the wind, shrank into themselves, trembling with cold. Panchito, whom I was leading by the bridle, followed me to the edge of the plateau, but drew back, trembling, from the dismal scene which lay stretched below. With a neigh of fear he laid his cold nose against my cheek, seeming to say: "Come back, master: what can take you to such a wretched place as that, where not even a blade of grass meets the eye?"

The descent on the eastern side is steep and sudden, and through a thick forest of pines, to the valley beneath. Trail there was none to direct us, and my half-breed knew nothing of the road, having passed but once before, and many years ago, but said it went somewhere down the pines. The evening was fast closing round us, and to remain where we were was certain death to our animals, if not to ourselves: I therefore determined to push for the valley, and accordingly struck at once down the pines.

Once amongst the trees there was nothing to do but reach the bottom as fast as possible, as it was nearly dark, and nothing was to be seen at the distance of a dozen yards, so dense was the forest. Before we had proceeded as many paces from the edge of the plateau, and almost before I knew where I was, horses, mules, &c., were rolling down the mountain all together, and were at last brought up in a snowdrift some twelve feet deep. There they all lay in a heap, the half-breed under one of the pack mules, and his swarthy face just peering out of the snow. Before a mule would stir every pack had to be removed; and this, with a temperature some ten degrees below zero, was trying to the fingers, as may be imagined. As it was impossible to reach the bottom from this point, we struggled once more to the top through six feet of snow and an almost perpendicular ascent. I had to beat a road for the animals, by throwing myself bodily on the snow, and pounding it down with all my weight. We were nearly frozen by this time, and my hands were perfectly useless—so much so that, when a large bird of the grouse species[8] flew up into a pine above my head, I was unable to cock my rifle to shoot at it. The mules were plunging into the snow at every step, and their packs were hanging under their bellies, but to attempt to adjust them was out of the question. It was nearly dark too, which made our situation anything but pleasant, and the mules were quite exhausted.

At last, however, we reached the top and struck down the mountain at another point, but it was with the greatest toil and difficulty that we reached the bottom long after dark, and camped shortly after near the creek which wound through the valley, or rather in its very bed. One of the mules had slipped its pack completely under the belly, and, the girth pinching her, she started off just before reaching the creek at full gallop, kicking everything the pack contained to the four winds of heaven. This pack happened to contain all the provisions, and, as the search for them in the dark would have been useless, we this night had no supper. To shelter ourselves from the wind, we camped in the bed of the creek, which was without water, but the wind howled down it as if it were a funnel, scattering our fire in every direction as soon as it was lighted, and tearing the blankets from our very bodies. The animals never moved from the spot where they had been unpacked; even if there had been grass, they were too exhausted to feed, but stood shivering in the wind, collapsed with cold, and almost dead. Such a night I never passed, and hope never to pass again. The hurricane never lulled for a single instant; all our efforts to build a fire were unavailing; and it was with no small delight that I hailed the break of day, when we immediately packed the mules and started on our journey.

The trail now led along the creek and through small broken prairies, with bluffs exhibiting a very curious formation of shale and sandstone. At one point the cañon opens out into a pretty open glade or park, in the middle of which is a large rock resembling a ruined castle; the little prairie is covered with fine grass, and a large herd

8 Called by the hunters *le coq des bois* (Scotch capercailzie). Ruxton's note.

of black-tailed deer were feeding in it. A little farther on we descried the timber on the Huérfano or Orphan Creek, so called from the remarkable isolated rock of sandstone[9] which stands in a small prairie on its left bank, and is a well-known landmark to the Indians. We camped on the Huérfano under some high cottonwoods, the wind blowing with unabated violence. The next morning all the animals were missing, and, following their trail, we found them on the other side of the creek, five or six miles from the camp, in a little prairie full of buffalo grass. As it was late in the day when we returned to camp, we did not leave till next morning, when we crossed on to the Cuernaverde or Greenhorn Creek.[10]

On a bluff overlooking the stream I had the satisfaction of seeing two or three Indian lodges and one adobe hovel of a more aspiring order. As we crossed the creek a mountaineer on an active horse galloped up to us, his rifle over the horn of the saddle, and clad in hunting shirt and pantaloons of deerskin, with long fringes hanging down the arms and legs. As this was the first soul we had seen since leaving Red River, we were as delighted to meet a white man (and him an American) as he was to learn the news from the Mexican settlements. We found here two or three hunters, French Canadians, with their Assinnaboin and Sioux squaws, who have made the Greenhorn their headquarters,[11] and game being abundant and the rich soil of the valley affording them a sufficiency of Indian corn, they lead a tolerably easy life, and certainly a lazy one, with no cares whatever to annoy them. This valley will, I have no doubt, become one day a thriving settlement, the soil being exceedingly rich and admirably adapted to the growth of all kinds of grain. The prairies afford abundant pasture of excellent quality, and stock might be raised upon them in any numbers.

The depreciation in the value of beaver skins has thrown the great body of trappers out of employment, and there is a general tendency amongst the mountain men to settle in the fruitful valleys of the Rocky Mountains. Already the plough has turned up the soil

[9] This Huérfano Butte, which gives its name to the stream and county, is a volcanic cone. It is beside Huérfano River, immediately east of where U. S. Highway 85 crosses the stream.

[10] So named for the Comanche chief, Cuerna Verde, who was killed here by Governor Juan B. de Anza in 1779. Greenhorn Creek is a branch of the St. Charles, which empties into the Arkansas.

[11] This pioneer settlement was at the present village of Crow.

within sight of Pike's Peak,[12] and a hardy pioneer, an Englishman, has led the way to the Great Salt Lake, where a settlement of mountaineers has even now been formed, three thousand miles from the frontier of the United States.[13]

From the Greenhorn an easy day's travel brought us to the banks of the San Carlos, which, receiving the former creek, falls into the Arkansa about two hundred and fifty miles from its source. The San Carlos is well timbered with cottonwood, cherry, quaking asp, box alder, and many varieties of shrubs, and many spots in the valley are admirably adapted for cultivation, with a rich loamy soil, and so situated as to be irrigated with great facility from the creek. Irrigation is indispensable over the whole of this region, rain seldom falling in the spring and summer, which is one of the greatest drawbacks to the settlement of this country, the labour of irrigation being very great. The San Carlos heads in a lofty range of mountains about forty miles from its junction with the Arkansa. Near its upper waters is a circular valley[14] enclosed by rugged highlands, through which the stream forces its way in a cañon whose precipitous sides overhang it to the height of three hundred feet. The face of the rock (of a dark limestone) is in many places perfectly vertical, and rises from the water's edge to a great elevation, piñons and small cedars growing out of crevices in the sides.

After leaving this creek we passed a barren rolling prairie with scanty herbage and covered with the *palmillas*[15] or soap plant. A few antelope were its only tenants, and these so shy that I was unable to approach them. Fourteen miles from the San Carlos we struck the Arkansa at the little Indian trading fort of the "Pueblo,"[16] which is

[12] At the settlement on Greenhorn Creek and at Pueblo Fort on the Arkansas, present site of the city of Pueblo.

[13] Ruxton doubtless refers to the trading post and ranch of Miles Goodyear and "the mysterious Captain Wells," at the site of Ogden, Utah. This post antedated the Mormons by at least two years. It was about 1500 miles, rather than 3,000, from the American frontier. Wells is "said to have been formerly a captain in the British army, who had previously lived some years in Santa Fé."—Charles Kelly and Maurice L. Howe, *Miles Goodyear, First Citizen of Utah; Trapper, Trader and California Pioneer* (Salt Lake City, 1937).

[14] The town of Beulah now nestles in this valley.

[15] The *palmilla* or soap-plant [yucca] is a species of cactus, the fibrous root of which the New Mexicans use as a substitute for soap. An abundant lather is obtained from it. Ruxton's note.

[16] There were trading houses here as early as 1839. A regular adobe fort existed in 1842. George Simpson and James P. Beckwourth both claimed to have been founders of the post.

situated on the left bank, a few hundred yards above the mouth of the Fontaine-qui-bouille, or Boiling Spring River, so called from two springs of mineral water near its headwaters under Pike's Peak, about sixty miles from its mouth. Here I was hospitably entertained in the lodge of one John Hawkens,[17] an ex-trapper and well-known mountaineer. I turned my animals loose, and allowed them to seek for themselves the best pastures, as in the vicinity of the fort the prairies were perfectly bare of grass, and it was only near the mountain that any of a good quality was to be found.

The Arkansa is here a clear, rapid river about a hundred yards in width. The bottom, which is enclosed on each side by high bluffs, is about a quarter of a mile across, and timbered with a heavy growth of cottonwood, some of the trees being of great size. On each side vast rolling prairies stretch away for hundreds of miles, gradually ascending on the side towards the mountains, and the highlands are there sparsely covered with piñon and cedar. The high banks through which the river occasionally passes are of shale and sandstone, and rise precipitously from the water. Ascending the river, the country is wild and broken until it enters the mountains, when the scenery is grand and imposing; but the prairies around it are arid and sterile, producing but little vegetation, and the grass, though of good quality, is thin and scarce. The Pueblo is a small square fort of adobe with circular bastions at the corners, no part of the walls being more than eight feet high, and round the inside of the yard or corral are built some half-dozen little rooms inhabited by as many Indian traders, *coureurs des bois*, and mountain men. They live entirely upon game, and the greater part of the year without even bread, since but little maize is cultivated. As soon as their supply of meat is exhausted they start to the mountains with two or three pack animals, and bring them back in two or three days loaded with buffalo or venison. In the immediate vicinity of the fort game is very scarce, and the buffalo have within a few years deserted the neighbouring prairies, but they are always found in the mountain valleys, particularly in one called Bayou Salado, which abounds in every species of game, including elk, bears, deer, bighorn or Rocky Mountain sheep, buffalo, antelope, &c.

Hunting in the mountains round the head of Fontaine-qui-bouille

---

[17]In his *Life in the Far West*, Ruxton indicates that his host at Pueblo was a nephew of the famous gunsmith of St. Louis. That gunsmith he calls Jake Hawken (pp. 35, 86, 100). See also Roy T. King, "Samuel Hawken, Gunsmith and Fifty-niner," *Colorado Magazine*, Vol. XIV, 31-35.

and Bayou Salado I remained for the rest of the winter, which was unusually severe—so much so, that the hunters were not unfrequently afraid to venture with their animals into the mountains. Shortly after my arrival on Arkansa, and during a spell of fine sunny weather, I started with a Pueblo hunter for a load or two of buffalo meat, intending to hunt on the waters of the Platte and the Bayou, where bulls remain in good condition during the winter months, feeding on the rich grass of the mountain valleys. I took with me my horse and three pack mules, as it was our intention to return with a good supply of meat.

Our course lay up the Fontaine-qui-bouille,[18] and on the third day we entered the pine-covered uplands at the foot of the mountain. Here we found deer so abundant that we determined to hunt here, rather than proceed across the ridge on to the waters of the Platte. We camped on a little mountain stream[19] running into the creek an hour or two before sunset, and, as we had no provisions, we sallied out to hunt as soon as we had unpacked the mules. We killed two deer almost immediately, and, returning to camp, made a good supper off some of the tidbits.

The next morning at daybreak, as soon as I had risen from my blanket, I saw a herd of deer feeding within a few hundred yards of camp, and seizing my rifle I immediately took advantage of some broken ground to approach them. Before, however, I could get within shot they ascended the bluffs and moved across a prairie, feeding as they went. I took a long circuit to get the wind of them, and, following a ravine, at length brought my rifle to bear, and knocked over a fine buck, the others running two or three hundred yards and then stopping to look round for their missing comrade. As I ran up to the dead one and took out my knife to cut the throat, another deer ran past and stopped between me and the herd, and, taking a long shot, I dropped the animal, which, however, rose again and limped slowly away. Leaving the dead one and my ramrod on its body, I followed the wounded deer, and, about half a mile from where I fired, found it lying dead. The process of butchering occupied about twenty minutes, and, packing the hams and shoulders on my back, I trudged back to my first victim. As I was crossing a ravine and ascending the opposite bluff, I saw the figure of a man crawling along

18 Present Fountain Creek, which enters the Arkansas at Pueblo.

19 This is probably the branch which enters Fountain Creek at the present town of Manitou and which is now known as Ruxton Creek, honoring our George F. Ruxton.

the bottom, evidently with the intention of approaching me. A close inspection assured me that it was an Indian; and as none but Arapahós were likely to be in the vicinity, and as these are the Indians most hostile to the white hunters, killing them whenever an opportunity offers, I made up my mind that a war party was about, and that myself and companion stood a very good chance of "losing our hair." As the Indian cautiously advanced, I perceived another was running round the prairie to cut me off from camp, and consequently I determined to make good my ground where I was, throwing down the meat and getting my rifle in readiness for work.

The only tribes of Indians who frequent this part of the mountains are the Yutas (or Eutaws·) [Utes] and the Arapahós, who are hereditary enemies, and constantly at deadly war with each other. A large band of the Yutas had been wintering in the Bayou Salado, to which one trail leads by the Boiling Spring River (where I was hunting), and another by the Arkansa. The former is the trail followed by the Arapahó war parties when on an expedition against the Yutas in the Bayou, and therefore I felt certain that none but the former Indians would be met with in this vicinity. However, as the Yutas are a very friendly tribe, I was loth to be the first to commence hostilities in case my antagonist might prove to belong to that nation, and therefore I awaited his approach, which he made stealthily, until he saw that I had discovered him, when, throwing himself erect, and gun in hand, he made directly towards me. With rifle cocked I watched his eye until he came within fifty yards, when suddenly, seeing my hostile appearance, he stopped, and, striking his hand thrice on his brawny chest, he exclaimed, in a loud voice—

"Arapahó, Arapahó!" and stood erect and still. This announcement was very nearly being fatal to him, for, on hearing him proclaim himself one of that hostile nation, my rifle was up to my shoulder in an instant, and covering his heart. As my finger was on the trigger, it flashed across my mind that I had heard that two Arapahós were amongst the hunters on the Arkansa, their sister being married to a mountaineer, and that probably the dusky gentleman at the end of my rifle was one of these, as indeed he proved to be. I accordingly made signals of peace, and he approached and shook me by the hand. That his intentions were not altogether honest I have no doubt, but, finding me prepared, he thought it more advisable to remain *en paz*. What strengthened me in this belief was the fact, which I shortly after discovered, that a war party of his nation were at that moment camped within a few hundred yards of us, whose vicinity he never apprised me of, and who, if they had seen us, would not have hesitated an instant to secure our scalps and animals.

When I returned to the spot where I had left the first deer, not a particle was visible except some hair scattered on the ground, but a few hundred yards from the spot a dozen wolves were engaged in dining off a lump of something, which, on approach, I found to be the remains of my deer, leaving behind them, when dispersed, a handful of hair.

The sagacity of wolves is almost incredible. They will remain round a hunting camp and follow the hunters the whole day, in bands of three and four, at less than a hundred yards' distance, stopping when they stop, and sitting down quietly when game is killed, rushing to devour the offal when the hunter retires, and then following until another feed is offered them. If a deer or antelope is wounded, they immediately pursue it, and not unfrequently pull the animal down in time for the hunter to come up and secure it from their ravenous clutches. However, they appear to know at once the nature of the wound, for if but slightly touched they never exert themselves to follow a deer, chasing only which have received a mortal blow.

I one day killed an old buck which was so poor that I left the carcase on the ground untouched. Six coyotes, or small prairie wolves, were my attendants that day, and of course, before I had left the deer twenty paces, had commenced their work of destruction. Certainly not ten minutes after, I looked back and saw the same six loping after me, one of them not twenty yards behind me, with his nose and face all besmeared with blood, and his belly swelled almost to bursting. Thinking it scarcely possible that they could have devoured the whole deer in so short a space, I had the curiosity to return, and, to my astonishment, found actually nothing left but a pile of bones and hair, the flesh being stripped from them as clean as if scraped with a knife. Half an hour after, I killed a large black-tail deer, and, as it was also in miserable condition, I took merely the fleeces (as the meat on the back and ribs is called), leaving four-fifths of the animal untouched. I then retired a short distance, and, sitting down on a rock, lighted my pipe, and watched the operations of the wolves. They sat perfectly still until I had withdrawn some threescore yards, when they scampered, with a flourish of their tails, straight to the deer. Then commenced such a tugging and snarling and biting, all squeaking and swallowing at the same moment. A skirmish of tails and flying hair was seen for five minutes, when the last of them, with slouching tail and evidently ashamed of himself, withdrew, and nothing remained on the ground but a well-picked skeleton. By sunset, when I returned to camp, they had swallowed as much as three entire deer.

We remained hunting in the mountains some days, and left the Boiling Spring River with our mules loaded with meat, having, almost by a miracle, been unmolested by the Arapahó war party, some of whom I saw hunting nearly every day, without being myself discovered. Nothing occurred on our return until the night of the second day, when we camped on the creek in a spot destitute of grass, and our animals took themselves off in search of food during the night, *where* we knew not.

The next morning my companion, thinking to find them close at hand, left me in camp cooking the breakfast while he went to bring the animals, but presently returned, saying that he could find neither them nor their track, but had discovered fresh Indian sign in the bottom, where several Indians had been but a few hours before, and that, doubtless, they had made "a raise." I instantly seized my rifle, and, taking a circuit round the camp, came presently upon the track of horses and mules, and struck at once after them, thinking that, of course, they were those made by our animals, as they tallied with the number, being two horses and three mules. I had followed up the track for ten miles, when, in crossing a piece of hard prairie which scarcely yielded to the impression of the hoofs, I, for the first time, observed that not one of the animals I was following was shod, and, knowing that most of my own were so, I began to think, and soon satisfied myself of the fact, that they were not those I was in search of. As soon as I had made up my mind to this I retraced my steps to camp, and immediately started again with my companion in another direction. This time we came upon the right track, and found that it took an easterly direction, and that the animals were not in the possession of the Indians, as their ropes still dragged along the ground, making a broad trail. Finding this, we returned to camp and "cached" our meat and packs in the forks of a cottonwood tree, out of reach of wolves; and without thinking of cooking anything, so anxious were we to find our animals, we started off at once in pursuit, carrying a lariat and saddle blanket to ride back on in case we found the mules. We followed the trail until midnight, by which time I felt not a little tired, as I had been on my legs since daybreak, and had not broken my fast since the preceding day. We therefore turned into the bottom, floundering through the bushes, and impaling ourselves at every step on the prickly pears which covered the ground,

and made a fire near the stream, in a thicket which in some degree
sheltered us from the cold. We had scarcely, however, lighted the
fire when a gale of wind burst upon us, and, scattering the burning
brands in every direction, quickly set fire to the dry grass and bushes
to leeward of the fire. All our efforts to prevent this were unavailing, and we were necessitated to put out our fire to prevent the whole
bottom from being burned. As the cold was intense, and I had no
covering but a paltry saddle blanket about four feet square, sleep
was out of the question if I wished to keep unfrozen, so that, after an
hour or two's rest and a good smoke, we again turned out, and by
the light of the moon pursued the trail. As it passed over prairies
entirely destitute of grass, the animals had never once stopped, but
continued a straight course, without turning to the right or left, in
search of pasture. We travelled on all night, and, halting for an hour's
rest in the morning, about noon, looking ahead, I descried four objects
feeding in the plain. I called out to my companion, who was a little
in rear, that there they were.

"Elk," he answered, after a long look, "or Injuns. They're no
mules, I'll lay a dollar; Arapahós, or I never see a redskin."

However, at that distance I recognised my mules, and, pushing
on, I found them quietly feeding with Panchito, my companion's
horse being alone missing, and they suffered me to catch them without
difficulty. As we were now within twenty miles of the fort, Morgan,
who had had enough of it, determined to return, and I agreed to go
back with the animals to the cache, and bring in the meat and packs.
I accordingly tied the blanket on a mule's back, and, leading the horse,
trotted back at once to the grove of cottonwoods where we had before encamped. The sky had been gradually overcast with leaden-
coloured clouds, until, when near sunset, it was one huge inky mass
of rolling darkness; the wind had suddenly lulled, and an unnatural
calm, which so surely heralds a storm in these tempestuous regions,
succeeded. The ravens were winging their way towards the shelter
of the timber, and the coyote was seen trotting quickly to cover,
conscious of the coming storm.

The black threatening clouds seemed gradually to descend until
they kissed the earth, and already the distant mountains were hidden
to their very bases. A hollow murmuring swept through the bottom,
but as yet not a branch was stirred by wind; and the huge cottonwoods, with their leafless limbs, loomed like a line of ghosts through
the heavy gloom. Knowing but too well what was coming, I turned
my animals towards the timber, which was about two miles distant.

With pointed ears and actually trembling with fright, they were as eager as myself to reach the shelter; but, before we had proceeded a third of the distance, with a deafening roar the tempest broke upon us. The clouds opened and drove right in our faces a storm of freezing sleet, which froze upon us as it fell. The first squall of wind carried away my cap, and the enormous hailstones, beating on my unprotected head and face, almost stunned me. In an instant my hunting shirt was soaked, and as instantly frozen hard; and my horse was a mass of icicles. Jumping off my mule—for to ride was impossible—I tore off the saddle blanket and covered my head. The animals, blinded with the sleet, and their eyes actually coated with ice, turned their sterns to the storm, and, blown before it, made for the open prairie. All my exertions to drive them to the shelter of the timber were useless. It was impossible to face the hurricane, which now brought with it clouds of driving snow; and perfect darkness soon set in. Still the animals kept on, and I determined not to leave them, following, or rather being blown, after them. My blanket, frozen stiff like a board, required all the strength of my numbed fingers to prevent it being blown away, and, although it was no protection against the intense cold, I knew it would in some degree shelter me at night from the snow. In half an hour the ground was covered on the bare prairie to the depth of two feet, and through this I floundered for a long time before the animals stopped. The prairie was as bare as a lake; but one little tuft of greasewood bushes presented itself, and here, turning from the storm, they suddenly stopped and remained perfectly still. In vain I again attempted to turn them towards the direction of the timber; huddled together, they would not move an inch; and, exhausted myself, and seeing nothing before me but, as I thought, certain death, I sank down immediately behind them, and, covering my head with the blanket, crouched like a ball in the snow. I would have started myself for the timber, but it was pitchy dark, the wind drove clouds of frozen snow into my face, and the animals had so turned about in the prairie that it was impossible to know the direction to take; and although I had a compass with me, my hands were so frozen that I was perfectly unable, after repeated attempts, to unscrew the box and consult it. Even had I reached the timber, my situation would have been scarcely improved, for the trees were scattered wide about over a narrow space, and, consequently, afforded but little shelter; and if even I had succeeded in getting firewood— by no means an easy matter at any time, and still more difficult now that the ground was covered with three feet of snow—I was utterly unable to use my flint and steel to procure a light, since my fingers were like pieces of stone, and entirely without feeling.

The way the wind roared over the prairie that night—how the snow drove before it, covering me and the poor animals partly—and how I lay there, feeling the very blood freezing in my veins, and my bones petrifying with the icy blasts which seemed to penetrate them —how for hours I remained with my head on my knees, and the snow pressing it down like a weight of lead, expecting every instant to drop into a sleep from which I knew it was impossible I should ever awake—how every now and then the mules would groan aloud and fall down upon the snow, and then again struggle on their legs—how all night long the piercing howl of wolves was borne upon the wind, which never for an instant abated its violence during the night—I would not attempt to describe. I have passed many nights alone in the wilderness, and in a solitary camp have listened to the roarings of the wind and the howling of wolves, and felt the rain or snow beating upon me, with perfect unconcern; but this night threw all my former experiences into the shade, and is marked with the blackest of stones in the memoranda of my journeyings.[20]

Once, late in the night, by keeping my hands buried in the breast of my hunting shirt, I succeeded in restoring sufficient feeling into them to enable me to strike a light. Luckily my pipe, which was made out of a huge piece of cottonwood bark, and capable of containing at least twelve ordinary pipefuls, was filled with tobacco to the brim; and this I do believe kept me alive during the night, for I smoked and smoked until the pipe itself caught fire, and burned completely to the stem.

I was just sinking into a dreamy stupor, when the mules began to shake themselves, and sneeze and snort; which hailing as a good sign, and that they were still alive, I attempted to lift my head and take a view of the weather. When with great difficulty I raised my head, all appeared dark as pitch, and it did not at first occur to me that I was buried deep in snow; but when I thrust my arm above me, a hole was thus made, through which I saw the stars shining in the sky and the clouds fast clearing away. Making a sudden attempt to straighten my almost petrified back and limbs, I rose, but, unable to

[20] He was in the vicinity of Fountain Creek or Black Squirrel, about twenty-five miles north of the Pueblo Fort. Horace Kephart, in telling of this experience in his edition of Ruxton (1916), incorrectly titles the chapter, "Blizzard in South Park." The blizzard caught Ruxton some fifty miles southeast of South Park.

"Wild Scenery—Making a Cache"
in a gorge of the Rockies (A. J. Miller)

Courtesy Walters Art Gallery

BLACKFOOT INDIANS
although powerful and vengeful foes, do not torture
their enemies, but offer hospitality and keep its laws
(A. J. Miller)

stand, fell forward in the snow, frightening the animals, which immediately started away. When I gained my legs I found that day was just breaking, a long grey line of light appearing over the belt of timber on the creek, and the clouds gradually rising from the east, and allowing the stars to peep from patches of blue sky. Following the animals as soon as I gained the use of my limbs, and taking a last look at the perfect cave from which I had just risen, I found them in the timber, and, singular enough, under the very tree where we had cached our meat. However, I was unable to ascend the tree in my present state, and my frostbitten fingers refused to perform their offices; so that I jumped upon my horse, and, followed by the mules, galloped back to the Arkansa, which I reached in the evening, half dead with hunger and cold.

The hunters had given me up for lost, as such a night even the "oldest inhabitant" had never witnessed. My late companion had reached the Arkansa, and was safely housed before it broke, blessing his lucky stars that he had not gone back with me. The next morning he returned and brought in the meat; while I spent two days in nursing my frozen fingers and feet, and making up, in feasting mountain fashion, for the banyans I had suffered.

The morning after my arrival on Arkansa, two men, named Harwood and Markhead[21]—the latter, one of the most daring and successful trappers that ever followed this adventurous mountain life, and whom I had intended to have hired as a guide to the valley of the Columbia the ensuing spring—started off to the settlement of New Mexico, with some packs of peltries, intending to bring back Taos whisky (a very profitable article of trade amongst the mountain men) and some bags of flour and Indian meal.

I found on returning from my hunt that a man named John Albert had brought intelligence that the New Mexicans and Pueblo Indians had risen in the valley of Taos, and, as I have before mentioned, massacred Governor Bent and other Americans, and had also attacked and destroyed Turley's ranch on the Arroyo Hondo, killing himself and most of his men. Albert had escaped from the house, and, charging through the assailants, made for the mountains, and, travelling night and day and without food, had reached the Greenhorn with the news, and after recruiting for a couple of days had come on to the Arkansa with the intelligence, which threw the fierce moun-

21 The death of these men is recorded presently by Ruxton. He gives additional data about Markhead in his *Life in the Far West*. Kit Carson told of saving Markhead's life.—D. C. Peters, *Kit Carson*, 95.

taineers into a perfect frenzy.[22] As Markhead and Harwood would have arrived in the settlements about the time of the rising, little doubt remained as to their fate, but it was not until nearly two months after that any intelligence was brought concerning them. It seemed that they arrived at the Río Colorado, the first New Mexican settlement, on the seventh or eighth day, when the people had just received news of the massacre in Taos. These savages, after stripping them of their goods, and securing, by treachery, their arms, made them mount their mules under the pretence of conducting them to Taos, there to be given up to the chief of the insurrection. They had hardly, however, left the village when a Mexican, riding behind Harwood, discharged his gun into his back; Harwood, calling to Markhead that he was "finished," fell dead to the ground. Markhead, seeing that his own fate was sealed, made no struggle, and was likewise shot in the back by several balls. They were then stripped and scalped and shockingly mutilated, and their bodies thrown into the bush by the side of the creek to be devoured by the wolves. They were both remarkably fine young men. Markhead was celebrated in the mountains for his courage and reckless daring, having had many almost miraculous escapes when in the very hands of hostile Indians. He had a few years ago accompanied Sir W. Drummond Stewart[23] in one of his expeditions across the mountains. It happened that a half-breed of the company absconded one night with some animals belonging to Sir William, who, being annoyed at the circumstance, said hastily, and never dreaming that his offer would be taken up, that he would give five hundred dollars for the scalp of the thief. The next day Markhead rode into camp with the scalp of the unfortunate horse thief hanging at the end of his rifle, and I believe received the reward, at least so he himself declared to me, for this act of mountain law. On one occasion, whilst trapping on the waters of the Yellow Stone, in the midst of the Blackfoot country, he came suddenly upon two or three lodges, from which the Indians happened to be absent. There was no doubt, from sign which he had previously discovered, that they were lying in wait for him somewhere on the stream to attack him when examining his

[22] John Albert afterwards lived for many years in Walsenburg, Colorado, and died there on April 24, 1899. For his account of the Arroyo Hondo fight, see L. R. Hafen, "Mountain Men—John D. Albert," *Colorado Magazine*, Vol. X, 56–62.

[23] Many of the paintings made for Sir W. Drummond Stewart by A. J. Miller are in possession of Mr. and Mrs. Clyde H. Porter in Kansas City. See Bernardo De Voto, *Across the Wide Missouri*, for additional information on Stewart. Some Miller paintings appear in the present volume.

traps, the Blackfeet, moreover, being most bitterly hostile to the white trappers, and killing them without mercy whenever an occasion offered. Notwithstanding the almost certainty that some of the Indians were close at hand, probably gone out for a supply of wood and would very soon return, Markhead resolved to visit the lodges and help himself to anything worth taking that he might find there. The fire was burning, and meat was actually cooking in a pot over it. To this he did ample justice, emptying the pot in a very satisfactory manner, after which he tied all the blankets, dressed skins, moccasins, &c., into a bundle, and, mounting his horse, got safely off with his prize.

It was not always, however, that he escaped scathless, for his body was riddled with balls received in many a bloody affray with Blackfeet and other Indians.

Laforey, the old Canadian trapper with whom I stayed at Red River, was accused of having possessed himself of the property found on the two mountaineers, and afterwards of having instigated the Mexicans to the barbarous murder. The hunters on Arkansa vowed vengeance against him, and swore to have his hair some day, as well as similar lovelocks from the people of Red River. A war expedition was also talked of to that settlement, to avenge the murder of their comrades, and ease the Mexicans of their mules and horses.

The massacre of Turley and his people, and the destruction of his mill, were not consummated without considerable loss to the barbarous and cowardly assailants. There were in the house, at the time of the attack, eight white men, including Americans, French Canadians, and one or two Englishmen, with plenty of arms and ammunition. Turley had been warned of the intended insurrection, but had treated the report with indifference and neglect, until one morning a man named Otterbees,[24] in the employ of Turley, and who had been dispatched to Santa Fé with several mule loads of whisky a few days before, made his appearance at the gate on horseback, and, hastily informing the inmates of the mill that the New Mexicans had risen and massacred Governor Bent and other Americans, galloped off. Even then Turley felt assured that he would not be molested, but, at the solicitations of his men, agreed to close the gate of the yard round which were the buildings of a mill and distillery, and make preparations for defence.

[24] Charlie Autobee—the name is variously spelled—later lived on the Huérfano near its confluence with the Arkansas River. A two-page list of goods taken to Taos by Autobee for Simeon Turley in August, 1845, and valued at $759.48, is among the Rich papers in the Huntington Library, San Marino.

A few hours after, a large crowd of Mexicans and Pueblo Indians made their appearance, all armed with guns and bows and arrows, and, advancing with a white flag, summoned Turley to surrender his house and the Americans in it, guaranteeing that his own life should be saved, but that every other American in the valley of Taos had to be destroyed; that the Governor and all the Americans at Fernández and the rancho had been killed, and that not one was to be left alive in all New Mexico.

To this summons Turley answered that he would never surrender his house nor his men, and that, if they wanted it or them, they "must take them."

The enemy then drew off, and, after a short consultation, commenced the attack. The first day they numbered about five hundred, but the crowd was hourly augmented by the arrival of parties of Indians from the more distant pueblos, and of New Mexicans from Fernández, La Cañada, and other places.

The building lay at the foot of a gradual slope in the sierra, which was covered with cedar bushes. In front ran the stream of the Arroyo Hondo, about twenty yards from one side of the square, and on the other side was broken ground, which rose abruptly and formed the bank of the ravine. In the rear, and behind the stillhouse, was some garden ground enclosed by a small fence, and into which a small wicket gate opened from the corral.

As soon as the attack was determined upon, the assailants broke, and, scattering, concealed themselves under the cover of the rocks and bushes which surrounded the house.

From these they kept up an incessant fire upon every exposed portion of the building where they saw the Americans preparing for defence.

They, on their parts, were not idle; not a man but was an old mountaineer, and each had his trusty rifle, with good store of ammunition. Wherever one of these assailants exposed a hand's-breadth of his person, there whistled a ball from an unerring barrel. The windows had been blockaded, loopholes being left to fire through, and through these a lively fire was maintained. Already several of the enemy had bitten the dust, and parties were constantly seen bearing off the wounded up the banks of the Cañada. Darkness came on, and during the night a continual fire was kept up on the mill, whilst its defenders, reserving their ammunition, kept their posts with stern and silent determination. The night was spent in running balls, cutting patches, and completing the defences of the building. In the morning the fight was renewed, and it was found that the Mexicans had effected a lodgment in a part of the stables, which were separated from the other portions of the building, and between which was an open space of a few feet. The assailants, during the night, had sought to break down the wall, and thus enter the main building, but the strength of the adobes and logs of which it was composed resisted effectually all their attempts.

Those in the stable seemed anxious to regain the outside, for their position was unavailable as a means of annoyance to the besieged, and several had darted across the narrow space which divided it from the other part of the building, and which slightly projected, and behind which they were out of the line of fire. As soon, however, as the attention of the defenders was called to this point, the first man who attempted to cross, and who happened to be a Pueblo chief, was dropped on the instant, and fell dead in the centre of the intervening space. It appeared an object to recover the body, for an Indian immediately dashed out to the fallen chief and attempted to drag him within the cover of the wall. The rifle which covered the spot again poured forth its deadly contents, and the Indian, springing into the air, fell over the body of his chief, struck to the heart. Another and another met with a similar fate, and at last three rushed at once to the spot, and, seizing the body by the legs and head, had already lifted it from the ground, when three puffs of smoke blew from the barricaded window, followed by the sharp cracks of as many rifles, and the three daring Indians added their number to the pile of corpses which now covered the body of the dead chief.

As yet the besieged had met with no casualties; but after the fall of the seven Indians, in the manner above described, the whole body of assailants, with a shout of rage, poured in a rattling volley, and two of the defenders of the mill fell mortally wounded. One, shot through the loins, suffered great agony, and was removed to the stillhouse, where he was laid upon a large pile of grain, as being the softest bed to be found.

In the middle of the day the assailants renewed the attack more fiercely than before, their baffled attempts adding to their furious rage. The little garrison bravely stood to the defence of the mill, never throwing away a shot, but firing coolly, and only when a fair mark was presented to their unerring aim. Their ammunition, however, was fast failing, and, to add to the danger of their situation, the enemy set fire to the mill, which blazed fiercely, and threatened destruction of the whole building. Twice they succeeded in overcoming the flames, and, taking advantage of their being thus occupied, the Mexicans and Indians charged into the corral, which was full of hogs and sheep, and vented their cowardly rage upon the animals, spearing and shooting all that came in their way. No sooner, however, were the flames extinguished in one place, than they broke out more fiercely in another; and as a successful defence was perfectly hopeless, and the numbers of the assailants increased every moment, a council of war was held by the survivors of the little garrison, when it was determined, as soon as night approached, that every one should attempt to escape as best he might, and in the meantime the defence of the mill was to be continued.

Just at dusk, Albert and another man ran to the wicket gate which opened into a kind of enclosed space, and in which was a number of armed Mexicans. They both rushed out at the same moment, discharging their rifles full in the faces of the crowd. Albert, in the confusion, threw himself under the fence, whence he saw his companion shot down immediately, and heard his cries for mercy, mingled with shrieks of pain and anguish, as the cowards pierced him with knives and lances. Lying motionless under the fence, as soon as it was quite dark he crept over the logs and ran up the mountain, travelled day and night, and scarcely stopping or resting, reached the Greenhorn, almost dead with hunger and fatigue. Turley himself succeeded in escaping from the mill and in reaching the mountain unseen. Here he met a Mexican, mounted on a horse, who had been a most intimate friend of the unfortunate man for many years. To this man Turley offered his watch (which was treble its worth) for the use of his horse, but was refused. The inhuman wretch, however, affected pity and commiseration for the fugitive, and advised him to go to a certain place, where he would bring or send him assistance; but on reaching the mill, which was now a mass of fire, he immediately informed the Mexicans of his place of concealment, whither a large party instantly proceeded and shot him to death.

Two others escaped and reached Santa Fé in safety. The mill and Turley's house were sacked and gutted, and all his hard-earned savings, which were considerable, and concealed in gold about the house, were discovered, and of course seized upon, by the victorious Mexicans.

The Indians, however, met a few days after with a severe retribution. The troops marched out of Santa Fé, attacked their pueblo, and levelled it to the ground, killing many hundreds of its defenders, and taking many prisoners, most of whom were hanged.

CHAPTER 12

Manitou Springs

Beaver has so depreciated in value within the last few years that trapping has been almost abandoned—the price paid for the skin of this valuable animal having fallen from six and eight dollars per pound to one dollar, which hardly pays the expenses of traps, animals, and equipment for the hunt, and is certainly no adequate remuneration for the incredible hardships, toil, and danger, which are undergone by the hardy trappers in the course of their adventurous expeditions. The cause of the great decrease in value of beaver fur is the substitute which has been found for it in the skins of the fur seal and nutria; the improved preparation of other skins of little value, such as the hare and rabbit; and, more than all, in the use of silk in the manufacture of hats, which has in a great measure superseded that of beaver. Thus the curse of the trapper is levelled against all the new-fashioned materials of Paris hats; and the light and (h)airy gossamer of twelve-and-six is anathematized in the mountains in a way which would be highly distressing to the feelings of Messrs. Jupp and Johnson, and other artists in the ventilating-gossamer line.

Thanks to the innovation, however, a little breathing-time has been allowed the persecuted castor; and this valuable fur-bearing animal, which otherwise would, in the course of a few years, have become extinct, has now a chance of multiplying, and will in a short time again become abundant; for, although not a very prolific animal, the beaver has perhaps fewer natural enemies than any other of the *ferae naturae*, and, being at the same time a wise and careful one, provides against all contingencies of cold and hunger, which in northern climates carry off so large a proportion of their brother beasts.

The beaver was once found in every part of North America from Canada to the Gulf of Mexico, but has now gradually retired from the encroachments and the persecutions of civilised man, and is met with only in the far, far West, on the tributaries of the great rivers, and the streams which water the mountain valleys in the great chain of the Rocky Mountains. On the waters of the Platte and Arkansa they are still numerous, and within the last two years have increased considerably in numbers; but the best trapping ground now is on the streams running through the Bayou Salado, and the Old and New Parks,[1] all of which are elevated mountain valleys.

The habits of the beaver present quite a study to the naturalist, and they are certainly the most sagaciously instinctive of all quadrupeds. Their dams afford a lesson to the engineer, their houses a study to the architect of comfortable abodes, while their unremitting labour and indefatigable industry are models to be followed by the workingman. The lodge of the beaver is generally excavated in the bank of the stream, the entrance being invariably under water; but not unfrequently, where the banks are flat, they construct lodges in the stream itself, of a conical form, of limbs and branches of trees woven together and cemented with mud. For the purpose of forming dams, for the necessary timber for their lodges, or for the bark which they store for their winter's supply of food, the beaver often fells a tree eight or ten inches in diameter, throwing it, with the skill of an expert woodsman, in any direction he pleases, always selecting a tree above stream, in order that the logs may be carried down with it to their destination. The log is then chopped into small lengths, and, pushing them into the water, the beaver steers them to the lodge or dam. These trees are as cleanly cut as they could be by a sharp axe, the gouging furrows made by the animal's strong teeth cutting into the very centre of the trunk, the notch being smooth as sawed wood.

With his broad tail, which is twelve or fourteen inches long, and about four in breadth, and covered with a thick scaly skin, the beaver plasters his lodge, thus making it perform all the offices of a hand. They say that when the beaver's tail becomes dry, the animal dies, but whether this is the case or not, I have myself seen the beaver when at work return to the water and plunge his tail into the stream, and then resume his labour with renewed vigour; and I have also seen them, with their bodies on the bank, thumping the water with their tails with a most comical perseverance.

The female seldom produces more than three kittens at a birth, but I know an instance where one was killed with young, having no less than eleven in her. They live to a considerable age, and I once ate

[1] Now known respectively as South Park, Middle Park, and North Park.

the tail of an old "man" beaver whose head was perfectly grey with age, and his beard was of the same venerable hue, notwithstanding which his tail was tender as a young raccoon. The kittens are as playful as their namesakes of the feline race, and it is highly amusing to see an old one with grotesque gravity inciting her young to gambol about her, whilst she herself is engaged about some household work.

The nutrias of Mexico are identical with the beavers of the more northern parts of America; but in South America, and on some parts of the western coast of North America, a species of seal, or, as I have heard it described, a hybrid between the seal and the beaver, is called nutria—quite a distinct animal, however, from the Mexican nutria.[2]

The trappers of the Rocky Mountains belong to a "genus" more approximating to the primitive savage than perhaps any other class of civilised men. Their lives being spent in the remote wilderness of the mountains, with no other companion than Nature herself, their habits and character assume a most singular cast of simplicity mingled with ferocity, appearing to take their colouring from the scenes and objects which surround them. Knowing no wants save those of nature, their sole care is to procure sufficient food to support life, and the necessary clothing to protect them from the rigorous climate. This, with the assistance of their trusty rifles, they are generally able to effect, but sometimes at the expense of great peril and hardship. When engaged in their avocation, the natural instinct of primitive man is ever alive, for the purpose of guarding against danger and the provision of necessary food.

Keen observers of nature, they rival the beasts of prey in discovering the haunts and habits of game, and in their skill and cunning in capturing it. Constantly exposed to perils of all kinds, they become callous to any feeling of danger, and destroy human as well as animal life with as little scruple and as freely as they expose their own. Of laws, human or divine, they neither know nor care to know. Their wish is their law, and to attain it they do not scruple as to ways and means. Firm friends and bitter enemies, with them it is "a word and a blow," and the blow often first. They may have good qualities, but they are those of the animal; and people fond of giving hard names call them revengeful, bloodthirsty, drunkards (when the wherewithal is to be had), gamblers, regardless of the laws of *meum* and *tuum*—in fact, "White Indians." However, there are exceptions, and I *have* met honest mountain men. Their animal qualities, however, are undeniable. Strong, active, hardy as bears, daring, expert in the use of their

2 In California the nutria was the otter.

weapons, they are just what uncivilised white man might be supposed to be in a brute state, depending upon his instinct for the support of life. Not a hole or corner in the vast wilderness of the Far West but has been ransacked by these hardy men. From the Mississippi to the mouth of the Colorado of the West, from the frozen regions of the North to the Gila in Mexico, the beaver hunter has set his traps in every creek and stream. All this vast country, but for the daring enterprise of these men, would be even now a terra incognita to geographers, as indeed a great portion still is; but there is not an acre that has not been passed and repassed by the trappers in their perilous excursions. The mountains and streams still retain the names assigned to them by the rude hunters; and these alone are the hardy pioneers who have paved the way for the settlement of the Western country.

Trappers are of two kinds, the "hired hand" and the "free trapper," the former hired for the hunt by the fur companies; the latter, supplied with animals and traps by the company, is paid a certain price for his furs and peltries.

There is also the trapper "on his own hook," but this class is very small. He has his own animals and traps, hunts where he chooses, and sells his peltries to whom he pleases.

On starting for a hunt, the trapper fits himself out with the necessary equipment, either from the Indian trading forts, or from some of the petty traders—*coureurs des bois*—who frequent the Western country. This equipment consists usually of two or three horses or mules—one for saddle, the other for packs—and six traps, which are carried in a bag of leather called a "trap sack." Ammunition, a few pounds of tobacco, dressed deerskins for moccasins, &c., are carried in a wallet of dressed buffalo skin, called a "possible sack." His "possibles" and "trap sack" are generally carried on the saddle mule when hunting, the others being packed with the furs. The costume of the trapper is a hunting shirt of dressed buckskin, ornamented with long fringes; pantaloons of the same material, and decorated with porcupine quills and long fringes down the outside of the leg. A flexible felt hat and moccasins clothe his extremities. Over his left shoulder and under his right arm hang his powder horn and bullet pouch, in which he carries his balls, flint and steel, and odds and ends of all kinds. Round the waist is a belt, in which is stuck a large butcher knife in a sheath of buffalo hide, made fast to the belt by a chain or guard of steel, which also supports a little buckskin case containing a whetstone. A tomahawk is also often added; and, of course, a long heavy rifle is part and parcel of his equipment. I had nearly forgotten the pipe-holder, which hangs round his neck, and is generally a *gâge d'amour*, and a triumph of squaw workmanship, in shape of a heart, garnished with beads and porcupine quills.

Thus provided, and having determined the locality of his trapping ground, he starts to the mountains, sometimes alone, sometimes with three or four in company, as soon as the breaking up of the ice allows him to commence operations. Arrived on his hunting grounds, he follows the creeks and streams, keeping a sharp lookout for "sign." If he sees a prostrate cottonwood tree, he examines it to discover if it be the work of beaver—whether "thrown" for the purpose of food, or to dam the stream. The track of the beaver on the mud or sand under the bank is also examined; and if the "sign" be fresh, he sets his trap in the run of the animal, hiding it under water, and attaching it by a stout chain to a picquet driven in the bank, or to a bush or tree. A "float stick" is made fast to the trap by a cord a few feet long, which, if the animal carry away the trap, floats on the water and points out its position. The trap is baited with the "medicine," an oily substance obtained from a gland in the scrotum of the beaver, but distinct from the testes. A stick is dipped into this and planted over the trap; and the beaver, attracted by the smell, and wishing a close inspection, very foolishly puts his leg into the trap, and is a "gone beaver."

When a lodge is discovered, the trap is set at the edge of the dam, at the point where the animal passes from deep to shoal water, and always under water. Early in the morning the hunter mounts his mule and examines the traps. The captured animals are skinned, and the tails, which are a great dainty, carefully packed into camp. The skin is then stretched over a hoop or framework of osier twigs, and is allowed to dry, the flesh and fatty substance being carefully scraped (grained). When dry, it is folded into a square sheet, the fur turned inwards, and the bundle, containing about ten to twenty skins, tightly pressed and corded, and is ready for transportation.

During the hunt, regardless of Indian vicinity, the fearless trapper wanders far and near in search of "sign." His nerves must ever be in a state of tension, and his mind ever present at his call. His eagle eye sweeps round the country, and in an instant detects any foreign appearance. A turned leaf, a blade of grass pressed down, the uneasiness of the wild animals, the flight of birds, are all paragraphs to him written in nature's legible hand and plainest language. All the wits of the subtle savage are called into play to gain an advantage over the wily woodsman; but with the natural instinct of primitive man, the white hunter has the advantages of a civilised mind, and, thus provided, seldom fails to outwit, under equal advantages, the cunning savage.

Sometimes, following on his trail, the Indian watches him set his traps on a shrub-belted stream, and, passing up the bed, like Bruce of old, so that he may leave no track, he lies in wait in the bushes until the hunter comes to examine his carefully set traps. Then, waiting until he approaches his ambushment within a few feet, whiz flies the home-drawn arrow, never failing at such close quarters to bring the victim to the ground. For one white scalp, however, that dangles in the smoke of an Indian's lodge, a dozen black ones, at the end of the hunt, ornament the campfires of the rendezvous.

At a certain time, when the hunt is over, or they have loaded their pack animals, the trappers proceed to the "rendezvous," the locality of which has been previously agreed upon; and here the traders and agents of the fur companies await them, with such assortment of goods as their hardy customers may require, including generally a fair supply of alcohol. The trappers drop in singly and in small bands, bringing their packs of beaver to this mountain market, not unfrequently to the value of a thousand dollars each, the produce of one hunt. The dissipation of the "rendezvous," however, soon turns the trapper's pocket inside out. The goods brought by the traders, although of the most inferior quality, are sold at enormous prices—coffee, twenty and thirty shillings a pint cup, which is the usual measure; tobacco fetches ten and fifteen shillings a plug; alcohol, from twenty to fifty shillings a pint; gunpowder, sixteen shillings a pint cup; and all other articles at proportionately exorbitant prices.

The "beaver" is purchased at from two to eight dollars per pound; the Hudson's Bay Company alone buying it by the pluie, or "plew," that is, the whole skin, giving a certain price for skins, whether of old beaver or kittens.

The rendezvous is one continued scene of drunkenness, gambling, and brawling and fighting, as long as the money and credit of the trappers last. Seated, Indian fashion, round the fires, with a blanket spread before them, groups are seen with their "decks" of cards, playing at euker, poker, and seven-up, the regular mountain games. The stakes are "beaver," which here is current coin; and when the fur is gone, their horses, mules, rifles, and shirts, hunting packs, and *breeches*, are staked. Daring gamblers make the rounds of the camp, challenging each other to play for the trapper's highest stake—his horse, his squaw (if he have one), and, as once happened, his scalp.

"There goes hos and beaver!" is the mountain expression when any great loss is sustained; and, sooner or later, "hos and beaver" invariably find their way into the insatiable pockets of the traders. A trapper often squanders the produce of his hunt, amounting to hundreds of dollars, in a couple of hours; and, supplied on credit with another equipment, leaves the rendezvous for another expedition, which has the same result time after time, although one tolerably successful hunt would enable him to return to the settlements and civilised life, with an ample sum to purchase and stock a farm, and enjoy himself in ease and comfort the remainder of his days.

An old trapper, a French Canadian, assured me that he had received fifteen thousand dollars for beaver during a sojourn of twenty years in the mountains. Every year he resolved in his mind to return to Canada, and, with this object, always converted his fur into cash; but a fortnight at the rendezvous always cleaned him out, and, at the end of twenty years, he had not even credit sufficient to buy a pound of powder.

These annual gatherings are often the scene of bloody duels, for over their cups and cards no men are more quarrelsome than your mountaineers. Rifles, at twenty paces, settle all differences, and, as may be imagined, the fall of one or other of the combatants is certain, or, as sometimes happens, both fall to the word "fire."[3]

A day or two after my return from the mountain, I was out in search of my animals along the river bottom, when I met a war party of Arapahós loping along on foot in Indian file. It was the same party who had been in the vicinity of our camp on Fontaine-qui-bouille, and was led by a chief called *Coxo*, "the game-leg." They were all painted and armed for war, carrying bows and well-filled quivers, war clubs and lances, and some had guns in deerskin covers. They were all naked to the waist, a single buffalo robe being thrown over them, and from his belt each one had a lariat or rope of hide to secure the animals stolen in the expedition. They were returning without a scalp, having found the Yutas "not at home"; and this was considered a sign by the hunters that they would not be scrupulous in "raising some hair," if they caught a straggler far from camp. However, their present visit was for the purpose of procuring some meat, of which

[3] The excellent foregoing description of the mountain man, and his life may be supplemented from the growing literature on the fur-trade period of the Rocky Mountain West. The basic work is still H. M. Chittenden, *The American Fur Trade of the Far West* (2 vols. 1935). For a good description of trapper life see Edwin L. Sabin, *Kit Carson Days* (2 vols., 1935).

they stood in need, as to reach their village they had to cross a country destitute of game. They were all remarkably fine young men, and perfectly cleanly in their person; indeed, when on the war path, more than ordinary care is taken to adorn the body, and the process of painting occupies considerable time and attention. The Arapahós do not shave their heads, as do the Pawnees, Caws, and Osages, merely braiding the centre or scalp lock, and decorating it with a gay ribbon or feather of the war eagle.

This war party was twenty-one in number, the oldest, with the exception of the chief, being under thirty, and not one of them was less than five feet eight inches in height. In this they differ from their neighbours the Yutas and Comanches, who are of small stature, the latter especially, when off their horses, presenting small ungainly figures, with legs crooked by constant riding, and limbs exhibiting but little muscular development. Not one of this Arapahó band but could have sat as a model for an Apollo. During their stay the animals were all collected and corralled, as their penchant for horseflesh, it was thought likely, might lead some of the young men to appropriate a horse or mule.

Each tribe of Prairie Indians has a different method of making mocassins, so that anyone, acquainted with the various fashions, is at no loss to know the nation to which any particular one belongs whom he may happen to meet. The Arapahós and Cheyennes use a "shoe" mocassin, that is, one which reaches no higher than the instep, and wants the upper side-flaps which mocassins usually have. I always used Chippewa mocassins, which differ from those of the Prairie make, by the seam being made up the centre of the foot to the leg, and puckered into plaits. This, which is the true fashion of the Forest Indian, who, by the by, is as distinct in character and appearance from him of the plains as a bear from a bluebottle, attracted the attention of the Arapahó warriors and caused a lively discussion amongst themselves, owing to the novelty of the manufacture. They all surrounded me, and each examined and felt carefully the unusual *chaussure*.

"Ti-yah!" was the universal exclamation of astonishment. The old chief was the last to approach, and, after a minute examination, he drew himself up and explained to them, as I perfectly understood by his gestures, that the people who made those mocassins lived far, far away from the sun, where the snow lay deep on the ground, and where the night was illuminated by the mystery fire (the aurora borealis), which he had seen, years ago, far to the north.

The vicinity of the pueblo affording no pasture, my *cavallada* had undertaken a voyage of discovery in search of grass, and had found a small valley up the bed of a dry creek, in which grew an abundance of bunch grass. As, however, the river was fast frozen, they were unable to find a watering-place themselves, and one day made their appearance in camp, evidently for the purpose of being conducted to water; I therefore led them to the river and broke a large hole, which they invariably resorted to every morning and evening at the same hour, although it was three or four miles from their feeding-place. This enabled me to catch them whenever I required, for at a certain time I had only to go to this hole, and I never failed to see them approaching leisurely, the mules following the horse in Indian file, and always along the same trail which they had made in the snow.

The grass, although to all appearance perfectly withered, still retained considerable nourishment, and the mules improved fast in flesh. Panchito, however, fell off in condition as the others improved, more, I think, from the severity of the winter than the scarcity of grass. When they had cleared the valley they sought a pasture still farther off, and, after losing sight of them for fifteen days, I found them fifteen miles from the river, at the foot of the mountain, in a prairie in which was a pool of water (which prevented their having recourse to the water hole I had made for them), and where was plenty of buffalo grass.

It was now always a day's work for me to catch my hunting mule, and the animals were becoming so wild that I often returned without effecting the capture at all, my only chance being to chase them on horseback and lasso the horse, when they all followed as quiet as lambs, never caring to forsake their old companion.

The weather in January, February, and March was exceedingly severe; storms of sleet and snow, invariably accompanied by hurricanes of wind, were of daily occurrence, but the snow rarely remained more than thirty hours on the ground, an hour or two of the meridian sun being sufficient to cause it to disappear. On the seventeenth of March the ice in the Arkansa "moved" for the first time, and the next day it was entirely broken up, and the arrival of spring weather was confidently expected. However, it froze once more in a few days as firm as ever, and the weather became colder than before, with heavy snowstorms and hard gales of wind. After this succeeded a spell of fine weather, and about the twenty-fourth the ice moved bodily away, and the river was clear from that date, the edges of the water only being frozen in the morning. Geese now made

233

their appearance in considerable numbers, and afforded an agreeable variety to our perpetual venison and tough bull meat, as well as good sport in shooting them with rifles. The bluebird followed the goose; and when the first robin was seen, the hunters pronounced the winter at an end.

When the river was clear of ice I tried my luck with the fish, and in ten minutes pulled out as many trout, hickory shad, and suckers, but from that time never succeeded in getting a nibble. The hunters accounted for this by saying that the fish migrate up the stream as soon as the ice breaks, seeking the deep holes and bends of its upper waters, and that my first piscatory attempt was in the very nick of time, when a shoal was passing up for the first time after the thaw.

Towards the latter end of March I removed my animals from their pasture, which was getting dry and rotten, and took them up Fontaine-qui-bouille into the mountains, where the grass is of better quality and more abundant. On the Arkansa and the neighbouring prairies not a vestige of spring vegetation yet presented itself, but nearer the mountains the grass was beginning to shoot. It is a curious fact that the young blade of the buffalo and bunch grass pierces its way through the old one, which completely envelops and protects the tender blade from the nipping frosts of spring, and thus also the weakening effects of feeding on the young grass are rendered less injurious to horses and mules, since they are obliged to eat the old together with the young shoots.

The farther I advanced up the creek, and the nearer the mountains, the more forward was the vegetation, although even here in its earliest stage. The bunch grass was getting green at the roots, and the absinthe and greasewood were throwing out their buds. As yet, however, the cottonwoods and the larger trees in the bottom showed no signs of leaf, and the currant and cherry bushes still looked dry and sapless. The thickets, however, were filled with birds, and resounded with their songs, and the plains were alive with prairie dogs, busy in repairing their houses and barking lustily as I rode through their towns. Turkeys, too, were calling in the timber, and the boom of the prairie fowl, at rise and set of sun, was heard on every side. The snow had entirely disappeared from the plains, but Pike's Peak and the mountains were still clad in white; the latter, being sometimes clear of snow and looking dark and sombre, would for an hour or two be hidden by a curtain of clouds, which rising displayed the mountains, before black and furrowed, now white and smooth with their snowy mantle.

On my way I met a band of hunters who had been driven in by a war party of Arapahós, who were encamped on the eastern fork of the Fontaine-qui-bouille. They strongly urged me to return, as, being alone, I could not fail to be robbed of my animals, if not killed myself. However, in pursuance of my fixed rule, never to stop on account of Indians, I proceeded up the river, and about fifty miles from the mouth encamped on the first fork,[4] where was an abundance of deer and antelope. In the timber on the banks of the creek I erected a little shanty, covering it with the bark of the prostrate trees which strewed the ground, and picqueting my animals at night in a little prairie within sight, where they luxuriated on plenty of buffalo grass. Here I remained for a day or two hunting in the mountain, leaving my *cavallada* to take care of themselves, and at the mercy of the Arapahós should they discover them. At night I returned to camp, made a fire, and cooked an appola of antelope-meat, and enjoyed my solitary pipe after supper with as much relish as if I was in a divan, and lay down on my blanket, serenaded by packs of hungry wolves, and sleeping as soundly as if there were no such people in existence as Arapahós, merely waking now and then and raising my hand to the top of my head, to assure myself that my topknot was in its place.

The next day I moved up the main fork, on which I had been directed by the hunters to proceed, in order to visit the far-famed springs from which the creek takes its name. The valley of the upper waters is very picturesque: many mountain streams course through it, a narrow line of timber skirting their banks. On the western side the rugged mountains frown overhead, and rugged cañons filled with pine and cedar gape into the plain. At the head of the valley, the ground is much broken up into gullies and ravines where it enters the mountain spurs, with topes of pine and cedar scattered here and there, and masses of rock tossed about in wild confusion. On entering the broken ground the creek turns more to the westward, and passes by two remarkable buttes of a red conglomerate, which appear at a distance like tablets cut in the mountainside. The eastern fork skirts the base of the range, coming from the ridge called "The Divide," which separates the waters of the Platte and Arkansa; and between the main stream and this branch, running north and south, is a limestone ledge which forms the western wall of the lateral valley running at right angles from that of the Fontaine-qui-bouille. The uplands are clothed with cedar and dwarf oak, the bottoms of the river with cot-

4 Near the site of Colorado Springs, where Fountain and Monument creeks join.

tonwood, quaking asp, oak, ash, and box alder, and a thick undergrowth of cherry and currant bushes.

I followed a very good lodge-pole trail, which struck the creek
before entering the broken ground, being that used by the Yutas and
Arapahós on their way to the Bayou Salado. Here the valley nar-
rowed considerably, and, turning an angle with the creek, I was at
once shut in by mountains and elevated ridges, which rose on each
side of the stream. This was now a rapid torrent, tumbling over rocks
and stones, and fringed with oak and a shrubbery of brush. A few
miles on, the cañon opened out into a little shelving glade; and on
the right bank of the stream, and raised several feet above it, was a
flat white rock in which was a round hole, where one of the celebrated
springs hissed and bubbled with its escaping gas. I had been cautioned
against drinking this, being directed to follow the stream a few yards
to another, which is the true soda spring.[5]

Before doing this, however, I unpacked the mule and took the
saddle from Panchito, piling my saddle and meat on the rock. The
animals, as soon as I left them free, smelt the white rock, and instantly
commenced licking and scraping with their teeth with the greatest
eagerness. At last the horse approached the spring, and, burying his
nose deep in the clear water, drank greedily. The mules appeared at
first to fear the bubbling of the gas, and smelt and retreated two or
three times before they mustered courage to take a draught; but when
they had once tasted the water I thought they would have burst themselves. For hours they paid no attention to the grass, continuing to
lick the rock and constantly returning to the spring to drink. For
myself, I had not only abstained from drinking that day, but, with
the aid of a handful of salt which I had brought with me for the purpose, had so highly seasoned my breakfast of venison, that I was in
a most satisfactory state of thirst. I therefore at once proceeded to the
other spring, and found it about forty yards from the first, but immediately above the river, issuing from a little basin in the flat white rock,
and trickling over the edge into the stream. The escape of gas in this
was much stronger than in the other, and was similar to water boiling smartly.

I had provided myself with a tin cup holding about a pint; but
before dipping it in, I divested myself of my pouch and belt, and
sat down in order to enjoy the draught at my leisure. I was half dead
with thirst; and, tucking up the sleeves of my hunting shirt, I dipped

[5] The Manitou Springs. The town of Manitou, which has grown up about
the mineral springs, is now a favorite tourist resort and watering place.

the cup into the midst of the bubbles, and raised it hissing and sparkling to my lips. Such a draught! Three times, without drawing a breath, was it replenished and emptied, almost blowing up the roof of my mouth with its effervescence. It was equal to the very best soda water, but possesses that fresh, natural flavour, which manufactured water cannot impart.

The Indians regard with awe the "medicine" waters of these fountains, as being the abode of a spirit who breathes through the transparent water, and thus, by his exhalations, causes the perturbation of its surface. The Arapahós, especially, attribute to this water god the power of ordaining the success or miscarriage of their war expeditions; and as their braves pass often by the mysterious springs, when in search of their hereditary enemies the Yutas, in the "Valley of Salt," they never fail to bestow their votive offerings upon the water sprite, in order to propitiate the "Manitou" of the fountain, and ensure a fortunate issue to their "path of war."[6]

Thus at the time of my visit the basin of the spring was filled with beads and wampum, and pieces of red cloth and knives, whilst the surrounding trees were hung with strips of deerskin, cloth, and mocassins, to which, had they been serviceable, I would most sacrilegiously have helped myself. The "sign," too, round the spring, plainly showed that here a war dance had been executed by the braves; and I was not a little pleased to find that they had already been here, and were not likely to return the same way; but in this supposition I was quite astray.

This country was once possessed by the Shos-shone or Snake Indians, of whom the Comanches of the plains are a branch; and although many hundred miles now divide their hunting grounds, they were once, if not the same people, tribes of the same grand nation. They still, however, retain a common language; and there is great analogy in many of their religious rites and legendary tales, which proves that at least a very close alliance must at one period have bound the two tribes together. They are even now the two most powerful nations, in point of numbers, of all the tribes of Western Indians; the Comanche ruling supreme on the eastern plains, as the Shos-shones are the dominant power in the country west of the Rocky Mountains, and in the mountains themselves. A branch of the latter is the tribe of Tlamath Indians, the most warlike of the Western tribes; as also

6 The Major S. H. Long exploring expedition of 1820 also noted beads and other Indian offerings in the Manitou Springs.

the Yutas, who may be said to connect them with the nation of Comanche.[7]

Numerically, the Snakes are supposed to be the most powerful of any Indian nation in existence.

The Snakes, who, in common with all Indians, possess hereditary legends to account for all natural phenomena, or any extraordinary occurrences which are beyond their ken or comprehension, have of course their legendary version of the causes which created, in the midst of their hunting grounds, these two springs of sweet and bitter water; which are also intimately connected with the cause of separation between the tribes of Comanche and the Snake. Thus runs the legend:

Many hundreds of winters ago, when the cottonwoods on the Big River were no higher than an arrow, and the red men who hunted the buffalo on the plains all spoke the same language, and the pipe of peace breathed its social cloud of kinnikinek whenever two parties of hunters met on the boundless plains—when, with hunting grounds and game of every kind in the greatest abundance, no nation dug up the hatchet with another because one of its hunters followed the game into their bounds, but, on the contrary, loaded for him his back with choice and fattest meat, and ever proffered the soothing pipe before the stranger, with well-filled belly, left the village—it happened that two hunters of different nations met one day on a small rivulet, where both had repaired to quench their thirst. A little stream of water, rising from a spring on a rock within a few feet of the bank, trickled over it, and fell splashing into the river. To this the hunters repaired; and whilst one sought the spring itself, where the water, cold and clear, reflected on its surface the image of the surrounding scenery, the other, tired by his exertions in the chase, threw himself at once to the ground and plunged his face into the running stream.

The latter had been unsuccessful in the chase, and perhaps his bad fortune, and the sight of the fat deer which the other hunter threw from his back before he drank at the crystal spring, caused a feeling of jealousy and ill-humour to take possession of his mind. The other, on the contrary, before he satisfied his thirst, raised in the hollow of his hand a portion of the water, and, lifting it towards the sun, reversed his hand, and allowed it to fall upon the ground—a libation to the Great Spirit who had vouchsafed him a successful hunt, and the blessing of the refreshing water with which he was about to quench his thirst.

[7] The Utes, Comanches, and Snakes are the major branches of the Shoshonean family.

Seeing this, and being reminded that he had neglected the usual offering, only increased the feeling of envy and annoyance which the unsuccessful hunter permitted to get the mastery of his heart; and the Evil Spirit at that moment entering his body, his temper fairly flew away, and he sought some pretence by which to provoke a quarrel with the stranger Indian at the spring.

"Why does a stranger," he asked, rising from the stream at the same time, "drink at the spring head, when one to whom the fountain belongs contents himself with the water that runs from it?"

"The Great Spirit places the cool water at the spring," answered the other hunter, "that his children may drink it pure and undefiled. The running water is for the beasts which scour the plains. Au-sa-qua is a chief of the Shos-shone; he drinks at the headwater."

"The Shos-shone is but a tribe of the Comanche," returned the other; "Waco-mish leads the grand nation. Why does a Shos-shone dare to drink above him?"

"He has said it. The Shos-shone drinks at the spring head; other nations of the stream which runs into the fields. Au-sa-qua is chief of his nation. The Comanche are brothers. Let them both drink of the same water."

"The Shos-shone pays tribute to the Comanche. Waco-mish leads that nation to war. Waco-mish is chief of the Shos-shone, as he is of his own people."

"Waco-mish lies; his tongue is forked like the rattlesnake's; his heart is black as the Misho-tunga (bad spirit). When the Manitou made his children, whether Shos-shone or Comanche, Arapahó, Shi-an [Cheyenne], or Pä-né [Pawnee], he gave them buffalo to eat, and the pure water of the fountain to quench their thirst. He said not to one, Drink here, and to another, Drink there; but gave the crystal spring to all, that all might drink."

Waco-mish almost burst with rage as the other spoke; but his coward heart alone prevented him from provoking an encounter with the calm Shos-shone. *He*, made thirsty by the words he had spoken—for the red man is ever sparing of his tongue—again stooped down to the spring to quench his thirst, when the subtle warrior of the Comanche suddenly threw himself upon the kneeling hunter, and, forcing his head into the bubbling water held him down with all his strength, until his victim no longer struggled, his stiffened limbs relaxed, and he fell forward over the spring, drowned and dead.

Over the body stood the murderer, and no sooner was the deed of blood consummated than bitter remorse took possession of his mind, where before had reigned the fiercest passion and vindictive hate. With hands clasped to his forehead, he stood transfixed with horror, intently gazing on his victim, whose head still remained immersed in the fountain. Mechanically he dragged the body a few paces from the water, which, as soon as the head of the dead Indian was withdrawn, the Comanche saw suddenly and strangely disturbed. Bubbles sprang up from the bottom, and, rising to the surface, escaped in hissing gas. A thin vapoury cloud arose, and, gradually dissolving, displayed to the eyes of the trembling murderer the figure of an aged Indian, whose long snowy hair and venerable beard, blown aside by a gentle air from his breast, discovered the well-known totem of the great Wan-kan-aga, the father of the Comanche and Shos-shone nation, whom the tradition of the tribe, handed down by skilful hieroglyphics, almost deified for the good actions and deeds of bravery this famous warrior had performed on earth.

Stretching out a war club towards the affrighted murderer, the figure thus addressed him:

"Accursed of my tribe! this day thou hast severed the link between the mightiest nations of the world, while the blood of the brave Shos-shone cries to the Manitou for vengeance. May the water of thy tribe be rank and bitter in their throats!" Thus saying, and swinging his ponderous war club (made from the elk's horn) round his head, he dashed out the brains of the Comanche, who fell headlong into the spring, which, from that day to the present moment, remains rank and nauseous, so that not even when half dead with thirst, can one drink the foul water of that spring.

The good Wan-kan-aga, however, to perpetuate the memory of the Shos-shone warrior, who was renowned in his tribe for valour and nobleness of heart, struck with the same avenging club a hard flat rock, which overhung the rivulet, just out of sight of this scene of blood; and forthwith the rock opened into a round clear basin, which instantly filled with bubbling, sparkling water, than which no thirsty hunter ever drank a sweeter or a cooler draught.

Thus the two springs remain, an everlasting memento of the foul murder of the brave Shos-shone, and the stern justice of the good Wan-kan-aga; and from that day the two mighty tribes of the Shos-shone and Comanche have remained severed and apart, although a long and bloody war followed the treacherous murder of the Shos-shone chief, and many a scalp torn from the head of the Comanche paid the penalty of his death.

The American and Canadian trappers assert that the numerous

springs which, under the head of Beer, Soda, Steamboat springs,[8] &c., abound in the Rocky Mountains, are the spots where his satanic majesty comes up from his kitchen to breathe the sweet fresh air, which must doubtless be refreshing to his worship after a few hours spent in superintending the culinary process going on below.

Never was there such a paradise for hunters as this lone and solitary spot. The shelving prairie, at the bottom of which the springs are situated, is entirely surrounded by rugged mountains, and, containing perhaps two or three acres of excellent grass, affords a safe pasture to their animals, which would hardly care to wander from such feeding and the salitrose rocks they love so well to lick. Immediately overhead Pike's Peak, at an elevation of 12,000 [14,110] feet above the level of the sea, towers high into the clouds; whilst from the fountain, like a granitic amphitheatre, ridge after ridge, clothed with pine and cedar, rises and meets the stupendous mass of mountains, well called "Rocky," which stretches far away north and southward, their gigantic peaks being visible above the strata of clouds which hide their rugged bases.

This first day the sun shone out bright and warm, and not a breath of wind ruffled the evergreen foliage of the cedar groves. Gay-plumaged birds were twittering in the shrubs, and ravens and magpies were chattering overhead, attracted by the meat I had hung upon a tree; the mules, having quickly filled themselves, were lying round the spring, basking lazily in the sun; and myself, seated on a pack, and pipe in mouth, with rifle ready at my side, indolently enjoyed the rays which, reverberated from the white rock on which I was lying, were deliciously warm and soothing. A piece of rock, detached from the mountainside and tumbling noisily down, caused me to look up in the direction whence it came. Half a dozen bighorns, or Rocky Mountain sheep, perched on the pinnacle of a rock, were gazing wonderingly upon the prairie, where the mules were rolling enveloped in clouds of dust. The enormous horns of the mountain sheep appeared so disproportionately heavy, that I every moment expected to see them lose their balance and topple over the giddy height. My motions frightened them, and, jumping from rock to rock, they quickly disappeared up the steepest part of the mountain. At the same moment a herd of black-tail deer crossed the corner of the glade within rifleshot of me, but fearing the vicinity of Indians, I refrained from

8 The towns of Soda Springs, Idaho, and Soda Springs and Steamboat Springs, Colorado, are located respectively at three of these famous springs.

firing before I had reconnoitred the vicinity for signs of their recent presence.

Immediately over me, on the left bank of the stream, and high above the springs, was a small plateau, one of many which are seen on the mountainsides. Three buffalo bulls were here quietly feeding, and remained the whole afternoon undisturbed. I saw from the sign that they had very recently drunk at the springs, and that the little prairie where my animals were feeding was a frequent resort of solitary bulls.

Perceiving that the game, which was in sight on every side of me, was unwarily tame, I judged from this fact that no Indians were in the immediate vicinity, and therefore I resolved to camp where I was. Ascending a bluff where had been an old Indian camp, I found a number of old lodge poles, and packed them down to the springs, near which I made my fire, but out of arrow-shot of the shrubbery which lines the stream. Instead of permitting the animals to run loose, I picqueted them close to and round the camp, in order that they might act as sentinels during the night, for no man or dog can so soon discover the presence or approach of an Indian as a mule. The organ and sense of smelling in these animals are so acute that they at once detect the scent peculiar to the natives, and, snorting loud with fear, and by turning their heads with ears pointed to the spot whence the danger is approaching, wake, and warn at the same moment, their sleeping masters of the impending peril.

However, this night I was undisturbed, and slept soundly until the chattering of a magpie overhead awoke me, just as Pike's Peak was being tinged with the first grey streak of dawn.

Daybreak in this wild spot was beautiful in the extreme. While the deep gorge in which I lay was still buried in perfect gloom, the mountaintops loomed grey and indistinct from out the morning mist. A faint glow of light broke over the ridge which shut out the valley from the east, and, spreading over the sky, first displayed the snow-covered peak, a wreath of vapoury mist encircling it, which gradually rose and disappeared. Suddenly the dull white of its summit glowed with light like burnished silver; and at the same moment the whole eastern sky blazed, as it were, in gold, and ridge and peak, catching the refulgence, glittered with the beams of the rising sun, which at length, peeping over the crest, flooded at once the valley with its dazzling light.

Blowing the ashes of the slumbering fire, I placed upon it the little pot containing a piece of venison for my breakfast, and, relieving my four-footed sentries from their picquet guard, sallied down the stream, the edges of which were still thickly crusted with ice, for the purpose of taking a luxuriously cold bath; and cold enough it was in all conscience. After my frugal breakfast, unseasoned by bread or salt, or by any other beverage than the refreshing soda water, I took my rifle and sallied up the mountain to hunt, consigning my faithful animals to the protection of the dryad of the fountain, offering to that potent sprite the never-failing "medicine" of the first whiff of my pipe before starting from the spot.

Climbing up the mountainside, I reached a level plateau, interspersed with clumps of pine and cedar, where a herd of black-tail deer were quietly feeding. As I had the "wind" I approached under cover of a cedar whose branches feathered to the ground, and, resting my rifle in a forked limb, I selected the plumpest-looking of the band, a young buck, and "let him have it," as the hunters say. Struck through the heart, the deer for an instant stretched out its limbs convulsively, and then bounded away with the band, but in a zigzag course; and unlike the rest, whose tails were lifted high, his black tufted appendage was fast "shut up." Whilst I, certain of his speedy fall, reloaded my rifle, the band, seeing their comrade staggering behind, suddenly stopped. The wounded animal with outstretched neck ran round and round for a few seconds in a giddy circle, and dropped dead within sixty yards of where I stood. The others, like sheep, walked slowly up to the dead animal, and again my rifle gave out its sharp crack from the screen of branches, and another of the band, jumping high in air, bit the dust. They were both miserably poor, so much so that I left all but the hind quarters and fleece, and hanging them upon a tree I returned to camp for a mule to pack in the meat.

The mountains are full of grizzly bears, but, whether they had not yet left their winter quarters thus early in the season, I saw but one or two tracks, one of which I followed unsuccessfully for many miles over the wildest part of the mountains, into the Bayou Salado [South Park]. Whilst intent upon the trail, a clattering as of a regiment of cavalry immediately behind me made me bring my rifle to the ready, thinking that a whole nation of mounted Indians were upon me; but, looking back, a band of upwards of a hundred elk were dashing past, looking like a herd of mules, and in their passage down the mountain carrying with them a perfect avalanche of rocks and stones. I killed another deer on my return close to camp, which I reached, packing in the meat on my back, long after dark, and found the animals, which received me with loud neighs of recognition and welcome, with well-filled bellies, taking their evening drink at the springs.

I spent here a very pleasant time, and my animals began soon to improve upon the mountain grass. Game was very abundant; indeed, I had far more meat than I possibly required; but the surplus I hung up to jerk, as now the sun was getting powerful enough for that process.

I explored all the valleys and cañons of the mountains, and even meditated an expedition to the summit of Pike's Peak, where mortal foot has never yet trod.[9] No dread of Indians crossed my mind, probably because I had remained so long unmolested; and I was so perfectly contented that I had even selected a camping ground where I intended to remain two or three months, and probably should be at the present moment, if I had not got into a "scrape."

The bears latterly began to move, and their tracks became more frequent. One day I was hunting just at the foot of the Peak, when a large she-bear jumped out of a patch of cedars where she had been lying, and with a loud grunt charged up the mountain, and, dodging amongst the rocks, prevented my getting a crack at her. She was very old, and the grizzliest of the grizzly. She was within a few feet of me when I first saw her. It was unluckily nearly dark, or I should have followed and probably killed her, for they seldom run far, particularly at this season, when they are lank and weak.

One day as I was following a band of deer over the broken ground to the eastward of the mountain, I came suddenly upon an Indian camp, with the fire still smouldering, and dried meat hanging on the trees. Robinson Crusoe could not have been more thoroughly disgusted at sight of the "footprint in the sand," than was I at this inopportune discovery. I had anticipated a month or two's undisturbed hunting in this remote spot, and now it was out of the question to imagine that the Indians would leave me unmolested. I presently saw two Indians, carrying a deer between them, emerge from the timber bordering the creek, whom I knew at once by their dress to be Arapahós. As, however, my camp was several miles distant, I still hoped that they had not yet discovered its locality, and continued my hunt that day, returning late in the evening to my solitary encampment.

The next morning I removed the animals and packs to a prairie a little lower down the stream, which, although nearer the Indian

[9] Dr. Edwin James, of Major Long's expedition, climbed to the summit of Pikes Peak in July, 1820.

camp, was almost hidden from view, being enclosed by pine ridges and ragged buttes, and entered by a narrow gap filled with a dense growth of brush. When I had placed them in security, and taken the precaution to fasten them all to strong picquet pins, with a sufficient length of rope to enable them to feed at ease, and at the same time prevent them straying back to the springs, I again sallied out to hunt. A little before sunrise I descended the mountain to the springs, and, being very tired, after taking a refreshing draught of the cold water, I lay down on the rock by the side of the water and fell fast asleep. When I awoke the sun had already set; but although darkness was fast gathering over the mountain, I was surprised to see a bright light flickering against its sides. A glance assured me that the mountain was on fire, and, starting up, I saw at once the danger of my position. The bottom had been fired about a mile below the springs, and but a short distance from where I had secured my animals. A dense cloud of smoke was hanging over the gorge, and presently, a light air springing up from the east, a mass of flame shot up into the sky and rolled fiercely up the stream, the belt of dry brush on its banks catching fire and burning like tinder. The mountain was already invaded by the devouring element, and two wings of flame spread out from the main stream, which roaring along the bottom with the speed of a racehorse, licked the mountainside, extending its long line as it advanced. The dry pines and cedars hissed and cracked, as the flame, reaching them, ran up their trunks, and spread amongst the limbs, whilst the long waving grass underneath was a sea of fire. From the rapidity with which the fire advanced I feared that it would already have reached my animals, and hurried at once to the spot as fast as I could run. The prairie itself was as yet untouched, but the surrounding ridges were clothed in fire, and the mules, with stretched ropes, were trembling with fear. Throwing the saddle on my horse, and the pack on the steadiest mule, I quickly mounted, leaving on the ground a pile of meat, which I had not time to carry with me. The fire had already gained the prairie, and its long, dry grass was soon a sheet of flame, but, worse than all, the gap through which I had to retreat was burning. Setting spurs into Panchito's sides, I dashed him at the burning bush, and, though his mane and tail were singed in the attempt, he gallantly charged through it. Looking back, I saw the mules huddled together on the other side, and evidently fearing to pass the blazing barrier. As, however, to stop would have been fatal, I dashed on, but before I had proceeded twenty yards my old hunting mule, singed and smoking, was at my side, and the others close behind her.

On all sides I was surrounded by fire. The whole scenery was illuminated, the peaks and distant ridges being as plainly visible as at noonday. The bottom was a roaring mass of flame, but on the other side, the prairie being more bare of cedar bushes, the fire was less fierce and presented the only way of escape. To reach it, however, the creek had to be crossed, and the bushes on the banks were burning fiercely, which rendered it no easy matter; moreover, the edges were coated above the water with thin ice, which rendered it still more difficult. I succeeded in pushing Panchito into the stream, but, in attempting to climb the opposite bank, a blaze of fire was puffed into his face, which caused him to rear on end, and, his hind feet flying away from him at the same moment on the ice, he fell backwards into the middle of the stream, and rolled over me in the deepest water. Panchito rose on his legs and stood trembling with affright in the middle of the stream, whilst I dived and groped for my rifle, which had slipped from my hands, and of course sunk to the bottom. After a search of some minutes I found it, and, again mounting, made another attempt to cross a little farther down, in which I succeeded, and, followed by the mules, dashed through the fire and got safely through the line of blazing brush.

Once in safety, I turned in my saddle and had leisure to survey the magnificent spectacle. The fire had extended at least three miles on each side of the stream, and the mountain was one sheet of flame. A comparatively thin line marked the progress of the devouring element, which, as there was no wind to direct its course, burned on all sides, actually roaring as it went.

I had from the first no doubt but that the fire was caused by the Indians, who had probably discovered my animals, but, thinking that a large party of hunters might be out, had taken advantage of a favourable wind to set fire to the bottom, hoping to secure the horses and mules in the confusion, without the risk of attacking the camp. Once or twice I felt sure that I saw dark figures running about near where I had seen the Indian camp the previous day, and just as I had charged through the gap I heard a loud yell, which was answered by another at a little distance.

Singularly enough, just as I had got through the blazing line, a breeze sprang up from the westward and drove the fire after me, and I had again to beat a hasty retreat before it.[10]

[10] This fire extended into the prairie, towards the waters of the Platte, upwards of forty miles, and for fourteen days its glare was visible on the Arkansa, fifty miles distant. Ruxton's note.

I encamped six or seven miles from the springs, and, whilst proceeding down the creek, deer and antelope continually crossed and recrossed the trail, some in their affright running back into the very jaws of the fire. As soon as I had secured the animals I endeavoured to get my rifle into shooting order, but the water had so thoroughly penetrated and swelled the patching round the balls that it was a long time before I succeeded in cleaning one barrel, the other defying all my attempts. This was a serious accident, as I could not but anticipate a visit from the Indians if they discovered the camp.

All this time the fire was spreading out into the prairies, and, creeping up the "divide," [between the drainages of the Arkansas and the South Platte] was already advancing upon me. It extended at least five miles on the left bank of the creek, and on the right was more slowly creeping up the mountainside; while the brush and timber in the bottom was one body of flame. Besides the long sweeping line of the advancing flame, the plateaus on the mountainside, and within the line, were burning in every direction, as the squalls and eddies down the gullies drove the fire to all points.

The mountains themselves being invisible, the air, from the low ground where I then was, appeared a mass of fire, and huge crescents of flame danced as it were in the very sky, until a mass of timber blazing at once exhibited the sombre background of the stupendous mountains.

I had scarcely slept an hour when huge clouds of smoke rolling down the bottom frightened the animals, whose loud hinnying awoke me, and, half-suffocated by the dense smoke which hung heavily in the atmosphere, I again retreated before the fire, which was rapidly advancing; and this time I did not stop until I had placed thirty or forty miles between me and the enemy. I then encamped in a thickly-timbered bottom on the Fontaine-qui-bouille, where the ground, which had been burned by the hunters in the winter, was studded like a wheatfield with green grass. On this the animals fared sumptuously for several days—better, indeed, than I did myself, for game was very scarce, and in such poor condition as to be almost uneatable. While encamped on this stream, the wolves infested the camp to that degree that I could scarcely leave my saddles for a few minutes on the ground without finding the straps of rawhide gnawed to pieces; and one night the hungry brutes ate up all the ropes which were tied on the necks of the animals and trailed along the ground; they were actually devoured to within a yard of the mules' throats. One evening a wolf came into camp as I was engaged in cleaning my rifle, one barrel of which was still serviceable, and a long hickory wiping stick in it at the time. As I was hidden by a tree, the wolf approached the fire within a few feet, and was soon tugging away at an apishamore or saddlecloth of buffalo calfskin which lay on the ground. Without dreaming that the rifle would go off, I put a cap on the useless barrel, and, holding it out across my knee in a line with the wolf, snap— ph-i-zz—bang—went the charge of damp powder, much to my astonishment, igniting the stick which remained in the barrel, and driving it like a fiery comet against the ribs of the beast, who, yelling with pain, darted into the prairie at the top of his speed, his singed hair smoking as he ran.

CHAPTER 13

Big Game

I<small>T IS A SINGULAR FACT</small> that within the last two years
the prairies, extending from the mountains to a hundred miles or more
down the Arkansa, have been entirely abandoned by the buffalo. Indeed, in crossing from the settlements of New Mexico, the boundary
of their former range is marked by skulls and bones, which appear
fresher as the traveller advances westward and towards the waters of
the Platte. As the skulls are said to last only three years on the surface
of the ground, that period has consequently seen the gradual disappearance of the buffalo from their former haunts.

With the exception of the Bayou Salado, one of their favourite
pastures, they are now rarely met with in large bands on the upper
waters of the Arkansa; but straggling bulls pass occasionally the foot
of the mountain, seeking wintering-places on the elevated plateaus,
which are generally more free from snow than the lowland prairies,
by reason of the high winds. The bulls separate from the cows about
the month of September and scatter over the prairies and into the
mountains, where they recruit themselves during the winter. A few
males, however, always accompany the cows, to act as guides and
defenders of the herd, on the outskirts of which they are always stationed. The countless bands which are seen together at all seasons
are generally composed of cows alone, the bulls congregating in
smaller herds, and on the flanks of the main body.

The meat of the cow is infinitely preferable to that of the male
buffalo; but that of the bull, particularly if killed in the mountains,
is in better condition during the winter months. From the end of
June to September bull meat is rank and tough, and almost uneatable;
while the cows are in perfection, and as fat as stall-fed oxen, the
dépouillé, or fleece, exhibiting frequently four inches and more of
solid fat.

249

Whether it is that the meat itself—which, by the way, is certainly the most delicious of flesh—is most easy of digestion, or whether the digestive organs of hunters are "ostrichified" by the severity of exercise and the bracing, wholesome climate of the mountains and plains, it is a fact that most prodigious quantities of fat cow may be swallowed with the greatest impunity, and not the slightest inconvenience ever follows the mammoth feasts of the gourmands of the Far West. The powers of the Canadian *voyageurs* and hunters in the consumption of meat strike the greenhorn with wonder and astonishment, and are only equalled by the gastronomical capabilities exhibited by Indian dogs, both following the same plan in their epicurean gorgings.

On slaughtering a fat cow, the hunter carefully lays by, as a titbit for himself, the "boudins" and medullary intestine, which are prepared by being inverted and partially cleaned (this, however, is not thought indispensable). The *dépouillé*, or fleece, the short and delicious hump-rib and "tender loin," are then carefully stowed away, and with these the rough edge of the appetite is removed. But *the* course is, par excellence, the sundry yards of "boudin," which, lightly browned over the embers of the fire, slide down the well-lubricated throat of the hungry mountaineer, yard after yard disappearing in quick succession.

I once saw two Canadians[1] commence at either end of such a coil of grease, the mass lying between them on a dirty apishamore like the coil of a huge snake. As yard after yard glided glibly down their throats, and the serpent on the saddlecloth was dwindling from an anaconda to a moderate-sized rattlesnake, it became a great point with each of the feasters to hurry his operation, so as to gain a march upon his neighbour, and improve the opportunity by swallowing more than his just proportion; each, at the same time, exhorting the other, whatever he did, to feed fair, and every now and then, overcome by the unblushing attempts of his partner to bolt a vigorous mouthful, would suddenly jerk back his head, drawing out at the same moment, by the retreating motion, several yards of boudin from his neighbour's mouth and stomach—for the greasy viand required no mastication, and was bolted whole—and, snapping up himself the ravished portions, greedily swallowed them; to be in turn again withdrawn and subjected to a similar process by the other.[2]

[1] The majority of the trappers and mountain hunters are French Canadians and St. Louis French Creoles. Ruxton's note.

[2] This paragraph is omitted by Horace Kephart in his edition of the Ruxton narrative.

"*Indians on the War Path*"
from a water color by Alfred Jacob Miller, who accompanied Sir William Drummond Stewart on his travels in the West and made a pictorial record of much of the country which Ruxton was to cross a few years later

"*The life and ornament of the boundless prairies*" concerning which Ruxton prophesied, "Notwithstanding the great and wanton destruction of the buffalo, many years must elapse before this lordly animal becomes extinct" (A. J. Miller)

From the Porter collection

No animal requires so much killing as a buffalo. Unless shot through the lungs or spine, they invariably escape; and, even when thus mortally wounded, or even struck through the very heart, they will frequently run a considerable distance before falling to the ground, particularly if they see the hunter after the wound is given. If, however, he keeps himself concealed after firing, the animal will remain still, if it does not immediately fall. It is a most painful sight to witness the dying struggles of the huge beast. The buffalo invariably evinces the greatest repugnance to lie down when mortally wounded, apparently conscious that, when once touching mother earth, there is no hope left him. A bull, shot through the heart or lungs, with blood streaming from his mouth, and protruding tongue, his eyes rolling, bloodshot, and glazed with death, braces himself on his legs, swaying from side to side, stamps impatiently at his growing weakness, or lifts his rugged and matted head and helplessly bellows out his conscious impotence. To the last, however, he endeavours to stand upright, and plants his limbs farther apart, but to no purpose. As the body rolls like a ship at sea, his head slowly turns from side to side, looking about, as it were, for the unseen and treacherous enemy who has brought him, the lord of the plains, to such a pass. Gouts of purple blood spurt from his mouth and nostrils, and gradually the failing limbs refuse longer to support the ponderous carcase; more heavily rolls the body from side to side, until suddenly, for a brief instant, it becomes rigid and still; a convulsive tremor seizes it, and, with a low, sobbing gasp, the huge animal falls over on his side, the limbs extended stark and stiff, and the mountain of flesh without life or motion.

The first attempts of a greenhorn to kill a buffalo are invariably unsuccessful. He sees before him a mass of flesh, nearly five feet in depth from the top of the hump to the brisket, and consequently imagines that by planting his ball midway between these points, it must surely reach the vitals. Nothing, however, is more erroneous than the impression; for to "throw a buffalo in his tracks," which is the phrase for making a clean shot, he must be struck but a few inches above the brisket, behind the shoulder, where alone, unless the spine be divided, a death-shot will reach the vitals. I once shot a bull, the ball passing directly through the very centre of the heart and tearing a hole sufficiently large to insert the finger, which ran upwards of half a mile before it fell, and yet the ball had passed completely through the animal, cutting its heart almost in two. I also saw eighteen shots, the half of them muskets, deliberately fired into an old bull, at six paces, and some of them passing through the body, the poor animal standing the whole time, and making feeble attempts to charge. The nineteenth shot, with the muzzle touching his body, brought him to the ground. The head of the buffalo bull is so thickly covered with coarse matted hair that a ball fired at half a dozen paces will not penetrate the skull through the shaggy frontlock. I have frequently attempted this with a rifle carrying twenty-five balls to the pound, but never once succeeded.

Notwithstanding the great and wanton destruction of the buffalo, many years must elapse before this lordly animal becomes extinct.[3] In spite of their numerous enemies, they still exist in countless numbers, and, could any steps be taken to protect them, as is done in respect to other game, they would ever remain the life and ornament of the boundless prairies, and afford ample and never-failing provision to the traveller over these otherwise desert plains. Some idea of the prodigious slaughter of these animals may be formed by mentioning the fact that upwards of one hundred thousand buffalo robes find their way annually into the United States and Canada; and these are the skins of *cows* alone, the bull's hide being so thick that it is never dressed. Besides this, the Indians kill a certain number for their own use, exclusive of those whose meat they require; and the reckless slaughter of buffalo by parties of white men, emigrants to the Columbia, California, and elsewhere, leaving, as they proceed on their journey, thousands of untouched carcases on the trail, swells the aggregate of this wholesale destruction to an enormous amount.

The grizzly bear is the fiercest of the *ferae naturae* of the mountains. His great strength and wonderful tenacity of life render an encounter with him anything but desirable, and therefore it is a rule with the Indians and white hunters never to attack him unless backed by a strong party. Although, like every other wild animal, he usually flees from man, yet at certain seasons, when maddened by love or hunger, he not unfrequently charges at first sight of a foe, when, unless killed dead, a hug at close quarters is anything but a pleasant embrace, his strong hooked claws stripping the flesh from bones as easily as a cook peels an onion. Many are the tales of bloody encounters with these animals which the trappers delight to recount to the greenhorn,

[3] The great slaughter came in the eighteen seventies, when special hunters killed the animals wholesale for the hides. See M. S. Garretson, *The American Bison*, and E. Douglas Branch, *The Hunting of the Buffalo*. The American Bison Society was instrumental in saving the buffalo from extinction.

to enforce their caution as to the foolhardiness of ever attacking the grizzly bear.

Some years ago a trapping party was on their way to the mountains, led, I believe, by old Sublette, a well-known captain of the West. Amongst the band was one John [Hugh] Glass,[4] a trapper who had been all his life in the mountains, and had seen, probably, more exciting adventures, and had had more wonderful and hairbreadth escapes, than any of the rough and hardy fellows who make the West their home, and whose lives are spent in a succession of perils and privations. On one of the streams running from the Black Hills, a range of mountains northward of the Platte, Glass and a companion were one day setting their traps, when, on passing through a cherry thicket which skirted the stream, the former, who was in advance, descried a large grizzly bear quietly turning up the turf with his nose, searching for yampa roots or pig nuts, which there abounded. Glass immediately called his companion, and both, proceeding cautiously, crept to the skirt of the thicket, and, taking steady aim at the animal, whose broadside was fairly exposed at the distance of twenty yards, discharged their rifles at the same instant, both balls taking effect, but not inflicting a mortal wound. The bear, giving a groan of pain, jumped with all four legs from the ground, and, seeing the wreaths of smoke hanging at the edge of the brush, charged at once in that direction, snorting with pain and fury.

"Harraw, Bill!" roared out Glass, as he saw the animal rushing towards them, "we'll be made meat of as sure as shootin'!" and, leaving the tree behind which he had concealed himself, he bolted through the thicket, followed closely by his companion. The brush was so thick that they could scarcely make their way through, whereas the weight and strength of the bear carried him through all obstructions, and he was soon close upon them.

About a hundred yards from the thicket was a steep bluff, and between these points was a level piece of prairie; Glass saw that his only chance was to reach this bluff, and, shouting to his companion to make for it, they both broke from the cover and flew like lightning across the open space. When more than half way across, the bear being about fifty yards behind them, Glass, who was leading, tripped over a stone and fell to the ground, and just as he rose to his feet, the beast, rising on his hind feet, confronted him. As he closed, Glass, never losing his presence of mind, cried to his companion to load up

---

[4] The story of Hugh Glass has been retold many times, including the narration in verse by John G. Neihardt, "The Song of Hugh Glass."

quickly, and discharged his pistol full into the body of the animal, at the same moment that the bear, with blood streaming from its nose and mouth, knocked the pistol from his hand with one blow of its paw, and, fixing its claws deep into his flesh, rolled with him to the ground.

The hunter, notwithstanding his hopeless situation, struggled manfully, drawing his knife and plunging it several times into the body of the beast, which, furious with pain, tore with tooth and claw the body of the wretched victim, actually baring the ribs of flesh and exposing the very bones. Weak with loss of blood, and with eyes blinded with the blood which streamed from his lacerated scalp, the knife at length fell from his hand, and Glass sank down insensible, and to all appearance dead.

His companion, who, up to this moment, had watched the conflict, which, however, lasted but a few seconds, thinking that his turn would come next, and not having had presence of mind even to load his rifle, fled with might and main back to camp, where he narrated the miserable fate of poor Glass. The captain of the band of trappers, however, dispatched the man with a companion back to the spot where he lay, with instructions to remain by him if still alive, or to bury him if, as all supposed he was, defunct, promising them at the same time a sum of money for so doing.

On reaching the spot, which was red with blood, they found Glass still breathing, and the bear, dead and stiff, actually lying upon his body. Poor Glass presented a horrifying spectacle: the flesh was torn in strips from his chest and limbs, and large flaps strewed the ground; his scalp hung bleeding over his face, which was also lacerated in a shocking manner.

The bear, besides the three bullets which had pierced its body, bore the marks of the fierce nature of Glass's final struggle, no less than twenty gaping wounds in the breast and belly testifying to the gallant defence of the mountaineer.

Imagining that, if not already dead, the poor fellow could not possibly survive more than a few moments, the men collected his arms, stripped him even of his hunting shirt and moccasins, and, merely pulling the dead bear off the body, mounted their horses, and slowly followed the remainder of the party, saying, when they reached it, that Glass was dead, as probably they thought, and that they had buried him.

In a few days the gloom which pervaded the trappers' camp, occasioned by the loss of a favourite companion, disappeared, and

Glass's misfortune, although frequently mentioned over the campfire, at length was almost entirely forgotten in the excitement of the hunt and Indian perils which surrounded them.

Months elapsed, the hunt was over, and the party of trappers were on their way to the trading fort with their packs of beaver. It was nearly sundown, and the round adobe bastions of the mud-built fort were just in sight, when a horseman was seen slowly approaching them along the banks of the river. When near enough to discern his figure, they saw a lank cadaverous form with a face so scarred and disfigured that scarcely a feature was discernible. Approaching the leading horemen, one of whom happened to be the companion of the defunct Glass in his memorable bear scrape, the stranger, in a hollow voice, reining in his horse before them, exclaimed, "Harraw, Bill, my boy! you thought I was gone under that time, did you? But hand me over my horse and gun, my lad; I ain't dead yet by a dam sight!"

What was the astonishment of the whole party, and the genuine horror of Bill and his worthy companion in the burial story, to hear the well-known, though now much altered, voice of John Glass, who had been killed by a grizzly bear months before, and comfortably interred, as the two men had reported, and all had believed!

There he was, however, and no mistake about it; and all crowded round to hear from his lips, how, after the lapse of he knew not how long, he had gradually recovered, and being without arms, or even a butcher knife, he had fed upon the almost putrid carcase of the bear for several days, until he had regained sufficient strength to crawl, when, tearing off as much of the bear's meat as he could carry in his enfeebled state, he crept down the river, and suffering excessive torture from his wounds, and hunger, and cold, he made the best of his way to the fort, which was some eighty or ninety miles from the place of his encounter with the bear, and, living the greater part of the way upon roots and berries, he after many, many days, arrived in a pitiable state, from which he had now recovered, and was, to use his own expression, "as slick as a peeled onion."

A trapper on Arkansa, named Valentine Herring,[5] but better known as "Old Rube," told me that once, when visiting his traps one morning on a stream beyond the mountains, he found one missing, at the same time that he discovered fresh bear "sign" about the banks. Proceeding down the river in search of the lost trap, he heard the

[5] Valentine Herring killed a trapper named Beer in a duel on the South Platte River in the winter of 1841–42, according to Rufus B. Sage, *Rocky Mountain Life*, 209. Ruxton tells more of Herring in his *Life in the Far West*.

noise of some large body breaking through the thicket of plum bushes which belted the stream. Ensconcing himself behind a rock, he presently observed a huge grizzly bear emerge from the bush and limp on three legs to a flat rock, which he mounted, and then, quietly seating himself, he raised one of his forepaws, on which Rube, to his amazement, discovered his trap tight and fast.

The bear, lifting his iron-gloved foot close to his face, gravely examined it, turning his paw round and round, and quaintly bending his head from side to side, looking at the trap from the corners of his eyes, and with an air of mystery and puzzled curiosity, for he evidently could not make out what the novel and painful appendage could be, and every now and then smelt it and tapped it lightly on the rock. This, however, only paining the animal the more, he would lick the trap, as if deprecating its anger and wishing to conciliate it.

After watching these curious antics for some time, as the bear seemed inclined to resume his travels, Rube, to regain his trap, was necessitated to bring the bear's cogitations to a close, and, levelling his rifle, shot him dead, cutting off his paw and returning with it to camp, where the trappers were highly amused at the idea of trapping a b'ar.

Near the same spot where Glass encountered his "scrape," some score of Sioux squaws were one day engaged in gathering cherries in a thicket near their village, and had already nearly filled their baskets, when a bear suddenly appeared in the midst, and, with a savage growl, charged amongst them. Away ran the terrified squaws, yelling and shrieking, out of the shrubbery, nor stopped until safely ensconced within their lodges. Bruin, however, preferring fruit to meat, albeit of tender squaws, after routing the petticoats, quietly betook himself to the baskets, which he quickly emptied, and then quietly retired.

Bears are exceedingly fond of plums and cherries, and a thicket of this fruit in the vicinity of the mountains is, at the season when they are ripe, a sure find for Mr. Bruin. When they can get fruit they prefer such food to meat, but are, nevertheless, carnivorous animals.

The game, par excellence, of the Rocky Mountains, and that which takes precedence in a comestible point of view, is the *carnero cimmarón* of the Mexicans, the bighorn or mountain sheep of the Canadian hunters. This animal, which partakes both of the nature of the deer and goat, resembles the latter more particularly in its habits, and its characteristic liking to lofty, inaccessible points of the mountains, whence it seldom descends to the upland valleys excepting in very severe weather. In size the mountain sheep is between the domestic animal and the common red deer of America, but more strongly made than the latter. Its colour is a brownish dun, the hair being tipped with a darker tinge as the animal's age increases, with a whitish streak on the hind quarters, the tail being shorter than a deer's, and tipped with black. The horns of the male are enormous, curved backwards, and often three feet in length with a circumference of twenty inches near the head. The hunters assert that, in descending the precipitous sides of the mountains, the sheep frequently leap from the height of twenty or thirty feet, invariably alighting on their horns, and thereby saving their bones from certain dislocation.

They are even more acute in the organs of sight and smell than the deer; and as they love to resort to the highest and most inaccessible spots, whence a view can readily be had of approaching danger, and particularly as one of the band is always stationed on the most commanding pinnacle of rock as sentinel, whilst the others are feeding, it is no easy matter to get within rifleshot of the cautious animals. When alarmed they ascend still higher up the mountain; halting now and then on some overhanging crag and looking down at the object which may have frightened them, they again commence their ascent, leaping from point to point and throwing down an avalanche of rocks and stones as they bound up the steep sides of the mountain. They are generally very abundant in all parts of the main chain of the Rocky Mountains, but particularly so in the vicinity of the "Parks" and the Bayou Salado, as well as in the range between the upper waters of the Del Norte and Arkansa, called the Wet Mountain by the trappers. On the Sierra Madre, or Cordillera of New Mexico and Chihuahua, they are also numerous.

The first mountain sheep I killed, I got within shot of in rather a curious manner. I had undertaken several unsuccessful hunts for the purpose of procuring a pair of horns of this animal, as well as some skins, which are of excellent quality when dressed, but had almost given up any hope of approaching them, when one day, having killed and butchered a black-tail deer in the mountains, I sat down with my back to a small rock and fell asleep. On awaking, feeling inclined for a smoke, I drew from my pouch a pipe, and flint and steel, and began leisurely to cut a charge of tobacco. Whilst thus engaged I became sensible of a peculiar odour which was wafted right into my face by the breeze, and which, on snuffing it once or twice, I immediately recognised as that which emanates from sheep and goats. Still I never thought that one of the former animals could be in the neighbourhood, for my mule was picqueted on the little plateau where I sat, and was leisurely cropping the buffalo grass which thickly covered it.

Looking up carelessly from my work, as a whiff stronger than before reached my nose, what was my astonishment at seeing five mountain sheep within ten paces, and regarding me with a curious and astonished gaze! Without drawing a breath, I put out my hand and grasped the rifle, which was lying within reach; but the motion, slight as it was, sufficed to alarm them, and with a loud bleat the old ram bounded up the mountain, followed by the band, at so rapid a pace that all my attempts to draw a bead upon them were ineffectual. When, however, they reached a little plateau about one hundred and fifty yards from where I stood, they suddenly stopped, and, approaching the edge, looked down at me, shaking their heads and bleating their displeasure at the intrusion. No sooner did I see them stop than my rifle was at my shoulder, and covering the broadside of the one nearest to me. An instant after and I pulled the trigger, and at the report the sheep jumped convulsively from the rock and made one attempt to follow its flying companions; but its strength failed, and, circling round once or twice at the edge of the plateau, it fell over on its side, and, rolling down the steep rock, tumbled dead very near me. My prize proved a very fine young male, but had not a large pair of horns. It was, however, "seal" fat, and afforded me a choice supply of meat, which was certainly the best I had eaten in the mountains, being fat and juicy, and in flavour somewhat partaking both of the domestic sheep and buffalo.

Several attempts have been made to secure the young of these animals and transport them to the States; and, for this purpose, an old mountaineer, one Billy Williams, took with him a troop of milch goats, by which to bring up the young sheep; but although he managed to take several fine lambs, I believe that he did not succeed in reaching the frontier with one living specimen out of some half-score. The hunters frequently rear them in the mountains, and they become greatly attached to their masters, enlivening the camp with their merry gambols.

The elk, in point of size, ranks next to the buffalo. It is found in all parts of the mountains, and descends not unfrequently far down into the plains in the vicinity of the larger streams. A full-grown elk is as large as a mule, with rather a heavy neck and body, and stout limbs, its feet leaving a track as large as that of a two-year-old steer. They are dull, sluggish animals, at least in comparison with others of the deer tribe, and are easily approached and killed. In winter they congregate in large herds, often numbering several hundreds, and at that season are fond of travelling, their track through the snow having the appearance of a broad beaten road. The elk requires less killing than any other of the deer tribe, whose tenacity of life is remarkable; a shot anywhere in the forepart of the animal brings it to the ground. On one occasion I killed two with one ball, which passed through the neck of the first and struck the second, which was standing a few paces distant, through the heart; both fell dead. A deer, on the contrary, often runs a considerable distance, strike it where you will. The meat of the elk is strong flavoured, and more like poor bull than venison: it is only eatable when the animal is fat and in good condition; at other times it is strong tasted and stringy.

The antelope, the smallest of the deer tribe, affords the hunter a sweet and nutritious meat, when that of nearly every other description of game, from the poorness and scarcity of the grass during the winter, is barely eatable. They are seldom seen now in very large bands on the grand prairies, having been driven from their old pastures by the Indians and white hunters. The former, by means of "surrounds," an enclosed space formed in one of the passes used by these animals, very often drive into the toils an entire band of antelope of several hundreds, when not one escapes slaughter.

I have seen them on the western sides of the mountains, and in the mountain valleys, in herds of several thousands. They are exceedingly timid animals, but at the same time wonderfully curious; and their curiosity very often proves their death, for the hunter, taking advantage of this weakness, plants his wiping-stick in the ground, with a cap or red handkerchief on the point, and, concealing himself in the long grass, waits, rifle in hand, the approach of the inquisitive antelope, who, seeing an unusual object in the plains, trots up to it, and, coming within range of the deadly tube, pays dearly for his temerity. An antelope, when alone, is one of the stupidest of beasts, and becomes so confused and frightened at sight of a travelling party that it frequently runs right into the midst of the danger it seeks to avoid.

I had heard most wonderful accounts from the trappers of an animal, the existence of which was beyond all doubt, which, although exceedingly rare, was occasionally met with in the mountains, but, from its supposed dangerous ferocity, and the fact of its being a cross between the devil and a bear, was never molested by the Indians or white hunters, and a wide berth given whenever the animal made its dreaded appearance. Most wonderful stories were told of its audacity and fearlessness—how it sometimes jumps from an overhanging rock on a deer or buffalo, and, fastening on its neck, soon brings it to the ground; how it has been known to leap upon a hunter when passing near its place of concealment, and devour him in a twinkling, often charging furiously into a camp, and playing all sorts of pranks on the goods and chattels of the mountaineers. The general belief was that the animal owes its paternity to the old gentleman himself; but the most reasonable declare it to be a cross between the bear and wolf.

Hunting one day with an old Canadian trapper, he told me that in a part of the mountains which we were about to visit on the morrow, he once had a battle with a *carcagieu*, which lasted upwards of two hours, during which he fired a pouchful of balls into the animal's body, which spat them out as fast as they were shot in. To the truth of this probable story he called all the saints to bear witness.

Two days after, as we were toiling up a steep ridge after a band of mountain sheep, my companion, who was in advance, suddenly threw himself flat behind a rock, and exclaimed in a smothered tone, signalling me with his hand to keep down and conceal myself, "*Sacré enfant de Gârce, mais* here's von dam *carcagieu!*"

I immediately cocked my rifle, and, advancing to the rock and peeping over it, saw an animal, about the size of a large badger, engaged in scraping up the earth about a dozen paces from where we were concealed. Its colour was dark, almost black; its body long, and apparently tailless; and I at once recognised the mysterious beast to be a glutton. After I had sufficiently examined the animal, I raised my rifle to shoot, when a louder than common *enfant de Gârce* from my companion alarmed the animal, and it immediately ran off, when I stood up and fired both barrels after it, but without effect, the attempt exciting a derisive laugh from the Canadian, who exclaimed, "Pe gar, may be you got fifty balls; vel, shoot 'em all at de dam *carcagieu*, and he not care a dam."[6]

The skins of these animals are considered "great medicine" by the Indians, and will fetch almost any price. They are very rarely met with on the plains, preferring the upland valleys and broken ground of the mountains, which afford them a better field for their method of securing game, which is by lying in wait behind a rock, or on the steep bank of a ravine, concealed by a tree or shrub, until a deer or antelope passes underneath, when they spring upon the animal's back, and, holding on with their strong and sharp claws,

[6] The carcajou, or wolverine, was sometimes called the "beaver-eater."

which they bury in the flesh, soon bring it bleeding to the ground. The Indians say they are purely carnivorous; but I imagine that, like the bear, they not unfrequently eat fruit and roots, when animal food is not to be had.

I have said that the mountain wolves, and, still more so, the coyote of the plains, are less frightened at the sight of man than any other beast. One night, when encamped on an affluent of the Platte, a heavy snowstorm falling at the time, I lay down in my blanket, after first heaping on the fire a vast pile of wood, to burn till morning. In the middle of the night I was awakened by the excessive cold, and, turning towards the fire, which was burning bright and cheerfully, what was my astonishment to see a large grey wolf sitting quietly before it, his eyes closed, and his head nodding in sheer drowsiness! Although I had frequently seen wolves evince their disregard to fires, by coming within a few feet of them to seize upon any scraps of meat which might be left exposed, I had never seen or heard of one approaching so close as to warm his body, and for that purpose alone. However, I looked at him for some moments without disturbing the beast, and closed my eyes and went to sleep, leaving him to the quiet enjoyment of the blaze.

This is not very wonderful when I mention that it is a very common thing for these animals to gnaw the straps of a saddle on which your head is reposing for a pillow.

When I turned my horse's head for Pike's Peak, I quite regretted the abandonment of my mountain life, solitary as it was, and more than once thought of again taking the trail to the Bayou Salado, where I had enjoyed such good sport.

Apart from the feeling of loneliness which anyone in my situation must naturally have experienced, surrounded by stupendous works of nature, which in all their solitary grandeur frowned upon me, and sinking into utter insignificance the miserable mortal who crept beneath their shadow, still there was something inexpressibly exhilirating in the sensation of positive freedom from all worldly care, and a consequent expansion of the sinews, as it were, of mind and body, which made me feel elastic as a ball of Indian rubber, and in a state of such perfect insouciance that no more dread of scalping Indians entered my mind than if I had been sitting in Broadway, in one of the windows of the Astor House. A citizen of the world, I never found any difficulty in investing my resting place, wherever it might be, with all the attributes of a home, and hailed, with delight equal to that which the artificial comforts of a civilised home would have caused, the, to me, domestic appearance of my hobbled animals, as they grazed around the camp, when I returned after a hard day's hunt. By the way, I may here remark that my sporting feeling underwent a great change when I was necessitated to follow and kill game for the support of life, and as a means of subsistence; and the slaughter of deer and buffalo no longer became sport when the object was to fill the larder, and the excitement of the hunt was occasioned by the alternative of a plentiful feast or a banyan; and, although ranking under the head of the most red-hot of sportsmen, I can safely acquit myself of ever wantonly destroying a deer or buffalo unless I was in need of meat; and such consideration for the *ferae naturae* is common to all the mountaineers who look to game alone for their support. Although liable to an accusation of barbarism, I must confess that the very happiest moments of my life have been spent in the wilderness of the Far West; and I never recall but with pleasure the remembrance of my solitary camp in the Bayou Salado, with no friend near me more faithful than my rifle, and no companions more sociable than my good horses and mules, or the attendant coyote which nightly serenaded us. With a plentiful supply of dry pine logs on the fire, and its cheerful blaze streaming far up into the sky, illuminating the valley far and near, and exhibiting the animals, with well-filled bellies, standing contentedly at rest over their picquet pins, I would sit cross-legged enjoying the genial warmth, and, pipe in mouth, watch the blue smoke as it curled upwards, building castles in its vapoury wreaths, and, in the fantastic shapes it assumed, peopling the solitude with figures of those far away. Scarcely, however, did I ever wish to change such hours of freedom for all the luxuries of civilised life, and, unnatural and extraordinary as it may appear, yet such is the fascination of the life of the mountain hunter, that I believe not one instance could be adduced of even the most polished and civilised of men, who had once tasted the sweets of its attendant liberty and freedom from every worldly care, not regretting the moment when he exchanged it for the monotonous life of the settlements, nor sighing, and sighing again, once more to partake of its pleasures and allurements.

Nothing can be more social and cheering than the welcome blaze of the campfire on a cold winter's night, and nothing more amusing or entertaining, if not instructive, than the rough conversation of the single-minded mountaineers, whose simple daily talk is all of exciting adventure, since their whole existence is spent in scenes of peril and privation; and consequently the narration of their everyday life is a tale of thrilling accidents and hairbreadth 'scapes, which, though simple matter-of-fact to them, appear a startling romance to those who are not acquainted with the nature of the lives led by these men, who, with the sky for a roof and their rifles to supply them with food and clothing, call no man lord or master, and are free as the game they follow.

A hunter's camp in the Rocky Mountains is quite a picture. He does not always take the trouble to build any shelter unless it is in the snow season, when a couple of deerskins stretched over a willow frame shelter him from the storm. At other seasons he is content with a mere windbreak. Near at hand are two upright poles, with another supported on the top of these, on which is displayed, out of reach of hungry wolf or coyote, meat of every variety the mountains afford. Buffalo *dépouillés*, hams of deer and mountain sheep, beaver tails, &c., stock the larder. Under the shelter of the skins hang his powder horn and bullet pouch; while his rifle, carefully defended from the damp, is always within reach of his arm. Round the blazing fire the hunters congregate at night, and whilst cleaning their rifles, making or mending mocassins, or running bullets, spin long yarns of their hunting exploits, &c.

Some hunters, who have married Indian squaws, carry about with them the Indian lodge of buffalo skins, which are stretched in a conical form round a frame of poles. Near the camp is always seen the "graining block," a log of wood with the bark stripped and perfectly smooth, which is planted obliquely in the ground, and on which the hair is removed from the skins to prepare them for being dressed. There are also "stretching frames," on which the skins are placed to undergo the process of dubbing, which is the removal of the flesh and fatty particles adhering to the skin, by means of the dubber, an instrument made of the stock of an elk's horn. The last process is the "smoking," which is effected by digging a round hole in the ground and lighting in it an armful of rotten wood or punk. Three sticks are then planted round the hole, and their tops brought together and tied. The skin is then placed on this frame, and all the holes by which the smoke might escape carefully stopped; in ten or twelve hours the skin is thoroughly smoked and ready for immediate use.

The camp is invariably made in a picturesque locality, for, like the Indian, the white hunter has ever an eye to the beautiful. The broken ground of the mountains, with their numerous tumbling and babbling rivulets, and groves and thickets of shrubs and timber, always afford shelter from the boisterous winds of winter, and abundance of fuel and water. Facing the rising sun the hunter invariably erects his shanty, with a wall of precipitous rock in rear to defend it from the gusts which often sweep down the gorges of the mountains. Round the camp his animals, well hobbled at night, feed within sight, for nothing does a hunter dread more than a visit from the horse-stealing Indians; and to be afoot is the acme of his misery.

CHAPTER 14

Homeward Bound

W<small>HEN I RETURNED</small> to the Arkansa I found a small
party were making preparations to cross the grand prairie to the
United States, intending to start on the first of May, before which
time there would not be a sufficiency of grass to support the animals
on the way. With these men I determined to travel, and in the meantime employed myself in hunting on the Wet Mountain, and Fisher's
Hole, a valley at the head of St. Charles, as well as up the Arkansa
itself. I observed in these excursions that vegetation was in a much
more forward state in the mountain valleys and the prairies con-
tiguous to their bases than on the open plains, and that in the vicinity
of the "pueblo" it was still more backward than in any other spot, on
the fifteenth of April not a blade of green grass having as yet made
its appearance round the fort. This was not from the effects of drought,
for several refreshing showers had fallen since the disappearance of
the snow; neither was there any apparent difference in the soil, which
is a rich loam, and in the river bottom, an equally rich vegetable mould.
At this time, when the young grass had not yet appeared here, it was
several inches high on the mountains and upland prairies, and the
cherry and currant bushes on the creeks were bursting into leaf.

Amongst the wives of the mountaineers in the fort was one
Mexican woman from the state of Durango, who had been carried
off by the Comanches in one of their raids into that department. Remaining with them several years, she eventually accompanied a party
of Kioways, allies of the Comanche, to Bent's Fort on the Arkansa,
Here she was purchased from them and became the wife of Hawkens,
who afterwards removed from Bent's and took up his abode at the
"pueblo," and was my hospitable host while on the Arkansa. It appeared that her Mexican husband, by some means or another, heard
that she had reached Bent's Fort, and, impelled by affection, under-

265

took the long journey of upwards of fifteen hundred miles to recover his lost wife. In the meantime, however, she had borne her
American husband a daughter, and when her first spouse claimed her
as his own and wished her to accompany him back to her own country,
she only consented on condition that she might carry with her the
child, from which she steadfastly refused to be separated. The father,
however, turned a deaf ear to this request, and eventually the poor
Durangueño returned to his home alone, his spouse preferring to
share the buffalo rib and venison with her mountaineer before the frijole and chile colorado of the bereaved ranchero.

Three or four Taos women, and as many squaws of every nation,
comprised the "female society" on the Upper Arkansa, giving good
promise of peopling the river with a sturdy race of half-breeds, if all
the little dusky buffalo-fed urchins who played about the corral of
the fort arrived scathless at maturity.

Amongst the hunters on the Upper Arkansa were four Delaware Indians, the remnant of a band who had been trapping for several years in the mountains, and many of whom had been killed by
hostile Indians, or in warfare with the Apaches while in the employ
of the states of New Mexico and Chihuahua. Their names were Jim
Dicky, Jim Swannick, Little Beaver, and Big Nigger. The last had
married a squaw from the Taos pueblo, and, happening to be in New
Mexico with his spouse at the time of the late rising against the
Americans, he very naturally took part with the people by whom he
had been adopted.

In the attack on the Indian pueblo it was said that Big Nigger
particularly distinguished himself, calling by name to several of the
mountain men who were amongst the attacking party, and inviting
them to come near enough for him, the Big Nigger, to "throw them
in their tracks." And this feat he effected more than once, to the cost
of the assailants, for it was said that the Delaware killed nearly all
who fell on the side of the Americans, his squaw loading his rifle and
encouraging him in the fight.

By some means or another he escaped after the capture of the
pueblo, and made his way to the mountains on the Arkansa; but as
it was reported that a price was put on his head, he retired in company with the other Delawares to the mountains, where they all lay
perdus for a time; and it was pretty well understood that any one
feeling inclined to reap the reward by the capture of Big Nigger
would be under the necessity of "taking him," and with every probability of catching a Tartar at the same time, the three other Dela-

wares having taken the delinquent under the protection of their rifles. Although companions of the American and Canadian hunters for many years, anything but an *entente cordiale* existed towards their white confreres on the part of the Delawares, who knew very well that anything in the shape of Indian blood is looked upon with distrust and contempt by the white hunters.

Tharpe, an Indian trader, who had just returned from the Cheyenne village at the "Big Timber" on the Arkansa, had purchased from some Kioways two prisoners, a Mexican and an American negro. The former had been carried off by the Comanche from Durango when about seven years old, had almost entirely forgotten his own tongue, and neither knew his own age nor what length of time he had been a captive amongst the Indians. The degraded and miserable existence led by this poor creature had almost obliterated all traces of humanity from his character and appearance. Probably not more than twenty-five years of age, he was already wrinkled and haggard in his face, which was that of a man of threescore years. Wrapped in a dirty blanket, with his long hair streaming over his shoulders, he skulked, like some savage animal, in holes and corners of the fort, seeming to shun his fellow men, in a consciousness of his abject and degraded condition. At night he would be seen with his face close to the rough doors of the rooms, peering through the cracks, and envying the, to him, unusual luxury within. When he observed anyone approach the door, he instantly withdrew and concealed himself in the darkness until he passed. A present of tobacco, now and then, won for me the confidence of the poor fellow, and I gathered from him, in broken Spanish mixed with Indian, an account of his miseries.

I sat with him one night on a log in the corral, as he strove to make me understand that once, long, long ago, he had been *muy rico* —very rich; that he lived in a house where was always a fire like that burning within, and where he used to sit on his mother's lap; and this fact he repeated over and over again, thinking that to show that once affectionate regard had been bestowed upon him was to prove that he had been at one time an important personage. "*Me quiso mucho, mucho,*" he said, speaking of his mother—"she loved me very, very much; and I had good clothes and plenty to eat; but that was many, many moons ago.

"*Mire,*" he continued, "from this size," putting his hand out about three feet from the ground, "*ni padre, ni madre, ni amigos he tenido yo*—neither father, mother, nor friends have I had—*pero patadas, bastante*—but plenty of kicks—*y poca carne*—and very little meat."

267

I asked him if he had no wish to return to his own country. His haggard face lighted up for an instant, as the dim memory of his childhood's home returned to his callous mind. "*¡Ay, Dios mío!*" he exclaimed, "*si fuera posible*—Ah, my God, if it were possible! But no," he continued after a pause, "*estoy ahora muy bruto, y así no me quadrara a ver mi madre*—I am now no more than a brute, and in this state would not like to see my mother. *Y de más*—and moreover—my compadre," as he called the man who had purchased him, "is going to give me a shirt and a sombrero. What can I want more? *Vaya, es mejor así*—it is better as it is." One night he accosted me in the corral in an unusual degree of excitement.

"*¡Mire!*" he exclaimed, seizing me by the arm—"look here! *estoy boracho*—I am drunk! *Me dió mi compadre un pedazo de aguardiente*—my godfather has given me a bit of brandy. *Y estoy tan feliz, y ligero como páxaro, como pa-x-ar-o,*" he hiccuped—"and I am as happy and as light as a bird. *Me vuelo*—I am flying. *Me dicen que estoy boracho. ¡Ay, qué palabra bonita!*—they tell me I am drunk: *drunk*—what a beautiful word is this! *En mi vida, nunca he sentido como ahora*—never in my life have I felt as I do now." And the poor wretch covered his head with a blanket, and laughed long and loud at the trick he had played his old friend misery.

The negro, on the contrary, was a characteristic specimen of his race, always laughing, singing, and dancing, and cutting uncouth capers. He had been a slave in the semicivilised Cherokee nation, and had been captured by the Comanches, as he himself declared, but more probably had run away from his master and joined them voluntarily. He was a musician, and of course could play the fiddle; and having discovered an old weather-beaten instrument in the fort, "Lucy Neal," "Old Dan Tucker," and "Buffalo Gals," were heard at all hours of the day and night; and he was, moreover, installed into the Weippert of the fandangos which frequently took place in the fort, when the hunters with their squaws were at the rendezvous.

Towards the latter end of April, green grass began to show itself in the bottoms, and myself and two others, who had been wintering in the mountains for the benefit of their health, made preparations for our departure to the United States. Packsaddles were inspected and repaired, apishamores made, lariats and lassos greased and stretched, mules and horses collected from their feeding grounds, and their forefeet shod. A small supply of meat was "made," *i.e.* cut into thin flaps and dried in the sun, to last until we reached the buffalo range, rifles

put in order and balls run, hobbles cut out of rawhide, parfleche mocassins cobbled up, deerskin hunting shirts and pantaloons patched,
and all our very primitive "kit" overhauled to render it serviceable
for the journey across the grand prairies, while the "possible sack"
was lightened of all superfluities—an easy task, by the way. When
everything was ready, I was delayed several days in hunting my animals. The Indian traders having arrived, bringing with them large
herds of mules and horses, my mules had become separated from the
horse and from one another, and it was with no small difficulty that I
succeeded in finding and securing them. Having once tasted the green
grass, they became so wild that, at my appearance, lasso in hand, the
cunning animals, knowing full well what was in store for them, threw
up their heels and scampered away, defying for a long time all my
efforts to catch them.

My two companions had left the United States the preceding
year, having been recommended to try the effect of change of climate
on a severe pulmonary disease under which both laboured. Indeed,
they were both apparently in a rapid consumption, and their medical
advisers had given up all hope of seeing them restored to health. They
had remained in the mountains during one of the severest winters ever
known, had lived upon game, and frequently suffered the privations
attendant upon a mountain life, and now were returning perfectly
restored, and in robust health and spirits.

It is an extraordinary fact that the air of the mountains has a
wonderfully restorative effect upon constitutions enfeebled by pulmonary disease; and of my own knowledge I could mention a hundred instances where persons whose cases have been pronounced by
eminent practitioners as perfectly hopeless have been restored to comparatively sound health by a sojourn in the pure and bracing air of
the Rocky Mountains, and are now alive to testify to the effects of
the revigorating climate.

That the lungs are most powerfully acted upon by the rarified
air of these elevated regions, I myself, in common with the acclimated
hunters, who experience the same effects, can bear witness, as it is
almost impossible to take violent exercise on foot, the lungs feeling
as if they were bursting in the act of breathing, and consequently the
hunters invariably follow game on horseback, although, from being
inured to the climate, they might be supposed to experience these
symptoms in a lesser degree.

Whatever may be urged against such a climate, the fact nevertheless remains, that the lungs are thus powerfully affected, and that

the violent action has a most beneficial effect upon these organs when in a highly diseased state.

The elevation above the level of the sea, of the plains at the foot of the mountains, is about four thousand feet, while the mountain valley of the Bayou Salado must reach an elevation of at least eight or nine thousand, and Pike's Peak has been estimated to exceed twelve thousand.[1]

On the thirtieth of April, having the day before succeeded in collecting my truant *mulada*, I proceeded alone to the forks of the Arkansa and St. Charles, where I had observed, when hunting, that the grass was in better condition than near the pueblo, and here I remained two or three days, the animals faring well on the young grass, waiting for my two companions, who were to proceed with me across the grand prairies. As, however, the trail was infested by the Pawnees and Comanche, who had attacked every party which had attempted to cross from Santa Fé during the last six months, and carried off all their animals, it was deemed prudent to wait for the escort of Tharpe,[2] the Indian trader, who was about to proceed to St. Louis with the peltries, the produce of his winter trade; and as he would be accompanied by a large escort of mountain men, we resolved to remain and accompany his party for the security it offered.

The night I encamped on the St. Charles the rain poured down in torrents, accompanied by a storm of thunder and lightning, and the next morning I was comfortably lying in a pool of water, having been exposed to the full force of the storm. This was, however, merely a breaking in for a continuation of wet weather, which lasted fifteen days without intermission, and at short intervals followed us to the Missouri, during which time I had the pleasure of diurnal and nocturnal shower baths, and was for thirty days undergoing a natural hydropathic course of wet clothes and blankets, my bed being the bare prairie, and nothing between me and the reservoir above but a single sarape.

On the second of May, my two fellow travellers arrived with the intelligence that Tharpe could not leave until a trading party from the north fork of the Platte came in to Arkansa, and consequently we started the next day alone. I may here mention that Tharpe started

[1] The elevation at Pueblo is 4,668 feet; the average in Bayou Salado (South Park) is about 9,500; and the summit of Pikes Peak is 14,110.

[2] William Tharpe, a trader with the Cheyennes, had a Mexican wife and two children. He joined the Bent and St. Vrain trading caravan and was killed by the Pawnees while en route to the States.

two days after us, and was killed on Walnut Creek by the Pawnees, while hunting buffalo at a little distance from camp. He was scalped and horribly mutilated.

The night before our departure the wolves ate up all the riatas by which our mules and horses were picqueted; and in the morning all the animals had disappeared but one. We saw by the tracks that they had been stampeded; and, as a very suspicious mocassin track was discovered near the river, we feared that the Arapahós had paid a visit to the *mulada*. One of my mules, however, was picqueted very near the camp, and was safe; and, mounting her, I followed the track of the others across the river, and had the good fortune to find them all quietly feeding in the prairie, with the ropes eaten to their very throats. This day we proceeded about twenty-five miles down the river, camping in the bottom in a tope of cottonwoods, the rain pouring upon us all night.

The next day we still followed the stream, and encamped about four miles above Bent's Fort, which we reached the next morning, and most opportunely, as a company of waggons belonging to the United States commissariat were at the very moment getting under way for Missouri. They had brought out provisions for the troops forming the Santa Fé division of the army of invasion, and were now on their return, empty, to Fort Leavenworth, under the charge of Captain —— [Enos], of the quartermaster general's department, who at once gave us permission to join his company, which consisted of twenty waggons, and as many teamsters, well armed.[3] A government train of waggons had been attacked, on their way to Santa Fé, the preceding winter, by the Pawnees, and the whole party—men, mules, and waggons—captured; the men, however, being allowed to continue their journey, without waggons or animals. They had likewise lately attacked a party under Kit Carson,[4] the celebrated mountaineer, who was carrying dispatches from Colonel Frémont, in California, to

[3] Lewis Garrard, who was in the company, gives the captain's name. He also tells of Ruxton's joining the party and thus describes him: "George F. Ruxton, the English traveler, with two men, here joined our party. Mr. R. was a quiet, good-looking man, with a handsome moustache. He conversed well, but sparingly, speaking little of himself. He has passed over the burning sands of Africa, penetrated the jungles of India [Ruxton was never in India], jogged on patient mule through the Tierra Caliente of Mexico, and laid down amid the snowdrifts of the Rocky Mountains."—*Wah-To-Yah and the Taos Trail* (Ralph (P. Beiber, ed.), 325.

[4] Kit Carson, Lieutenant E. F. Beale, and others left San Diego, California, February 25, 1847.—Sabin, *op. cit.*, II, 550.

the government of the United States, and in fact every party who had passed the plains; therefore, as a large number of loose stock was also to be carried in with the waggons, an attack was more than probable during the journey to the frontier.

Bent's Fort is a square building of adobe, flanked by circular bastions loopholed for musketry, and entered by a large gateway leading into the corral or yard. Round this are the rooms inhabited by the people engaged in the Indian trade; but at this time the Messrs. Bent themselves were absent in Santa Fé, the eldest brother, as I have before mentioned, having been killed in Taos during the insurrection of the Pueblo Indians. We here procured a small supply of dried buffalo meat, which would suffice until we came to the buffalo range, when sufficient meat might be procured to carry us into the States.

We started about noon, proceeding the first day about ten miles, and camped at sundown opposite the mouth of the Purgatorie—the Pickatwaire[5] of the mountaineers, and "Las Ánimas" of the New Mexicans—an affluent of the Arkansa, rising in the mountains in the vicinity of the Spanish Peaks. The timber on the Arkansa becomes scarcer as we proceed down the river, the cottonwood groves being scattered wide apart at some distance from each other; and the stream itself widens out into sandy shallows, dotted with small islands covered with brush. At this camp we were joined by six or seven of Frémont's men,[6] who had accompanied Kit Carson from California; but, their animals giving out here, had remained behind to recruit them. They were all fine, hardy-looking young fellows, with their faces browned by two years' constant exposure to the sun and wind, and were fine specimens of mountaineers. They were accompanied by a Californian Indian, a young centaur, who handled his lasso with a dexterity which threw all the Mexican exploits I had previously seen into the shade, and was the means of bereaving several cows of their calves when we were in the buffalo range.

Our next camping place was the "Big Timber," a large grove of cottonwoods on the left bank of the river, and a favourite wintering place of the Cheyennes. Their camp was now broken up, and the village had removed to the Platte for their summer hunt. The debris of their fires and lodges were plentifully scattered about, and some stray horses were running about the bottom. On the fifth and

[5] The full Spanish name was Las Ánimas Perdidas en Purgatorio, which French trappers shortened and changed to Purgatoire. The Americans altered this to Picketwire, by which it is locally known today.

[6] Garrard names several of these men in his book, *op. cit.,* 325.

sixth we moved leisurely down the river, camping at Sandy Creek, and in the "Salt Bottom," a large plain covered with saltirose efflorescences. Here we proceeded more cautiously, as we were now in the outskirts of the Pawnee and Comanche country. The waggons at night were drawn up into a square, and the mules enclosed after sunset within the corral. Mine, however, took their chance outside, being always picqueted near my sleeping place, which I invariably selected in the middle of a good patch of grass, in order that they might feed well during the night. A guard was also placed over the corral, and everyone slept with his rifle at his side.

Near the Salt Bottom, but on the opposite side of the river, I this day saw seven bulls, the advanced party of the innumerable bands of buffalo we shortly passed through.

On the seventh, as I rode two or three miles in advance of the party, followed by my mules, I came upon fresh Indian sign, where a village had just passed, with their lodge poles trailing on the ground; and presently, in a level bottom on the river, the white conical lodges of the village presented themselves a short distance on the right of the trail. I at once struck off and entered it, and was soon surrounded by the idlers of the place. It was a Cheyenne village; and the young men were out, an old chief informed me, after buffalo, and that they would return an hour before sunset, measuring the hour with his hand on the western horizon. He also pointed out a place a little below for the waggons to encamp, where he said was plenty of wood and grass. The lodges, about fifty in number, were all regularly planted in rows of ten; the chief's lodge being in the centre, and the skins of it being dyed a conspicuous red. Before the lodges of each of the principal chiefs and warriors was a stack of spears, from which hung his shield and arms; whilst the skins of the lodge itself were covered with devices and hieroglyphics, describing his warlike achievements. Before one was a painted pole supporting several smoke-dried scalps, which dangled in the wind, rattling against the pole like bags of peas.

The language of signs is so perfectly understood in the Western country, and the Indians themselves are such admirable pantomimists, that, after a little use, no difficulty whatever exists in carrying on a conversation by such a channel; and there are few mountain men who are at a loss in thoroughly understanding and making themselves intelligible by signs alone, although they neither speak nor understand a word of the Indian tongue.

The waggons shortly after coming up, we proceeded to the spot indicated by the chief, which is a camping-place well known to the Santa Fé traders by the name of the "Pretty Encampment." Here we were soon surrounded by men, women, and children from the village, who arrived in horse-loads of five or six mounted on the same animal, and, begging and stealing everything they could lay their hands upon, soon became a perfect nuisance. An hour before sundown the hunting party came in, their animals tottering under heavy loads of buffalo meat. Twenty-one had gone out, and in the chase had killed twenty-one bulls, which were portioned out, half the animal to each lodge. During the night a huge cottonwood, which had been thoughtlessly set on fire, fell, a towering mass of flame, to the ground, and nearly into the midst of my animals, who, frightened by the thundering crash and the showers of sparks and fire, broke their ropes and ran off. In the morning, however, they returned to camp at daybreak, and allowed me to catch them without difficulty.

The next night we encamped on a bare prairie without wood, having recourse to the *bois de vâches*, or buffalo chips, which strewed the ground, to make a fire. This fuel was so wet that nothing but a stifling smoke rewarded our attempts. During the day an invalid died in one of the waggons, in which upwards of twenty poor wretches were being conveyed, all suffering from most malignant scurvy. The first waggon which arrived in camp sent a man to dig a hole in the prairie; and on the waggon containing the dead man coming up, it stopped a minute to throw the body into the hole, where, lightly covered with earth, it was left, without a prayer, to the mercies of the wolves and birds of prey.

Bent's Fort had been made a depot of provisions for the supply of the government trains passing the grand prairies on their way to New Mexico, and the waggons now returning were filled with sick men suffering from attacks of scurvy.[7] The want of fresh provisions and neglect of personal cleanliness, together with the effects of the rigorous climate, and the intemperate and indolent habits of the men, rendered them proper subjects for this horrible scourge. In Santa Fé, and wherever the volunteer troops were congregated, the disease made rapid progress, and proved fatal in an extraordinary number of cases.

As I was riding with some of the Californians in advance of the train, a large white wolf limped out of the bottom, and, giving chase, we soon came up to the beast, which on our approach crouched to the ground and awaited its death-stroke with cowardly sullenness. It was miserably poor, with its bones almost protruding from the skin,

[7] Called "black leg" in Missouri. Ruxton's note.

and one of its forelegs had been broken, probably by a buffalo, and trailed along the ground as it ran snarling and chopping its jaws with its sharp teeth.

On the ninth, as I rode along ahead, I perceived some dark objects in the prairie, which, refracted by the sun striking the sandy ground, appeared enormous masses, without form, moving slowly along. Riding towards them on my mule, I soon made them out to be buffalo, seventeen bulls, which were coming towards me. Jumping off the mule, I thrust the picquet at the end of her lariat into the ground, and, advancing cautiously a few paces, as the prairie was entirely bare and afforded not even the cover of a prairie-dog mound to approach under, I lay down on the ground to await their coming. As they drew near, the huge beasts, unconscious of danger, picked up a bunch of grass here and there, sometimes kicking up the dust with their forefeet, and, moving at the slowest walk, seemed in no hurry to offer me a shot. Just, however, as they were within a hundred paces, and I was already squinting along the barrel of my rifle, a greenhorn from the waggons, who had caught a glimpse of the game, galloped headlong down the bluff, and before the wind. He was a quarter of a mile off when the leading bull, raising his head, snuffed the tainted air, and with tail erect scampered off with his companions, leaving me showering imprecations on the head of the "muff" who had spoiled my sport and supper. Whilst I was lying on the ground, three wolves, which were following the buffalo caught sight of me, and seemed instantly to divine my intentions, for they drew near, and, sitting within a few yards of me, anxiously gazed upon me and the approaching bulls, thinking, no doubt, that their persevering attendance upon them was now about to be rewarded. They were doubtless disgusted when, as soon as I perceived the bulls disappear, I turned my rifle upon one cur which sat licking his chaps, and knocked him over, giving the others the benefit of the remaining barrel as they scampered away from their fallen comrade. I now rode on far ahead, determined not to be disturbed; and by the time the waggons came into camp, I had already arrived there with the choice portions of two bulls which I killed near the river. We encamped on the ninth at Choteau's Island, called after an Indian trader named Choteau,[8] who was here beleaguered by the Pawnees for several weeks, but eventually made his escape in safety. Every mile we advanced, the buffalo became more plentiful, and the camp was soon overflowing with fresh meat.

[8] A. P. Chouteau, who had brought trappers up the Arkansas to the mountains in 1815.

The country was literally black with immense herds, and they were continually crossing and recrossing the trail during the day, giving us great trouble to prevent the loose animals from breaking away and following the bands.

On the twelfth, a man was found dead in one of the waggons on arriving in camp, and was buried in the same unceremonious style as the first. In the evening I left the camp for a load of meat, and approached an immense herd of buffalo under cover of a prairie-dog town, much to the indignation of the villagers, who resented the intrusion with an incessant chattering. The buffalo passed right through the town, and at one time I am sure that I could have touched many with the end of my rifle, and thousands were passing almost over me; but, as I lay perfectly still, they only looked at me from under their shaggy brows, and passed on. One huge bull, and the most ferocious-looking animal I ever encountered, came to a dead stop within a yard of my head, and steadily examined me with his glaring eyes, snorting loudly his ignorance of what the curious object could be which riveted his attention. Once he approached so close that I actually felt his breath in my face, and, smelling me, he retreated a pace or two and dashed up the sand furiously with his feet, lashing his tail at the same time about his dun sides with the noise of a carter's whip, throwing down his ponderous head, and shaking his horns angrily at me. This old fellow was shedding his hair, and his sleek skin, now bare as one's hand in many parts, was here and there dotted with tufts of his long winter coat. From the shoulder backwards the body was, with these exceptions, perfectly smooth, but his head, neck, and breast were covered with long shaggy hair, his glowing eyes being almost hidden in a matted mass, while his coal-black beard swept his knees. His whole appearance reminded me strongly of a lion, and the motion of the buffalo when running exactly resembles the canter of the king of beasts. At last my friend began to work himself up into such a fury that I began to feel rather uncomfortable at my position, and, as he backed himself and bent his head for a rush, I cocked my rifle, and rose partly from the ground to take a surer aim, when the cowardly old rascal, with a roar of affright, took to his heels, followed by the whole band, but as one sleek, well-conditioned bull passed me within half a dozen yards, I took a flying shot, and rolled him over and over in a cloud of dust, levelling to the ground, as he fell, a well-built dog house.

No animals in these Western regions interested me so much as the prairie dogs. These lively little fellows select for the site of their towns a level piece of prairie with a sandy or gravelly soil, out of which they can excavate their dwellings with great facility. Being of a merry, sociable disposition, they, unlike the bear or wolf, choose to live in a large community, where laws exist for the public good, and there is less danger to be apprehended from the attacks of their numerous and crafty enemies. Their towns equal in extent and population the largest cities of Europe, some extending many miles in length, with considerably regularity in their streets, and the houses of a uniform style of architecture. Although their form of government may be styled republican, yet great respect is paid to their chief magistrate, who, generally a dog of large dimensions and imposing appearance, resides in a house conspicuous for size in the centre of the town, where he may always be seen on his housetop, regarding with dignified complacency the various occupations of the busy population —some industriously bearing to the granaries the winter supply of roots, others building or repairing their houses; while many, their work being over, sit chatting on their housetops, watching the gambols of the juveniles as they play around them. Their hospitality to strangers is unbounded. The owl, who on the bare prairie is unable to find a tree or rock in which to build her nest, is provided with a comfortable lodging, where she may in security rear her round-eyed progeny; and the rattlesnake, in spite of his bad character, is likewise entertained with similar hospitality, although it is very doubtful if it is not sometimes grossly abused; and many a childless dog may perhaps justly attribute his calamity to the partiality of the epicurean snake for the tender meat of the delicate prairie pup. However, it is certain that the snake is a constant guest; and, whether admitted into the domestic circle of the dog family, or living in separate apartments, or in copartnership with the owl, is an acknowledged member of the community at large.

The prairie dog, a species of marmot, is somewhat longer than a guinea pig, of a light brown or sandy colour, and with a head resembling that of a young terrier pup. It is also furnished with a little stumpy tail, which, when its owner is excited, is in a perpetual jerk and flutter. Frequently, when hunting, I have amused myself for hours in watching their frolicksome motions, lying concealed behind one of their conical houses. These are raised in the form of a cone, two or three feet above the ground, and at the apex is a hole, vertical to the depth of three feet, and then descending obliquely into the interior. Of course, on the first approach of such a monster as man, all the dogs which have been scattered over the town scamper to their holes as fast as their little legs will admit, and, concealing all but their heads and tails, bark lustily their displeasure at the intrusion. When they have sufficiently exhibited their daring, every dog dives into his burrow, but two or three who remain as sentinels, chattering in high dudgeon, until the enemy is within a few paces of them, when they take the usual summerset, and the town is silent and deserted. Lying perfectly still for several minutes, I could observe an old fellow raise his head cautiously above his hole, and reconnoitre; and if satisfied that the coast was clear, he would commence a short bark. This bark, by the way, from its resemblance to that of a dog, has given that name to this little animal, but it is more like that of a wooden toy dog, which is made to bark by raising and depressing the bellows under the figure. When this warning has been given, others are soon seen to emerge from their houses, and, assured of their security, play and frisk about. After a longer delay, rattlesnakes issue from the holes, and coil them-selves in the sunny side of the hillock, erecting their treacherous heads, and rattling an angry note of warning if, in his play, a thoughtless pup approaches too near; and, lastly, a sober owl appears, and, if the sun be low, hops through the town, picking up the lizards and cameleons which everywhere abound. At the first intimation of danger given by the sentinels, all the stragglers hasten to their holes, tumbling over owls and rattlesnakes, who hiss and rattle angrily at being disturbed. Everyone scrambles off to his own domicile, and if, in his hurry, he should mistake his dwelling, or rush for safety into any other than his own, he is quickly made sensible of his error, and, without cere-mony, ejected. Then, every house occupied, commences such a volley of barking, and such a twinkling of little heads and tails, which alone appear above the holes, as to defy description. The lazy snakes, re-gardless of danger, remain coiled up, and only evince their conscious-ness by an occasional rattle; while the owls, in the hurry and con-fusion, betake themselves, with sluggish wing, to wherever a bush of sage or greasewood affords them temporary concealment.

The prairie dog leads a life of constant alarm, and numerous enemies are ever on the watch to surprise him. The hawk and the eagle, hovering high in air, watch their towns, and pounce suddenly upon them, never failing to carry off in their cruel talons some un-happy member of the community. The coyote, too, a hereditary foe, lurks behind a hillock, watching patiently for hours until an unlucky straggler approaches within reach of his murderous spring. In the winter, when the prairie dog, snug in his subterranean abode, and with granaries well filled, never cares to expose his little nose to the icy blasts which sweep across the plains, but, between eating and sleeping, passes merrily the long, frozen winter, he is often roused from his warm bed, and almost congealed with terror, by hearing the snorting yelp of the half-famished wolf, who, mad with hunger, assaults with tooth and claw, the frost-bound roof of his house, and, with almost superlupine strength, hurls down the well-cemented walls, tears up the passages, plunges his cold nose into the very chambers, snorting into them with his earth-stuffed nose, in ravenous anxiety, and drives the poor little trembling inmate into the most remote corners, too often to be dragged forth and unhesitatingly devoured. The rattlesnake, too, I fear, is not the welcome guest he reports himself to be; for often I have slain the wily serpent, with a belly too much protuberant to be either healthy or natural, and bearing in its outline a very strong resemblance to the figure of a prairie dog.

A few miles beyond a point on the river known as the Caches, and so called from the fact that a party of traders, having lost their animals, had here cached, or concealed, their packs, we passed a little log fort,[9] built by the government employes, for the purpose of erecting here a forge to repair the commissariat waggons on their way to Santa Fé. We found the fort beleaguered by the Pawnees, who killed everyone who showed his nose outside the gate. They had carried off all their stock of mules and oxen, and in the vicinity had, two or three days before, attacked a company under an officer of the United States Engineers, running off with all the mules belonging to it. We were now, day after day, passing through countless herds of buffalo. I could scarcely form an estimate of the numbers within the range of sight at the same instant, but some idea may be formed of them by mentioning, that one day, passing along a ridge of upland prairie at least thirty miles in length, and from which a view extended about eight miles on each side of a slightly rolling plain, not a patch of grass ten yards square could be seen, so dense was the living mass that covered the country in every direction.

On leaving the Caches, the trail, to avoid a bend in the Arkansa, strikes to the northeast over a tract of rolling prairie, intersected by many ravines, full of water at certain seasons, known as the Coon Creeks. On this route there is no other fuel than *bois de vâches*, and the camps are made on naked bluffs, exposed, without the slightest shelter, to the chilling winds that sweep continually over the bare

[9] Fort Mann, built by Captain McKissack and named for D. P. Mann, an army teamster.—Bieber, *op. cit.*, 330–32.

plains. I scarcely remember to have suffered more from cold than in passing these abominable Coon Creeks. With hunting shirt saturated with the rain, the icy blasts penetrated to my very bones, and, night after night, lying on the wet ground in wet clothes, after successive days of pouring rain I felt my very blood running cold in my veins, and as if I never could again imbibe heat sufficient to warm me thoroughly.

One night, while standing guard round the camp, which was about two miles from the river, I heard an inexplicable noise, like distant thunder, but too continuous to proceed from that source, which gradually increased, and drew nearer to the camp. Placing my ear to the ground, I distinguished the roaring tramp of buffalo thundering on the plain; and as the moon for a moment burst from a cloud, I saw the prairie was covered by a dark mass, which undulated, in the uncertain light, like the waves of the sea. I at once became sensible of the imminent danger we were in; for when thousands and hundreds of thousands of these animals are pouring in a resistless torrent over the plains, it is almost impossible to change their course, particularly at night, the myriads in the rear pushing on those in front, who, spite of themselves, continue on their course, trampling down all opposition to their advance. Even if we ourselves were not crushed by the mass of beasts, our animals would most certainly be borne away bodily with the herd, and irrevocably lost. I at once alarmed the camp, and all hands turned out, and, advancing towards the buffalo, which were coming straight upon us, by shouting and continued firing of guns we succeeded in turning them, the wind being, luckily, in our favour; and the main body branching in two, one division made off into the prairie, while the other crossed the river, where for hours we heard their splashing, sounding like the noise of a thousand cataracts. In the daytime even our *cavallada* was in continual danger, for immense bands of buffalo dashed repeatedly through the waggons, scarcely giving us time to secure the animals before they were upon us; and on one occasion, when I very foolishly dismounted from Panchito to fire at a band passing within a few yards, the horse, becoming alarmed, started off into the herd, and, followed by the mules, was soon lost to sight amongst the buffalo, and it was some time before I succeeded in recovering them.

As might be inferred, such gigantic sporting soon degenerates into mere butchery. Indeed, setting aside the excitement of a chase on horseback, buffalo-hunting is too wholesale a business to afford much sport—that is, on the prairies; but in the mountains, where they are met with in small bands, and require no little trouble and expertness to find and kill, and where one may hunt for days without discovering more than one band of half a dozen, it is then an exciting and noble sport.

There are two methods of hunting buffalo—one on horseback, by chasing them at full speed, and shooting when alongside; the other by "still hunting," that is, approaching, or stalking, by taking advantage of the wind and any cover the ground affords, and crawling to within distance of the feeding herd. The latter method exhibits in a higher degree the qualities of the hunter, the former those of the horseman. The buffalo's head is so thickly thatched with long shaggy hair that the animal is almost precluded from seeing an object directly in its front; and if the wind be against the hunter, he can approach, with a little caution, a buffalo feeding on a prairie as level and bare as a billiard table. Their sense of smelling, however, is so acute that it is impossible to get within shot when to windward, as, at the distance of nearly half a mile, the animal will be seen to snuff the tainted air and quickly satisfy himself of the vicinity of danger. At any other than the season of gallantry, when the males are, like all other animals, disposed to be pugnacious, the buffalo is a quiet, harmless animal, and will never attack unless goaded to madness by wounds, or, if a cow, in sometimes defending its calf when pursued by a horseman; but even then it is seldom that they make any strong effort to protect their young.

When gorged with water, after a long fast, they become so lethargic that they sometimes are too careless to run and avoid danger. One evening, just before camping, I was, as usual, in advance of the train, when I saw three bulls come out of the river and walk leisurely across the trail, stopping occasionally, and one, more indolent than the rest, lying down whenever the others halted. Being on my hunting mule, I rode slowly after them, the lazy one stopping behind the others, and allowing me to ride within a dozen paces, when he would slowly follow the rest. Wishing to see how near I could get, I dismounted, and, rifle in hand, approached the bull, who at last stopped short, and never even looked round, so that I walked up to the animal and placed my hand on his quarter. Taking no notice of me, the huge beast lay down, and while on the ground I shot him dead. On butchering the carcass, I found the stomach so greatly distended that another pint would have burst it. In other respects the animal was perfectly healthy and in good condition.

One of the greatest enemies to the buffalo is the white wolf. These persevering brutes follow the herds from pasture to pasture, preying upon the bulls enfeebled by wounds, the cows when weak at the time of calving, and the young calves whenever they straggle from the mothers. In bands of twenty and thirty they attack a wounded bull, separate him from the herd, and worry the poor animal until, weak with loss of blood and the ceaseless assaults of his active foes, he falls hamstrung, a victim to their ravenous hunger.

On one of the Coon Creeks I was witness to an attack of this kind by three wolves on a cow and calf, or rather on the latter alone, which by some accident had got separated from the herd. My attention was first called to the extraordinary motions of the cow—for I could neither see the calf nor the wolves on account of the high grass —which was running here and there, jumping high in air and bellowing lustily. On approaching the spot, I saw that she was accompanied by a calf about a month old, and all the efforts of three wolves were directed to get between it and the cow, who, on her part, used all her generalship to prevent it. Whilst one executed a diversion in the shape of a false attack on the cow, the others ran at the calf, which sought shelter under the very belly of its mother. She, poor animal! regardless of the wounds inflicted on herself, sought only to face the more open attack; and the wolf in rear, taking advantage of this, made a bolder onslaught, and fastened upon her hams, getting, however, for his pains such a well-delivered kick in his stomach as threw him a summerset in the air. The poor cow was getting the worst of it, and the calf would certainly have fallen a victim to the ravenous beasts if I had not most opportunely come to the rescue; and, waiting until the battle rolled near the place of my concealment, I took advantage of a temporary pause in the combat, when two of the wolves were sitting in a line, with their tongues out and panting for breath, to level my rifle at them, knocking over one dead as a stone, and giving the other a pill to be carried with him to the day of his death, which, if I am any judge of gunshot wounds, would not be very distant. The third took the hint and scampered off, a ball from my second barrel whistling after him as he ran; and I had the satisfaction of seeing the cow cross the river with her calf and join in safety the herd, which was feeding on the other side.

A SURROUND
the Indian's method of taking game (A. J. Miller)

From the Porter collection

"Trappers and Snake Indians Conversing by Signs"
(A. J. Miller)

CHAPTER 15

Crossing the Plains

W E REACHED Pawnee Fork of the Arkansa without any *novedad*, but found this creek so swollen with the rains that we feared we should experience no little trouble in crossing. We here met a train of waggons detailed by the above cause on their way to Santa Fé, and we learned from them that a party of Mexican traders had been attacked by the Pawnees at this very spot a few days before, losing one hundred and fifty mules, one Indian having been killed in the fight, whose well-picked skeleton lay a few yards from our camp. Pawnee Fork being considered the most dangerous spot on the trail, extraordinary precautions were taken in guarding against surprise, and the animals belonging to the train were safely corralled before sundown, and a strong guard posted round them. Mine, however, were picqueted as usual round my sleeping place, which was on a bare prairie at some distance from the timber of the creek. Such a storm as poured upon our devoted heads that night I have seldom had the misfortune to be exposed to. The rain, in bucketsful, Niagara'd down as if a twenty years' supply was being emptied from the heavens on that one night; vivid forked lightning, in continuous flashes, lit up the flooded prairie with its glare; and the thunder, which on these plains *is* thunder indeed, kept up an incessant and mammoth cannonade. My frightened mules crept as near my bed as their lariats would allow them, and, with water streaming from every extremity, trembled with the chilling rain.

In the early part of the night, when the storm was at its height, I was attracted to a fire at the edge of the encampment by the sound of a man's voice perpetrating a song. Drawing near, I found a fire, or rather a few embers and an extinguished log, over which cowered a man sitting cross-legged in Indian fashion, holding his attenuated hands over the expiring ashes. His features, pinched with the cold, and lank and thin with disease, wore a comically serious expression, as the lightning lit them up, the rain streaming off his nose and prominent chin, and his hunting shirt hanging about him in a flabby and soaking embrace. He was quite alone, and sat watching a little pot, doubtless containing his supper, which refused to boil on the miserable fire. Spite of his situation, which could be termed anything but cheering, he, like Mark Tapley, evidently thought that now was the very moment to be jolly, and was rapping out at the top of his voice a ditty, the chorus of which was, and which he gave with peculiar emphasis,

> *How happy am I!*
> *From care I'm free:*
> *Oh, why are not all*
> *Contented like me?*

Not for an instant intending it as a satire upon himself, but singing away with perfect seriousness, raising his voice at the third line, "Oh, why are not all," particularly at the "Oh," in a most serio-comical manner. During the night I occasionally shook the water out of my blanket, and raised my head to assure myself that the animals were safe, lying down to sleep again, perfectly satisfied that not even a Pawnee would face such a storm, even to steal horses. But I did that celebrated thieving nation gross injustice; for they, on that very night, carried off several mules belonging to the other train of waggons, notwithstanding that a strict guard was kept up all night.

The next day, as there was no probability of the creek subsiding, it was determined to cross the waggons at any risk; and they were accordingly, one after the other, let down the steep bank of the stream, and, several yokes of oxen (which had first been swum over) being attached, were hauled bodily through the water, some swimming, and others, if heavily laden, diving across. I myself crossed on Panchito, whose natatory attempt, probably his first, was anything but first-rate; for on plunging in, and at once, into deep water, instead of settling himself down to a quiet swim, he jumped up into the air, and, sinking to the bottom, and thus gaining a fresh impetus, away he went again, carrying me, rifle, and ammunition under water at every plunge, and holding on by his neck like grim death. All my kit was contained in a pair of mule packs, which I had had made of waterproof material. Unfortunately one had a hole in the top, which had escaped my notice. This admitted the water, which remained in the pack, several inches deep, for a fortnight. This pack contained all my papers, notes, and several manuscripts and documents relative to the history of New Mexico and its Indian tribes, which I had collected with considerable trouble and expense. On opening the trunk, I found all the papers completely destroyed, and the old manuscripts, written on bad paper, and with worse ink, reduced to a pulpy mass; every scrap of writing being perfectly illegible.[1]

At length all the waggons were got safely over, with the exception of having everything well soaked; and as the process had occupied the whole day, we camped on the other side of the creek. Every day we found greater difficulty in procuring fuel; for, as we were now on the regular Santa Fé Trail, the creeks had been almost entirely stripped of firewood, and it was the work of hours to collect a sufficiency of brush to make a small fire to boil a pot of water. On arriving at camp, and having unpacked the mules, the first thing was to sally forth in quest of wood—an expedition of no little danger, for it was always more than probable that Indians were lurking in the neighbourhood, and therefore the rifle always accompanied the fuel hunter.

Between Pawnee Fork and Cow Creek all our former experiences of buffalo-seeing were thrown into the shade, for here they literally formed the whole scenery, and nothing but dense masses of these animals was to be seen in every direction, covering valley and bluff, and actually blocking up the trail. Nothing was heard along the line of march but pop—bang—pop—bang every minute; and the Californian Indian lassoed the calves and brought them in in such numbers that many were again set free. I had hitherto refrained from "chasing," in order to save my poor horse; but this day, a fine band of cows crossing the trail on a splendid piece of level prairie, I determined to try Panchito's mettle. Cantering up to the herd, I singled out a wiry-looking cow (which sex is the fleetest), and, dashing at her, soon succeeded in separating her from the rest. As I steered Panchito right into the midst of a thousand of these animals, he became half mad with terror, plunging and snorting and kicking right and left; but he soon became tamer and more reconciled when the chase was a trial of speed between him and the flying cow, and he then was as much excited as his rider. The cow held her ground wonderfully well, and for a quarter of a mile kept up a couple of lengths astern, which distance my horse seemed hardly to wish to decrease. As he became warm, however, I pushed him up to her just as she entered a large band, where she doubtless thought to have found refuge; but, running through it, she

---

[1] Only his book of brief notes, which he carried elsewhere, survived. This was obtained from descendants of the family in England.

again made for the open prairie, and here, after a burst of a few hundred yards, I again came up with her; but Panchito refused to lay me alongside, darting wildly on one side if I attempted to pass the animal. At last, pushing him with spur and leg, I brought him to the top of his speed, and, shooting past the flying cow in his stride, and with too much headway on him to swerve, I brushed the ribs of the buffalo with my mocassin, and, edging off a little to avoid her horns, discharged my rifle into her side, behind the shoulder. Carried forward a few paces in her onward course, she fell headlong to the ground, burying her horns deep into the soil, and, turning over on her side, was dead. She was so poor that I contented myself with the tongue, leaving the remainder of the carcase to the wolves and ravens.

We continued to find the buffalo in similar abundance as far as Cow Creek, a little beyond which we saw the last band; and on Turkey Creek the last straggler, an old grizzly bull, which I killed for a last supply of meat.

After passing the Little Arkansa, the prairie began to change its character; the surface became more broken, the streams more frequent, and fringed with better timber, and of a greater variety, the eternal cottonwood now giving place to aspen, walnut, and hickory, and the short curly buffalo grass to a more luxuriant growth of a coarser quality, interspersed with numerous plants and gay flowers. The dog towns, too, disappeared; and, in lieu of these little animals, the prairie hen boomed at rise and set of sun, and, running through the high grass, furnished ample work for the rifle. Large game was becoming scarcer; and but few antelope were now to be seen, and still fewer deer.

No scenery in nature is more deary and monotonous than the aspect of the grand prairies through which we had been passing. Nothing meets the eye but a vast undulating expanse of arid waste; for the buffalo grass, although excellent in quality, never grows higher than two or three inches, and is seldom green in colour; and, being but thinly planted, the prairie never looks green and turf like. Not a tree or shrub is to be seen, except on the creeks, where a narrow strip of unpicturesque cottonwood only occasionally relieves the eyes with its verdant foliage. The sky, too, is generally overcast, and storms sweep incessantly over the bare plains during all seasons of the year, boisterous winds prevailing at all times, carrying with them a chilling sleet or clouds of driving snow. It was therefore a great relief to look upon the long, green, waving grass, and the pretty groves on the streams; although our animals soon exhibited the consequences of the change of diet, between the rich and fattening buffalo grass, and the rank, although more luxuriant, herbage they now fed upon.

On approaching Council Grove, the scenery became very picturesque; the prairie lost its flat and monotonous character, and was broken into hills and valleys, with well-timbered knolls scattered here and there, intersected by clear and babbling streams, and covered with gaudy flowers, whose bright colours contrasted with the vivid green of the luxuriant grass. My eye, so long accustomed to the burnt and withered vegetation of the mountains, revelled in this refreshing scenery, and never tired of gazing upon the novel view. Council Grove is one of the most beautiful spots in the Western country. A clear rapid stream runs through the valley, bordered by a broad belt of timber, which embraces all the varieties of forest trees common to the West. Oak, beech, elm, maple, hickory, ash, walnut, &c. here presented themselves like old friends; squirrels jumped from branch to branch, the hum of the honeybee sounded sweet and homelike, the well-known chatter of the blue jay and catbird resounded through the grove; and in the evening the whippoorwill serenaded us with its familiar tongue, and the drumming of the ruffed grouse boomed through the grove. The delight of the teamsters on first hearing these well-known sounds knew no bounds whatever. They danced, and sang, and hurrahed, as, one after the other, some familiar note caught their ear. Poor fellows! they had been suffering a severe time of it, and many hardships and privations, and doubtless snuffed in the air of the johnnycakes and hominy of their Missouri homes.

"Wagh!" exclaimed one rawboned young giant, as a bee flew past, "this feels like the old 'ooman, and mush and molasses at that, if it don't, I'll be doggone!"

"Hurroo for old Missouri!" roared another; "h'yar's a hos as will knock the hind sights off the corn-doins. Darn my old heart if thar arn't a reg'lar-built hickory—makes my eyes sweat to look at it! This child will have no more mountains; hurroo for old Missouri! Wagh!"

A trader amongst the Caw Indians had erected himself a log house at the grove, which appeared to us a magnificent palace. Himself, his cows, and horses looked so fat and sleek that we really thought them unnaturally so; and so long had I been used to see the rawboned animals of Mexico and the mountains that I gravely asked him what he gave them, and why he made them so unwieldy. When he told me that his stock were all very poor, and nothing to what they were when they left the States a month before, I thought the man was taking a "rise" out of me; and when I showed him my travel-worn animals, and bragged of their, to me, plump condition, he told me that where he came from it would be thought cruel to work such starved-looking beasts. There was one lodge of Caw Indians at the grove, the big village being out on the prairie, hunting buffalo. On the opposite side of the stream was a party of Americans from Louisiana, who had been out for the purpose of catching calves; and round their camp some thirty were feeding, all they had been able to keep alive out of upwards of a hundred.

From Council Grove to Caw, or Kansas, River, the country increases in beauty, and presents many most admirable sports for a settlement; but as it is guaranteed by treaty to the Caw and Osage Indians, no white man is allowed by the United States government to settle on their lands.

The night before reaching Caw River, we encamped on a bare prairie, through which ran a small creek, fringed with timber. At sundown the wind, which had blown smartly the whole day, suddenly fell, and one of those unnatural calms succeeded, which so surely herald a storm in these regions. The sky became overcast with heavy inky clouds, and an intolerably sultry and oppressive heat pervaded the atmosphere. Myriads of fireflies darted about, and legions of bugs and beetles, and invading hosts of sandflies and mosquitoes droned and hummed in the air, swooping like charging Cossacks on my unfortunate body. Beetles and bugs of easy squeezability, Brobdingnag proportions, and intolerable odour, darted into my mouth as I gasped for breath; while sandflies with their atomic stings probed my nose and ears, and mosquitos thrust their poisoned lances into every part of my body. Hoping for the coming storm, I lay without covering, exposed to all their attacks; but the agony of this merciless persecution was nothing to the thrill of horror which pervaded my very bones when a cold clammy rattlesnake crawled over my naked ankles, a flash of lightning at the moment revealing to me the reptile, as with raised head it dragged its scaly belly across my skin, during which time, to me an age, I feared to draw a breath lest the snake should strike me. Presently the storm broke upon us; a hurricane of wind squalled over the prairie, a flash of vivid lightning, followed by a clap of deafening thunder, and then down came the rain in torrents. I actually revelled in the shower bath; for away on the instant were washed bugs and beetles, mosquitos were drowned in millions, and the rattlesnakes I knew would now retire to their holes and leave me in peace and quiet for the remainder of the night.

We now passed through a fine country, partially cultivated by the Caw Indians, whose log shanties were seen scattered amongst the timbered knolls. Caw River is the headquarters of the nation, and we halted that night in the village, where, in the house of a white farmer, I ate the first civilised meal I had tasted for many months, and enjoyed the unusual luxury of eating at a table with knife and fork; moreover sitting on a chair, which, however, I would gladly have dispensed with, for I had so long been accustomed to sit Indian fashion on the ground, that a chair was at first both unpleasant and awkward. The meal consisted of hotcakes and honey, delicious butter, and lettuce and radishes. My animals fared well too, on Indian corn, and oats in the straw; and the whole expense, eleven horses and mules having been fed the better part of a day and one night, amounted to one dollar and a half, or six shillings sterling.

A troop of dragoons from St. Louis to Fort Leavenworth met us on the road on their way to the latter station, from whence they were about to escort a train of waggons, containing specie, to Santa Fé. They were superbly mounted: the horses, uniting plenty of blood with bone, so great a desideratum for cavalry, were about fifteen hands high, and in excellent condition. The dragoons themselves were all recruits, and neither soldierlike in dress nor appearance.

We passed the Kansas or Caw River by a ferry worked by Indians, and, striking into a most picturesque country of hill and dale, well timbered and watered, entered the valley of the great Missouri. A short distance from the river, on the left of the trail, is a tabular bluff of most extraordinary formation, being the exact and accurately outlined figure of a large fortification, with escarpments, counterscarps, glacis, and all details perfectly delineated. A little farther on, we came in sight of the garrison of Fort Leavenworth, the most western military station of the United States, and situated on the right bank of the Missouri in the Indian Territory. The fort is built on an eminence overhanging the river, but, although called a fort, has no pretensions to be a military work, the only defence to the garrison being four wooden blockhouses, loopholed for musketry, placed at each corner of the square of buildings. The barracks, stables, and officers' quarters surrounded this square, which is planted with trees and covered with luxuriant grass. The accommodation for the men and officers is excellent, the houses of the latter being large and commodious, and quite unlike the dirty pigsties which are thought good enough for the accommodation of British officers. The soldiers' barrack rooms are large and airy, but no attention appears to be paid to cleanliness, and the floors, walls, and windows were dirty in the extreme. The beds are all double, or rather the bedsteads, for the bedding is separate, but in close contact. What struck me more than anything was the admirable condition of the horses, and their serviceable appearance; I did not see a single troop horse in the squadron which would not have sold in England for eighty guineas, the price paid for them here, that is, the government contract price, being from fifty to eighty dollars, or from ten to twenty pounds.

The garrison constitutes the whole population of the place. With the exception of the sutler's store for the use of the soldiers, there are neither shops, taverns, nor private buildings of any description; and I should have fared but badly if it had not been for the hospitality of Captain Enos, of the quartermaster general's department, who most kindly assigned to me a room in his own quarters in the garrison, and made me a member of his mess.

The officers of the dragoons, who may be said to be buried for life in this wilderness, are mostly married, and their families constitute the only society the place affords. I remember to have been not a little struck at the first sight of many very pretty, well-dressed ladies, who, after my long sojourn amongst the dusky squaws, appeared to me like the houris of paradise; and I have no doubt that I myself came in for a share of staring, for I was dressed in complete mountain costume, with my mahogany-coloured face shaded by a crimson turban *à la Indien,* and in all the pride of fringed deerskin and porcupine quills; and I was paid the compliment of being more than once mistaken for an Indian chief, and on one occasion I was appealed to by two of the dragoons to decide a bet as to whether I was a white man or a redskin. One day I was passing through the dragoons' stables when the men were cleaning their horses, and my appearance created no little difference of opinion amongst the troopers as to what tribe of Indians I belonged to.

"That's a Pottawatomie," said one, "by his red turban."

"How long have you been in the West," cried another, "not to know a Kickapoo when you see him?"

"Pshaw!" exclaimed a third, "that's a white trapper from the mountains. A regular mountain boy that, I'll bet a dollar!"

One smart-looking draggon, however, looked into my face and, turning round to his comrades, said, "Well, boys, I'll just bet you a dollar all round that that Injun's no other than a British officer. Wagh! And what's more, I can tell you his name." And, sure enough, my acquaintance proved to be one of the many deserters from the British army belonging to the dragons, and one who had known me when in the service myself.

After a few days' stay at Fort Leavenworth, I made preparations for my departure to St. Louis, getting rid of my mountain traps and, what caused me no little sorrow, parting with my faithful animals, who had been my companions in a long and wearisome journey of more than three thousand miles, during the greater part of which they had been almost my only friends and companions. I had, however, the satisfaction of knowing that whilst with me they had never experienced a blow or an angry word from me, and had always fared of the very best—when procurable; and many a mile I had trudged on foot to save them the labour of carrying me. For Panchito I found a kind master—exacting, in return for the present, a promise that he should not be worked for the next three months; and, before leaving, I had the satisfaction of knowing that, in company with three old acquaintances who had pastured with him in the mountains, he was enjoying himself in veritable "clover," and corn unlimited, where, I doubt not, he soon regained his quondam beauty and condition. The disposal of the mules gave me greater anxiety, as there was such a demand for these animals at the moment to send with the government trains to New Mexico, that I knew to give them away would be only to put their value in the pocket of a stranger, and the animals themselves into the first waggon which crossed the plains. I therefore sold them to the commissary at the fort, and paid them daily visits in the government stables, where they revelled in the good things of this life, and had, moreover, a kindhearted master in the shape of the Missourian teamster who had the charge of them, and who, on my giving him a history of their adventures, and a good and true account of their dispositions and qualities, promised to take every care of the poor beasts, and, indeed, was quite proud of having under his charge such a travelled team. The parting between Panchito and the mules was heart-rending, and for two or three days they all refused to eat and be comforted; but at the end of that time their violent grief softened down into a chastened melancholy, which gradually merged into a steady appetite for the "corn doins" of the liberal master of the mules; and before leaving I felt assured, from their sleek and well-filled appearance, that they were quite able to start on another expedition across the plains.

A steamboat touching at the fort, bound for the Mississippi and St. Louis, I availed myself of the opportunity, and secured myself a berth for the latter city. After running upon sand bars every half-hour, about thirty miles below Independence we at last stuck hard and fast, and, spite of the panting efforts of the engine, there we remained during the night, and until noon the next day. A steamboat then made its appearance, bound, like ourselves, down the river, and, coming up alongside, the two captains held a consultation, which ended in *ours* recommending his passengers to "make tracks" into the other boat, as he did not expect to get off; which interchange being effected, and our fares paid to the other boat, a hawser was attached to the one aground, and she was readily hauled off—we, the passengers, having been done pretty considerably brown in the transaction. However, such rascalities as these, on the Western waters, are considered no more than "smart," and are taken quite as a matter of course by the free and enlightened citizens of the model republic.

I must say that since a former visit to the States, made three years ago, I perceived a decided improvement, thanks to the Trollope and Boz castigations, in the manners and conduct of steamboat travellers, and in the accommodations of the boats themselves. With the exception of the expectorating nuisance, which still flourishes in all its disgusting monstrosity, a stranger's sense of decency and decorum is not more shocked than it would be in travelling down the Thames in a Gravesend or Herne Bay steamer. There is even quite an arbitrary censorship established on the subject of dress and dirty linen, which is, since it is passively submitted to by the citizens, an unmistakable sign of the times. As a proof of this, one evening, as I sat outside the cabin, reading, a young man, slightly "corned," or overtaken in his drink, accosted me abruptly:

"Stranger, you haven't are a clean shirt to part with, have you? The darned—(hiccup)—capen says I must go ashore bekase my 'tarnal shirt ain't clean."

And this I found to be the fact, for the man was actually ejected from the saloon at dinnertime, on his attempting to take his seat at the table in a shirt which bore the stains of julep and cocktail.

The miserable scenery of the muddy Missouri has been too often described to require any additional remarks. The steamboat touched occasionally at a woodpile, to take in fuel; and sallow, aguish faces peered from the log shanties as we passed. We had the usual amount of groundings on sand bars and thumping against snags and sawyers, passed the muddy line of demarcation between the waters of the Missouri and the "Father of Streams," and, in due course, on the fourth day ran alongside the outer edge of three tiers of huge steamboats which lined the wharf at St. Louis.

We had but one exciting episode during the voyage, in the shape of a combat between one of the "hands" of the boat, a diabolical-looking Mexican, and the mate. The latter, at a wooding station, thinking that the man was not sufficiently spry, administered a palthogue, which not meeting the approbation of the *Mejicano*, that worthy immediately drew his knife and challenged the aggressor. The mate, seizing a log from the pile, advanced towards him, and the Mexican, likewise, dropping his knife, took up a similar weapon and rushed to the attack. After a return of blows they came to close quarters, hugged, and fell, the Yankee uppermost, whose every energy was now directed to gouge out the eye of his prostrate foe, while he on his part, seized the eye-scooper by his long hair, tugged, with might and main, to pull him to the ground. With a commendable spirit of fair play, the other "hands" danced round the combatants, administering well-directed kicks on the unfortunate Mexican's head and body, in all the excitement of unrestrainable valour. The captain, however, interfered, and secured a fair field for the gallant pair; but at length, tired of the bungling attempts of his mate to screw his antagonist's eye out of its socket, pulled him off, and, giving the Mexican a friendly kick in the ribs, desired him to get up. That worthy rose undismayed, and, ramming the end of his thumb into his eye, to drive that organ into its proper place, exclaimed, "*¡Qué carajo es este, qui no sabe pelear!*—what a cur is this, who does not know how to fight!" and, shaking himself, sat upon a log and proceeded coolly to make himself a shuck cigar.

A negro came up to me at Fort Leavenworth, and asked me to allow him to accompany me down to St. Louis. On my saying that I did not require a servant for so short a distance, he told me that, although himself a free negro, yet no black was allowed to travel without a master, and that if he attempted it he would, in all probability, be seized and imprisoned as a runaway slave.

This reminded me that I was in that transcendently free country, ever boasting of its liberty and equality, which possesses, in a population of some eighteen millions, upwards of three millions of fellow men in most abject yet lawful slavery—a foul blot upon humanity, which has every appearance of being perpetuated until the evil grows to such a height as will end in curing itself.

This subject, which necessarily forces itself upon the mind of all travellers in the *Slave States*, is one which, having received the attention of the most enlightened philanthropists of both hemispheres, it would scarcely become me to dilate upon, or even notice, did I not feel that everyone, however humble, should raise his voice in condemnation of that disgraceful and inhuman INSTITUTION, which, in a civilised country and an enlightened age, condemns to a social *death*, and degrades, by law, to the level of the beasts of the field, our fellow men, subjecting them to a moral as well as physical slavery, and removing from them every possible advantage of intellectual culture or education, by which they might attain any position a grade higher than they now possess—the human beasts of burthen of inhuman masters.

It is adduced as an argument against the abolition of slavery, of course by those whose interest it is to uphold the evil, that the emancipation of the slaves would, in the present state of feeling against the negro race, be productive of effects which would convulse the whole social state of the country, or, in other words, that the whites would never rest until the whole race was exterminated in the United States. That there is a physical impossibility to any amalgamation in the Southern states is as certain as that, year by year, the difficulty of removing the evil is surely increasing; and its very magnitude and the moral cowardice of the American people prevent this evil being grappled with at once, and some steps taken to oppose its perpetuation.

The three arguments brought forward by those who endeavour to palliate or uphold slavery, in feeble sophistry, plainly exhibit the weakness of the cause. First, they say, we admit the evil, but the cure will be worse than the disease. We have inherited it; the blame rests not upon us, but our fathers. If the negroes be emancipated, what is to become of them? They cannot, and *shall not*, remain in our community, on an equality with us and our children, and enjoying the privileges of white men. This *cannot* be. Moreover, the burden of supporting them will fall upon us, for they will not work unless compelled.

Secondly: We deny the sinfulness of the institution. Negroes are *not men*, but were sent into the world to be slaves to the white man. To support this they are ready with quotations from the Scripture, and I blush to say that I have heard well-educated and liberal-minded men take no other ground than this to support the cause.

And, thirdly, they say no legislation can reach the evil. Law cannot deprive a citizen of his property; if so, away with liberty at once, if one act confirms rights and another removes them.

The abolitionist of the North raves at the slaveowner of the South; but let a foreigner converse with the former, and he will at once turn round and take the part of the slaveowner. It is like a third person interfering in the quarrels of man and wife. "No, no, my good sir," they say, "let us settle this question amongst ourselves; this is a family affair." No one could deny the justice of this, if they really made a bona fide attempt to grapple the evil; but I must confess that abolitionism in the United States appears to me to be anything but genuine and honest, and that, if left to themselves, the question is very, very far from any chance of settlement, unless, as I believe will be the result, the slaves themselves cut the Gordian knot of the difficulty.

The great difficulty to be combated in America, in freeing the country from the curse of slavery, is prejudice. The negro is not recognised (startling as this assertion may be) as a fellow creature—I mean by the mass of the people. This anomaly, in a country where the very first principle of their social organism is the axiom, the incontrovertible truth, that "all men are born equal," is the more palpable, since the popular and universal outcry is, and ever has been, the same sentiment which animated the Fathers of the Revolution, when they offered to the world, as a palliation for the crime of rebellion, the same watchword which is now so prodigally used by every American tongue, and so basely and universally prostituted. "All men are born equal. Liberty, therefore, and equal rights to all"—except to those whose skins are black!

I have heard clergymen of the American church affirm their belief that the negro was placed on earth by God to be the white man's slave. I have heard many educated, and in every other respect moral and conscientious, Americans assert that negroes were not made in God's image, but were created as a link between man and the beast, to minister to the former's wants, and to support him by the toil of their hands and the sweat of their brows.

And when I add that by law it is felony to teach a negro to read or write, what argument can be offered to combat such unnatural prejudices? I believe that slaves are *generally* well treated in the United States, although many instances could be adduced where the very reverse is the fact, particularly on the Western frontier. But this good treatment is on the same grounds that we take care of our horses and cows and pigs, because it is the owner's interest to do so; and the well-being—that is, the physical healthiness—of slaves is attended to in the same degree that we feed and clothe our horses, in order that they may be in condition to work for us, and thereby bring in a return for the care we have bestowed upon them.

That this question will one day shake to its very centre, if it does not completely annihilate, the union of the American States, is as

palpable as the result is certain. This belief is very generally entertained by both parties, and yet in spite of it the evil is allowed to increase, although its removal or cure thereby becomes hourly more
difficult.

Hundreds of plans have been suggested for the abolition of
slavery, but all have been found to be impracticable, if not impossible
to be carried out. Perhaps the most feasible and practicable was that
proposed by the late Mr. King many years ago, and which at the time
met with the fate of every other suggestion on the same subject. Mr.
King, as sound and practical a statesman as the country every produced, proposed that a certain yearly sum should be laid aside out of
the revenue derived from the sale of public lands, to be devoted to
the emancipation of slaves by the purchase of their freedom. This
process, however slow, at the same time that it would effect the gradual abolition of slavery, and at all events effectually prevent its increase and perpetuation, and offer a final, although distant termination
to the evil, was at the same time less calculated to alarm the interested
minds of the slaveowners; since, as the emancipation would be gradual, and the compensation proportionable to the loss sustained, their
interests were not so materially affected as they would be by the entire removal, at one swoop, of their vested rights of property and
possession. As it is, however, there is no evidence of any positive
action being taken by the legislature to effect the removal of this disgraceful stain on the national character. So rabid and intolerant is
the temper of the Southern people when this question is mooted, and
so fraught with danger to the union is the agitation even of the subject,
that all discussion is shunned and avoided, and the evil hour protracted
and put off, which will, as surely as that the sun shines in the heavens,
one day plunge the country into a convulsion dreadful to think of or
anticipate. Meanwhile the plague spot remains; the foul cancer is eating its way, and only by its extirpation can the body it disfigures regain its healthfulness and beauty, and take its place in the scale of
humanity and civilisation, from which the loathsome pestilence has
outpaled it.

As I have said, I notice the subject merely to add my humble
voice to the cry for humanity's sake, which should never cease to stun
the ears of the unholy men who, in spite of every law both human
and divine, use their talents, and the intellect which God has given
them, to uphold and perpetuate the curse of slavery.

CHAPTER 16

Return Home

PROCEEDING, on my arrival at St. Louis, to an excellent hotel called the Planter's House, I that night, for the first time for nearly ten months, slept upon a bed, much to the astonishment of my limbs and body, which, long accustomed to no softer mattress than mother earth, tossed about all night, unable to appreciate the unusual luxury. I found chairs a positive nuisance, and in my own room caught myself in the act more than once of squatting cross-legged on the floor. The greatest treat to me was bread; I thought it the best part of the profuse dinners of the Planter's House, and consumed prodigious quantities of the staff of life, to the astonishment of the waiters. Forks, too, I thought were most useless superfluities, and more than once I found myself on the point of grabbing a tempting leg of mutton mountain fashion, and butchering off a hunter's mouthful. But what words can describe the agony of squeezing my feet into boots, after nearly a year of mocassins, or discarding my turban for a great boardy hat, which seemed to crush my temples? The miseries of getting into a horrible coat—of braces, waistcoats, gloves, and all such implements of torture—were too acute to be described, and therefore I draw a veil over them.

Apart from the bustle attendant upon loading and unloading thousands and thousands of barrels of grain upon the wharf, St. Louis appeared to me one of the dullest and most commonplace cities of the Union. A great proportion of the population consists of French and Germans; the former congregating in a suburb called Vide Poche, where they retain a few of the characteristics of their lighthearted nation, and the sounds of the fiddle and tambourine may be nightly heard, making the old-fashioned, tumble-down tenements shake with the tread of the merry dancers. The Dutch and Germans have their beer gardens, where they imbibe huge quantities of malt and honey-

Ruxton *of the Rockies*

dew tobacco; and the Irish their shebeen shops, where Monongahela is quaffed in lieu of the "rale crather."

The town was full of returned volunteers from the wars. The twelvemonth's campaign they had been engaged in, and the brilliant victories achieved by them, which, according to the American newspapers, are unparalleled in the annals of the world's history, have converted these rowdy and vermin-covered veterans into perfect heroes; and every batch on arriving is feasted by the public, addresses are offered to them, the officers presented with swords and snuff boxes, and honours of all kinds lavished upon them in every direction.

The intense glorifications at St. Louis, and in every other part of the United States, on the recent successes of their troops over the miserable Mexicans, which were so absurd as to cause a broad grin on the face of an unexcited neutral, make me recur to the subject of this war, which hitherto I have avoided mentioning in the body of this little narrative.

It is scarcely necessary to trace the causes of the war at present raging between two republics of North America. The fable of the wolf and lamb drinking at the same stream may be quoted, to explain to the world the reason why the *soi-disant* champion of liberty has quarreled with its sister state "for muddying the water" which the model republic uses to quench its thirst.

A lesson has been read to the citizens of the United States which ought to open their eyes to the palpable dishonesty of their government, their unblushing selfishness, and total disregard to the interests of the country, when those of themselves or of their party are at stake; and although in the present instance President Polk has overreached himself, and raised a storm which he would be only too glad to lay at any cost, yet, in the whole history of the Mexican war, the violence of party and political feeling is evident, from the ninth of May, 1846, when the first shot was fired at Palo Alto, to the date of the last half-score dispatches which inform the world that General Scott "still remained at Puebla," waiting reinforcements.

It is enough to observe that the immediate cause of hostilities was the unjustifiable invasion of Mexican territory by the Army of the United States to take possession of a tract of country of which the boundary line had been disputed between the Mexican government and one of its revolted states, and which had been annexed to the American Union before its recognition as an independent state by the country from which it had seceded.[1]

There can be no question but that the United States had deep cause of complaint against Mexico, in the total disregard evinced by the latter to the spirit of international treaties, and the injuries inflicted upon the persons and property of American citizens—all redress of which grievances was either totally refused, or procrastinated until the parties gave up every hope of ultimate compensation. The acquisition of Texas, however, was in any case a balancing injustice, and should have wiped out all old grievances, at least those of a pecuniary nature; while, if a proper spirit of conciliation had been evinced on the part of the Americans, at the period when the question of annexation was being mooted, all danger of a rupture would have been removed; and Mexico would have yielded her claims to Texas with a better grace, if taken as a receipt in full for all obligations, than in suffering a large portion of her territory to be torn from her, against all laws held sacred by civilised nations.

It is certain that such consequences as have resulted from the advance of the American troops from the Nueces to the Río Grande, were never anticipated by the President of the United States, whose policy in bringing on a quasi crisis of the state affairs on the Mexican frontier, and provoking the Mexicans to overt acts which could at any moment be converted into a *casus belli*, was not for the sake of territorial aggrandizement, but for a purpose which, it is known to those in the secret of his policy, had an object more remote, and infinitely more important, than a rupture with the Mexican government.

At that time the position taken up by Mr. Polk and his party with regard to the Oregon question involved, as a natural consequence, the probability of a war with England; nay, more—if such position were persisted in, the certainty of a war with that power. That a majority of the people, and all the right-thinking and influential classes were opposed to such measures as would hazard or produce such a rupture, was so palpable, that the government was conscious that any proposal for making preparations for a war with England, which they knew a perseverance in their policy would assuredly bring about, would not be favourably received, or even tolerated, and therefore they looked about them for a means of attaining their object, by blinding the eyes of the people as to their ulterior designs. Mexico was made the scapegoat. A war with that weak and powerless state would be popular, since its duration, it was supposed, could be but for a very brief period, the government having no resources whatever, and being

1 Ruxton's own nation, Great Britain, had recognized the independence of Texas in 1843.

sadly deficient in any of the sinews of war; and, moreover, such a war would be likely to flatter the national pride and conceit of the American people.

To bring, therefore, affairs to such a critical position on the Texan frontier, that a "state of war" could at any moment be assumed, and its imminence be actually very apparent, was the stroke of policy by which Polk and his party hoped to blind the people, and, profiting by it, make such preparations as would enable them to carry out their plans in connection with the Oregon question and the probable war with England. They thought that, even if hostilities broke out with Mexico, that power would at once succumb; and, in the meantime, that the war fever in the United States would spread, and that the people would sanction an increase in the army and navy in such a case, which could at any time be made available for another purpose.[2]

The first shot fired on the Río Grande changed their views. Until then the Americans were in utter ignorance of the state of Mexico and the Mexicans. They never anticipated such resistance as they have met with; but, judging from the moral and physical inferiority of the people, at once concluded that all they had to do was *venire, videre, et vincere*. Children in the art of war, they imagined that personal bravery and physical strength were the only requisites for a military people; and that, possessing these qualities in as great a degree as the Mexicans were deficient in them, the operations in Mexico would amount to nothing more arduous than a promenade through the table-lands of Anahuac—the "Halls of Montezuma," in which it was the popular belief that they were destined "to revel," being the goal of their military *paseo* of six weeks.

As soon, however, as the list of killed and wounded on the fields of Palo Alto and Resaca de la Palma reached Washington, President Polk saw at once the error into which he had fallen. It became evident to him that all the resources of the country would be required to carry on the war with one of the most feeble powers in the world, and that the sooner he pulled his foot out of the hot water, which at the temperature of 54° 40' was likely to scald him, the better for him and his country; for it naturally occurred to him that, if such a *scrimmage* as the Mexican war gave him considerable trouble, an affair with such a respectable enemy as England was likely to prove anything but an agreeable pastime; and hence the very speedy acceptance

[2] The facts do not justify Ruxton's conclusion that the Mexican War was provoked to produce preparations for war on Great Britain over the Oregon Question.

of Lord Aberdeen's ultimatum, and the sudden settlement of the Oregon question.[3]

As affairs now stand, and unless the United States very materially modify the conditions under which they signify their willingness to withdraw the avowedly pacific proposals of Commissioner Trist, it is difficult to assign any probable period for the termination of the war; and it is certain that, as the Mexican armies, one after the other, dissolve before the American attacks, and the farther the latter penetrate into the country, the greater are the difficulties which they will have to surmount. Harassed by hordes of guerrillas, with a long line of country in their rear admirably adapted by nature for the system of warfare pursued by irregular troops, and through which all supplies have to pass, to defeat an army is but to increase the conquerors' difficulties, since, while before they had one tangible enemy in their front, now they are surrounded by swarms of hornets, who never run the risk of defeat by standing the brunt of a regular engagement.

Neither have the invariable and signal defeats the Mexicans have met with, the same moral effect which such reverses have amongst more civilised nations. They take them as matters of course, and are not dispirited; while, on the other hand, the slightest success instils new life and energy into their hearts. Until the whole country is occupied by American troops, the war, unless immediately concluded, will be carried on, and will eventually become one of conquest. But, in the meantime, the expenses it entails upon the treasury of the United States are enormous, and hourly increasing; and it would seem that the amount of compensation for the expenses of the war, which, in money or territory, is a *sine qua non* in the peace proposals of the American commissioner, is consequently increasing *pari passu*, and therefore the settlement of the question becomes more difficult and uncertain.

It is extremely doubtful if the Mexican people will consent to a surrender of nearly one-third of their territory, which will most probably be required as compensation for the expenses of the war, or, what is the same thing, be demanded as a security for the payment of a certain sum of money, and whether they will not rather prefer war to the knife to the alternative of losing their nationality. In reality, this war does them little harm. They were in such a state of misery

[3] The Oregon Treaty was signed June 15, 1846. Aberdeen's proposal should not be called an ultimatum; in fact, it gave up the former British claim to the Columbia and accepted the American proposal of the forty-ninth parallel as a boundary.

301

and anarchy before it commenced, and have been for so long a period tyrannised over by the *republican* despots who have respectively held the reins of power, that no change could possibly make their condition more degraded; and the state of confusion and misrule attendant upon the war in such a country as Mexico is so congenial to the people, that, from my own observations, I believe them to be adverse, even on this account alone, to the termination of hostilities. Moreover, the feeling against the Americans, which was at first mere apathy, has increased to the bitterest of hatred and animosity, and is sufficient in itself to secure the popular support to the energetic prosecution of the war; and the consciousness of the justice of their cause, and the injustice of the unprovoked aggression on the part of the United States, ought, and I have no doubt will, keep alive *one* spark of that honour which prompts a people to resent and oppose a wilful and wanton attack on their liberties and nationality.[4]

After a stay of a few days in St. Louis, in order to rig myself out in civilised attire, I went on board a steamboat bound for the Illinois River and Peoria, intending to cross the prairies of Illinois to Chicago, and thence down the Canadian lakes to New York.

This river is more picturesque than the Missouri or Mississippi; the banks higher, the water clearer, and the channel dotted with pretty islands, between which the steamboat passes, almost brushing the timber on the banks. At Peoria we were transferred to stagecoaches, and, suffering a martyrdom of shaking and bad living on the road— if road it can be called—we arrived at last at Chicago—the city, that is to be, of the Lakes, and which may be termed the City of Magnificent Intentions.

Chigago, or Chicago, is situated at the southwestern corner of Lake Michigan, and on the lake shore. In spite of the pasteboard appearance of its houses, churches, and public edifices, all of wood, it is a remarkably pretty town, its streets wide and well laid out; and it will, doubtless, after it has been burned down once or twice, and rebuilt of stone or brick, be one of the finest of the Western cities. It has several excellent hotels, some of which are of gigantic dimensions, a theatre, courthouse, and an artificial harbour, constructed at the expense of the city.

[4] Ruxton's forecast of the final phases of the war and its termination was at considerable variance with what actually occurred. The Treaty of Guadalupe Hidalgo was signed February 2, 1848; it was ratified by the United States Senate on March 10, and by the Mexican Congress on May 24, 1848.

An American stagecoach has often been described: it is a huge lumbering affair with leathern springs, and it creaks and groans over the corduroy roads and unmacadamized causeways, thumping, bumping, and dislocating the limbs of its "insides," whose smothered shrieks and exclamations of despair often cause the woodsman to pause from his work, and, leaning upon his axe, listen with astonishment to the din which proceeds from its convulsed interior.

The coach contains three seats, each of which accommodates three passengers; those on the centre, and the three with their backs to the horses, face each other, and, from the confined space, the arrangement and mutual convenience of leg-placing not unfrequently leads to fierce outbreaks of ire. A fat old lady got into the coach at Peoria, whose uncompromising rotundity and snappishness of temper, combined with a most unaccommodating pair of limbs (legs on this side the Atlantic), rendered her the most undesirable vis-à-vis that a traveller could possibly be inflicted with. The victim happened to be an exceedingly mild Hoosier, whose modest bashfulness prevented his remonstrating against the injustice of the proceeding; but, after unmitigating sufferings for fifty miles, borne with Christian resignation, he disappeared from the scene of his martyrdom, and his place was occupied by a hard-featured New Yorker, the captain of one of the Lake steamboats, whose sternness of feature and apparent determination of purpose assured us that he had been warned of the purgatory in store for him, and was resolved to grapple gallantly with the difficulty. As he took his seat, and bent his head to the right and left over his knees, looking as it were, for some place to bestow his legs, an ominous silence prevailed in the rocking coach, and we all anxiously awaited the result of the attack which this bold man was evidently meditating, the speculations being as to whether the assault would be made in the shape of a mild rebuke, or a softly spoken remonstrance and request for a change of posture.

Our skipper evidently imagined that his pantomimic indications of discomfort would have had a slight effect, but when the contrary was the result, and the uncompromising knees wedged him into the corner, his face turned purple with emotion, and, bending towards his tormentor, he solemnly exclaimed, "I guess, marm, it's got to be done anyhow sooner or later, so you and I, marm, must jist 'dovetail.' "

The lady bounded from her seat, aghast at the mysterious proposal.

"Must what, sir-r-?"

303

"Dovetail, marm; you and I have got to dovetail, and no two ways about it."

"Dovetail me, you inhuman savage!" she roared out, shaking her fist in the face of the skipper, who shrank, alarmed, into his corner; "dovetail a lone woman in a Christian country! If thar's law on airth, sir-r, and in the state of Illinoy, I'll have you hanged!

"Driver, stop the coach," she shrieked from the window; I go no farther with this man. I believe I ar' a free 'ooman, and my name is Peck. Young man," she pathetically exclaimed to the driver, who sought to explain matters, whilst we, inside, were literally convulsed with laughter, "my husband shall larn of this, as shiure as shiooting. Open the door, I say, and let me out!" And, spite of all our expostulations, she actually left the coach and sought shelter in a house at the roadside; and we heard her, as we drove off, muttering "Dovetail me, will they? the Injine savages! If ther's law in Illinoy, I'll have him hanged!"

It is unnecessary to say that "dovetailing" is the process of mutually accommodating each other's legs followed by stagecoach and omnibus passengers; but the term—certainly the first time I had ever heard it used in that sense—shocked and alarmed the modest and the worthy Mrs. Peck of Illi*noy*.

A canal is in course of construction in the state of Illinois, to connect the waters of the Lakes with the Mississippi—a gigantic undertaking, but one which will be of the greatest benefit to the Western country. When this canal is completed, the waters of Lake Superior will, therefore, communicate with the Gulf of Mexico by way of the Mississippi, as they do already with the North Atlantic by means of the Welland and Rideau canals, which pass through Canada; and, even already, vessels have been spoken in mid-ocean, built on Lakes Michigan and Huron, cleared from Chicago, and bound for England, passing inland navigation of upwards of three thousand miles.

Leaving Chigago, I crossed the lake to Kalamazoo, whence I "railed" across the Michigan peninsula to Detroit, the chief city of the state of Michigan. This railroad was a very primitive affair, with but one line of rails, which, in very many places, were entirely divested of the iron, and in these spots the passengers were requested to "assist" the locomotive over the "bad places." However, after killing several hogs and cows, we arrived safe enough at Detroit.

I remarked that, since a former visit to the United States, three or four years ago, there had been a very palpable increase in the feeling of jealousy and dislike to England and everything British which has very generally characterized the free and enlightened citizens from the affair of Lexington to the present time. I must, however, do them the justice to declare that in no one instance have I ever perceived that feeling evinced towards an individual; but it exists most assuredly as a national feeling, and is exhibited in the bitterest and most uncompromising spirit in all their journals, and the sayings and doings of their public men. Thus, in travelling through the United States, an Englishman is perpetually hearing his country and its institutions abused. Everything he admires is at once seized upon, to be tortured into a comparison with the same thing in England. But what is more amusing is that it is a very general belief that, from the Queen down to the gruel-stirrer in Marlyebone workhouse, everybody's time is occupied with the affairs of the United States, and all their pleasures turned to gall and wormwood by the bitter envy they feel at her well-being and prosperity.

In passing down the Lakes, I took a passage from Detroit to Buffalo in a Canadian steamer, which, by the way, was the most tastefully decorated and best-managed boat on the lake. As we passed down the Detroit River, which connects Lakes Erie and St. Clair, we had a fine view of the Canadian as well as the American shore; and the contrast between the flourishing settlements and busy cities of the latter, and the quaint, old-fashioned villages of the French Canadians, was certainly sufficiently striking. As the boat passed Malden, celebrated as being the scene of stirring events in the Indian wars, and the more recent one of 1812, I ascended, spite of the burning sun, to the upper deck, in order to obtain a view of the shore, which at this point, where the river enters the lake, is very picturesque and beautiful. I found a solitary passenger seated on the roof, which was red hot with the burning rays of the sun, squirting his tobacco juice fast and furiously, and with his eyes bent on the shore, and a facetious and self-satisfied grin on his lank, sallow countenance. His broad-brimmed brown beaver hat, with dishevelled nap, suit of glossy black, including a shining black satin waistcoat, of course proclaimed him to be a citizen. Waving his hand towards the Canada shore, he asked me in a severe tone,

"What do you call this, sir? Is this the land of the Queen of England, sir?"

"Well, I guess it ain't nothing else," answered, for me, the pilot of the boat. "But," he continued, "it ain't agoing to be so much longer."

"Longer, sir!" quoth my severe interrogator; "too long by half has that unfortunate country been oppressed by British tyrants. Look thar, sir," waving his arm towards the opposite shore; "thar's a sight, sir, where a man can look up to God A'mighty's heavens, and bless him for having made him a citizen of the United States."

"A fine country," I observed; "there's no doubt of it."

"A fine country, sir! the first country in the world, sir; and feeds the starving English with what it can't consume itself, sir. The philanthropy of our country"—he took me for a citizen—"flies on the wings of the wind, sir, and bears to the hungry slaves of the Queen of England corn, sir, and bread doins of every description. Yes, sir! and to show them, sir, that we can feed 'em with one hand and whip 'em with the other, we send it over in a ship of war, which once carried their flag, until it was lowered to the flag of freedom. I allude, sir"— turning to me—"to the frigate *Macedonian*, and the stars and stripes of our national banner."

This speech, delivered in the most pompous manner, and with exuberant gesture, was too much for my gravity, and I exploded in an immoderate fit of laughter.

"Laugh, sir," he resumed, "pray laugh. I perceive you are not a native, and your countrymen had ort to laugh without loss of time; for soon, sir, will their smile of triumph be turned to a howl of despair, when Liberty treads to the earth your aristocracy—your titled lords, and the star-spangled banner waves over Windsor Palace." Saying which, and squirting over the deck a shower of tobacco-spray, he turned magnificently away.

"A smart man that, stranger," said the pilot to me, giving the wheel a spoke to port—"one of the smartest men in these parts." This I easily believed.

We had the misfortune to damage a part of the machinery just after entering Lake Erie, and were compelled to wait until another steamboat made her appearance, and towed us back to Detroit, where it took twenty-four hours to repair damages.

From Buffalo I travelled by railroad to Albany, on the Hudson, and, descending that magnificent river, reached New York early in July, in eight travelling days from St. Louis, a distance of—I am afraid to say how many thousand miles.

From New York the good ship *New World* carried myself and a dozen fellow passengers, spite of contrary winds, in thirty days to Liverpool, where I arrived, *sin novedad*, some time in the middle of August, 1847.

CHAPTER 17

Going West

[U]PON HIS ARRIVAL back home in Britain, Ruxton must have worked diligently to complete the manuscript on his recent experiences in Mexico and the American West. The narrative was first published in Murray's "Home and Colonial Library," as numbers 52 and 53, issued in paper bindings at 2s. 6d. each. It was received with general enthusiasm. The reviewer in the *Westminster and Foreign Quarterly* remarked, "It is not often that one meets with a hand equally practiced with the long rifle, 'bowie knife and Colt's revolver' and at the same time so apt with the pen."[1] And Dr. Richard King, in his biographical sketch of Ruxton, in the Ethnological Society *Journal* for 1848, remarked that it was "merely necessary to mention the title under which this accomplished traveller wrote . . . in order to call forth anew that admiration for the author which has seldom been bestowed so universally upon one of the contributors to the series of the Home and Colonial Library, of which these adventures form a part. It divides with Madame Calderón de la Barca's well-known volumes, the merit of being the best narration extant of travel and general observation in modern Mexico."

Before the end of the year 1847, the narrative also appeared in regular book form, published in London by John Murray. This is the volume which has provided the story used in the preceding eleven chapters.

During the winter and the spring of 1848, Ruxton prepared a number of articles based upon his recent observations and study. From this same period came his most ambitious literary work, *Life in the Far West*, which was to run serially in *Blackwood's Edinburgh Magazine* from June to November, 1848, and then to appear in book form early in 1849.

[1] Issue of April, 1848, p. 102. The work was favorably reviewed also in the *Athenaeum* (January 29, 1848), 108, and in the *Journal* (Vol. XVIII) of the Royal Geographical Society, of which Ruxton was a member. See Voelker, *loc. cit.*, 87.

In the spring of 1848, while preparing his articles for publication, the restless young Ruxton was eagerly planning new adventures. But his body was no longer a match for his valiant spirit. To a friend he confessed in May: "I have been confined to my room for many days, from the effects of an accident I met with in the Rocky Mountains, having been spilt from the bare back of a mule, and falling on the sharp picket of an Indian lodge on the small of my back. I fear I injured my spine, for I have never felt altogether the thing since, and shortly after I saw you, the symptoms became rather ugly. However, I am now getting round again."[2]

A letter of May 4, to his mother, reveals the condition of his health and purse, as well as his concern for her:

"I send you ten pounds and am sorry that I am not at present able to help you with more; but my little money comes in by fits and starts and I have been several weeks in arrears of rent—and doctors' fees, as you know, run away with not a little. However, this much I can spare you *without the slightest inconvenience*, so do not distress yourself with the idea that I am hard up. I dare say I can let you have another ten in a month, if you want it. But this illness of mine throws me back, as I am not able to work.

"I have only this day come to the club for an hour.[3] I have been three days in bed. I am suffering from a fall I got from a mule, when in the Rocky Mountains; I was thrown violently on a stump and injured my spine. It has been coming on for months, but as there were no decided symptoms until very lately, I never knew what was the matter with me."

Having made up his mind to go again to his beloved Rockies, he wrote a final letter to Blackwood's:

"As you say, human natur can't go on feeding on civilised fixings in this 'big village'; and this child has felt like going West for many a month, being half froze for buffler meat and mountain doins. My route takes me *via* New York, the Lakes, and St. Louis, to Fort Leavenworth, or Independence, on the Indian frontier. Thence packing my 'possibles' on a mule, and mounting a buffalo horse, (Panchito, if he is alive,) I strike the Santa Fé trail to the Arkansa, away up that river to the mountains, winter in the Bayou Salade, where Killbuck and La Bonté joined the Yutes, cross the mountains next spring to Great

---

[2] "The Late George Frederick Ruxton," *Blackwood's Edinburgh Magazine* (November, 1848), 594.

[3] The original letter is written on stationery embossed "Army and Navy Club."

Salt Lake—and that's far enough to look forward to—always supposing my hair is not lifted by Comanche or Pawnee on the scalping route of the Coon Creeks and Pawnee Fork.

"If anything turns up in the expedition which would 'shine' in Maga, I will send you a despatch."[4]

To obtain money for the trip, Ruxton sold his royalty rights in *Life in the Far West* to his friend Charles S. Dickson.[5] Then, upon setting out, he sent this farewell note:

"My dear Mother,

"I always think it better not to say good-bye, therefore only tell you to keep a lookout for me one of these days.

"This will be my last trip; but it was necessary for me to leave England—more on account of my health than any other reason. I am convinced if I were to remain here I should not live, for I am arrived at my grand climacteric, and it just depends upon the next six months, whether I get strong again, or break up completely.

"When I return I intend to settle down for good.

"I cannot tell you where to address me. There are not posts where I am going. I may be away six months or a year.

"However, I hope to return within that time and in good health, for I have not known what it was to be well for the last eight months, and have been in continual pain.

"I hope I will see you all well when I come back. Don't say anything to dear old granny about my going, but give my love to her, Dash, and Billy, and believe me ever affectionately,

G. F. R."[6]

En route to the West, Ruxton visited his brother Augustus Alexander at Halifax.[7] At Buffalo, on his way to St. Louis, he chanced to meet a companion with whom he had travelled down the Arkansas River the year before. This was Lewis Garrard, a young man who had journeyed over the Santa Fé Trail to New Mexico and was pres-

4 "The Late George Frederick Ruxton," *loc. cit.*, 594.

5 Dickson's letter of December 1, 1848, to W. Blackwood, Esq. Later, by letter of November 4, 1850, Dickson accepted fifty guineas for his rights to *Life in the Far West*. See letters in the Blackwood Papers, National Library of Scotland, in Edinburgh.

6 Original in our Ruxton papers.

7 In a letter to his brother William, Augustus wrote of George on September 20 from Halifax, Nova Scotia: "It was but five weeks ago that he was sitting in my room and promised to come back and stay some time with me."

ently to write an excellent account of his experiences. In that volume, *Wah - To - Yah and the Taos Trail*, Garrard writes this note:

"When in Buffalo, in August, 1848, I saw in the throng, awaiting admission to the dining room, a moustache which struck me as familiar. After dinner, advancing to the wearer, I said,—'How do you do, Mr. Ruxton?' He did not recognize me; my greasy buckskins, old wool hat, hickory shirt, and moccasins having been exchanged for more civilized habiliments; and to aid his memory I said, 'Don't you recollect the wolf-chase near Tharpe's bottom; the little sorrel mule, Bonita, and its owner stopping at Mann's Fort?' He then immediately called me by name. Retiring to one side, we had a talk of the old scenes, his book, and other matters. Of the Blackwood series of 'Life in the Far West,' then in course of publication, he acknowledged the authorship.[8] He was then on his way to the mountains—that afternoon he left. . . .''[9]

Ruxton, travelling with his friend Captain Andrew Cathcart, reached the Planters House in St. Louis on August 15.[10] Ruxton became ill, and in his impaired health succumbed to the epidemic dysentery that was raging in the city that summer. He died on August 29, 1848. The best account of George's sickness and death is contained in the letter of his brother Augustus[11] to their mother, written from Boston on October 31, 1848:

"I am now on my return to Halifax from St. Louis, and I am happy to say that it will be a consolation to me for the rest of my life, having made a pilgrimage to poor George's grave, and ascertaining how satisfactorily everything had been done, both as regards his burial, and the care taken of him during his illness. You must not be surprised at not hearing from me before this—for since the 22d of September I have been travelling night and day. St. Louis is in the State of Missouri, the extreme end of the United States, near the Rocky Mountains. To give you an idea of the distance, I have been

[8] The author was not indicated when the series was first published.
[9] Garrard, *op. cit.*, 333.
[10] *Daily Missouri Republican*, August 16, 1848.
[11] Upon reading in the papers of George's death, Augustus immediately obtained leave and made preparations to proceed to St. Louis. To his eldest brother, Hay, he wrote: "I am about to start on a most melancholy expedition to St. Louis in the United States, from whence I have only just got intelligence of poor George's death—I enclose the newspapers in which I saw it and my intention is, should the report turn out to be true, to see that the poor fellow has been properly interred, and raise some small monument to his memory."

over (not including the sea voyage from Halifax) five thousand miles.

"Part of the country is almost unexplored, and I had to get along, in consequence of the Ohio River being shallow, sometimes in a canoe, canal boat, wagon or anything I could get hold of. Captain Cathcart, with whom poor George was traveling, had gone on from St. Louis, leaving him, by poor George's express desire, as he was getting quite well from an attack of dysentery, and was to have followed as soon as he got better. The day after Cathcart left, poor George had a re-lapse, and was so ill that the doctors,[12] two of whom attended him, decided to remove him to the hospital, where he would be under the care of the Sisters of Charity.[13] He kept getting weaker and weaker, and the third day after his removal internal hemmorhage came on, which carried the poor fellow off, but so suddenly that he was not at all aware of his approaching end. An American gentleman who told me this, was with him an hour before his death. He was then in good spirits, talking of joining Cathcart. This gentleman left him with one of the Sisters of Charity in whose arms he died—the doctor being present at the time. He had been staying some time in the town and was pretty generally known. In consequence of this, and his being a literary man, which goes a great way with the Americans, a great many attended his funeral. The body was enclosed in a coffin of oak, and then in another of massive walnut, and covered with purple vel-vet. It was drawn in a hearse with four horses, four mourning coaches, and sixteen private carriages, besides a great many on foot. Poor Cathcart! The moment he heard of his death he returned to St. Louis and was so shocked, and felt so much for poor George that he be-

[12] Cathcart's letter to Augustus Ruxton lists Drs. Lane and Clarke. There were two doctors named Lane in St. Louis at the time—Dr. William Carr Lane, the first mayor of St. Louis, and his cousin, Dr. Hardage Lane. The latter had a large and lucrative practice among the best families of the city and gave his attention closely to professional duties, so that he was less conspicuous in political circles and not so generally known as his cousin Mayor Lane.

No Dr. Clarke was listed in 1847 and 1848; however, a business directory of 1850 does list a Dr. Clarke, but gives no first name. In 1848, Dr. Joseph J. Clark was listed at 21 Locust Street.

[13] The hospital conducted in St. Louis by the Sisters of Charity was known in 1848 as the St. Louis Mullamphy Hospital, or Sisters Hospital. It was first organized in 1828 by four sisters and these were joined in 1831 by four more. In that year the cornerstone was laid for the brick building which they occupied until 1874, on the corner of Fourth and Spruce streets. It was the first hospital of its kind established west of the Mississippi. According to Scharf, it was not a public charity in the general acceptance of the term. The public was to use it, but it was to be self-sustaining.

came ill himself, otherwise he intended to come to me in Halifax and then return home. He remained in St. Louis three weeks, and only left two days before I arrived,[14] he never dreamt of my coming there. He had written me all the particulars,[15] and concerning what he left in the way of property. These I shall find on my return to Halifax and I will send them on to you by the next packet. I send you this merely to set your mind at ease, and to assure you that had the poor fellow been under your own roof, he could not have met with more kindness. Cathcart had erected a simple white marble monument, and all I could do, was to have the space where the grave is, completely bricked up with a large slab and the monument put on top—the whole enclosed with an iron railing. There is an acacia tree at the head of the grave from which I broke a small branch. This shall be sacred in my keeping until I can give it to you myself.

"In great haste, ever your affectionate son.

Augustus."

News of Ruxton's death reached England in late September. The report, published in the *London Times* and other papers, was followed by obituary notices and biographical sketches in various British journals.

Blackwood's Edinburgh Magazine, which had been running serially his *Life in the Far West*, followed the final installment in the issue of November, 1848, with a fine tribute to the young author:

"The readers of *Blackwood's Magazine*, who for six succeeding months have followed La Bonté and his mountain companions through the hardships, humours, and perils of 'Life in the Far West,' will surely not learn with indifference, that the gallant young author of those spirited sketches has prematurely departed to his long home, from that Transatlantic land whose prairies and forests he so well loved to tread, and the existence and eccentricities of whose wildest sons he so ably and pleasantly portrayed. . . .

"As regards his second work, we shall not, under the circumstances, be deemed egotistical, if we here, at the close of its final por-

---

[14] Cathcart accompanied J. C. Frémont on his tragic winter expedition into the San Juan Mountains, where all of the company's 120 mules, and 11 of the 33 men, perished in the snow.

[15] The first two pages of Cathcart's letter to Augustus Ruxton telling of George's death are not to be found. The last two pages are in the collection and list his money, clothes, and equipment.

tion, express our very high opinion of its merits. Written by a man untrained to literature, and whose life, from a very early age, had been passed in the field and on the road, in military adventure and travel, its style is yet often as remarkable for graphic terseness and vigour, as its substance every where is for great novelty and originality. . . .

"Few men, so prepossessing on first acquaintance, gained so much by being better known. With great natural abilities, and the most dauntless bravery, he united a modesty and gentleness peculiarly pleasing. Had he lived, and resisted his friends' repeated solicitations to abandon a roving life, and settle down in England, there can be little doubt that he would have made his name eminent on the list of those daring and persevering men, whose travels in distant and dangerous lands have accumulated for England, and for the world, so rich a store of scientific and general information. And, although the few words we have thought it right and becoming here to devote to his memory, will doubtless be more particularly welcome to his personal friends, we are persuaded that none will peruse without interest this brief tribute to the merits of a gallant soldier, and accomplished English gentleman."

Perhaps the fullest biographical sketch was the one prepared by Dr. Richard King and read by him before the Ethnological Society on December 20, 1848. In it he gave this appraisal:

"Many individuals, even in the most enterprising periods of our history, have been made the subjects of elaborate biography, with far less title to the honour than Mr. Ruxton. Time was not granted him to embody, in a permanent shape, more than a tithe of his personal experiences and strange adventures in three-quarters of the globe; indeed, when we consider the amount of physical labour which he endured, and the extent of the fields over which his wanderings were spread, we are almost led to wonder how he could have found leisure even to have written so much."

We regret that Augustus Ruxton's long trip to St. Louis to insure his brother's remains a permanent resting place, well marked, did not achieve its desired objective.[16] In later years the Episcopal Ceme-

16 Ruxton was buried in old Christ Church Cemetery, with Bishop Cicero Hawks of the Episcopal church conducting the services.—*Daily Missouri Republican*, August 31, 1848, and Christ Church "Records of Burials," No. 101. Cited by Voelker, *loc. cit.*, 89.

tery was abandoned and a building rose upon the grounds. The dis-interred were removed to the New Wesleyan Cemetery, which has since been abandoned, and Ruxton's stone has never been found.[17]

George Ruxton's life and achievements were truly amazing. His thirst for adventure and knowledge seemed insatiable. Mr. Horace Kephart, a student of Ruxton's life and an editor of his works, said that he "belonged to that picked company of born explorers who not only knew how to observe but how to fare in wild regions, and endure. Nothing came amiss: he was equally at home in a mansion or hovel, or bedded on the bare earth of a cold windswept plain. He was, too, a citizen of the world, with a happy aptitude for assimilat-ing with any company that chance might offer. Tactful but daunt-less, he could go anywhere—alone if need be—and get through. Noth-ing escaped his shrewd powers of observation, to which were joined a knack of vivid description and a hearty sense of humor that en-livened every situation in which he was thrown. There was a hard vein in him, like that which showed in nearly all our frontiersmen, but that very hardness was often priceless amid the dangers and diffi-culties that beset his path."[18]]

Ruxton was not a trained literary man, but native ability illumi-nates his writings. His gripping pen pictures of adventures have won him a permanent place in the literature of the American West.

[17] Christ Church Cemetery, which was bounded approximately by Cali-fornia and Ohio avenues and La Salle and Caroline streets, was abandoned in 1884 and the bodies were removed to New Wesleyan Cemetery, at the southeast corner of Olive Street and Hanley Roads.—Voelker, *loc. cit.*, 89.

[18] From the Introduction to Kephart's edition of *Adventures in Mexico*.

"Western Log Cabin"
a comfortable home on the edge of the wilderness
(A. J. Miller)

BROAD OAK
boyhood home of George Ruxton, on a wooded hilltop
overlooking the village of Brenchley, in Kent, southeast
of London

Index

Aberdeen, Lord: ultimatum, 301
Abert, Lieut. J. W.: 106, 166n., 181n., 182n.
Africa, North: Ruxton in, 87–88
Africa, South: Ruxton's trip to, 89–91; experiences in, 92–103; natives, 94, 96–97; slaves, 100
Africana, chief: 99, 100
Aguas Calientes, Mexico: 121–22
Albatrosses: 91, 92
Albert, John: 219, 220n.; carries news of Arroyo Hondo fight, 224
Albuquerque: 176
Alec: Ruxton's hunting companion, 56
Alexander, Sir J.: 98, 99
Algier, Señor: 106n.
Algonquin Indians: 45
American frontiersmen: shooting match, 83; house, 84; trade with, 84–85
American people: 108
American troops: in Mexican War, 166–70
Americans: characterized, 108; opinion of in Mexico, 114, 143; teamsters in Mexico, 132, 137; tragedy in desert, 139–41; merchant in Mexico, 144; atrocities to Indians, 149; invading Mexico, 151; captives at El Paso, 162; as soldiers, 169; New Mexicans hostile toward, 188; killed at Turley's mill, 221; attitude towards England, 303–306
Amherstburg, Canada: 37

Amrol, African chief: 99
Angel, Señor (mozo): 136, 137
Angra Pequeña: 95, 96
Antelope: in Mexico, 133, 149, 164; in New Mexico, 170; up the Arkansas, 200, 201; at Bayou Salado, 211; near Manitou Springs, 247; description of, 259, 286
Anza, Gov. Juan B. de: kills Comanche chief, 209n.
Apaches: 185; horse thieves, 129; scalped, 146; murdered, 148; make bread of mesquite beans, 151; in Mexico, 155, 161, 163, 164; marauding, 162; in New Mexico, 165, 171
Aragón: 13
Arapaho Indians: 27, 213, 244; war party, 215, 231, 235, 236; customs, 232; duty to Manitou, 237
Architecture: in Mexico, 111–13
Arkansa River: 107, 151, 265, 309; traders on, 192; divide, 206; trading fort on, 210; description of, 211; beaver on, 226; ice moves, 233; no grass on, 234; timber on, 272
Armijo, Gov. Manuel: 132–33, 147, 151, 176, 187n.
Armijo, Señora: 176
Armijo Family: 176
Arroyo Hondo: 190, 192, 193, 194, 195
Atlantic: 33; Ruxton's crossing, 43, 108
Autobee, Charlie: 221n.

Barbados: 108

UNIVERSITY OF OKLAHOMA PRESS

NORMAN